AWAKEN THE WORLD WITHIN
By Professor Hilton Hotema

ANCIENT WISDOM

Printed in the United States of America.

AWAKEN THE WORLD WITHIN

PROLOGUE

The last book of the Bible is the enigma of the Christian World. Of it Thomas Jefferson said:

"It has been 50.or 60 years since I read the Apocalypse, and I considered it then merely the ravings of a maniac ... What has no meaning admits of no explanation".

Wm. McCarthy, who died in 1959 at the age of 93, wrote a book titled Bible, Church and God. In it he reviewed from the literal word each book of the Bible, and of Revelation he said:

"In the oldest MMS the title is simply Apocalypse. The book is wholly a composition. Its material was taken from many sources, yet the compiler studiously refrains from indicating its source. In fact, he endeavors to make it appear the material was original with him.

"Some of its symbolisms were taken from Daniel and Ezekiel. It embodies Egyptian, Babylonian and Greek mythology, all worked over and woven together with the author's imagination and forging pen. Its writer or compiler was an unknown Jew. ...When it first appeared, it was rejected as fraudulent in both the East and the West. ... Luther placed it with Jude, James and Hebrews. Zwingli rejected it. Calvin doubted it. During the 19th Century the Western Church broke down this opposition. And so, the book, a fraud for sixteen hundred years, suddenly became the Word of God of the West and a fraud in the East.

"To the early church men of the West, prone
to believe anything labeled Word Of God, the book
was chiliastic, i.e., Christ was to return immediately, and reign personally over the world for a
thousand years (Chap. 20). Satan was to be chained
to the post, fed on bread and water, and made to be
good for all that time. Then he was to be 'loosed
for a little while'. At the final, or second resurrection, he, the devil, was to be locked in hell, to
remain there forever.

"Millions (of fools) believed this (stupid) doctrine. But Christ did not return, old Satan was not
locked up, and humanity, by spending all its time
dodging the devil and preparing for heaven, became
but little better, and much filthier, than animals.
The church had made a promise, the people believed
it--result: More than a thousand years of misery,
ignorance, filth, and depravity--the Dark Ages".

Today few people know that pre-historic man
had no religion. What we know as religion is a system that was created by the priesthood, and its purpose was to exalt them and enslave the masses.

The ancient scrolls from which the Bible was
compiled were not of a religious character and did
not treat of any God. They were scientific works,
and dealt symbolically with the mystery of Creation, the nature of Life, and the constitution of Man.
The designing crooks who compiled the collection
of writings called the Bible, had a dark plot in mind.
They made the Bible to serve the Church and to con--
trol the multitude. Then they burnt the scrolls to
hide the fact that the scrolls did not tell the same
story the Bible tells.

The last book of the Bible deals allegorically
with the Kingdom of Life within (Luke 17:21). The

(2)

Book with Seven Seals (Rev. 5), is man's body. It has Seven Vital Control Centers, and they are called Seals because in the average individual they are in a semi-dormant state, which reduces Consciousness to a very low level, below that of the beasts and fowls.

These Control Centers were called Chakras by the Hindu Masters. They are located in the body as described in this work, and are numbered from the bottom up, the 6th and 7th being located in the brain.

In the last book of the Bible the Masters presented certain functions of the organism relative to Creative Power. They discovered that when this Power is diverted from its procreative function, it produces amazing effects that are highly beneficial to the organism, and when controlled and guided, increases the activity of the Seven Centers mentioned, resulting in a surprising increase in Consciousness that makes such man a Seer.

That is the reason why the Masters guarded this discovery with such jealous care, imparting the secret only to the Neophyte in the Ritual of Initiation in the Ancient Mysteries.

And that is the story, allegorically related, in Revelation.

The student is advised that this work, Awaken The World Within, is a printed, revised, improved version of Son of Perfection.

Professor Hilton Hotema.

Honolulu, 1962.

Happy is the man that findeth wisdom, and the man that getteth understanding.

For the merchandise of it is better than the merchandise of silver, and the gain thereof than fine gold.

She is more precious than rubies; and all the things thou canst desire are not to be compared unto her.

Length of days is in her right hand; and in her left hand riches and honor.

Her ways are ways of pleasantness, and all her paths are peace.

She is a tree of life to them that lay hold upon her; and happy is every one that retaineth her.

With all thy getting, get understanding.

—Proverbs of Solomon.

TABLE OF CONTENTS

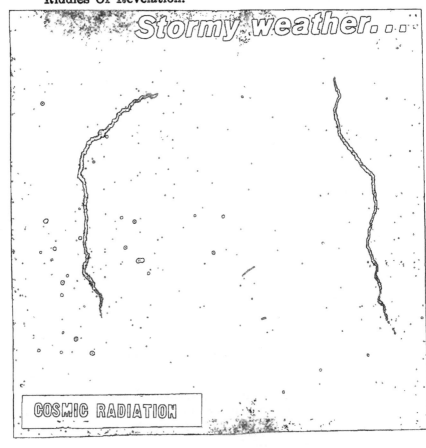

The Ancient Masters used the Pentacle to symbolize Man. He is constituted of Fire, Air, Water, Earth and Life. Two Pentacles were required to signify Birth and Death. The Black Pentacle fall of the Ego into Matter, Birth, and was called Crucifixion, due to confinement of the Ego in a prison. The Blazing Pentacle indicated release of the Ego from its prison by Death, and was termed Resurrection. The Masters said, "The day of (thy) Death (is better) than the day of one's Birth" (Eccl. 7:1). This is the esoteric meaning of the biblical statement, "Death is swallowed up in victory" (1 Cor. 15:54).

MYSTERY INCREASES

The Mystery of Creation increases as materialistic science discovers more about the metaphysical constitution of Creation. There are two great areas of knowledge: the physical and the metaphysical. Science recognized only the physical, and scientists deny the existence of the metaphysical. We live in an age of scientists, not an age of science. Science is knowledge based on facts. Scientists are men with all the frailties, emotions, prejudices and errors of other men.

Scientists are more embarrassed with their great ideas coming so simply. After years of diligent research, patient experiments, laboratory observations, they end in a blind alley. Then suddenly the idea filled their mind. How come? They can't explain. We don't understand the manner in which great discoveries originate. It is a process beyond the reach of reason. In physics, the rigid Universe disappeared in 1905 when Einstein showed that energy has mass. The energy a man would expend in a life-time of heavy manual labor can be weighed. It would amount to about 1/60000 of an ounce.

This page is composed of swarming atoms, which are made up of electrons, which are composed of radiation. In the past, scientists saw huge masses of materials and formulated laws to describe their functions. They then assumed these laws were correct and would apply universally. This was error in their logic. Certain laws of physics apply to large masses, but not to electrons, to atoms, or even to small aggregations of electrons or atoms.

Biologists tend to be greater physicists. Biology remains a descriptive system, classifying and arranging facts of animative activity.

John Rowland indicated that mysteries in the living world reach far beyond the materialism of biology. These mysteries are not dispelled by using the word Evolution. That term merely describes a process and explains nothing.

Dr. J. B. Rhine said, "At the heart of life, as at the heart of the atom, there is a mystery not yet even suspected. There is not even a theory that pretends to deal with it." As long as Life itself remains an unsolved mystery, we shall never discover and understand the higher functions of the human body.

Sacred Wisdom

KNOWLEDGE

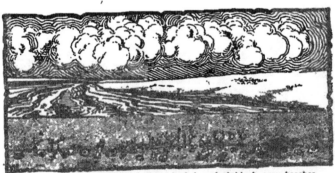

The first land, where gray waters rippled against bleak gray beaches.

THE DAWN OF LIFE

VIII

INTRODUCTION

In this course I have embodied many valuable secrets, collected with great care and long labor from the treasured wisdom of the Ancient Masters.

This knowledge will give you better understanding of mysteries and miracles which may have confused you in the past. It will open your eyes to many strange things, and prove to be a "guide, philosopher and friend."

I hope you will come to regard it as the greatest boon that has ever come into your life.

This new knowledge will invest you with courage, hope, power, length of days, a radiant countenance and a happier personality.

Your world is made by your Mind. Your training and education have been designed to keep you in darkness by controlling your Mind.

If you digest this work, you will no longer remain on the social pattern level. Your Mind will be fed by "forbidden" food that will force you to think and rise above the rank and file of the masses.

This work will show you a New World that you will never forsake for the old one in which you have lived. Have you the courage to proceed?

You will be shocked to see how slyly the Mind is deceived and how surely Man is enslaved by the powers that invent the laws and control the customs that rule civilization.

These lessons show how the higher faculties of Mind and Soul may be aroused and activated, thus enabling the body, through which the Real Man contacts the physical plane, to express the highest impulses and the noblest characteristics.

Thus if you are seeking the highest spheres of mental physical and spiritual existence, you should find in these lessons the help and guidance you need.

May my message linger long with you and bring you a world of light and life, and beauty, radiant with joy and youth.

Professor Hilton Hotema

MAGIC Story

"Occultism is the intellectual side of Spiritualism, and teaches the student the latent powers of his own spirit."
— Stainton Moses "More Spirit Teachings" pp. 81, 1951 edition.

WHEEL of KNOWLEDGE
KEEP IT ROLLING
BOOKS ARE ROADS TO KNOWLEDGE

Phoenix — Immortality

THE BIG QUESTION

Is man mortal or immortal?

The Bible definitely answers that question:

Old Testament—

"Then shall the dust (dead body) return to the earth as it was; and the Spirit (animating principle) shall return to God who gave it" (Eccl. 12:7).

New Testament—

"God is Spirit . . . It is Spirit that quickeneth" (animates the body) (Jn. 4:24; 6:63).

"Ye are the Temple of God, and God Dwelleth in you" (and therefore is you) (1 Cor. 3:16).

The Church teaches that man is mortal; that immortality is the "gift" of God to those who believe that Jesus was the son of God; and that immortality for all men is a lie given by Satan to Adam and Eve in the Garden of Eden.

The Bible itself proves different.

The Ancient Scriptures teach that Man is Immortal. According to the doctrine of the Ancient Masters, the term "man" is merely a name applied to Incarnated God-Spirit on the physical plane.

The flesh-eating Tyranosaurus attacking the armoured Ceratopsia. An elephant would have been an easy victim for this vicious thirty-foot monster.

Was the gospel Jesus man or myth? Did he live as a man, or did he represent on the Stage of Life some Cosmic Principle of the Universe?

For 1600 years the church has taught that Jesus was not only a great man, the greatest that ever lived, but that he was the Savior of humanity.

It seems strange that a man so great has no history at all outside of the New Testament. It appears that the only reason why the New Testament was written was to bring this Savior into being and give him some semblance of a history.

There is strong suggestion of the Mystery Drama in the New Testament. In the gospels the stage is set, Jesus appears, speaks his lines, and makes his exit.

But no actor, no mythical man, and no actual man has ever affected the world so profoundly as he has.

Many great men have lived, and many pages of history are devoted to them and their work. None of these ever affected mankind so deeply as Jesus has,—and yet he has no history except a brief story in the New Testament.

Little is said of his birth and infancy. Then the gospels are silent and no mention is made of Jesus except in the Luke, when he was 12 years old. After that, the gospels are silent again until he is 30. Then for three short years he preaches to a few thousand people in a small region around Galilee, and disappears.

It is certain from all the evidence that Jesus was not a man. It is just as certain that he was invented as an actor for a definite purpose, and that such invention was the work of a great power with great wealth.

Only as such, with wealth and power back of him, could this character called Jesus have affected the world so widely and so profoundly. That fact we shall clearly show in this discussion of

THE MYSTERY MAN OF CHRISTIANITY
AND
THE SACRED SCIENCE OF THE ANCIENT MASTERS

The former will show who was the real man of the gospels; and the latter will show what Cosmic Principles the actor Jesus represented.

It will amaze the reader to see how skilfully the Masters saved their Sacred Science from destruction and preserved it, in symbol and allegory, in the Fictitious Life of the Fabulous Christ Jesus.

Many rulers of the past had made vigorous attempts to crush the Sacred Science into oblivion. The Emperor Constantine was determined to have the job well done. He would invent a new religion, sell it to the people of his vast realm, and by this means destroy the Ancient Arcane Science.

The Masters were too clever to be outwitted by Constantine. They met him at his own game, prepared the New Testament as he directed,—but skilfully made the gospel Jesus play a double role.

For the exoteric, he was the Lord and Savior of humanity; but for the esoteric, he was the Symbol of Cosmic Principles and Spiritual Processes.

There was nothing new in that. The writings of the Masters always contained dual messages,—one intended for the profane and one intended for the initiates and disciples.

For 1600 years the world has been given by the church the exoteric message contained in the New Testament. This work has been prepared to give the reader the esoteric message concealed in the Hidden Life of Christ Jesus.

COSMIC CONSCIOUSNESS

THE MYSTERY MAN

The Sacred Science of the Ancient Masters and the Mystery Man of Christianity are so inseparably connected that both must be considered together.

The Mystery Man gave us those fragments of the Sacred Ancient Science that are contained in the New Testament. But for a secret reason he was deposed as the author and replaced by another who "died on the cross" to save man from the just penalty of his evil deeds,—a doctrine so preposterous and so contrary to all the known laws of the Universe that faith must rise superior to Intelligence in order for a sane person to believe it.

This deposed author is the most mysterious man the world has ever known, and was made such for a peculiar and definite reason.

That reason was that he became the Jesus Christ of the New Testament, the Paul of the Epistles, and the John of Revelation,—and yet few know his true identity.

He was the greatest sage, seer, master, philosopher and author of the first century A.D., and from his voluminous writings the New Testament was compiled in the fourth century. Yet he is the least known man in history, and the world has not one scrap of his writings in his own name.

He raised from the "dead" a bride who died on her wedding day, and the maid's parents were so excited and joyful that they gave him 150,000 drachnas, which he gave to the girl as a wedding present. This event, somewhat distorted appears in the New Testament as the work of its Jesus.

He lived the greatest life that history records, changed the destiny of man, and was worshipped by millions. Of all the characters listed in the New Testament, he is the only one that actually lived, and he is the only one that is not mentioned by name.

Why is this man surrounded by all this secrecy and mystery?

Because for certain reasons he became the most feared of all men that was ever born. His very name was expunged from the pages of history. Encyclopedias declare that he was only a mythical character, and that writings about him are "religious work of fiction."

Because of him, millions were murdered, cities depopulated, and blood flowed in streams. His writings were burned after they were used to make the New Testament, and men were forbidden even to mention his name. Few people now living ever heard of him.

This mystery man became the god of a new religion, under a new name, and people were forced to worship him as "the only begotten Son of God" or suffer death.

That caused the crash of the greatest nation on earth, and plunged Europe into a reign of terror and darkness that lasted for more than a thousand years.

Even the disappearance of this strange man is a mystery. No one ever knew whether he died or what happened to him. Some said that he went to live with the Masters in the Himalayas. Emperor Aurelian and others claimed they saw him and heard him preach two hundred years after he vanished.

These stories, and other reports that some of his writings had been found, circulated for centuries. As they filtered back to Rome, the church that Constantine had founded in the fourth century grew worried.

Something had to be done to keep the Mystery Man from being known. It was done. The Crusades were organized, and the leaders were ordered to bring back the Mystery Man dead or alive, and to destroy all his writings that might be found.

The Book They Blamed on God

EVOLUTION OF THE EARTH

Apatosaurus, harmless vegetarians as large as Pullman coaches.

Lesson No. 1

ANCIENT WISDOM

Science now says that it requires 220,000,000 years for our Sun to make one revolution of its vast orbit, and that it has made thousands, and perhaps hundreds of thousands, of complete revolutions. If it has made but a thousand, that covers a period of two hundred and twenty billion years.

Certain scientists say that man is millions of years old. The evidence dug from the ruins of past ages shows that thousands of years ago man had a Science of Human Life so much superior to what we now have, that the Ancient Masters were competent to write in symbol and allegory a description of that science which is incomprehensible to the most advanced scholars of this day and time.

That science was concealed in the Ancient Zodiac, which was used as a chart to teach select students the Mysteries of Life. As the first vow of the candidate was silence, no description of the initiatory ceremonies was ever permitted in writing that could be understood by the profane.

The whole purpose of initiation was to teach the worthy ones the Secret Knowledge of Man and his relation to the Universe. The Initiate was bound by a terrible oath never to divulge the secret to anyone not entitled to receive it.

The only written record of this ancient wisdom that the western world has, appears as the last book of the New Testament. Had that book been written in clear language so its contents could be understood, it had been destroyed and never found a place in the Christian canon.

Scores are the number of those who have tried to interpret the book of "Revelation" in the Bible. Prof. Roswell D. Hitchcock, D.D., LL.D., says in his Analysis of the Bible, published in 1886, that—

"1. Chapter I-III. 'Things which are,' or the then present condition of the churches. This portion, besides an account of the manner in which the writer was commissioned to write, contains seven separate addresses of epistles, to the seven principal churches of Asia, which distribute warnings, reproofs, and praises, as is deserved.

2. Chapter IV-XIX. 'Things which shall be,' or a prophetic view of future ages. It is this later portion of the

1

Revelations that has given rise to such an infinite number and variety of interpretations."

As the student proceeds he will be amazed to learn how little the Christian authorities know of the scriptures they use as the foundation of their religious system.

In the eyes of the orthodox, the "wicked" are those who belong to no church and are bound by no man-made creed. Those who do belong are those who fear the wrath to be meted out to the "wicked" by a God that is claimed to be "all love."

The Apocalypse does not treat of "things which are," nor of "things which shall be." It treats of Man and his Redemption, not by a "Redeemer" but by himself.

The only Redeemer is a Clear Conscience, and the only Heaven is a state of the Mind.

Lesson No. 2

THE APOCALYPSE

Emanuel Swedenborg was a prominent Mystic. He was one of Hitchcock's eighty commentators on the Apocalypse who are worth reading. He wrote in Latin a book of 1200 pages, published in 1874. The English translation was made by Rev. T. B. Hayward, and revised by Rev. John Worcester at Boston. On the title page appears this statement:

"The Apocalypse Revealed: wherein are disclosed the Arcana there foretold, which have hitherto remained concealed."

The Preface begins with this statement:

"Many there are who have toiled in the explanation of the Apocalypse; but, as the spiritual sense of the Word has been hitherto unknown, they were unable to see the Arcana which lie stored up in it, for these the spiritual sense alone discloses; on which account expositors have conjectured various things, and the most of them have applied the things about ecclesiastical matters. The Apocalypse, like the whole Word, does not in its spiritual sense treat at all of worldly things, but of heavenly things; consequently not of empires and kingdoms, but of heaven and the church."

The Preface ends with this statement:

"Every one can see that the Apocalypse can by no

means be explained but by the Lord alone; for each word therein contains arcana, which would in no wise be known without a particular enlightenment, and thus revelation: on which account it has pleased the Lord to open the sight of my (Swedenborg's) spirit, and to teach me. Do not believe, therefore, that I have taken anything herein from myself, not from any angel, but from the Lord alone. The Lord also said to John through the angel, 'Seal not the words of the prophecy of this Book' (Chap. 22:10); by which it means that they are to be made manifest."

For centuries an attempt was made to give the Apocalypse an historical interpretation. Failing in that, it was next interpreted as prophecy. Then Swedenborg stepped in with his mystic knowledge and sought to show what "The Apocalypse Revealed." We shall see that he lived in darkness as dense as did the many before him, "who have toiled in the explanation of the Apocalypse," and failed to find that it does not at all treat "of heaven and the church."

It is only too true that this book can be explained but by one possessed of a particular enlightenment. Such enlightenment has little relation to "heaven" and none to the "church."

The book treats of both terrestrial and spiritual things. It treats of Man, the subject of the Bible, as a dual entity, related to the temporal and eternal worlds, and describes his Redemption —not by a Redeemer but by **himself.**

As some doctors, for profit and power, teach people to believe that "disease" is a mysterious demon that can be subdued only by them, so some of the clergy, for the same purpose, teach people to believe that man's Redemption can be accomplished only by their work.

Had the body not the power to correct its disturbed equilibrium, it could not be corrected; and had man not the power to achieve his own Redemption, it could not be achieved.

Swedenborg, a noted Mystic, used 1200 pages to try to explain the text of the Apocalypse, and explained nothing. He increased the confusion. He beheld the book in the wrong light. He believed that it treated of "heaven and the church." The Master who wrote it knew of synagogs but never heard the word "church"; and he knew that "heaven" is a state of the Mind and not a region in space, and said so (Rom. 14:17).

FORGERY AND INTERPOLATION

In the oldest manuscript of the book, the title is simply

"Apocalypse." As it appears in the New Testament, it is shot through and through with forgery and interpolation. Many times it has been taken apart and reassembled, and much material added.

There have been many versions of the book, of which six are ancient. Our Bible's version is taken from the Latin Bible and its Vulgate Edition. Of this version, there are eight different manuscripts written between the sixth and fifteenth centuries. Then there are the Syriac, Armenian, Egyptian, Sahidic, Ethiopic, Arabian et al versions.

These versions are all different, as each country made the book appear as "the Revelation" of its god, "which God gave unto him, to show unto his servants things which must shortly come to pass" (Rev. 1:1).

MORE PIOUS FRAUD

The Apocalypse is purported to be the work of "St. John The Divine," who is also accredited with the fourth gospel. The Bible says that he was an ignorant, unlearned fisherman (Mk. 1:19; Acts 4:13).

The fourth gospel and the Apocalypse are not the work of the same man. The fourth gospel was compiled from a biography of Apollonius, written by Damis, a Greek historian, and the most beloved disciple of the Master that he loved so well. The compiler had orders to delete the name Apollonius wherever it appeared and insert the name Jesus. Then the original manuscript was to be destroyed, but it was not.

Damis was not an ignorant, unlearned fisherman. That class does not produce philosophy. He was a prominent writer, and in the fourth gospel he defined Life (6:63) in the words of his Master. That is more than modern science has been able to do.

The Apocalypse contains in symbol and allegory the Science of Man and the Secret of Regeneration. Modern science has not yet gone that far.

The Apocalypse is the great parable of the New Testament. It deals with the allegory of Genesis as to the Fall of Man. Both books refer to the human body and its deepest functions.

The Ancient Masters taught the science of unfolding the faculties of the higher nature by means of self-discipline. By this technique spiritual truths are capable of reverification by each generation. That secret science is contained in the Apocalypse.

In his book published in 1892, J. M. Roberts states that the

4

Apocalypse is the work of Apollonius, the great philosopher of the First Century, who retired to the Isle of Patmos in 69 A.D. and remained there for approximately two years. In that retirement the desire came to him to write an allegorical account of the initiatory ceremonies of the Sacred Ancient Mysteries, of which he was a Master. Roberts is partly correct and partly not.

The Apocalypse is a scripture of extreme antiquity, written many ages before anyone ever heard of the gospel Jesus, and reproduces what is far older than itself.

The book is a sublime Kabalistic summary of all the occult figures. It divides its images into three Septenaries, after which there is a silence in heaven. There are seven seals to be opened, i.e., seven mysteries to know, seven difficulties to conquer, seven trumphets to sound, and seven cups to empty.

The book is as obscure to the profane as the Sohar. It is written hieroglyphically with numbers and images in order to conceal from the profane the secret knowledge the Masters taught to their Initiates. The author often appeals to the Intelligence of the Initiated. **"Let him who hath knowledge, understand! Let him who understands, calculate!"** he often says after an allegory or the mention of a number.

The work is the completest embodiment of Occultism. It contains far more meaning than the words convey. Its expressions are as figurative as poetry, and as exact as numbers.

The text of the Apocalypse as it appears in the Bible, did not become fixed in its present form until the art of printing put a stop to biblical fogery and interpolation. It was not until the 16th century that the Bible in English took its present shape.

THE CHRISTIAN BIBLE

Bronson C. Keeler, in his "History of the Bible," says that the Bible, as we have it today, is scarcely more than three centuries old (p. 126).

Roman Catholicism was founded as the Roman state religion in 325 A.D., and was financed and promoted by the power and tax-money of the great Roman Empire. Churches were established and trusted bishops were appointed to supervise and systematize the work.

In the fifth century one of these bishops named Theodore made to his superior a report in which he said:

"I found more than 200 such books (ancient scriptures) in our churches that had been received with respect; and, having gathered them all up, I caused them to be burnt, and in their place introduced the gospels of the Four Evangelists" (Fab. 1:20).

What did the burnt scriptures teach? Not the Christian doctrine. They were burnt because they taught the Sacred Science of the Ancient Masters, that man has eternal life and needs no "Redeemer." That truth made the gospel Jesus useless, and that truth set man free of the priesthood (Jn. 8:32). For that very good reason the ancient scriptures were destroyed.

There are said to be extant three great manuscripts of the Greek Bible, and Sinaitic, the Vatican, and the Alexandrine. They are the high courts of appeal in all cases of disputed texts.

The Sinaitic was found by Tischendorf in a convent of St. Catherine, Mt. Sinai, in 1859, and is probably the oldest of the New Testament codices in existence, dating back to the later part of the fourth century A.D. It contains the four gospels, the fourteen Pauline Epistles, the Acts, the Seven Catholic Epistles, the Revelation, the Epistles of Barnabas, and part of the Shepherd of Hermas, the last two being later rejected and removed from the Bible.

The Vatican manuscript belongs to the latter part of the fourth century, and ends by mutilation of Hebrews 9:14. The Alexandrine belongs to the fifth century.

For thirteen hundred years the church tried to collect from ancient scriptures a Bible agreeable to all the church authorities by letting the bishops settle the question among themselves. That course failed. It led only to a violent clashing of opinions, and an ominous revolt was breaking out in the northern part of the Roman Empire.

As the contents of the Bible was the key to the situation, the church was forced to take in hand the whole question of the canon, and fix it once and for all. Then the writings put in the Bible became the "word of God."

Lesson No. 3

THE FISH GOD

According to its title in the Greek text, the Apocalypse is an account of the Initiation of Ioannes. In the subtitle the author calls it "The Initiation of Anointed Iesous," that is, of his own illuminated Nous, the "witness" for the universal Logos, as Ioannes is the Material World, the "slave" of the true Self, the "witness" for the individual Logos.

6

Whence comes the name Ioannes? According to ancient mythology, the earliest instructor of man in letters, sciences and arts, especially in architecture, geometry, and all other useful knowledge, was the **Fish God Oannes.**

We observe that Joshua begins where Moses ends: "Now after the death of Moses the servant of the Lord, it came to pass, that the Lord spake unto Joshua, the son of Nun" (Jos. 1:1).

Here we have the Fish God. Nun is Semitic for Fish, and Joshua means savior. Fish and Cross Symbols embodied the ancient idea of generation.

Ichthys is Greek for Fish. This word appeared on many seals, rings, urns, tombstones, etc., in the early days of Christianism. The word had a mystical meaning, for each character formed an initial letter of the words Iesous Christos, Theou Hyios, Soter; that is, Jesus Christ, Son of God, Savior.

In the Talmud the Messiah is called "The Fish."

The Fish was sacred among the Babylonians, Assyrians and Phoenicians. It was sacred also to Venus, and the Romanites still eat Fish on the very day of the week that was called "Dies Vernes," Venus' Day; Fish Day.

A Fish was a symbol of fecundity. The most ancient symbol of the productive power was a Fish. It is the universal symbol upon many of the earliest coins.

Pythagoras and his followers ate no Fish, as they associated Fish with the productive power. A Fish was the earliest symbol of the gospel Jesus, and appears as a design in the catacombs.

The Rev. Dr. Geikie, in his "Life and Words of Christ," says that a Fish stood for his name, from the significance of the Greek letters in the word that expressed the idea, and for that reason he was called a Fish.

At Kouyunjik there was a colossal statute to the Fish-God Oannes.

In the biblical allegory, Jonah was swallowed by a big fish, and was in its belly three days and nights. Then it vomited him out upon dry land (Jno. 1:17; 2:10).

A similar Hindu allegory states that Saktideva was swallowed by a big fish, and came out unhurt.

In Grecian fable, Hercules was swallowed by a big fish, and after three days "he came out bald-pated after his sojourn there."

Commentators assert that these heroes, remaining three days and nights inside the Fish symbolize the Sun at the Winter Solstice, from December 22nd to the 25th. For three days and nights the Sun remains in the Lowest Region, in the bowels of the

Earth, in the belly of the Fish. It is then cast forth and renews its career.

Other commentators hold that these personages are symbols of the secret doctrine. They are personifications of the Seed with the fishy odor.

Fish are drawn from the water, and the Seed of Man comes from the River of Living Water.

All the characters represented as a man emerging from a fish's mouth are all benefactors of mankind. So is the Seed.

The Masters taught that the oily substance with a fishy odor, excreted by the gonad glands, enters the blood and is carried to all parts of the body. It is the Seed (Son) of Man, and is the highest and purest fluid in the body. In Greek it was termed "Chrism"— the "blood of Christ" (Heb. 10:19; 1 Pet. 1:2; 1 Jn. 1:7).

That is the "Christ in Man" (Col. 1:26,27). That is the Christ that liveth in me. I travail in birth until Christ be formed in you (Gal. 2:20; 4:19). Christ is all and in all (Col. 3:11).

That symbolical Christ died at the First Council of Nicea in 325 A.D., and was replaced by a man.

Bryant, in his "Analysis of Ancient Mythology," says that "the great Patriarch who preached philosophy and righteousness to the Antediluvians is styled 'Oan" and 'Oannes," which is the same as Joshua, Jonah, John and Jesus" (Vol. 2, p. 291).

In due time we shall learn the literal meaning of the allegorical statements, "Christ was raised up from the dead." "Christ being raised from the dead dieth no more" (Rom. 6:4, 9). Then shall we understand the teachings of the Ancient Masters, that an .oily substance with a fishy odor flows down the spinal cord to the sacral plexus, cave or manger, where it remains three days and nights, and is then "raised up from the dead."

From the Book of Enoch we quote:

> "The Masons .hold their grand festival on the day of St. John, not knowing that therein they merely signify the Fish-God Oannes, the first Hermes and the first founder of the Mysteries, the First Messenger to whom the Apocalypse was given, and whom they ignorantly confound with (St. John the Divine) the fabulous author of the common Apocalypse" (Vol. 2 p. 154).

This evidence indicates that the Apocalypse was written long ages before the time of Apollonius. It shows that "the common Apocalypse" was copied by him from a very ancient manuscript.

Then after he inserted interpolations to make it fit his purpose, the founders of Christianism edited and revised it to make it fit their purpose.

Lesson No. 4

APOKALYPSIS

It is not generally known that the ancient scriptures, from Genesis to Revelation, and all others omitted from the Bible for certain reasons, are a compilation of allegories, parables, fables, fiction and symbols dealing only with Man, his Fall and his Redemption.

In the Ancient Mysteries, suppressed by Constantine and his successors, the Gnosis, or Ancient Arcane Science, taught the Initiate that man is complete. His constitution is such that he corresponds with the two kingdoms, the spiritual and the terrestrial, the eternal and the temporal.

That was secret knowledge and was guarded with jealous care, being imparted only to those found worthy of initiation, according to the maxim, "Many are called, but few are chosen." That is true today of Freemasonry.

In the Ancient Greek Mysteries, also called the "perfecting" or "finishing" rites, the candidates, after receiving some preparatory training in the semi-exoteric lesser rites, were termed Mystai, "veiled ones," while the Initiates were called Epoptai, "those having super-sight," or Seers.

The Greek word Apokalypsis, "unveiling," is a substitute for Epopteia (initiated into seership). The original title of the book indicated that the **Mysteries of Life had been unveiled and revealed to the Initiate.** The biblical forgery terms it "The Revelation of Jesus Christ."

. The author of the Apocalypse did not intend that the title of his occult description of Initiation into the Mysteries and the results thereof, should convey to the profane the meaning "revelation."

Strong evidence of that fact appears in the work itself, which is the despair of theology. The clergy admit that it must be regarded as an unsolved, and possibly insoluable, enigma. They translate its title "Revelation"—yet to them, the uninitiated, it reveals nothing.

The work is not only profoundly esoteric and couched in the mystery language of the ancient Zodiac, but also has its meaning so impregnably intrenched behind symbolism, allegorism, ana-

9

grammatism, number-words, and other puzzling devices, that it has successfully resisted the assaults of "those without" (exotericists, uninitiated—Mk. 4:11) for nearly two millenniums. Its subtitle also, by the word symbolized (esemanen), likewise indicates that it was not written as literature for the profane.

It is true that the "authorized" translators render the verb "signified"; yet with bland inconsistency they ascribe the sense of "miracle" to the substantive semeion, which properly means a symbol, as a constellation or sign of the Zodiac.

DANGEROUS INVENTION

Things are dangerous to organized institutions when they reveal truth and disclose fraud.

The invention of printing put a stop to biblical forgeries, and caused Cardinal Wolsey of London, in a convocation of his clergy in 1474, to say:

"If we do not destroy this dangerous invention (Printing Press), it will one day destroy us" (Doane, Biblical Myths, p. 438).

After the art of printing was invented, established institutions have sought to control publishing. This was done at first by licensing the printers. As more men learned the art, clandestine shops printed books that contained much revealing truth. That "danger" was met by the "List of Forbidden Books." Such books were burned when found, and in many instances the author was burned too.

The gullible public think this could not happen now, as all people want knowledge based on truth. The facts show otherwise. In the New York Herald of May 7, 1901, the Rev. Mr. Harney, conducting a mission in St. Peter's R.C. Church, New Brunswick, New Jersey, is quoted as stating:

"I do not doubt, if they were strong enough, that the Catholic people would hinder, **even by death if necessary,** the spread of heretical errors among the people, and I **say rightly so."**

In this case, the "spread of heretical errors" means the dissemination of knowledge that feeds the Mind and frees the Man from the snares of the social pattern.

We are attacking no creed, but are facing cold facts. If your

10

creed is so contrary to the laws of God that it cannot face facts, your faith rests on a mighty frail foundation.

SPIRITUAL LIFE

Modern science and modern theology know nothing about Physical Life and Spiritual Life. ·

Modern science is based on the theory that the atom was solid and eternal, indivisible and indestructible.

The atom is found to be as empty as the air appears to us. If an atom were magnified to the size of a large room, internal whirling particles could be seen. According to science, these particles are whirling centers of energy.

The whirling particles in the atom are intangible. They are called electrical. That means little, for no one knows what electricity is. The word Spiritual could as well be used. Perhaps better.

Material science boycotts the terms spirit and spiritual because they were used by the Ancient Masters to designate Invisible Cosmic Force. Things spiritual modern science condemns as heathenish superstition.

It seems more sensible and scientific to speak of Spiritual Life within us than to term it Energy or Electrical Life.

Electricity appears as undirected force without intelligence that makes nothing. Spirit appears as directed Cosmic Force with Intelligence that makes everything. Proof of that appears in the things made. If not so made, then how made? To that question science is silent.

Atoms are kept in motion by a force termed energy by science. The Ancient Masters called it Spiritual Intelligence, and declared that it is omnipresent, pervading all things.

Then came the curtain of darkness in the 4th century A.D., and men were led astray into believing that God was far away, beyond, separate. Modern science was fated to prove what it has denied. It was fated to prove the omnipresent existence of God while denying Him.

Lesson No. 5

KEY OF THE GNOSIS

The Apocalypse is the Key of the Sacred Ancient Science. It is in truth the Key of the Gnosis.

Incomprehensible as the book may seem to the exoteric scholar, however great his intellectual attainments, keen his mental acumen, and vast his store of erudition, to the mere tyro in the Sacred Science the general meaning of the Apocalypse is perfectly clear.

The book is unintelligible to the conventional scholar because its subject-matter, veiled in symbolical language, relates to the Sacred Ancient Mysteries, the esoteric teachings of which it was not lawful to reveal to the profane, the uninitiated.

Great secrecy was always maintained regarding the Sacred Science, so as to guard it from those morally unworthy to receive it. For the power its possession confers would be destructive to them and injurious to their fellow-men.

This reason applies not so forcibly to the Apocalypse. Much that is presented in it had already been overtly stated in the writings of Plato and other Greek Initiates, as well as in the Buddhistic and Brahmanical scriptures.

While the Apocalypse treats very fully of the spiritual and psychic forces in man, **it nowhere reveals even a clue to the process by which these forces can be increased and aroused into action.**

In the introductory part, the author clearly intimates that it is intended for the guidance of those who, without any esoteric instruction, find these forces awakened within them by the purity of their nature and the intensity of their aspiration for the higher life.

Evidently the author had another motive for resorting to the symbology and ingenious puzzles which have baffled the uninitiated for so many centuries. This motive is easily percieved. Had he written the book in clear language, it had almost certainly been destroyed, and had never been included in the Christian canon.

From the concluding portion of the fourth gospel, it is plain that the great Seer and Initiate clearly foresaw the fate of the Ancient Science and the loss of the esoteric doctrine.

Hence, it would seem a reasonable supposition that he wrote the Apocalypse for the purpose of preserving the secret doctrine in the records, carefully concealing it under the most extraordinary symbols, checked off by a numerical key and by similar puzzles, so that the meanings would be clearly demonstrated from the text itself, and concluding it with a dread imprecation against anyone who should add to or take from the text of the book.

Now, when modern biblical criticism, scholarly accurate, conventionally exoteric, and remorselessly unsparing, has demonstrated the unsoundness and instability of the modern theological structure, and has so weakened it that it is tottering to its fall, appears to be the intended and appropriate time for the Seals of the Apocalypse to be broken, and the secret contents of the book made known to the world.

Throughout the long centuries the orthodox church has treasured this mysterious, unintelligible book as part of its sacred scriptures and a place to which it is justly entitled, as it is the Masterpiece of the Great Master Apollonius. But the church has never realized that it was especially designed for the purpose of the undoing of modern orthodoxy. Its purpose is to preserve the Sacred Science of Antiquity, the revelation of which ipso facto destroys all faith in modern theology.

When the compilers of the New Testament named John as the author of the fourth Evangel and the Apocalypse, they had the evidence and knew what they were doing. They knew both writings described the work of the same man, one by himself, and the other in which his work was described by his disciple, Damis.

The Greek of the Apocalypse is somewhat inferior to that of the fourth Evangel because the former was written by Appollonius in his native language, the Samaritan, and he who translated it to Greek was not so proficient in writing Greek as the Greek historian Damis, who is mentioned as Demas in Col. 4:14; 2d Tim. 4:10; and Phil. 24.

The Apocalypse is the Key of that divine Gnosis which is the same in all ages, and is superior to all faiths and philosophies—that secret science of Man which is secret only because it is hidden and locked in the inner nature of every human being, however ignorant and humble. For none but he can turn the Key that fills the Mind with Light.

From its very nature it is impossible for the Gnosis itself ever to be "revealed." It pertains to the realm of the Demiurgic Mind, the Spiritual Consciousness, and lies beyond the scope of mere intellection, which can never rise higher than speculative philosophy. But the Key of the Gnosis, the scientific method by which this higher knowledge may be attained, can be placed in possession of any intelligent person who is intuitive enough to appreciate its value and apply it in practice.

Lesson No. 6

THE MYSTERY MAN

1. He was the most wonderful man the world has ever known.

13

2. He lived the greatest life that history records.

3. He changed the destiny of man and was worshipped by millions.

4. Then he became the most feared of any man that ever lived.

5. His very name was erased from the pages of history.

6. Encyclopedias declare that he was only a mythical character.

7. Because of him people were slaughtered, cities depopulated, and blood flowed in streams.

8. His writings were burned and men were forbidden to speak his name.

9. He then became the god of a new religion under a new name.

10. That caused the crash of the greatest nation on earth, and a reign of darkness that lasted for a thousand years.

This is the man to whom the modern world is indebted for the possession of a peculiar manuscript, written in symbol and allegory so profound, that men in the last sixteen hundred years have been unable to interpret it.

As great as this strange man was, it is evident that he could not have been the original author of that manscript. The work is so profound and contains so much of the mysterious, that it must have been ages in preparation. It embodies in symbol and allegory the Science of Man and his Redemption as known only to the Great Masters of Antiquity, and was used by them as a chart in the marvellous ceremonies of Initiation in the Ancient Mysteries.

We refer to the Apocalypse, the last book of the New Testament. It appears as the greatest work in symbol and allegory ever prepared by man. It is so mysterious in character that it has defied the best brains of modern times to analyze it.

Christianism presents this document as "The Revelation of Jesus Christ, which God gave unto him, to shew unto his servants things which must shortly come to pass; and he sent and signified it by his angel unto his servant John" (Rev. 1:1),—all of which is rank forgery.

This biblical copy of the Apocalypse is full of glaring interpolations that a high school student should be able to detect.

As we sift out the spurious interpolations, we find that the work is foreign to Christianism, to the gospel Jesus and to his teachings.

It is certain from the evidence that the gospel Jesus knew nothing about the context of the Apocalypse. It is also certain

14

that the system now known as Christianism did not stem from him.

The records show that a new religious system was founded in the early part of the fourth century. This came to be known as Roman Catholicism, with Jesus as its god and leader. He did not create the system. It created him. For no trace of him appears in history until that system was invented.

After the system was born, a textbook was needed. That was prepared by the church and presented as the New Testament. The church wrote its own Bible.

A study of this work reveals the presence of a Mystery Man preaching to the people of Asia Minor. He appears as the man who did most of the work described in the New Testament. Eliminate him and his Epistles from it, and little is left.

The great man of the New Testament should be the gospel Jesus; but he is not. That man is a shadowy figure who says:

"But I certify you, brethren, that the gospel (god-spell) which was preached of me is not after man. For I neither received it of man, neither was I taught it" (Gal. 1:11,12).

This Mystery Man further says:

"If ye continue in the faith grounded and settled, and be not moved away from the hope of the gospel, which ye have heard, and which was preached to every creature which is under heaven; whereof I Paul am made a minister" (Col. 1:23).

A very old gospel. That is not the gospel of Jesus. It had long been preached and was well established ages before the gospel Jesus was ever known.

This Mystery Man calls himself Paul. Without warning or introduction he appears out of nowhere, being first abruptly mentioned in Acts 7:58 as a young man "whose name was Saul," and was strangely and subsequently changed to Paul.

It is peculiar and irregular that nothing is said about this Paul, or why he was there so suddenly introduced. That is unusual if he were truly an historical character. This appears as evidence that there was some good reason for concealing his background. That reason shall be noticed in due course.

From that time on, this Paul becomes the key and central figure of what is termed the New Testament. Jesus himself is overshadowed and outshone by this Mystery Man. Why is his history hidden? If his real identity could be discovered it might disclose some startling facts. It would not only reveal the authorship of the so-called Pauline Epistles, but also the source and origin of Christianism.

The evidence clearly shows that the gospel Jesus was merely an incidental character, an after thought, invented when the so-called Pauline Epistles had been considered and accepted as part of the New Testament. This arouses our suspicion.

The context of the Epistles proves the truth of this assertion. For a child can almost see that they have been interpolated, doctored and distorted to bring the gospel Jesus into being.

Lesson No. 7

THE TERRIBLE PERSECUTOR

By clever design, as the work of a high school student, this Paul is made to figure at first as a terrible persecutor of Christians.

No Christian writer has ever attempted to explain why no mention was made by contemporaneous writers of any Christians existing at that day, nor of that terrible Paul, the persecutor. The word "Christian" appears but thrice in the New Testament, and then no doubt was interpolated by some monk or bishop. These facts should arouse the suspicion of everyone able to think.

It is well further to observe that when this mysterious Paul was miraculously convinced of his error, as alleged in Chapter 9 of the Acts, he suddenly knew, without previous instruction, all about the gospel Jesus and his doctrine. In fact, he then and there becomes the foremost Christian on earth, and knew more about Jesus and his doctrine than did the famous Peter, "the Rock" on which was built the Roman Catholic Church (Mat. 16:18).

No one at Ephesus, Antioch, Athens or Rome ever heard of this Paul who led the Christian cause so efficiently and figured so prominently in the work at the time he lived, and preached, and wrote.

Pomponius Mela, a prominent Roman geographer who died about 60 A.D., said there was no one to his knowledge who knew aught about a man or minister named Paul as described in the New Testament.

PAUL'S SILENCE AS TO JESUS

In not one of the Pauline Epistles is there a word concerning the "annunciation," or of Mary, or of the voice and the dove at

16

the baptism, or of Lazarus, and the boy at Nain, and the daughter of Jairus.

This silence seems the more perplexing because Paul was reared and educated at Jerusalem. He was "brought up" in Jerusalem, "at the feet of Gamaliel, and taught according to the law of the fathers" (Acts 22:3; 26:4, 5).

This was at the very time of the preaching and crucifixion of Jesus, according to the gospels, when his fame went out to the whole world (Mat. 4:24; 9:26; 14:1), and great multitudes came together to hear him (Lu. 5:15). Where was Paul that he knows nothing about such stirring events?

It is probable that Paul was at the Passover when Jesus was crucified. He had probably seen Jesus (1 Cor. 9:1; 2 Cor. 5:16). From his lips he must have heard the beautiful saying that is nowhere cited save in Acts (20:35) that "It is more blessed to give than to receive."

Paul might possibly omit the wondrous incidents of the career of Jesus when preaching at Jerusalem or to the Jews. How could he omit these in his writings to the Gentiles?

The populace at Lystra was anxious to worship Paul for merely curing a cripple; those at Melite said he was a god because he was not killed by the bite of a serpent (Acts 28:6); those at Ephesus found full efficacy in apparel worn by him (19:12); yet Paul never once relates, in letter or sermon, the wonders Jesus wrought or that were wrought for him which, it should seem from Paul's own experience, would most easily have brought these people to a realization of the divine nature of his Master Jesus.

On the contrary, it was not these events and incidents on which Paul relied, to which he referred, or which he maintained. He never once cites any sign or wonder wrought by or for Jesus. More than once he refers to his own thaumaturgy (2 Cor. 12:12), but fails to discuss any save those "signs" wrought through himself by the aid of Jesus (Rom. 15:18, 19).

If any controversy or report was current in his day as to the miracles worked by Jesus, Paul had no contention as to them, or ever mentioned them. It was for referring to the resurrection of the dead, both the just and the unjust, that he was called in question by the Jews (Acts 23:6; 24:15-21); and for asserting that Jesus was arisen (25:19); and for urging the Jews to repentance and good works (26:23); and for teaching that "the hope of Israel" was extended to the Gentiles (28:20, 28).

"If Christ be not risen," he declared, "our preaching is vain" (1 Cor. 15:14); and within eleven verses he formulates his whole creed of salvation and all the gospel he taught (1 Cor. 15:1-11).

17

In this appears the central assertion of the physical revivification of Jesus as the seal of his divinity (Rom. 1:4), as well as evidence of the bliss or woe in the physical nature that would attach to mankind after death.

It seems strange that when Paul desires to convince his audience that Jesus was the Christ, he cites no evidence about that life described in the four gospels, but quotes from the Old Testament prophets, which his audience, as devout Jews, should believe "must needs have been fulfilled."

Paul attempts to show from the scriptures that the death and resurrection of Jesus were necessary (Acts 12:2, 3; 18:28), but he makes no attempt to demonstrate anything by quoting any acts or words of the Jesus he mentions, nor any appeal to tradition or history. In fact, he regards himself as the originator of his philosophy, which has for its basis the code of ethics which he designates as his own gospel (Gal. 1: 11, 12). He preached a doctrine about a spiritual being known as "Christ" who had previously inspired the man Jesus, and not a doctrine of a divinely born Jesus who worked miracles.

Perhaps in this clear evidence appears the reason why the Christian Fathers disliked Paul and his Epistles, and why Tertullian referred to him as the "apostle of the heretics."

Justin Martyr, Hegesippus, and others whose writings have come down to us as orthodox, ignored the work of Paul and based their system upon apocryphal or lost scriptures which were the precursors of the canonical gospels.

Lesson No. 8

TESTIMONY OF ANTIQUITY

Dr. Westcott's work titled, "On the Canon of the New Testament," calls the first two centuries A.D. the "dark age of Christian literature" so scant was it. He conceded that the four gospels were not in existence up to 250 A.D. by declaring:

"A few letters of consolation and warning, two or three apologies addressed to heathens, a controversy with a Jew, a vision, and a scanty gleaning of fragments of lost works, comprise all the literature that may be called Christian up to the middle of the second century A.D."

According to the New Testament, Paul appears as the first and leading Christian author. In his Epistles he makes no mention of the four gospels; makes no quotations from them, and makes not the slightest reference to them. To him they are unknown and do not exist.

The Apostolic Fathers are they who immediately followed the so-called Apostles who were men of straw and never existed.

The first of these was Clement of Rome, 97 A.D. The next were Ignatius and Polycarp, 116 A.D. Then came Papias, 150 A.D. None of these knew anything of the four gospels and its Jesus.

We come next to Justin Martyr, 175 A.D. He was the first polemical writer that Christianity had, and the church has made every effort to show that he knew of the four gospels. He made 314 quotations from the Old Testament, and in 197 of them he named the book from which he quoted. He seems to know nothing of a New Testament. He quotes certain statements from the "Memoirs of the Apostles," and calls them "gospels," but they are not the four gospels of the New Testament.

The first man to mention four gospels by name was Irenaeus who flourished about 200 A.D. The gospels he mentioned are not those now contained in the New Testament. Some think that his mention of the gospels is another church forgery.

This includes all the "testimony of antiquity," up to the third century, as to the four gospels and their Jesus. Almost a hundred years after the alleged death of Jesus, there appears the first evidence of four gospels.

It appears from reliable evidence that a learned man named Marcion (Mark), found in Antioch, some thirty years after the demise of Paul (Pol, Polos, Apollonius), some writings of the latter. These he copied, making such alterations as would conceal their true authorship, and first introduced them to the public in Rome about 130 A.D. He then became the leader of a large body of Essenes, and charged another sect, that later became orthodox Christians, with making interpolations in the Pauline Epistles to make them harmonize with the writings they were using.

In the middle of the second century this Marcion, whom the church later called St. Mark, was teaching in Rome from the Pauline Epistles a system of philosophy that was later labeled heresy.

It was from these writings, as edited and revised by Marcion, that were later compiled and presented as the first three gospels and the Pauline Epistles. These are the gospels to which Irenaeus referred in the second century. And as yet the church interpolators had not doctored them to make them refer to the gospel Jesus.

The leading man of the New Testament was Paul. His writings constituted the original creed of Christianity. The whole system rests on his writings. That makes his identity highly important. Who was he? What did he teach? Do we have his teachings in the New Testament? Or were his writings doctored and distorted so as to eliminate his doctrine and replace it with another?

If we can definitely identify this Mystery Man, we may expose the whole system of Christianism as a fraud, and uncover that skeleton in the Christian closet which has been carefully concealed for more than sixteen hundred years.

The Mystery Man has been found. He appears in authentic history as the son of wealthy parents, born at Tyana, in Cappadocia, Asis Minor, February 16, A.D. 2, and lived to be 98 years old. Some say he passed the century mark. His name was Apollonius, a name derived from "Apollo" the Sun God of Greece.

From a history of his life, written by the learned scholar Philostratus, we excerpt the following data:

Before his birth a god appeared to his mother and informed her that he himself should be born of her. She was greatly shocked by this information. At the time of her delivery, the most marvelous things occurred. All the people of the country acknowledged that the child was the Son of God. Are the rest of us the children of apes?

As the child grew in stature, his powers, greatness of memory, and striking beauty attracted the attention of all. Much of his time he spent as a youth among the philosophers, the disciples of Plato, Chrysippus, and Aristotle. When he attained manhood he became an admirer and follower of Pythagoras, spending six years studying Pythagorean philosophy under the Master Euxenes.

He prepared himself for this task with the terrible Five Year Silence; abstained from all animal food, wine and women; subsisted on herbs and fruit, dressed only in linen; went barefooted and uncovered head, and wore hair and beard uncut.

During his five years of complete silence, he traversed Asia Minor in all directions, but never opening his lips. The vow of silence he enforced upon himself did much to enhance his reputation of holiness. His fame spread far and wide; and just his presence on a scene was sufficient to hush the noise of the warring factions of the cities of Celicia and Pamphylia.

Francis Barrett in his "Biographia Antigua," mentioned Apollonius as follows:

"Apollonius was one of the most extraordinary persons that ever appeared on earth. At the age of sixteen he became a rigid disciple of Pythagoras, renouncing flesh, wine and women, wearing no shoes, wearing his hair and beard uncut, and making his abode in a temple of Aesculapius where many sick people resorted to be cured by him."

"He lived six years without speaking a word, although during this silence he quelled several seditions in Cilicia and Pamphilia. That which he stopped at Aspenda was the worst of all to appease, as the task was to make those harken to reason whom famine had driven to revolt."

"Some rich men had caused this commotion by monopolizing all the corn which occasioned a great scarcity in the city. Apollonius quelled this popular commotion without speaking a word to the enraged multitude. He had no occasion for words, as his Pythagoric silence did all that the finest figures of oratory could effect."

To his poor relatives he gave his large patrimony, and went to Ephesus, where people flocked about him. Then he went to Antioch, a center of learning, and preached the Pythagorean philosophy. He became a Master of the Temple of Apollo Daphne at Antioch, where he was taught the mysteries of its priesthood.

Lesson No. 9

IN JERUSALEM

After some time at Antioch, he went to Jerusalem, arriving there when he was 33 years old. The renown of his fame had preceded him, and when the people heard of his coming, they took branches of palm trees and went forth to meet him, shouting Hosanna; blessed is he that cometh in the name of the Lord. While at Jerusalem he performed some unusual work.

This event is recorded in the gospels, but when they were compiled and revised in the fourth century for the New Testament, the name of Apollonius was deleted and that of Jesus inserted (Mat. 21:9; Mk. 11:9; Jn. 12:13).

At Rome, in the case of a dead maiden, he demonstrated a fact well known to the Masters. When the body, apparently dead, is yet fresh and warm, as in the case of a man who drowns, one whose faith in God is strong, power is great, will is indomitable, and knows certain secrets of the body, can often cause the Spirit to return to the temple of God.

21

In this way the "dead" may be raised to life. That fact is often demonstrated in modern times, in cases of those who drown or are badly shocked by an electric wire, and are restored to life. We think little of it; but it becomes a supernatural event when it appears in the Bible.

Damis, a disciple of Apollonius, recorded the story in his biography of his Master. A young bride died on her wedding day. Meeting the funeral bier, Apollonius said to the attendants: "Set down the bier and I will dry thy tears for the maid." He asked for her name, then touched the body, spoke to her in a low tone, and she awakened from the death-like sleep.

The relatives of the maid were overjoyed, and presented him with 150,000 drachinas. He gave the sum to the girl "as a marriage portion."

The compilers of the New Testament interpolated this story in the synoptic gospels (Mat. 9:25; Mk. 5:39-42; Lu. 8:54, 55).

GOES TO INDIA

About 36 A.D. Apollonius went to India and studied under the Hindu Masters for two years. On his return he brought back some of the Hindu scriptures and used them to introduce in Asia Minor the religious system of the Hindu gods, Krishna and Buddha.

He later made another trip to India, and remained there from about 45 to 50 A.D. He was initiated into the Mysteries of the Brahmans, and presented with some rare Hindu manuscripts. He studied under the Hindu Masters five years. To him they said:

"We know everything because we begin by knowing Man, for Man is an epitome of the Universe. We regard salvation as embracing both the spiritual and physical man. For the spiritual man is the Divine Essence and the physical man is its temple." (1 Cor. 6:19).

On his return to Europe from India, Apollonius was saluted as a great Magician and recieved with much reverence by both the priesthood and the people.

When he went to Alexandria, a large crowd greeted him. As he was entering the gates of the city, he met the sad procession of ten criminals being taken to execution. He asked the guards to go as slowly as they could and to delay the execution as much as possible, as one of the prisoners was innocent. As they cut off the heads of eight, a rider came with the news of the reprieve of one who, while innocent, had confessed under torture. This remarkable event earned great reverence for him.

From Alexandria, Apollonius went up the Nile to the very confines of Ethiopia. As they sailed up the Nile they met a bark steered by a youth named Timaison. Apollonius asked the boy to give some account of his life, but Timaison blushed and kept silent. Then Apollonius, by the power of spiritual vision, told his disciples Timaison's whole life history. The youth, greatly amazed, confessed that it was true.

The return of Apollonius from India to the Hellenic world created great interest in his teachings and strong reverence for his person. Oracles mentioned him and commanded the sick to seek him for relief. His features, strength and habits riveted on him the attention of all. Cities sent him embassies for counsel in building temples and in difficult decisions.

When the Master took passage to Greece, many crowded on the ship desiring to take passage on it, believing that he had power over storms. To accommodate the large crowd, he took passage on a bigger boat (Mk. 4:39; Lu. 8:24).

In Olympia he preached often, but left when the Lacedaemonians were ready to celebrate in his honor the ceremonies of a theophany, receiving him as a god.

He was initiated into the Mysteries of Apollo by the very Hierophant whose name he had predicted four years previously.

After his last return from India, Apollonius founded a school in which he taught his version of the Hindu scriptures. The principle of Initiation is expressed in the famous Text: "Thou art a priest forever after the order of Melchisedek."

The meaning of this is, A priest after the order of the Sun, the King of Day, High Priest of the Heavens, the Solar Orb, personified in the New Testament as a human being and high priest in order to decieve and mislead.

The Sun is a king without father, or mother, or descent, and without beginning or end of life (Ps. 2:7, 8; 110:4; Heb. 5:4-6; 7:1-4).

On a certain occasion, Vespasian called on Apollonius, meeting him in the temple and saying to him, "Make me emperor." Apollonius answered, "That is what I made thee; for in that I prayed for an emperor who should be just, noble, paternal and moderate."

Vespasian was delighted and exclaimed, "May it be given me to rule over wise men, and may wise men ever rule over me." Vespasian did become emperor of Rome.

23

After his first visit to Jerusalem, it was thirty-two years before he went there again. On his later return, he was employed by Vespasian as Oracle in his army camp at the overthrow of Jerusalem.

This Emperor had the highest intellect of his great empire from which to choose, and it was Apollonius whom he consulted for advice on the management of his kingdom.

Lesson No. 10

SPIRITUAL VISION

Apollonius claimed the power of spiritual vision and of foreseeing the future. He was preaching at Ephesus when Domitian was assassinated and saw the deed done.

At first his voice dropped as if he were terrified. Then, with less vigor, he continued to preach as one who, between words, saw glimpses of something foreign to his subject. At last he lapsed into silence, as one interrupted in his discourse.

Staring at the ground, he advanced a few paces from his pulpit and cried: "Courage, Stephanus; smite the tyrant,"—not as one who derives from a mirror a faint image of the event, but as one who sees it with his own eyes.

Then after a short pause, he continued: "Rejoice, my friends, for the tyrant dies this day. Yea, the very moment in which I was silent, he suffered for his crimes. He dies." The announcement was later confirmed by a messenger from Rome.

The great philosopher was a master of all practices of hypnotism, and by that means is said to have relieved many of their ailments. Ostensibly by the use of hypnotic suggestion he performed many "miracles" in apearance that were identical to those alleged to have been performed by the gospel Jesus.

Came the time when the Master was well along in years, and he wrote a long letter to Emperor Nerva, full of good advice. Then he asked Damis to deliver it. The latter obeyed, but against his better judgment. For he had a premonition that he would never again see his beloved Master.

The Seer was preparing to retire into complete obscurity, following his own precept, "Seek to live obscurely."

To pass from the stage without witnesses, he sent Damis away, with these significant words, "O Damis, when thou shalt philosophize for thyself, keep me before thine eyes."

One account says that while he had reached the century mark, his powers were not weakened, nor his mind dull, and that he died at Ephesus in 103 A.D. at the age of 101.

The story of his death states that he went to the temple of Diktyana in Éphesus late at night. Fierce dogs guarded the place; but they did not molest him. They came up and fawned on him.

The guards of the shrine seized and bound him for a magician and a thief, in that he had thus charmed the dogs. Later he loosened his bonds, then called to him those who had bound him, that they might witness what was to happen. He then ran to the doors of the temple, which strangely opened at his command, without apparent help of human hands. After he had passed within, they closed behind him just as mysteriously; and from within the astonished guards heard a chorus of maidens singing within the temple. Their song was this: "Hasten thou from earth; hasten thou to Heaven, hasten" (Philostratus, Vol. II, p. 401).

This great philosopher understood many languages, and was the best grammarian of his time. He appeared to know the "inmost thoughts of men" (Jn. 1:42, 47), and, "according to tradition, he ascended bodily to heaven, appearing after death to certain persons who had doubts of a future life," wrote Philostratus (Mat. 28:17; Mk. 16:12; Lu. 24:51; Jn. 26).

According to tradition, after Apollonius had passed from earthly life, he still preached of the Soul and Immortality (1 Cor. 15:51).

There was a certain youth in Tyana who was powerful in debate. He did not agree to the true doctrine of the Soul and Immortality.

After quite extended reasonings of the subject among the younger people of Tyana, the youth declared that it could not be so, for the great Apollonius was so completely dead that he could not appear to any one, although he himself had, for ten months, besought Apollonius to appear to him, if Immortality of the Soul were a true doctrine.

Five days later, having once more discussed the subject, he fell into a deep sleep and was awakened with such a shock that perspiration streamed from his face. Crying out, he said, "Do you not see Apollonius, how he is watching your studies, and singing rapsodies about the Soul?"

The others could not see the Master nor hear his song; and the youth recited to them what he caught of it, as follows:

"The Soul is immortal, and 'tis no possession of thine but of Providence.

"After the body has fallen, like a swift horse freed of its bonds,

25

"The Soul leaps forward and mingles with the fluid air;
"Repelling the harsh yoke of servitude it has endured.
"What use is this now to you which you'll see when your body is done?
"And to what end this searching while still among men?"

Lesson No. 11

PAUL'S GHOST RETURNS

In a few clean cut words in the fifteenth chapter of 1st Corinthians appears all we have in the New Testament of the true doctrine of the Soul and Immortality as taught by the Mystery man.

"Behold, I show you a mystery; we shall not sleep, but we shall be changed" (vs. 51).

The Masters taught that man's body is individualized matter and his Soul is individualized Spirit. At death the body dissolves and returns to the Cosmic Reservoir of Substance, and the Soul returns to God (Eccl. 12:7).

The modern minister hides his ignorance in a cloud of words, and the words too often are mere combinations of sounds without meaning. Our consciousness and our senses are mysteries to us, and we are mysteries to ourselves. We may know the attributes of the Soul, its thoughts and its perceptions, but we know nothing of the Soul itself which perceives and thinks.

The great truth of the Ancient Wisdom was that the Soul is Immortal; not the result of organization, not an aggregate of modes of motion of matter; not a succession of phenomena and perception, but an Existence, one and identical, a living spirit, a spark of the Great Central Light, that hath entered into and dwells in the body, to be separated from it at death (born again), and return to God, the Great Unit; that doth not disperse nor vanish at death, like fog or smoke, nor can be annihilated; but eternally exists and possesses activity and intelligence, even as it exists in God before imprisoned in the body.

"We do not sleep in death," said the Master. We change from physical consciousness to spiritual consciousness. Death is the "born again" process by which the Soul is freed from its material prison.

As Stradivarius became the "king of violin makers" by living

94 years and making fiddles all his life. So Apollonius became the king of prophets by living 101 years and preaching the Immortality of the Soul all his life.

Even after his disappearance from among men, the Spirit of Apollonius appeared to many, according to reports. The youth at Tyana saw him in spiritual vision and, with his spiritual sense of hearing, heard him preach after physical demise.

The most famous of these visitations was that which occurred nearly one hundred seventy-five years after Apollonius disappeared, and which saved his native city, Tyana, from destruction by Emperor Aurelian. On this point Frances Barrett, in his "Biographia Antiqua," writes:

"It is related that (in 274 A.D.) Aurelian had decided, and publically declared his intentions, to demolish the city of Tyana, but that Apollonius, an ancient philosopher and prophet of great renown, a true friend of the gods and himself honored as a deity, appeared to him in his usual form as he retired into his tent, and addressed him thus:

" 'Aurelian, if you desire to be victorious, think no more of the destruction of my fellow citizens.

" 'Aurelian, if you desire to rule, abstain from the blood of the innocent.

" 'Aurelian, if you will conquer, be merciful.'

"Aurelian being acquainted with the features of this ancient philosopher, having seen his images in several temples, vowed to erect a temple and statue to him; and therefore altered his resolution of sacking Tyana.

"This account we have from men of credit, and have met with it in books in the Olpian library; and we are the more inclined to believe it on account of the dignity of Apollonius. For was there ever anything among men more holy, venerable, noble and divine than Apollonius? He restored life to the dead, he did and said many things beyond human reach; which, whoever would be informed of, may meet with many accounts of them in the Greek histories of his life."

These reports circulated for centuries after the Master's death. They filtered back to Rome to the effect that "Paul" had returned to earth and was again preaching to the multitude.

The rumors increased and the church was worried. Something had to be done and it was done. The Crusades were organized, and the leaders ordered to bring back the Mystery Man dead or alive.

Again we meet pious fraud. We are told in histories and encyclopedias, written and censored by Romanism since 325 A.D. down to the present, that the purpose of the Crusades was to "deliver the Holy Land from the Mahommedans."

"As chivalry directed the layman to defend what was right, so the preaching of the Crusades directed him to attack what was wrong— the possession by 'infidels of the Sepulchre of Christ'."

"The knight who joined the Crusades might thus still indulge the bellicose side of his genius—under the aegis and at the bidding of the church and in so doing he would also attain what the spiritual side of his nature ardently sought—a perfect salvation and remission of sins. He might butcher all day, till he waded ankle-deep in blood, and at nightfall kneel, sobbing for joy, at the altar of the Sepulchre—for was he not red from the winepress of the Lord?"

"Nor was the church merely able, through the Crusades, to direct the martial instincts of a feudal society; it was also able to pursue the object of its own immediate policy, and to attempt the universal diffusion of Christianity, **even at the edge of the sword,** over the whole of the known world."—Ency. Brit., Vol. 7-8, p. 524.

Contemporaries regarded the Crusades as "holy wars" and pilgrims' progress towards Christ's Sepulchre."

There is the historical version of the Crusades. That is the only version the world has, and it was prepared by the church.

HIS WRITINGS DESTROYED

Apollonius is shown by ancient records to have been the greatest philosopher, prophet, preacher and author of the first century. He spent his long life visiting various countries, studying their religious systems, preaching and writing.

No one in his time wrote and left to the world so many valuable manuscripts as he, all devoted to the subject of the Soul and Immortality. But not one fragment of his writings, under his name, has escaped the hand of those who destroyed the ancient records to conceal their fraudulent work, concerning which we shall learn more as we proceed.

No one, not even the church, ever claimed that the gospel Jesus wrote one line of the New Testament. Yet he is the hero of that work and the god of a religious system. Men of straw do not write. Those who make them do their writing.

In the more than two hundred years between Apollonius and the Nicene Council in 325 A.D., many eminent men lived and wrote, such as Justin, Tatian, Bardesanes, Clement of Alexandria, Clement of Rome, Julius Africanus, Tertullian, Minucius Felix, Ignatius, Polycarp, Papias, Justin Martyr, Irenaeus, and scores of others.

Some of the writings of all these men remain and we have them. They lived and wrote in the first three centuries of the Christian era. Search through such of their writings as the church has permitted to come down to us, and in them one cannot find the least notice of that great man of the first century. Even his name we cannot find. But we do find the names of Saul, Apollo, Pol, Paul, Polos, and Paulus.

This total silence regarding that eminent philosopher and brilliant preacher should make intelligent people think. Why is it? It is not the work of chance or accident.

It can be accounted for in only one way: It was imperative utterly to ignore the Great Master, his teachings and his writings in his own name, in order for the church to put in his place the name of its Jesus Christ. The evidence is so overwhelming that it would convince any court on earth.

Of all the men named above, the complete works of none of them have been allowed by the church to come down to us. Why?

The writings of the first three centuries had to pass through the censorial hands of Pope Sylvester I., Eusebius, and their coadjutors and successors who, from the early part of the fourth century down to the day when the art of printing stopped it, were assiduously engaged in interpolating, mutilating, and distorting every fragment of ancient writings that revealed the true identity of their Jesus Christ and the origin of their religious system that came to be known as Christianism.

We now know the reason why Archbishop Chrysostom was so happy when he boasted in the middle of the fifth century A.D. that, "Every trace of the old philosophy and literature of the ancient world has now vanished from the face of the earth" (Bible Myths, Doane, p. 438).

The church fathers destroyed it and admitted it, but they failed for good reason to state why they did it. We are learning the reason why.

It is not by chance nor accident that nowhere in the books of the New Testament is there one single, definite mention of Apollonius by that name. And why were the names of Saul and

29

Paul given to this active character who, according to the testimony of the New Testament, did the most that was done to establish Christianism?

Overwhelming evidence shows that his real name was Apollonius.

The evidence shows there is no history of the gospel Jesus except that contained in the New Testament. He was unknown until the compilers wrote the New Testament in the fourth century.

There was a man born in the reign of Caesar Augustus (Lu. 2:1), who visited Jerusalem and who was called the "Light of the World," a famous oracle, magician, and spiritual leader. His name was Apollonius.

This leader, called Paul in the New Testament, was evidently an Essenean. He taught a doctrine which, divested of spurious additions and interpolations, was the same as that of the early Buddhistic spiritualist. The most convincing indication that he was an Essenean comes from the gospels themselves.

The fact that this man was identified with an unnamed religious sect, apparently organized after the Pythagorean pattern, as opposed to the two dominant Jewish sects co-existing with it is Palestine (the scene of his visit), appears to indicate that he was an Essenean. So the obvious reason why the compilers of the New Testament did not definitely mention the Essenes by name, was because of their leader and his record.

At the Nicene Council in 325 A.D. one of the many bitter arguments arose as to the identity of this great oracle, philosopher and prophet, who had been selected to head the new religion, and who had been dead for more than two hundred years.

One faction claimed that he was a famous Greek Oracle, venerated throughout the world, the story of whose life had been stolen by the Roman Bishops to support their fading power.

The other faction, supporting Constantine, denounced that view and said, in order to disguise their purpose, that he was "very God" incarnate, having adopted the name Apollo, derived from the Greek symbolism of the Sun.

After a heated debate this latter motion carried by the vote of Constantine's faction, and the results of the deliberations were set forth as the Trinity creed.

Lesson No. 12

THE CHALLENGE OF HIEROCLES

As the new religion and its Messiah Jesus began to be preached in Rome in the reign of Diocletian, a learned statesman and Roman pro-consul named Hierocles boldly charged upon the priests their plagiarism of the writings of the great Pythagorean philosopher, Apollonius.

The history of Apollonius, declared Hierocles in his "Candid Words to the Christians," was the original of the stories of the gospel Jesus which, with the epistles and other scriptures by Apollonius (reinterpreting yet older writings), formed the basis of the Christian (Kristosite) scriptures as finally set forth by the Nicene Council.

This charge by Hierocles showed that the fraudulent work of the Christian fathers had been discovered, and caused them to see the urgent necessity of using every means at their command to conceal their fraud.

So the writings of Hierocles were destroyed by Eusebius of Caesarea (264-349 A.D.), who called himself Eusebius Pamphili.

All we know of these writings of Hierocles comes from the reply of Eusebius to the charge, from which we can judge the nature of the revelations Hierocles made.

In that reply, Eusebius wrote "a spirited defense of the Christian faith" and condemned Apollonius as "the noted impostor."

If the charge were false it appears irregular that the Christian fathers, with nothing to fear from other religious systems, were so anxious and careful to destroy every trace of evidence concerning both Apollonius and Hierocles.

A true, honest religion does not fear the differences of opinion; but that attitude has never been assumed by Roman Catholicism.

BIOGRAPHY OF APOLLONIUS

In the third century A.D. the cultured empress Julia Domna, wife of Emperor Serverus, observing how Apollonius was worshipped by the Romans in her day, managed to secure possession of the biography of the great Master that had been written by Damis who, from 43 to 98 A.D., had accompanied Apollonius on his philosophical journeys in Rome, Spain, Egypt, Africa, Iona, Babylonia and India.

At his death Damis had bequeathed his writings to one of his relatives and they finally found their way into the hands of Julia. She urged Philostratus, an eloquent sophist of high repute, to write the biography of Apollonius, giving him the manuscript of Damis which she had preserved in her library.

The Emperor Hadrian (117-138 A.D.) had collected all of

31

the accessible writings of Apollonius that he could find and preserved them in his palace at Antium. Julia managed to secure these also and gave them to Philostratus.

Of Apollonius, Philostratus wrote, "He lived in times not long gone by nor again quite of our own day, yet **men knew him not** because of the true wisdom which he practiced as a Sage."

The compilers of the New Testament paraphrased that statement as follows: "He was in the world . . . and the world knew him not" (Jn. 1:10).

PRIESTHOOD EXCITED

Great was the consternation produced in the fourth century by the translation of Philostratus' "Life of Apollonius of Tyana" into the modern tongues of Europe.

The priesthood was so excited that it cast discretion to the wind and floundered into the bog from which it was their chief aim to escape.

Dr. Lardner admits that all through the third century frequent mention was made of Apollonius and his teachings. It was not until Hierocles, in the fourth century, boldly charged upon the Roman priesthood their plagiarism of the teachings and writings of the great Master, that they saw the fraud had been discovered and found it necessary to set at work every means they could muster that would help to conceal the shocking truth which Hierocles proclaimed with such portentous force, and for which his writings were destroyed and he was silenced.

Paulinus, first archbishop of York, in 622, stated that he was one of the first translators of the Scriptures from the Gallic into the Saxon tongue. He said, "I substituted, as did Eusebius, Jesus Christ of Judea for Apollonius of Tyana," to make "them correspond with Eusebius' version" (Antiquity Unveiled, p. 544).

The life, labors and letters of Apollonius were suppressed by orders of the priesthood of Greece and Rome. In that suppression they conveniently became the life, labors and teachings of the gospel Jesus, who "have sent mine angel to testify unto you these things in the churches, and washed us from our sins in his own blood" (Rev. 1:5; 22:16).

The name Apollonius signifies the personification of the Light of the world (Apollo), in accordance with the practice by which Initiates of the Mysteries were given symbolical names.

So the compilers of the New Testament have their Jesus say, **"I am the light of the world; he that followeth me shall not walk in darkness, but shall have the light of life"** (Jn. 8:12).

It is certain that the biography of Apollonius suffered greatly at the hands of the priesthood, and was much mutilated and caricatured, the real truth being obtainable only by careful scrutiny.

At the zenith of his immense popularity, Apollonius travelled extensively over all parts of the then civilized world, from Spain to India and back again; but most of his preaching was done in Asia Minor to the north of Jerusalem, in the region of Antioch and Ephesus.

The great Master lived at an early age in Tarsus, alleged birthplace and home of Paul. He travelled over the Roman world to the very places Paul is said to have visited—and many more. Both were Esseneans; both were Roman citizens, and both became involved in difficulties with the government.

In the Pauline epistles there is no doubt that it is Damis, the disciple of Apollonius, who is called Demas, the companion of Paul (Col. 4:14). The latter is occasionally mentioned as "Apollos," which is said to be listed as "Apollonius" in the ancient manuscript of the first Corinthians, called the Codex Beza, found in a monastery in France by a Huguenot soldier.

The New Testament articles show evidence of an old and highly developed ecclesiastical system already existing at the time they are supposed to have been written, and are based upon other writings, which also were already in existence.

Such names as Pontius Pilate, Herod, Caiaphas, etc., along with certain historical episodes, were lifted bodily from the works of Josephus.

George Brandes shows in his work "Jesus, A Myth," that many passages in the New Testament were copied literally from the so-called Old Testament, and from other supposedly Jewish works. Other episodes, such as the virgin birth and the crucifixion story, were taken from contemporary writings of older religions that filtered out from the Ancient Mysteries, then those writings were destroyed to hide the source.

APOLLONIUS AND JESUS

Concerning the gospel Jesus, Tischendorf wrote:

"Author after author, volume after volume, of the life of Christ may appear until the archives of the Universe are filled, and yet all we will have of the Life of Jesus appears in the New Testament. Not one person especially associated with Jesus impinges history."

Taylor's Diegesis says:

"We have investigated the claims of every document possessing a plausible claim to be investigated which history has preserved the transactions of the first century A.D. and not so much as a single passage, purporting to have been written at any time within the first hundred years, can be produced to show the existence of such a man as Jesus Christ, or of such a set of men as could be accounted to be his disciples."

Regarding the actual existence of Jesus of the gospels, Gauvin wrote:

"If Christ were an historical character, why was it necessary to forge documents to prove his existence? Did any one ever think of forging documents to prove the existence of any person who was really known to have lived? The early Christian forgeries are tremendous testimony of the weakness of the Christian cause" (Did Jesus Christ Really Live, p. 46).

The gospel story of Jesus is a myth, and the gospel life of Jesus is one of miracles, regarding which Dean Farrar remarks:

"If miracles be incredible," Christianity is false."

Bishop Westcott stated:

"The essence of Christianity lies in a miracle. If it can be shown that a miracle is either impossible or incredible, all further inquiry into the details of its history is superfluous."

In his "Bible Myths," Doane makes this statement:

"The reader should compare this (remark by Wescott) with Pope Leo X's avowal that 'it is well-known how profitable this faith of Christ has been to us'" (p. 438).

In his work on Apollonius, Reville said:

"Jesus is presented as the offspring of obscure people; his doctrine was but the refinement of a paltry local tra-

34

dition; his life, of which nothing is known outside of the New Testament, was extremely short. He soon fell victim, to the attacks of two or three priests, a petty ruler, and a prosecutor, and a few progidies alone distinguish him from a crowd of other existences which had nothing to do with the destinies of man."

"On the contrary, Apollonius is a well-known historical character, was the son of wealthy parents, and had stored his vast intellect with the religious doctrines of the whole world, from Spain to India, and his life extended over a century, one author asserting that he lived to the age of 130. Like a luminous meteor he traversed the earth, in constant intercourse with kings and the powerful ones of the world, who venerated and feared him. If he ever met with opposition, he triumphed over it majestically, always stronger than his tyrants, never subject to humiliation, never brought into contact with public executioners."

In his book, "Apollonius of Tyana," F. A. Campbell wrote:

"A striking, distinctive figure, clad in white linen, with feet unsandled and with locks unshorn; austere, reserved, and of meager mein; with eyes cast upon the ground as was his manner, Apollonius drew all simple folks to him with something of a saint's attraction, and yet won as intimates the Emperors of Rome."

"Through his love for all life and swift appreciation of the beauty of the human form, he drew nigh to the sufferings of the body and became acquainted with the sufferings of the soul. He sought to heal, or at least to soothe, some of the distresses, physical and spiritual, of poor humanity; and to such singular degree of skillfulness did he attain in the healing arts of his day, that even the sacred orgies of Agaea and of Delphi pronounced him more than mortal, referred the distempered body and the smitten soul to him for relief, knowing that from his very presence proceeded a peculiar virtue, a benign influence, an almost theurgic power.

"By years of silence and contemplation, by extensive travel, and by a continuous spiritual and worldly experience, he deepened, to a large measure, an originally powerful and intense personality; and so it was that at length he became the admiration not only of all countries

35

through which he passed, but of the whole Roman and Hellenic world.

"Cities sent envoys and embassies to him decreeing him public favors; monarchs bestowed special dignities upon him, counting him worthy to be their counsellor; incense was burnt before his altars; and after his death divine honors were paid to his images, which had been erected, with great enthusiasm, in all the temples of the gods.

"Nor did his fame evanesce. All down through the ages (of the first three centuries A.D.) his name has carried in it something of a hurricane. For speculative critics of both early and later days have thought to find in the life of this extraordinary man a parallel to the life of (the gospel) Christ, and to ground thereon an argument against the supernal claims for the 'Son of Man.'

"Hence for centuries even the name of Apollonius was odious to Christians; for it seemed that the very Gospel of the 'Son of Man' was at stake. The Christian apologists, on their part, in self defence, were not lacking in fiercely attacking their adversaries' champion and to denounce him as little better than an imposter, a socerer and a magician.

"On this account they have generally failed to understand Apollonius. They have lacked, at least in their combative approach to him, that sweet affection for signal worth, that gracious patience for nobleness, which is absolutely essential to comprehend a new or startling character or mode of life."

J. M. Roberts wrote:

"We have abundant proof that Jesus Christ is founded on the known life of Apollonius, the earthly existence of whom has never been questioned, to which is added passages from the lives of various personages and teachings of the mythical gods of other lands.

"The Christians will find that their ideal Jesus is but a phantom—a myth. They can chase it as a child would a butterfly through the meadows on a summer's day, and it will elude their grasp. The Christian Jesus is nothing more than the Krishna of the Hindus" (Ant. Unveiled).

The strict avoidance of all notice of the philosophical and religious teachings of Apollonius definitely shows the consciousness of the priesthood that Apollonius was the real Jesus, Paul and John of the New Testament. In fact, the original compilers of the New Testament knew this was true, as they had the evidence to prove it in the scriptures they used to make the New Testament.

Every picture presented as that of the gospel Jesus is that of Apollonius, painted by the artist of Vespasian while Apollonius was his Oracle.

It was the followers of Apollonius, and not the so-called Christians, who were persecuted by the Roman authorities, and they were Essenes.

The active part of the life of this Master extended through the reigns of the Roman Emperors Tiberius, Caligula, Claudius, Nero, Vespasian, Titus, Domitian, Nerva, and into the reign of Trajan.

A DANGEROUS BOOK

In the early part of the third century A.D. Philostratus wrote his biography of Apollonius. After the new religion was established in 325 A.D., the first act of the founders was to burn all writings they could find, especially those of the first few centuries that mentioned Apollonius as the great spiritual leader of the first century.

It was for this reason that they burned the ancient libraries, including the famous Alexandrian Library with its 400,000 manuscripts and scrolls of ancient history, which was burnt under the edict of the Roman Emperor Theodosius.

The chief librarian, learning of the plot, secretly removed from the library some of the most valued writings and sent them to the east for safety. Among these was the "Life of Apollonius" by Philostratus.

As though God intended that truth should prevail and the greatest fraud on earth be exposed, this work, thus saved from the flames, was regarded by the church as the most dangerous of all heretical writings.

From the burning of the Alexandrian Library until the suppression of Blout's first English translation of the "Life of Apollonius," the church made every effort to destroy this work and keep it from the public. But the work survived through the centuries, escaping all attempts to destroy it.

During the Dark Ages this work was preserved among the Arabs, and was not introduced into Europe until early in the sixteenth century, when it was immediately put under ecclesiastical ban, with the result that at present, even among the well educated, there prevails in the western world a general ignorance of the very existence of the Great Master of the first century.

Only a few centuries ago all the writings and records of antiquity were in the hands of the church, and it is easily understood why knowledge of the life and teachings of Apollonius was not permitted to pass out to the modern world.

The "Life of Apollonius" was not permitted to be published in Europe until 1501 A.D., when Aldus Manutins printed the first Latin edition to appear in Europe.

It was not until 1680 that Charles Blount made the first English translation of the first two of the eight manuscripts written by Philostratus; and his notes on what he translated raised such a storm, that in 1693 the translation was condemned by the church and further publication prohibited.

Concerning the effects of Blount's translation, F. A. Campbell, in his "Apollonius of Tyana," said:

"Fierce passions were let loose. Sermons, pamphlets
and volumes descended upon the presumptous Blount like
fireballs and hailstones, and his adversaries did not rest
until the church authorities had forbidded him to publish
the remaining six manuscripts."

All Blount said in his notes on the work was to point out that we must admit the truth of the apparent miracles of Apollonius as well as those of the gospel Jesus, or, if the former were false, there is less ground to believe in the latter.

It was not until 1809 that Edward Berwick made the first complete English translation of the Life of Apollonius by Philostratus. The church destroyed this work so fast that in 1907 two London book shops of world-wide reputation searched and advertised in vain for a copy.

GREAT POPULARITY OF THE MASTER

Today hardly any one can be found, even among the highly educated, who ever heard of Apollonius of Tyana, much less know aught about his work.

But "there was a day," writes Campbell, "when the name of Apollonius was on the tongue of every educated Englishman, even though sectarian prejudice against him characterized every writer prior to the nineteenth century."

So remarkable was Apollonius as a wonder-worker, that after his death he was deified and worshipped by Emperor Antonius Caracella as a Divine, while Emperor Alexander Severus (A.D. 205-235) set up in his private shrine a statue of the Master. Other Roman Emperors showered upon high honors and held him in great esteem.

Many temples were erected in his name and dedicated to him. One such temple was erected at Tyana by the Roman Emperors, who considered him worthy to be honored in a measure in which they themselves were honored in turn.

Philostratus stated that at the time he wrote the biography of Apollonius, in the third century, the Master was worshipped by the Romans in the days of Septimius Severus (146-211 A.D.) as the "Savior of Men."

The feats held by the Romans in honor of Apollonius were always celebrated with the Star dedicated to him. This was a star of the zodiac constellation Aris, the Lamb (Jn. 1:29), the sign in which the Sun crossed the equinoctial line at the vernal equinox, thus identifying Apollonius as the "Crucified Lamb," whose "crucifixion redeemed the world" from the desolation and death of Winter.

Pliny, the Younger, was appointed by Trajan as procurator of Bythinia and Pontus the latter part of the first century A.D. He reported to Trajan that he found the Essenes, not Christians as reported in history, were accustomed to meet on a fixed day before dawn and sing in turns a hymn to Apollonius as a god.

The encyclopedias say that this correspondence with Trajan was apparently preserved in a single manuscript which "disappeared." In 1888 E. G. Hardy found the "copy" that was supplied to the printers of the Aldine text. The words Apollonius and Essenes were deleted from the "copy" and replaced by the words Jesus Christ and Christians.

Had the original manuscript not "disappeared," we would learn more of the powerful influence of Apollonius on the people, and of how the ancient records were doctored, distorted and destroyed to eliminate his name and put in its place the gospel Jesus.

The remarkable popularity of the Great Master in the first three centuries A.D. stands in sharp contrast to his almost complete oblivion today. Then he was worshipped by the multitude as a god. Today modern encyclopedias give him a short paragraph, stating that—

"The narratives of his work are so full of the miraculous that many have regarded him as an imaginary character. The work of Philostratus, composed at the instance of Julia, wife of Severus, is generally regarded as a religious work of fiction" (Enc. Brit. Vol. 1-2, p. 188).

Thus are we deceived by the histories and the encyclopedias.

Barret said, "Was there ever any one among men more holy, venerable, noble, and divine than Apollonius? He restored life to the dead, he did and said many things beyond human reach, which things, whoever would be informed of them, may meet with many accounts of them in the Greek histories of his life."

While ancient histories contain numerous accounts of Apollonius and his work, they do not so much as mention the name of the gospel Jesus.

HIS MYSTERIOUS DISAPPEARANCE

Philostratus says that no grave of the Great Master was ever found, but everywhere he met with marvelous tales about his "disappearance."

Some said that his last great miracle was his final disappearance, and that he re-appeared to his disciples. Others said that he secretly left for the Himalayas to rejoin his Brahman teachers and spend his days with them in seclusion.

Several Roman Emperors, including Caracella who erected a temple to Apollonius, investigated the matter in vain.

It is amazing to know that some centuries later there appeared in Spain an Arab philosopher named Artephius, who claimed to be Apollonius.

This Artephius seems to have lived in Granada and Cadiz, places where Apollonius had stayed for some time, and where Artephius had a high reputation among the Hermetic Philosophers of his day. They came to him from the most distant regions in order to consult him.

Artephius, like Apollonius, professed the Pythagorean philosophy and studied the art of compounding talismans and divination by the character of the planets and the song of the birds. He had been able, he claimed, to prolong his life in a miraculous way by means of certain secret knowledge.

There is considerable evidence that after his mysterious disappearance from the court of Domitian, as proof of which Philostratus quotes court records extant in this day, and a period of time spent in the Himalayas, Apollonius went to the Near East, where he continued to live among the Arabians who preserved his writings during the Dark Ages, and were instrumental in introducing the Hermetic Sciences of astrology and alchemy which, after the Crusades, were brought to Europe and constituted the beginnings of modern science.

· Phillmore refers to the identity of Apollonius and a man known as Balinus in the following words:

· "Who was this Apollonius? With the Balinus of eastern legend we might be content; had Moeragenes survived we might have had some certitude. (Moeragenes wrote a biography of Apollonius that was destroyed by the church.) Something uncommon there must have been in the personality that gave Philostratus a theme on which to embroider."

There is a tradition that Apollonius lived among the Arabians under the name of Balinus.

Djildeki wrote about a book by Balinus on the Seven Figures (planets). Iznik mentioned a work by Balinus on Alchemy. Albert der Grosse cites from the work the following:

"The Seven," by Balinus, which starts with. "Balinus said that Apollo (Apollonius) dictated the book, which is cited in an anonymous astrological-magical compilation in the year 926 in Fjabiribn Atlah's book on Palmistry."

Under the name of Balinus, Apollonius is supposed to have been the author and inspirer of Arabian sciences, according to a Spanish translation from the Arabic of a work, "Book on the Forms and Images that are in Heaven," by Befehl Alfons X, who refers to Apollonius as Belyanus, and says, "Always he creates magic, or astrology or magical cures."

As previously stated, it was these reports and rumors regarding the appearance of Paul's Ghost that worried the church in Rome and inspired the Crusades. The church was excited and anxious to get its hands on the man it feared so greatly, whose name it had deleted from the pages of history, whose writings it had burned, and whose very name it had forbidden men to mention.

The history of Apollonius was further obliterated by the Roman Church in the utter destruction of Ephesus by the Roman army. That was the city where he was last seen and in which it was said he died and was buried.

Ephesus was once the greatest city in all Asia Minor and the principal emporium of trade in the East. It was known as one of the eyes of Asia, Smyrna being the other.

The Great Philosopher did much of his teaching in Ephesus. His beloved disciple Damis, a Greek historian, was born there; and is mentioned in the New Testament (Col. 4:14; 2d Tim. 4:10; Phil. 24). He joined Apollonius in that city, accompanied him in his travels, and wrote an account of them, in which he inserted the discourses and prophecies of his Master.

41

To make certain the destruction of these writings, and of all memory and trace of Apollonius and Damis in and around Ephesus, history states that "None of the ancient cities have been so completely destroyed as was Ephesus."

That is more evidence to show how greatly Romanism feared the work and memory of this man, whose life it used as that of its Jesus, and whose writings it used as the Pauline Epistles.

Lesson No. 13

THE PATH OF POWER

As few students may be expected to have sufficient acquaintance with ancient philosophy and the rather detailed knowledge of psycho-physiology necessary for even a superficial survey of the Apocalypse, a brief sketch will be given of the topics that must be considered in interpreting it.

The point where the ancient arcane system sharply diverges from all the conventional schools of thought, is in the means of acquiring knowledge.

The conventional scientist and orthodox religionist rely for knowledge on the physical senses, the psychic emotions, and the intellectual faculties as they are in the present stage of human development.

The scientist enlarges the scope of the senses by the use of microscope, telescope and other mechanical devices which can never reach beyond the material. The religionist puts his faith in ancient scriptures that are misleading to the exoteric because they were never written to be understood by any but the initiates.

The esotericist, refusing to be confined within the narrow limits of the physical senses and mental faculties, and realizing that the gnostic powers of the Soul are hopelessly obstructed by the imperfect instrument, the physical organism, through which it functions, devotes himself to what may be termed intensive self-evolution, the conquest and utilization of all the forces and faculties that lie latent in that fontal essence within his own body, which is the primary source of all the elements and powers of his Being, or all that he is, has been, and will be. The Kingdom of God is within.

By gaining conscious control of the concealed potencies that are the proximate cause of his individual evolution, man seeks to traverse the path leading to spiritual illumination and liberation from physical bondage, moving forward, as it were, toward that goal which mankind, as a whole, will never reach, because great skill and knowledge are required to aid the Seeker of

42

Light in avoiding the snares and traps set along the path by despots and their henchmen.

The difficult task of the Seeker of Light is not so much to know as to become. To know is easier than to become. Herein lies the powerful import of the Delphic inscription, "Know Thyself," and the ancient admonition, "He that overcometh shall inherit all things" (Rev. 21:7).

Regardless of the greatness of our knowledge, if not intelligently and persistently applied it is worthless.

That is the key-note of esotericism and ancient wisdom. We have little of it now because, as the great Carrel wrote, "Our ignorance (of the body and its functions) is profound."

If the clergy knew aught about man's psycho-physiological nature, they would not attempt to interpret the Apocalypse as treating of "heaven and the church."

The esotericist understands that true self-knowledge can be attained only through self-development in the highest sense of the term,—a development that begins with a healthy body and an introspection and the awakening of the regenerative forces which slumber in modern man's inner protoplasmic nature, like the vivific potency in the female ovum, and which, when roused into activity, transforms man ultimately into a divine being, clothed with a deathless ethereal form.

This course of transcendental self-conquest, the development from the concealed essence of one's own embryonic nature of a self-luminous, immortal being, is the sole subject matter of the Apocalypse, which contains, in symbol and allegory, an almost complete outline of the psycho-physiological process of regeneration.

ABSOLUTE REALITY

In the esoteric philosophy Absolute Deity is considered as beyond the spheres of evistence and ulterior to Being itself.

The world of true Being is that of the Logos, or Nous, the Demiurgos of the Gnostics, the realm of divine thought, or archetypes, which are the eternal patterns, so to say, of all things in the manifested Universe.

By a paradox that defies the reasoning faculty, but which is readily resolved intuitively, God is said to be apart from, and independent of, the Universe, and yet to permeate every atom of it.

God is abstract Unit, the origin of all number, but which never loses its unit-value, and cannot be divided into fractions.

The Logos in the manifested or collective Unit, a deific Individuality, the collectivity of a countless host of Logoi, who are differentiated into Seven Hierarchies, constituting in the aggregate the Second Logos, the uttered Thought or Word.

As a mediate principle for the manifestation of the Logos in and from God, Apollonius, in the fourth gospel, puts the Archeus as the primary element or substratum of substantive objectivity,—that which becomes the differentiation from the subtil, and then the gross material elements of the manifested worlds.

If this primary substance is related back to God, and considered as being prior to the Logos, the result is the refined dualism that mars some of the old systems of philosophy. In the prologue the Logos is really coeval with the Archeus. The Logos is (subsists) in the Archeus, and the latter becomes, in the Logos, the principle of manifest Life that irradiates as Light.

The Light of the Logos is identical with the Pneuma, the Breath or Spirit, and, esoterically, it is the pristine force that underlies matter in every stage, and is the producer of all the phenomena of Being. It is the Great Force from which differentiate all the forces in the Cosmos.

From the (1) Archetypal world, that of the Logos, emanate successively the (2) Psychic and the (3) Physical Realms. To these three may be added a fourth, usually included by ancient authors in the Psychic, but in reality it is distinct from it. The fourth department, which may be called the Phantasmal, is the realm of phantoms, evil spirits, and psychic garbage generally.

MAN IS THE UNIVERSE

Within himself man contains all the universes, systems, planets and globes. He is the temple of the living God (1 Cor. 3:16), the epitome of all worlds and all things. He is the focusing and condensing point of innumerable electro-magnetic currents. The origin of man is in God, and his real self, or individuality, is a Logos, a manifested phase of God.

Analogous with the Universe or Macrocosm, man, the microcosm, has three departments or bodies, termed the spiritual, the psychical, and the physical. In the Upanishads they are termed the casual body, the subtil body, and the gross body.

In mystic writings these bodies are made to correspond to the four occult elements, fire, air, water and earth, and also to the sun and moon. Hence they were termed the solar body, fire body, lunar body, air body, water body and earth body.

The spiritual (pneumatic) body is not actually a body, but only an ideal, archetypal form, ensphered by the pneuma or primor-

44

dial principle which, in the duality of manifestation, generates all forces and elements. It is called the "casual body" because from its sphere all the other bodies are engendered.

The lower forms are enveloped by the same circumambient aura, called in the New Testament the "radience" or "glory," which was actually visible to the Masters as a faint, oviform film of bluish haze.

THE SERPENTINE FIRE

Semi-latent within this pneumatic ovum is the Paraklete,—the Light of the Logos which, in energizing, becomes what may be called the living, conscious, vital electricity, of incredible voltage, but hardly comparable to the form of electricity known to physicists.

In ancient symbology this was the "good serpent." Taken from the pneumatic ovum, it was also represented by the symbol of the Egg and the Serpent. In Sanskrit writings it was called the Kundalini, the annular or ring-form force, and in Greek, Speirema, the serpent-coil.

In the telestic work or cycle of initiation, this force weaves from the primal substance of the auric ovum, upon the ideal form or archetype it contains, and conforming thereto, the immortal Augoeides, or Solar Body (Soma Heliakon), so-called because in its visible appearance it is self-luminous like the sun, with a golden radiance. Its aureola displays an opalescence. This Solar Body is of atomic, non-molecular substance.

The psychic (lunar) body, through which the Nous (Mind) acts in the psychic world, is molecular in structure, but of far finer substance than the elements composing the gross physical form, to which organism it closely responds, having organs that match the five physical senses, which, in fact are the exteriorized representatives of the psychic body.

In appearance, the psychic body has a silvery luster, tinged with delicate violet; and its aura is of palest blue, with an interchanging play of all the prismatic colors, rendering it irridescent.

There is a fourth body that is sometimes mentioned in mystic writings. In Sanskrit it is called Kama Rupa, the form engendered by lust. It comes into existence only after somatic death, save in the exceptional case of the extremely evil socerer who has become morally dead while physically alive.

This body is of phantasm shape, from the dregs and effluvia of matter by the image-creating power of the gross animal mind.

Of such nature are the "unclean spirits" of the New Testament, where also the "abominable stench" seems to be a covert allusion to this malodorous shade. This phantasm has the shadowy semblance of the physical body from which it was derived, and is surrounded by a cloudy aura of brick-red hue.

NOTHING DEAD

In the esoteric cosmogony the theory of "dead" matter has no place.

The Universe is a manifestation of life, of consciousness, from the Logos down to the very atoms of the material elements. In fact, in the atom abides the intelligence of the Universe.

In ancient philosophy a sharp distinction was made between Being and Existence. The Logos, the Archetypal World, is that of True Being, changeless, eternal; while existence is a moving outward into the worlds of becoming, of ceaseless change and transformation.

Lesson No. 14

CYCLES OF LIFE

The Universe and all its parts move in cycles, according to cosmic law. The Nous (immortal man) comes under this law. It enters upon a cycle of incarnations, passing in due order from one mortal body to another, leaving the old and building a new one.

The Ancient Masters taught that the body is but a temporary dwelling place of Immortal Spirit (1 Cor. 3:16), which has fashioned that material form, moulds it, leaves it in due course, and builds another, repeating that process over and over for seven times, in harmony with the cosmic Law of Seven.

This ancient doctrine was explained in the old philosophy destroyed by Romanism when its founders plunged Europe into darkness in order to carry out their nefarious scheme of a crucified savior. They knew it would be fatal to the church for the masses to know aught about reincarnation.

In fact, the doctrine of reincarnation had always prevailed throughout the world, except in modern times and among western people.

It was taught by Pythagoras and Plato; it was one of the principles of the Druid faith. Caesar found it among the Gauls. It was found in the old races of Mexico, Central and South America. Among modern philosophers, Kant and Scopenhauer upheld it. Bruno, Goethe and Emerson found it agreeable to their thoughts. Mystics and poets have professed faith in it. Huxley,

46

archpriest of mid-Victorian materialistic science, wrote of it:

> "None but very hasty thinkers will reject it on the ground of inherent absurdity. The doctrine has its roots in the world of reality, and it can claim such support as the great argument of analogy is capable of supplying."

Eternal existence, interrupted by death and resumed from one physical life to another, would explain better than any other theory, the vast difference between persons, of the same families, in the kind and degree of their abilities, capacities, and the conditions of their existence.

If Mozart composed music at the age of six, if Bernini modelled statues when he was seven, and if DeQuincey, at thirteen, could have harangued an Athenian mob in its own language, may it not have been because each had developed his capacities in these directions during antecedent earthly lives?

The powers and faculties with which we are endowed may be in the nature of automatic remembrances of things learned slowly in past existences, quite in analogy with those transformations experienced by the human embryo in the months of its antenatal life, during which it rapidly passes through the various stages of the physical life of the species.

All such cycles appear as the Law of the Universe. As in the childish jingle of "The House That Jack Built," the cosmic process repeats each preceding phrase and then adds another line for subsequent repetition.

On what other interpretation of cosmic processes than that presented by reincarnation, is it possible to discover any semblance of essential justice; or account for the feeling we all have had at one time or another, of "I have been here before," or "This has been thus before," as expressed by Rosetti in "Sudden Light"?

On what other theory are explicable the secret likings and antipathies that urge men to seek out their fate; the haunting charm to the eye of certain faces; to the ear of certain voices; the kinship to the mind of certain fields of knowledge—different fields to different minds—or the vividness of the imagination of particular periods of past history.

It is an axiom of science that in the absence of evidence which is conclusive, that theory is best which most completely and successfully accounts for and correlates the greatest number of unexplained phenomena.

The most ancient teaching to the effect that man, through successive lives, is self-rewarded, self-punished, reaps as he sows, and builds, good or bad, the house (body) he inhabits; that failure is at most only postponement, and success but a steppingstone to greater effort, satisfies not only the head but the heart as well.

When Krishnamurti was asked about reincarnation, he said: "Reincarnation is a fact, but what good will that do you now?"

He probably meant to imply that preoccupation with one's past or future diverts the mind from concentration on the NOW, which is the only point of contact with physical reality and the only door through which any newness can enter.

It is fairly well established that past and future are illusions of the physical consciousness, which creates its own time element. Ouspensky said:

"We know already by our intellect that everything exists in infinite spaces of time—nothing is made, nothing becomes, all is" (Tertium Organum).

The Universe is a unit. It had no beginning and has no end. All things in it and all its parts partake of that same perpetual quality. Man is as eternal as the stars themselves. He makes his own limitations. They rise from his faulty education, designed to fit him in the orthodox social pattern, on which modern civilization rests, and to preserve which, all knowledge must be curtailed and controlled.

The Ancient Masters taught that man is eternal. According to their doctrine, the term "man" is merely a name applied to God-Spirit in the flesh on the physical plane.

They held that man appears as the incarnated God-Spirit, Know ye not that your body is the temple of God-Spirit, which is in you, which is you. God-Spirit that dwelleth in man does the work. What work? Everything done by man (Jn. 4:24; 6:63; 14:10; 1 Cor. 3:16; 6:19).

Language could not be plainer nor more explicit. Most men cannot comprehend these plain propositions because they are taught to look for a god in the distant sky.

The Bible explains what man is. It destroys the dogma of vicarious atonement and clearly shows that man has eternal life.

It is common knowledge that universal electricity luminates all electric light on earth. If we cut off the current, the lights expire, but the electricity has not changed nor been annihilated.

It should be as easy to understand that Universal God-Spirit animates all living forms. When the material form expires, becomes lifeless, God-Spirit has neither changed nor been annihilated.

The Bhagavad Gita says:

"As the Soul, wearing this material body, experienceth the stages of infancy, youth, manhood, and old age, even so shall it, in due time pass on to another body, and in other incarnations shall it again live, and move and play its part. Those who have attained the wisdom of the Inner Doctrine, know these things, and fail to be moved by aught that cometh to pass in the world of change—to such Life and Death are but words, and both are but surface aspects of the deeper Being" (p. 26).

Eternal Life is a fact. The dogma of a crucified savior is false. Christianity has no foundation. It falls as its fraudulent Christ fails.

Because physical life is time for man, because he is embedded in it, he cannot realize by experience the truth of that which his intellect assures him, nor conceive of himself otherwise than as conditioned by time. For him time is not; for him time does not exist.

The theory that at least seven incarnations are required for the attainment of that higher state of consciousness which was the goal of the Masters, and yet that this can occur in a moment, are reconcilable when we consider the nature of the change.

Physics provides an excellent analogy for this understanding: When heat is applied to solid substance, while its temperature rises, to all external appearance it remains the same. But the moment the degree of heat is reached which marks the melting point, the solid begins to become liquid, changing shape and seemingly its very nature. The same kind of transformation occurs when liquid changes into gas.

These natural changes in state are produced by an expansion of the molecules and an increase in the rate of vibration of the constituent particles of any given substance.

Yoga is like that. It is a self-induced raising of one's rate of vibration with the result that when the rate reaches a certain intensity, there ensues that expansion of consciousness which effects a change of state or condition, a release of power, a freedom of movement in a more ample medium, in which the time element disappears, or changes to something else, and physical laws, as known to us, fade into spiritual laws unknown to physical man.

Although the heating process for man may be a slow one,

resumed and repeated life after life, because no necessary step can be omitted, the final apotheosis may be sudden and surprising, like the volatilization of liquid into gas.

The fact of reincarnation, instead of being mysterious and difficult of proof, is very prosaic and simple, and has always been treated as exoteric in all archaic religions and philosophies.

Positive knowledge of its truth, on a basis of personal experience, is one of the first results discovered by him who enters upon the initial stages of self-conquest. It is then a fact as apparent to him as are the cognate facts of physical birth and death. Just as simple and just as mysterious.

The telestic work has for its object to achieve deliverance from the ordeal or reincarnation, and this is complete and final only when the eternal Solar Body is formed, and the Perfected Man is thereby freed from the process of reincarnation in the mortal physical and psychic forms.

THE PHYSICAL BODY

In elucidating the Apocalypse, the physical body, in its physiological relation to psychology, must be noticed somewhat in detail.

The physical body may itself be considered an objective microcosm, an epitome of Nature, of the Material World, to every department of which its organs and functions correspond and are in direct relation. Furthermore, as the object through which the Soul contacts the visible world, its organs correspond to, and are the respective instruments of, the powers and faculties of the Soul.

Thus the body has four chief vital centers that are analogues of the four kingdoms, and of the four manifested generic powers of the Soul. These four somatic divisions are:

1. Brain, the organ of the Nous or higher mind
2. Lungs and heart, the seat of the lower mind
3. Navel region, the center of the passional nature
4. Generative center, seat of the vivifying powers on the animal plane.

For the purpose at hand, it is unnecessary to go deeper into details as to these correspondences, save only in regard to the nerve system and the vital force operating through it.

The nerve system is a unit with dual aspects as follows:

(1) the cerebro-spinal, consisting of brain and spinal cord,
(2) the sympathetic or ganglionic department.

While virtually distinct, these two systems are intimately related in their ramifications in the body.

The sympathetic system consists of a series of distinct nerve-centers, or ganglia. They are small masses of vascular neurine, extending on each side of the spinal column from the head to the coccyx.

Lesson No. 15

ASTRAL PLANE

As long as modern science refuses to recognize planes of existence beyond the material, and as long as theology remains in darkness, the masses will never realize how great the Ancient Masters were in knowledge and intelligence.

No understanding of the recondite phases of the Apocalypse is possible for those with little knowledge of the structures of the body, and especially of those structures that function in correspondence with realms beyond the material. For the body's structures function in correspondence with every plane of being.

In addition to the structures of his body that function on the material plane, the Masters taught that man has an occult, astral or fourth dimensional anatomy, or structures that function in harmony with the fourth dimensional plane.

Ancient allegories contain many references to the Astral Plane; but orthodox scientists refuse to recognize that plane, and orthodox religionists have no clear conception of it, nor of the astral body of man. Hence we must consider this phase of the subject in order to understand the profound allegories of the Apocalypse that puzzle the church.

There are Seven Planes of Being according to the Masters. The lowest is the Material. Second in order is that known as the Plane of Forces; the third is known as the Astral, and the fourth is the Mental Plane.

Beyond these four planes of vibration are three higher ones known to occultists. They have no names that can be understood by those dwelling exclusively on the lower planes, and the terms are incapable of explanation to those on the lower planes.

There are but few of the controlled minds competent to break the bonds of the social pattern and grasp some of the things described in this work.

We must first form a clear conception of the term "plane."

51

In consulting dictionaries the student may get the impression that planes are places or series of level layers, or strata.

Such error rises from considering planes as composed of matter. The densest form of matter, stone and steel, is composed of vibratory waves. The forces of the Cosmos are but manifestations of waves of vibration.

Planes do not rise above one another. They are graded as to their respective degrees of vibration. They are planes of vibration and not planes of matter. Matter is the lowest degree of vibration.

The various planes have not spatial distinction nor degree. They interpenetrate one another in the same point of space. A single point of space may have its manifestations of all the seven planes of being.

PLANE A STATE

The Masters said, "A plane of being is not a place of being, but a state of being."

In the scriptures they wrote that Heaven is not a place in space, but a state of Mind (Rom. 14:17).

They taught that the kingdom of Heaven is not a material plane in space, but a state of man's consciousness (Lu. 17:21).

They said that when man dies, he does not ascend to heaven nor descend to hell. There is simply a **change of consciousness** from the material to the spiritual (1 Cor. 15:51).

In the ceremonies of the Ancient Mysteries, Eternal Life was actually demonstrated to the neophyte by a secret ritual that has remained unknown to the profane unto this day. It was never revealed by the Initiates.

By a secret process known only to the Masters, the neophyte was put into a deep, hypnotic sleep, and it lasted three days. Then his unconscious body was exposed to the Rays of the Rising Sun in the ceremony that restored him to physical consciousness.

This ceremony was termed the Last Resurrection. When the neophyte was "raised from the dead" and his physical consciousness returned, he knew that he had Life Eternal. He knew that man is a dual being of both the temporal and eternal worlds. For during the days of his physical unconsciousness, he was in the Realm of Spiritual Consciousness, and actually saw the kingdom of God (Jn. 3:3).

It was to prepare the neophyte for this mystic ordeal that he was required to pass through the rigid preparatory training. If he failed, he was rejected as unworthy of the great blessings of the Initiatory Ceremonies.

52

Students of the Ancient Mysteries know that the raising of Lazarus by the gospel Jesus is an allegory which refers to this ritual (Jn. 11:44).

As explained in our course titled "Immortalism," every man, at the moment of his demise, realizes his duality. For a certain period, a few moments to a few minutes, his physical consciousness remains functional, fading out slowly, while his spiritual consciousness is increasing.

During the time it takes the physical consciousness to fade out entirely man knows that he is a dual being. At that moment he can see the material world from his spiritual state. The material world disappears as the material consciousness fades entirely out.

Clear light contains all the colors of the rainbow. It is invisible-to our eye because of its rapid vibration. When any obstruction retards the vibratory rate, the eye can then see the slower vibrations, and they appear as colors. The difference in colors is the difference in planes of vibration. The difference between the material plane and the astral is the difference in vibratory rate.

Our terminology is not competent to give a better explanation of, or aid to, the correct mental conception of the idea of a "plane of being."

Each clear beam of sunlight contains many different colors, each with its own rate of vibration. By the proper laboratory apparatus each color of light may be separated from the others. The difference in colors rises from the difference in etheric vibrations, as explained above.

The Astral Plane is the fourth dimensional quality that lies relative to the material plane. It is the plane of Divine Creation, in which the Divine expresses all of the potential or uncreate qualities of the Godhead, and from which the material world receives all things that appear on the visible plane.

In the Astral Plane is located the essence of the Divine City, the new Jerusalem (Rev. 21:2). It is not up nor out, but occupies the same space as the material world, being separated from it by its vibratory octave, and quality and kind of manifestation of Divine attributes that are inherent in that plane.

THE ASTRAL BODY

Man's body is so complex that it corresponds to all the planes of being. His astral body corresponds to the astral plane.

Man's physical body does not have to disintegrate nor de-

53

materialize in order to vibrate in harmony with the astral plane. There are two avenues of approach: (1) By the employment of the astral senses, and (2) by visiting in the "astral body."

THE ASTRAL SENSES

The astral senses are a higher set, corresponding in office to the five physical senses that function on the material plane. When the astral senses are functional, man is able to receive impressions on the Astral Plane.

Each physical sense has its astral counterpart, which functions on the astral plane as the physical senses function on the material plane. Man has, in latency, the power of seeing, hearing, feeling, smelling, and tasting on the astral plane by means of the astral senses.

The Masters knew that man really has seven physical senses, instead of five. These two additional senses are not sufficiently developed for use in the average person. These two extra physical senses also have their astral counterparts.

In cases of those who, accidentally or through proper training, have developed the power of astral vision, the scenes of the astral plane are perceived as clearly as are those of the material.

The Master Apollonius, whose life, labors and letters became those of Jesus, Paul and John of the New Testament, was preaching in Ephesus when the Roman Emperor Domitian was assassinated, and saw the deed done.

At first, his voice dropped, as if he were terrified, and then, with less vigor, he continued his exposition, like one who, between the words, caught glimpses of something foreign to his subject. At last he lapsed into silence, as one who has been interrupted in his discourse.

With a concentrated glance at the ground, he stepped forward a few paces from his pulpit and cried: "Courage, Stephanus; smite the tyrant,"—not as one who derives from a mirror a faint image of the event, but as one who sees it with his own eyes.

Then, after a pause, he continued: "Rejoice, my friends, the tyrant dies this day. This day do I say? The very moment in which I was silent, he suffered for his crimes. He dies." This announcement was later confirmed by a messenger from Rome.

The ordinary clairvoyant has flashes of astral vision, as a rule, and is not able to sense astrally by an act of will. The trained occultist is able to shift from one set of senses to the other, by an act of will, as he desires to do so. He may function on both planes at the same time if he so wishes.

ASTRAL BODY STRUCTURES

According to the Masters, the Astral Body of man is so complex that it contains 420,000 Nadis or channels, three of which are termed major, and a fourth dimensional channel that runs relative to the spinal column. This last begins approximately at the Pons Varoli part of the brains and extends down the spine to terminate at the tip of the spine in a hollow channel called the Kanda. The Masters called this channel Sushumna.

Beginning at each nostril and extending down the sides of the spine are two other major channels terminating in the Kanda. These channels (nerves) are called the Ida at the left nostril, and the Pingala at the right. They carry the etheric force (Prana), positive and negative in polarity, inhaled from the air.

As the air passes into the nose, a tiny valve at the root of the nostrils opens, and as oxygen, nitrogen, hydrogen, krypton and other gases pass down into the lungs, the etheric vitality passes down through the Ida and Pingala channels to the Kanda. Extending from the Kanda are thousands of tiny channels, leading to the various organs of the body, carrying the etheric vitality (Prana).

The Masters taught that there are Seven Chakras, or special nerve centers, in or attached to the Sushumna, the central channel. These nerve ganglia are listed as follows:

1. Sacral (sacred) ganglion (Muladhara)
2. Prostatic (Adhishthana)
3. Epigastric (Manipuraka)
4. Cardiac (Anahata)
5. Pharyngeal (Vishuddhi)
6. Cavernous (Ajna)
7. Conarium (Sahasrara)

The lowest, at the bottom of the spine, Muladhara, was symbolized as a lotus with four petals.

The highest, located in the brain, called Sahasrara (pineal gland) was symbolized as the thousand-petalled lotus.

The pineal gland is a small conical, dark-grey body, located in the brain immediately behind the extremity of the third ventricle, in a groove between the nates, and above the cavity filled with sabulous matter said to be composed of phosphate and carbonate of lime.

The pineal gland, believed by modern anatomists to be the vestige of an atrophied eye, is termed by them "the unpaired eye."

According to the Masters, there are twelve spiritual centers in the brain relative to the twelve major pairs of nerve terminals in the cave of the brain, and they surround the pineal gland. These twelve spiritual centers are the twelve houses of the Zodiac in the true spiritual astrology. In every man one is open and dominant, and the cause of this is that the power which flows through them impells man through life.

The twelve centers and the pineal gland, called the Royal Center by the Masters, was another symbol adopted by the church from the Ancient Mysteries and used to represent Jesus and his twelve disciples.

The twelve disciples represent the twelve spiritual channels, and Jesus represents the Shekinah, the Pineal Gland, which is the doorway to Brahm, the gateway into absolute bliss. By some it was called the Holy King, by others the three feasts, and Jesus called it the Eye Single. When he said, "if thine eye be single, thy whole body also is full of light" (Mat. 6:22; Lu. 11:34), he meant let all our consciousness be placed in that single eye.

In the Ancient Mysteries this symbolism was carried out in the Golden Plate, the Holy of Holies, and the twelve stones represented the twelve spiritual powers. Later the spiritual centers were the twelve great knights of the round table, while King Arthur represented the third eye, and the quest of the Holy Grail was the quest for the subjugation of lust.

In modern man the pineal gland is atrophied physically, but is still the organ of spiritual vision when its higher function is restored by the vivifying force of the Speirema, or Paraklete, and it is therefore called esoterically "the third eye," or the eye of the Seer.

The pineal gland is the first center of power in the body that must be awakened before one can rise to the higher plane.

In the ancient allegory, the Kundalini, the Serpent Fire, the Divine Power that must be raised (resurrected) in order to gain spiritual vision, was said to lie coiled in the Kanda like a sleeping serpent.

DUCTLESS GLANDS

In the Ancient Mysteries the candidate was taught the secret of the Endocrine System, the ductless glands recently discovered by medical art, and considered as another "great stride of medical science." The function of the endocrine system is yet but vaguely understood by modern doctors, but the functions of these glands were well understood by the Masters.

When the right course of living activates the dormant Serpent Fire, it displaces the sluggish nerve force or neuricity and becomes the agent of the telestic or perfecting work.

As the power passes up from one chakra to the next, its voltage is increased, the chakra or ganglia acting as so many electric cells coupled for intensity. Furthermore, in each chakra the power is liberated and partakes of the quality peculiar to that center, and is then said to "conquer" the chakra.

In Sanskrit mystic literature great stress is put on this "conquering of the chakras," and in due course we shall see why.

The currents of the Kundalini (Serpent Fire), as also the channels they pursue, are called Nadis, pipes, or tubes, of which we said there are 420,000. The three principal ones are (1) Sushumna, which passes from the terminus of the spinal cord to the top of the head; (2) Pingala, which corresponds to the right sympathetic nerve; and (3) Ida, which corresponds to the left sympathetic nerve.

The force, as specialized in the ganglionic system, becomes the Seven Tattvas, referred to in Zech. 4:10 as "the eyes of the Lord, which run to and fro through the whole earth" (body), and in the Apocalypse as the Seven Pneumata (breaths), since they are differentiations of the Great Breath, the World-Mother, symbolized by the Moon.

Concurrent with these seven lunar forces are five solar forces pertaining to the cerebro-spinal system, called the five Pranas, "vital airs," or "life-winds," which in the Apocalypse are termed "winds."

Lesson No. 17

THE ZODIAC

The Apocalypse represents these twelve forces, the seven breaths, and the five winds as corresponding to the twelve signs of the Zodiac, of which only a brief description will be given here since the Zodiac is more fully covered in our course titled "Immortalism."

The Zodiac is a belt of the celestial sphere, about seventeen degrees in breadth, containing the twelve constellations that the sun traverses during the year in passing round the ecliptic.

Within this zone are confined the apparent motions of the moon and major planets.

The zodiac circle was divided by the Ancient Masters into twelve equal portions called signs, which were designated by the names of the constellations then adjacent to them in the following order: Aries, Taurus, Gemini, Cancer, Leo, Virgo,

Libra, Scorpio, Sagittarius, Capricornus, Aquarius and Pisces.

Due to the precession of the equinoxes, the signs of the ecliptic are now about one place ahead of the corresponding zodiac constellations, which constitute the fixed Zodiac.

Aside from its astronomical utility, the scheme of the Zodiac was used to symbolize the relation between the macrocosm and the microcosm, each of the twelve signs being designed to correspond to one of the twelve greater god-symbols of the ancient pantheon and assigned to the "house" of one of the seven sacred planets; each sign, moreover, being said to govern a particular portion of the human body.

AWAKENING SPIRITUAL POWERS

The foregoing statements cover the topics that must necessarily be noticed in elucidating the recondite meaning of the Apocalypse. To convey a clearer conception of its practical and psychological application, further explanation will now be given of the action of the Serpentine Fire (Speirema) in the telestic or perfective work.

The task of preparing for initiation in the Ancient Mysteries was preceded by the most rigid purificatory discipline. This included strict celibacy and abstemiousness, and it is possible only for the man or woman who has attained a high state of mental and physiological purity. It requires a sound Mind in a sound Body, which requirements exclude most of the degenerates that constitute civilization in this day and time.

To him who is gross and sensual, or whose mind is sullied by evil thoughts or constricted by bigotry, the holy Paraklete comes not. The unpurified person who rashly attempts to invade the adytum of his Spiritual Kingdom within, can arouse only the lower psychic forces of his animal nature, which forces are cruelly destructive and never regenerative. So we find the words celibacy and chastity written in letters of fire in all the ancient scriptures (Rom. 6:13, 21; 8:6, 7; 1 Cor. 5:1, 13, 18; 7:1).

The neophyte who has acquired the purifying virtues before entering upon the systematic course of introspective meditation by which the spiritual powers are awakened, must also, as a necessary preliminary, gain almost complete control of his thoughts, with the ability to focus his mind undeviatingly upon a single detached idea or abstract concept, excluding from his mental field all associated ideas and irrelevant notions.

If successful in this mystic meditation, he eventually obtains the power of arousing the Speireme, or Paraklete, and can thereby enter at will into the state of manteia, the sacred trance of seership.

The four mantic states are not psychic trances nor somnambulic conditions. They pertain to the noetic, spiritual nature; and in every stage of the manteia, complete consciousness and self-command are retained, whereas the psychic trances rarely transcend the animalistic phrenic nature, and are usually accompanied by unconsciousness or semi-consciousness.

Proficiency in the noetic contemplation, with the arousing of the Speirema and the conquest of the life-centers, leads to knowledge of spiritual realities, the science of which constitutes the Gnosis, and the acquirement of certain mystic powers. This culminates in emancipation from physical existence through the "birth from above" when the eternal solar body has been fully formed.

This telestic work requires the unremitting effort of many years. But almost in its initial stages the consciousness of the aspirant becomes disengaged from the mortal phrenic mind and centered in the immortal noetic mind, **so that from incarnation to incarnation the memory carries over,** more or less clearly according to the degree he has attained, the knowledge acquired. With this unbroken memory and certainly of knowledge, he is in fact immortal.

RESURRECTION

In resurrecting the Serpentine (Kundalini) Power by conscious effort in meditation, the Sushumna, while it is the highly important force, is ignored, and the Mind is concentrated on the two side-currents.

The Sushumna cannot be vitalized alone, and it does not commence activity until the Ida and Pingala have preceded it, forming a positive and negative current along the spinal cord.

On reaching the sixth chakra situated back of the nasal passages, these dual currents radiate to right and left, along the line of the eyebrows. Then the Sushumna, starting at the base of the spinal cord, proceeds along the spinal marrow, its passage through each section thereof, corresponding to a sympathetic ganglion, being accompanied by a shock, or rushing sensation, due to the accession of force—increased voltage—until it reaches the conarium, and thence passes outward through the brahmarandra, the three currents thus forming a cross in the brain.

In the initial stage, the seven psychic colors are seen. When the Sushumna impinges upon the brain, there follows the lofty consciousness of the Seer, whose mystic "third eye" now becomes, as it has been poetically expressed, "a window into space."

In the next stage, as the brain centers are successively "raised from the dead" by the Serpentine Fire, the seven "spiritual sounds" are heard in the tense and vibrant aura of the Seer.

In the succeeding stage, the senses of sight and hearing become blended into one, by which colors are heard and sounds are seen. Or colors and sound become one, and are perceived by the sense that is neither sight nor hearing, but both.

Similarly, the psychic senses of taste and smell become unified; and next the two senses, thus reduced from four, are merged in the interior, intimate sense of touch, which in turn vanishes into the epistemonic faculty, the gnostic power of the Seer—exalted above all sense-perception—to cognize eternal realities.

This is the sacred trance, called Samadhi in Sanskrit, and Manteia in Greek. In the ancient literature of these languages, four such trances are described.

These stages of seership are but the beginning of the telestic labor, the culmination of which, as before stated, is rebirth in the Immortal Solar Body.

As the Apocalypse has for its sole theme this spiritual re-birth, it should be apparent why that book has been a puzzle to the conventional theologian, and never yielded its secrets to the mere man of letters who believed that it treated of "heaven and the church."

Lesson No. 18

RIDDLES OF REVELATION

As we sift out of the Apocalypse the spurious interpolations of Eusebius and his successors, made as they compiled the books of the New Testament, we see that this work of Apollonius is a coherent whole, symmetrical, with every detail put in its place with great care.

In its orderly arrangement and concise statements, the book is a model of precise literary workmanship. It purposely presents a series of elaborate puzzles, thereby serving to vex the orthodox and to verify the correct interpretation of the more important symbols. As a detailed description of these in this analysis would interrupt the interpretation of the book as a whole, for the sake of clearness the solution of these puzzles will be given in advance.

The four animal symbols are conspicuous dramatis personae:

(1) A Lamb, with seven horns and seven eyes, is identified as Iesous, and becomes "the Conqueror";

(2) a beast resembling a leopard, with bear's feet and lion's mouth, with seven heads and ten horns;

(3) a red dragon, having seven heads and ten horns, who represents carnal lust; and

(4) a beast having two horns like a Lamb, but speaking like a dragon, and who is called the Pseudo-Seer, or false teacher.

Of these four, the leopard is particularly mentioned as "the beast"; and concerning it the Apocalyptist says:

"Here is cleverness (sophia); he who has the Nous,
let him count the number of the beast; for it the number
of a man, and his number is 666."

The "cleverness" of this puzzle lies in its simpleness. The words "the Nous," the familiar term in Greek philosophy for the higher mind, or man, naturally suggests the correct answer, the Phren, the cognate term for the lower mind, or physical man.

As numbers are expressed in Greek by letter of the alphabet, and not by arithmetical figures, the number of a name is simply the sum of the numerical values of the letters composing it. Thus the numberical value of "he phren" is 666.

If this were the whole of the puzzle, it would be almost puerile. It is only part of and the clue to an elaborate puzzle which, in its entirety, is remarkably ingenious.

1. The Beast (phrenic mind) is the faculty ruling one of the four somatic divisions of the body. From this the logical inference in drawn that the other three are also the regents of the other three somatic divisions. .

2. The Lamb would therefore represent the highest of these, the Nous (Iesous). The word Iesous gives the sum 888. The "Lamb of God" means the head-sign of the Zodiac, Aries, the Ram, a mature Lamb. For this reason "Lamb" usually refers to man's head.

3. The red Dragon, "the archaic serpent," symbolizes the epithumetic nature, and fits into place as the ruler of the third somatic division, Epithumia, which word yields the number 555.

4. The fourth beast, the "False Prophet," takes its place in the fourth division as the procreative principle, Akrasia, "sensuality," the number of its name being 333. The "False Prophet" deceives by yielding pleasure while destroying the body.

Plato applies to this principle the word "Akolasia," which has the same meaning and same numerical value.

Placing these four names, and their numbers, in the four of a diagram of the four somatic divisions of the body, it becomes apparent that the puzzle is still only partly solved. For evidently a complete series of numbers is intended.

A space is left where the diagram, to complete the meaning, requires that very ancient symbol, the Cross, and another space for another very ancient symbol, the "good serpent," the regenerative force; the "bad serpent," carnal lust that leads to generation and degeneration, being already included. The number of the Cross, Stauros, is 777.

The spiraling electric force, "the coil of the serpent," is the Speirema, which word gives the number 444.

The action of this force on the brain, where its triple current forms the Cross, gives the noetic perception, direct cognition, the epistome or highest degree of knowledge, so beautifully defined by Plato. To express this in the diagram makes it necessary to insert the word "Epistemon," the philosophic and esoteric equivalent for the exoteric word Krishna (Christos); its numerical value being 999.

Further, he who has risen to this higher knowledge forthwith becomes the Conquorer. As "The Conquerer" is the hero of the Apocalyptic Drama, his name must be placed at the head of the list, as Ho Nikon, with his number 1,000.

The diagram, thus completed, clarifies the basic teaching of the Apocalypse, which treats of the Speirema and its energizing power through the vital centers as the Conquorer masters them and builds for himself, out of that primordial substance, his immortal vehicle, the monogenetic or Solar Body.

This phase of the subject is so vital that a separate chapter will be devoted to it in due time.

This eternal solar vesture is symbolized as a City, coming down out of the sky, the new Jerusalem enveloped in the radiance of God, and it is portrayed with poetic imagery of exquisite beauty (Rev. 21).

The description, with its wealth of detail should be sufficient to show clearly what the City actually is. The author has supplied conclusive proof of the meaning by inserting in the description a puzzle that reads as follows:

> "The Divinity, who was talking with me, had for a measure a golden reed, to measure the City, its gateways, and its wall. The City lies foursquare, and the length is as large as the breadth. He measured the City with the reed, by stadia, 12,000. The length and breadth and height are equal. And he measured its wall, 144 cubits, the measure of a man, that is, of a Divinity" (Rev. 21: 15-17).

As the expression "by stadia" shows that the measurement should not be taken in stadia, it follows that it should be reduced to miles. Dividing 12,000 by 7½, the number of stadia to the Jewish mile, the quotient is 1,600. That is the numerical value of the words "Soma Heliakon," the Solar Body.

In the authorized version the preposition "epi" (by) is not translated, being omitted as redundant—which shows the untrustworthiness of an empirical translation.

That version also reads, "a hundred and forty and four cubits, (according to) the measure of a man, that is, of an angel," the spuriously interpolated words making the passage meaningless.

The "wall" of the Solar Body is its aura, or radiance, "he doxa"; but the letters of that term amount to only 143.

As a puzzle, that number would be too transparent, nor would it harmonize with the other numbers listed in relation to the City, as 12,000 stadia, twelve gateways, twelve foundations, etc., all of which have a direct reference to the ancient Zodiac.

Hence, the number was increased to 144, the square of twelve, by adding another alpha, which is called "the measure of a man."

In the formula, "I am the Alpha and Omega, the first and the last," Alpha is the symbol of the Divine Man, or Divinity, before descent into matter (before birth on the physical plane), and Omega is the symbol of the Perfect Man who gains perfection by passing through the Cycle of Resurrection and regaining spiritual consciousness.

The City is described as having the form of a cube. To solve this phase of the puzzle, it is necessary only to unfold the six sides of the cube, thereby forming the Cross, which represents man with arms extended.

Mention is made of measuring "the city, its gateways, and its wall," but no measurement of the gateways is given for the obvious reason that it is unnecessary, as the word "gateways" sufficiently indicates their character. They are the orifices of the human body.

"The gates shall not be shut at all by day, for there shall be no night there," further indicates the character of the City. The body functions incessantly, without stop, from birth to death.

In the Upanishads the human body is often called poetically the twelve-gate city of God's abode.

Apollonius wrote a work titled "Key to the Initiated," which was destroyed by the church. This explained that the Apocalypse was a combination of the teachings of the Brahman and Buddhist orders of priests with reference to man.

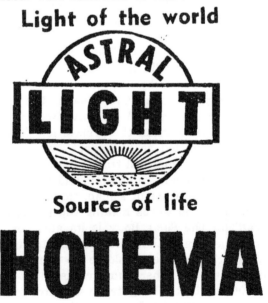

64

TABLE OF CONTENTS

ROMAN CATHOLIC ACTION

Harold Lamb wrote a book of 320 pages in which he said, "Charles the Great, king of the Franks and the Roman Empire of the West, was called Charlemagne. In the Dark Ages he was the ruler of all Europe. This Catholic Warrior and Conqueror was a passionate champion of Catholicism. In one day HE BEHEADED 4500 PROTESTANT SAXONS as a lesson for the others."

In 1567 A. D. Philip II, king of Spain, condemned to death all the people of the Netherlands. This was the most bloodthirsty decree in the whole history of the world. The Dutch had forsaken Catholicism and adopted Protestantism. To save time, the Spanish Inquisition simply decreed that all of the three million people of the country should die. They were to be burned to ashes. King Philip gave his approval in a Royal Proclamation, and sent the Duke of Alva to Holland with an army to destroy the people. This Catholic Army did its best to execute the people. Some 18,600 were burned. But the Dutch did not just stand there like docile slaves and wait to be burned. They staged a bitter battle against their Catholic Destroyers, and finally won their Independence from their cruel, ruthless Catholic oppressors

Lesson No. 19

SELF CONQUEST

In literary construction, the Apocalypse follows somewhat the conventional model of Greek drama. In narrative form, it divides logically into acts or scenes, in each of which the scenic setting is vividly pictured, and interspersed with the action are monologues, dialogues, and choruses, and even "god-on-a-string" plays a part.

As a mere literary device, these scenes are represented in a series of visions. In this the author adopted the style of the Hindu seers, from whom he took much of the quaint symbolism, ornate imagery, and mystifying phraseology that he used, and which was used in the Ancient Mysteries.

With the material obtained from these sources, the author skilfully combined symbols drawn from the ancient Greek and the Essenean arcana, reaching out occasionally to draw from the Egyptian, Chaldaic and other systems, and weaving these into a harmonious whole, wonderfully systematic and complete. having all details worked out with careful exactness.

Then, having thus darkly veiled his work by this eclectic symbolism, utterly baffling to the conventional symbolist, he ingeniously supplied means for verifying the import of each of the principal symbols. This was accomplished by word-numbers and other puzzles. The work of a great Master.

By the sentimental literalists, the Apocalypse is generally considered a record of "visions" experienced by "the Seer of Patmos," although it requires but little discrimination to perceive that the visionary style is an artifice, adopted by the author for the purpose of introducing the fabulous character of his drama and mystifying his readers.

It is only the psychics, the mystai, or "veiled ones," who see symbolical visions. The true Seer, the Epoptes, beholds the phenomena of Nature as they actually are, and not as they seem. He perceives that all forms and processes of the visible realm are but the shadowy symbols of the eternal Ideas of the intelligible world, and passes beyond this fabric of materialism and psychic glamour, this veil by which the Real is covered and concealed, and penetrates to the First Principles of phenomena, the archetypal, spiritual realities.

MANY ACTORS

Many actors apparently play their part in the Apocalyptic

drama. They are symbols, not persons. They represent Cosmic Forces. The only person involved is the neophyte himself. He is taught in the initiatory ceremony how to awaken all the slumbering forces of his organism. How to resurrect the "Christ" in him (Col. 1:27).

That is what Paul meant when he said, "I travail in birth until Christ is formed in you (Gal. 4:19). If "Chrism" (Christ, Seed) is not raised, "then is our preaching vain" (1 Cor. 15:14). The secret meaning of these remarks will be literalized in due course.

When the neophyte passed through the terrible ordeal of the purificatory discipline and the telestic labors, he formed and raised the "Christ" in him and emerged as the Conquerer, the self-perfected Man who had regained his place among the deathless Gods. He was the hero of, and the sole actor in, the drama.

All the other dramatis personae are the personifications of the principles, faculties, forces and elements of Man, that minor world so vast and mysterious, whose ultimate destiny is to become co-extensive with the illimitable Universe.

In the Sacred Ancient Mysteries the candidate witnessed a wonderful drama, staged to instruct him in the Mysteries of Life. Every power of creation, displayed in natural phenomena, was symbolized by well-trained actors and actresses, who skilfully performed the parts assigned to them.

In the brief prologue to the drama, the Anointed Iesous, the illuminated Mind, is depicted as the first-born from the dead, the moribund inner faculties, the ruler of the lower powers, having been crucified by them on the Cross of Matter (the physical body). Now, at his coming, they who wounded him shall weep and wail over him.

In the New Testament allegory, there are two crucifixions: one relating to the Soul's imprisonment in matter at the birth of the physical form, and the other to its ascent to spirit, or regeneration in the Solar Body.

. Then, "in the Breath," that is, in Samadhi (the sacred trance), Ioannes has a vision of the Logos, his own Spiritual Self, in the self-luminous pneumatic body, of which he gives a magnificent description, partly literal and partly symbolical.

He visualizes himself as walking to and fro among seven lamp-stands, and holding in his right hand seven stars; announcing himself to be the ever-living Self, who was "dead" (incarnated), but is now alive throughout the aeons. The Logos explains that the lamp-stands symbolize the "seven Societies in Asia," and the seven stars, their Divinities. That is, they

66

represent the Seven Rays of Light of the Logos (Seven Forces), and the Seven Centers or chakras in the body, through which they energize.

Asia was the native land of Ioannes (Apollonius), therefore typifying the body, the physical home of the Soul; and the Seven Societies (chakras) are designated by the names of Asian cities, each of which, by some well-known characteristic or something for which it was noted, calls to mind the somatic centers of the body it represents.

These cities are listed in the same order in the Apocalypse as are the chakras in the Upanishads, thus:

1. Muladhara, sacral ganglion; Ephesos, a city celebrated for its great temple of Diana, the "many-breasted mother," who appears in the Apocalypse as the Woman clothed with the Sun, the Moon underneath her feet, the lunar goddess (Isis) and the Apocalyptic heroine alike, personifying the regenerative forces, the Sushumna, mystically called the World Mother.

2. Adhishthana, prostatic ganglion; Smyrna, noted for the fig industry, the fig being preeminently a phallic symbol.

3. Manipuraka, epigastric ganglion; Pergamos, celebrated for its temple of Esculapius; the epigastric, or solar plexus, is the controlling center of the vital processes of the body, and of the forces utilized in all systems of psychic healing.

4. Anahata, cardiac ganglion; Thyateira, a city noted for the manufacture of scarlet dyes; the name being thus a covert reference to the blood and circulatory system.

5. Vishuddhi, laryngeal ganglion; Sardeis, a name which suggests the sardion, sardine or carnelian, a flesh-colored stone, thus alluding to the laryngeal protuberance commonly called "Adam's apple."

6. Ajna, cavernous ganglion; Philadelphia, a city which was repeatedly destroyed by earthquakes. The manifestation of the serpentine fire at this sixth center is especially violent. So Ioannes describes the opening of the sixth seal, identical with the sixth Society, as being accompanied by a "great earthquake."

7. Sahasrara, conarium, or pineal gland, the "third eye"; Laodikeia, noted for the manufacture of the so-called "Phrygian powder," which was esteemed a sovereign remedy for sore and weak eyes, presumably the "eye-salve" mentioned by Ioannes in the message to this seventh Society.

To each of these Societies the Logos sends a message. In these communications which he dictates to Ioannes, the nature and function of each center is indicated. A particular aspect of the Logos is presented to each, a good and a bad quality being ascribed to each center, and a prize is promised, specifying the

67

spiritual results accruing to "the Conqueror" from the conquest of each chakra.

SEVEN CENTERS OF CONSCIOUSNESS

These Seven Societies symbolize the Seven Centers of Consciousness. The Apocalypse, in symbol and allegory, covers the unfoldment of these centers, as the subject was scientifically taught by the Great Masters in the Sacred Ancient Mysteries.

The neophyte was taught that man's world is no larger than the horizon of his state of consciousness. It is the state of consciousness of man which is the real attainment that ranks above all other factors in the great drama on the earth plane.

The mere intellect of man, although highly educated, is of little consequence compared to the higher unfoldment of his spirit consciousness.

There are many faculties of the Soul yet undiscovered by modern science. The Masters knew how to awaken and unfold these dormant faculties through greater understanding of the Cosmos.

Conscious unfoldment is the sine qua non of human existence. The body is the Temple of the Living Soul. It is the instrument by which pure spirit consciousness is competent to contact the material world.

In order that the Great Spirit within may unfold in consciousness, it is endowed with the physical body that has five physical senses and seven principle centers of consciousness strung like pearls along a golden chain. These are:

1. The desire of inner impulse of the consciousness of anger hatred, selfishness, etc., is the consciousness of the lowest center of consciousness in the body, located near the lower end of the spinal axis of this mystic chain.

2. Next above is the sex center of consciousness, easily realized by the most primitive neophyte.

3. Next above that is the abdominal brain, or solar plexus or the life center that is conscious of all the needs and wants that carry on physical existence and gives us the consciousness of the want of air, imperfect circulation, digestion, elimination, or the sense of well-being, despondency, lack of life force, etc.

The combined consciousness of these three lower centers constitute the consciousness of the physical, the animal, the egoistic, the actual selfish ego man.

4. Next above these three centers is the heart center of consciousness. We know the thrill of the heart center when joyful news arrives, or its depression when sad. This is the center of

68

conscious feeling that we term emotion. This is that state of consciousness we call unselfish, altruistic, sympathetic, merciful, loving, and the desire to serve humanity. This is the center of soul-consciousness that we feel, realize, and know, but not understood by the masses.

5. The next center of this division is the thyroid or throat center. Its consciousness ever guards and keeps pure the Body Temple from the entrance of poison, so that poisons may not harm the two conscious centers above.

For instance, if we get a morsel of food into our mouth unfit for the Body Temple, we gag, retch and eject the poison. That is the consciousness of this center in one of its functions.

These two centers, the heart and thyroid taken together, constitute the purified man, the feeling, unselfish, pure spiritual man.

6. The next center above is at the base of the brain, a powerful conscious center, with many wonderful, subtle powers and potentialities, and many subtle psychic powers yet to unfold.

Here dwells the consciousness of Higher Intuition, the power to perceive the inner meaning of things, that faculty we term the Inner Vision and the small voice within.

7. The center next above is the highest and most wonderful of all, located in the cortex and convolutions of the cranial brain.

This is the Master Center, the summum bonum of all conscious life. This center, with the sixth, constitute the Spiritual Man, the God-like man, the Image of God man.

The unfoldment of these centers of consciousness is the true philosophy of life and transcends all forms of religion. This is the ancient philosophy which the church, in the fifth century, boasted had disappeared from the face of the earth.

This is the philosophy of Paganism that was "unfit" for the followers of the gospel Jesus to know anything about. For it turned one away from the false religion of Romanism to the true religion of the only true God.

Man is truly the culmination of all creation. He is truly a miniature Universe, a replica of the whole. Within him is the kingdom of God and all the elements of the Cosmos.

"As above so below. As it is with God so it is with man. He is the Microcosm. The Universe is the Macrocosm." God actually abides in us.

Within man are the various states of consciousness, from the lowest to the highest, from the brute to the angel. The Masters taught that the lower states of consciousness must be controlled, neutralized, transmuted to higher states of consciousness.

This is the unfoldment of consciousness to higher planes,

the actual transmutation from the sub-conscious animal state to the super-conscious spiritual state. This is the very essence of all religion, and this is the philosophy taught by the Ancient Masters.

As we proceed we shall realize that the strange story contained in the Apocalypse is the accumulation of The Ancient Wisdom of the Ages; for it transcends the brain capacity of any one man.

LOGOS ENTHRONED IN THE SKY

In the next vision appears the Logos enthroned in the sky, with his four septenary powers.

Here Ioannes has constructed a simple little puzzle by employing redundant symbols and by inverting the order of the forces, enumerating the lesser ones first and the greater ones last. He places twenty-four Ancient ("elders," hours of the day) circling the throne (Sun), before which also are Seven Breaths ("spirits," consciousness) and a crystaline sea (psychic centers); after which he describes four Zoa ("living creatures"), each of whom has six wings. He makes it apparent later that the Zoa are superior to the Ancients and next in rank to the Logos.

The four Zoa are the four manifested "Beasts," whose nature, as the regents of the four somatic divisions of the body, has been explained.

As the Zoa are septenates, they are said to have six wings each. These wings are identical with the twenty-four Ancients; and the seven Breaths before the throne are likewise identical with the highest septanate, the noetic Zoon.

This seemingly complicated assemblage thus resolves itself simply into the Nous centered in the brain, with its four septenary powers; and the "Glassy sea" is the ether vibrating in the mystic "eye" of the Seer. For the "sky" in the Apocalypse is not the "heaven" of the profane, the celestial world believed by the masses to be somewhere in the far depths of space.

The four Zoa are the Lion, Bull, Man and Eagle. These symbols represent the four cardinal signs of the Zodiac, constituting the so-called Cross of the Zodiac: Leo, Taurus, Aquarius, and Scorpio.

The constellation Aquila, the Eagle, though extra-zodiacal, rising at the same time as Scorpio, is frequently substituted for it.

The word Zodiac is derived from zodion, "a little animal," a diminutive form of zoon, "an animal." Hence, the zodiac signs being called zodia, the four principal ones are the zoa.

A SCROLL

A scroll (book) is the next symbol introduced. It is the human body, esoterically considered.

The book is "written inside and at the back," referring to the sympathetic and cerebro-spinal nerve systems, and "closed with seven seals," which are the seven major chakras of the spinal column.

The sacrificial Lamb is the neophyte who has attained to the intuitive, noetic consciousness, which is symbolized by his having seven horns and seven eyes—that is, mental powers of action

ZODIAC.

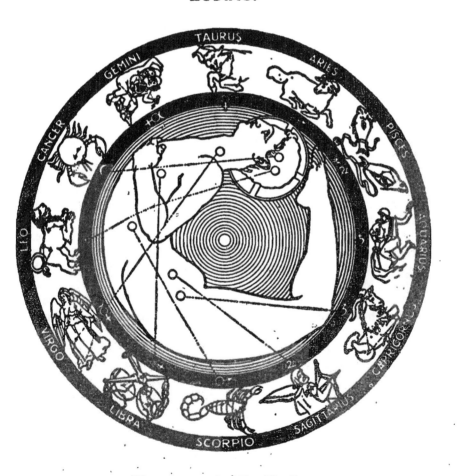

The Apocalyptic Zodiac

and perception. He opens the seals (arouses the chakras) successively.

As they are opened, they change to zodiac signs, the Zodiac being applied to the microcosm (man) as shown in the diagram here presented, the man being depicted as lying in a circle, and not standing upright as in the exoteric Zodiac.

The seven planets are assigned to the twelve signs of the Zodiac in the order followed by Porphyrios and, in fact, by all ancient and modern authorities.

In the sacred Sanskrit scriptures the planets are made to correspond also to the seven chakras in the following order, beginning with Muladhara, Saturn, Jupiter, Mars, Venus, Mercury, Moon and Sun.

According to this zodiac scheme, seven signs, with their planets, extend along the cerebro-spinal region of the body, and correspond to the seven chakras, which are the focal centers of the Tattvas, and have the same planets; while the rest of the signs pertain to the five pranas.

As the Lamb opens one of the seals, one of the four Zoa thunders, "Come." A white horse appears, its rider having a bow. This is Sagittarius, the Bowman.

Ioannes thus starts the mysterious Kundalini Current at the second chakra, and correctly so, for the Sushumna does not energize until Ida and Pingala have reached the forehead. Then it starts from the first center, corresponding to the terminus of the spinal cord. So he avoids calling this the first seal, but says, "one of the seals," and then numbers the others merely in the order in which opened.

The second seal being opened, the second Zoon says, "Come." A red horse comes forth. To its rider is given a great sword, and power to take away peace from the earth. This is Scorpio, the house of Mars, the War God.

At the opening of the third seal, the third Zoon says, "Come." A black horse appears, its rider having a balance in his hand. This is Libra, the Balance.

As the fourth seal is opened, the fourth Zoon says, "Come." A pale (chloros, "yellowish") horse appears, and its rider is Death, accompanied by Hades. They are given power over one quarter of the earth, to kill with sword, famine and death, and by the wild beasts.

This is Virgo, the astrological sign of the uterus. In the New Testament, as in the Upanishads and other mystic literature, "Death" is the term frequently applied to the productive, generative world, in which birth, decay and death hold sway.

At the birth of man, when the Soul becomes imprisoned in

72

the material body, that was considered by the masters as the death of the Soul insofar as the Soul can die.

In her character of the bad virgin, "a queen and not a widow," Virgo appears later in the drama in the role of the Woman in scarlet, seated on the red Dragon, in the epithumetic nature. But here she is associated with a higher center that relates to the psychic consciousness, and therefore Hades, the psychic realm, is said to ride with Death; and the evil thoughts, desires, passions and lust of the psycho-physical consciousness devastate the earth to the extent that they dominate.

The four horses, corresponding to the four Zoa, as also to the four beasts, are the four somatic divisions of the human organism.

The general belief of the orthodox clergy is that "The Four Horsemen of the Apocalypse" are the grim figures of Conquest, War, Famine and Death.

The fifth seal opened is the cavernous ganglion, to which corresponds the sign Cancer. While Leo precedes Cancer in the Zodiac, its corresponding chakra, the conarium, is the last of the centers to be aroused; for Ida and Pingala (nerves) branch out to right and left at the forehead, and it is only the Sushumna, starting at the sacral ganglion, that reaches the conarium.

But the influence of the two nerve currents, at this stage, produces a partial awakening of the lower centers in the brain.

This is revealed by Ioannes in an ingenious little allegory about the uneasy ghosts (souls) of those who had been sacrificed (atrophied) because of the evidence they held. For it is by the atrophy of these noetic centers that man loses the evidence of Spiritual Realities. The lost powers of civilized man.

The sixth seal opened is the sacral plexus, to which corresponds the sign Capricorn.

When this chakra is awakened, the Sushumna flows along the spinal cord and impinges upon the brain.

Words cannot adequately describe the sensations of the neophyte as he first experiences the effects produced by this mighty power of nerve force. It is as if the earth instantly crumbled to nothingness, and sun, moon and stars were swept from the sky, so that he suddenly found himself to be but an unbodied Soul alone in the black abyss of empty space, struggling against dread and terror.

Thus Ioannes pictures it, in terms of cosmic phenomena, as a seismic cataclysm, seemingly the end of the world.

To the neophyte, unprepared for this ordeal, failure may mean merely a short period of unconsciousness, or instant death. For this vital electricity has the destructiveness, when misdirected, of the thunder-belt.

This sixth center, ajna, is the great lunar chakra, where the currents bifurcate. At this point the resurgent solar fires, those related to the cerebro-spinal system, form a Cross in the brain. and·their force is intensified.

These solar forces are symbolized as five Divinities, of whom, four stand at the corners of the earth, presiding over the four winds, and a dominant Divinity, the fifth, who, bearing the signet-ring of the living God, ascends from the fifth direction of space, "the birthplace of the Sun"—quite naturally, as he is, in fact, an aspect of that Sun, the Nous.

Lesson No. 21

ISRAEL

With his signet-ring he seals 144,000 out of the twelve tribes of the children of Israel (Ch. 7:4).

The twelve tribes are symbols of the twelve zodiac signs. So are the twelve disciples of the gospel Jesus. These represent the twelve forces of the Logos, which differentiate into numerous minor powers.

In the microcosm, these are the nadis of the Upanishads, which enumerate variously the nadis centering in the brain, and usually place the number at 75,000.

It is well to digress here and reveal another secret that is well hidden. Each nation and race of antiquity had various names for God. In Arabia, it is Allah; in India, Brahma; in Hebrew, Yod, Jod, Jehovah; in Egypt, Is-Ra-El, which also means the whole visible universe or body of God.

The Hebrews claimed they were the Children of Israel, God's own "chosen people" (Deut. 7:6). All races can make that claim, for they are all God's children.·

The Hebrews took the word Israel from the Egyptians. It is a compound of three Egyptian words: Is, Ra, and El. "IS" was an Egyptian symbol of God as Universal Mother; "RA" was a symbol of God as Universal Father; and "EL" was a symbol of God as Universal Son. The Egyptian words IS RA EL meant the three Universal Principles of God—Father, Mother, Son—the Trinity.

A mystery ceases to be such when explained. To understand what we read, we must understand the basic meaning of the words we read.

There is not one book on earth in which one may find an unbiased, unprejudiced, truthful answer to many puzzling questions that arise concerning the origin of religious systems and their various dogmas and doctrines.

God said unto Moses, I AM THAT I AM. Say unto the children of Israel, I am hath sent me (Ex. 3:14).

The Hebrews took this from the Egyptians. "I AM" is another name of God. The "I" means Spirit, and "AM" means eternity.

Over the doors of pre-Egyptian Temples, ten thousand years ago, were inscribed the words, "Nuk Pu Nuk," which mean, I AM THAT I AM.

In 1937 David Livingston wrote a book of 339 pages on the subject "I AM." The whole secret is here related in a few words. The Hebrews copied it from the Egyptians. They copied everything they had. Much of the Pentateuch was copied from Egyptian writings, for which reason many Egyptian words appear in the Bible.

ZODIAC

Ioannes follows the zodiac scheme. As each zodiac sign is subdivided into twelve minor signs, he multiplies these by 1,000 —a number often used in mystic writings to express indefinite terms—and so arrives at a total of 144,000.

There appears after this a great multitude, from all nations and men of all languages, white-robed and pure, who wave palm-branches and sing a paean before the throne. They are said to be those "coming out of the great ordeal."

This "great ordeal" is reincarnation, the misery of being bound for ages to the cosmic wheel of birth and death, similar to vapor that becomes ice and then vapor again. This concourse of the "redeemed" who sing the chorus in this scene, are the liberates elements of the aspirant's own nature. They are not a throng of people exterior to him, but his own body cells.

By evoking the marvelous potencies of his spiritual selfhood, the Conqueror thereby regerminates all that was good, beautiful and true in each of his past incarnations, and so he can say, in the magnificent language of the Gospel of Phillip:

"I have united myself, assembling myself together from the four quarters of the Universe, and joining together the members that were scattered abroad."

LEO (LION)

The seventh seal is the conarium, its zodiac correspondence being Leo, the house of the Sun.

Here reigns the Silence from which issue the seven spiritual "voices," or sounds. These mystic sounds Ioannes describes allegorically as trumpet-calls sounded successively by seven Divinities. They become audible as the chakras in the brain are awakened and activated.

The first four relate to the four somatic divisions of the body, and react on them; hence Ioannes ascribes to the trumpet-calls an obscuring or destructive effect on the earth, the sea, the rivers and springs, and the sky, which correspond to the four somatic divisions.

At this stage of the telestic meditation, the physical body is already in a state of trance, and it is now the lower psychic consciousness that is to be temporarily dormantized or placed in abeyance. So, leaving the physical consciousness out of the reckoning, Ioannes terms the psychic the "third" as applied to each of the four planes, to which correspond the first four trumpet calls.

The results produced by the three remaining trumpet-calls he terms "woes," since they entail trying ordeals, the issue of which is certain failure to the unpurified neophyte, of whom it has been said:

"His vices will take shape and drag him down. His sins will raise their voices like the jackal's laugh and sob after the sun goes down; his thoughts become as an army and bear him off a captive slave."

Thus, at the fifth trumpet-call appears "a star fallen from the sky to the earth," who is the "Divinity of the abyss" and has the key to its crater, or opening, and whose name is Apollyon, "he who utterly destroys," the "Murderer"; he opens the crater of the abyss, and from it emerges a locust-swarm of centaurs, who, with their scorpion-like tails, inflict torments on man.

This "star" is Lucifer, the fallen "son of the morning," the debased psychic mind of man, which is indeed the ruler over the absymal depths of desire, the bottomless pit of the passional nature, and the "murderer" truly of all that is pure, beautiful and true.

This fifth trumpet-call refers to the carnal mind energizing in the sympathetic nerve system, the seat of the epithumetic consciousness, "the throne of the Beast."

The sixth trumpet-call bears relation to the cerebro-spinal axis, the Apocalyptic "river Euphrates," and to what may be termed the psycho-religious consciousness, which manifests itself in the emotional worship of the false mental images of Deity

—the lower phase of religion that indulges in irrational theologies, superstition, sorcery, fanaticism and persecution, such as that which prevails now and has prevailed since the destruction of the Ancient Wisdom.

The neophyte who has not freed his mind from these pseudoreligious illusions will inevitably fail in the mystic meditation, which requires that all thought-images and preconceptions must be excluded from the mind, so as to present it a clean page for the inscription of Truth.

After this sixth trumpet-call, the four Divinities fettered at the river Euphrates are loosed. They are the solar regents of the seasons, ruling the quaternary divisions of the year, month, day and hour.

The liberation of these forces is followed by the appearance upon the scene of an army of warriors mounted on lion-headed, serpent-tailed horses, which symbolize the countless powers of the Noùs.

A "strong" Divinity, the fifth, then descends from the sky, enveloped in a cloud, with a rainbow round his head; his face luminous like the Sun, and his feet resemble pillars of fire.

This description of him is similar to that of the Logos. He is, in fact, the Nous, for he and the four Euphratèan Divinities are the analogues, on the purely intellectual plane, of the Logos and the four Zoa.

The strong Divinity cries out with the roar of a lion, and seven thunders utter their voices.

Ioannes is very reticent concerning the utterances of these seven thunders. As the Greek language has but the one word (phone) for both "voice" and "vowel," the meaning is obviously that the "great voice" of the Logos, who is the seven vowels in one, is echoed by the seven vowels, the sounds by which the higher forces are evoked,—and these the Seer is forbidden to record.

As this stage of the sacred trance the neophyte, having attained to the noetic consciousness, begins to receive the mystery-teachings, the "sacred, unspeakable words" which, as Paulos says, "it is not lawful for man to disclose."

When the neophyte shall have mastered the next noetic center, the "third eye" of the Seer, he passes beyond the illusions of time and space. "There shall be time no longer" (Rev. 10:6), and "the God-mystery shall be perfected."

When the sixth sense (Manas—Pituitary) has awakened the seventh (Buddhi, Pineal), the spiritual light radiating from the seventh (Third Eye) illuminates the Field of Infinitude in man's physical consciousness; and his Spiritual Consciousness, being

77

thus aroused from its dormant state in the last Resurrection, becomes active; and for that period of time man becomes omniscient. The Past and the Future, Space and Time, disappear and become for him the Present, which is Eternity

It is not the fault of God but of man that he lives and labors in mental darkness—a slave of the institutions by which he is controlled (Ibid.).

The Divinity gives a little scroll to Ioannes, who eats it; and while honey-sweet in his mouth, it makes his belly bitter.

The scroll symbolizes the esoteric instructions he has received, which are bitter indeed to the lower man, for they inculcate the utter extirpation of the epithumetic nature.

He is then told that he must become a teacher, opposing the exoteric beliefs of the masses who are controlled by the social pattern and taught false precepts and doctrines that keep people in darkness (Rev. 10:11).

The scribe of the Matthew wove the substance of this into his gospel by having his resurrected Jesus say: "All power is given unto me in heaven and in earth. Go ye therefore, and teach all nations" (Mat. 28:18, 19).

By a side-scene, a parenthetical explanation is given of the adytum or shrine of the God and the "two witnesses" of the "strong" Divinity, the Nous.

The adytum, the temple-cell or fane in which the God is enthroned, is the seventh of the noetic centers; and the two witnesses are the Ida and Pingala nerves, the Sushumna being the third witnesses, "the believable and true."

Here are the two thieves crucified with Jesus, with him (the Sushumna) in the center.

When the seventh trumpet-call is sounded, there is a choral announcement that the God, the true Self, has come to his own and will reign throughout the aeons.

The adytum is opened, disclosing the ark, the mystic receptacle in which were placed the "tablets" (generative organs) whereon was inscribed the contract of God with man. That contract extends to all living creatures that reproduce themselves in the generation of offspring, and to all of the vegetal kingdom.

Thereupon appears the Woman clothed with the Sun, star-crowned and standing on the Moon; travailing, she gives birth to a male child.

She symbolizes the Light of the Logos, the World-Mother, the pristine force-substance of which is moulded the Solar-Body— her "Man-child."

The red Dragon, symbolizing the epitheumetic nature, seeks

78

to devour her child; but the child is caught up to the God's throne, and the Woman flees to the desert, where she is nourished three and a half years.

This symbolizes the fact that after the formation of the Solar Body has begun, any strong passion or emotion may disintegrate and destroy it; and that during the first half of the cycle of initiation into the Ancient Mysteries, here placed at seven years, the nascent body remains in the spiritual world, as it were, while the Sushumna force of the body abides in its "place" in the material form, symbolized by "desert."

For, strictly speaking, the Solar Body is not really formed at this stage, but only has its inception. In the allegory, Ioannes could hardly employ more accurate but less delicate mystery-representation of the Eleusinia.

Lesson No. 22

THE SKY BATTLE

The sacred trance ends here for the present; and the next follows a battle in the sky.

The Dragon and the Divinities are hurled down from the sky by Mikael and his hosts—that is, the Mind is now purified from the taint of impure thoughts.

Mikael and his fellow Chief-Divinities, Uriel, Raphael and Gabriel, of whom he alone is named, are the four Zoa in another guise. But the Dragon, while ejected from the intellectual nature, continues his persecutions on the lower plane.

The Beast (phrenic nature) is described next. One of his seven heads (the seven dominant desires) has been slain, but comes to life. It represents the desire for sentient existence, the principle which causes the soul to reincarnate.

This will to live, this passionate clinging to sensuous life, is expatiated on by Plato.

Although the aspirant has apparently extirpated this longing, so far as the grosser affairs of the material world are concerned, it revives when he enters into the subtler planes of consciousness and perceives the psychic realms of existence.

In Buddistic literature it is termed tanha, the trishna of Sanskrit philosophical works. In one ritual it is said, "Kill love of life; but if thou slayest tanha, take heed lest from the dead it rise again."

Because this principle keeps man under the sway of reincarnation, Ioannes significantly says, "If any one welcomes cap-

79

tivity, into captivity he goes; if any one shall kill with the sword, with the sword must he be killed" (Mat. 26:52).

"Every word Eusebius put into the mouth of his Jesus can be traced back to very ancient scriptures.

Appears another beast, who is the symbol of the procreative principle. He participates in the nature of each of the other beasts; for he has two horns like the Lamb, talks like the Dragon, and has the magic powers of the Beast. He is called the Pseudo-Seer. His false seership is a low form of psychism which, while not necessarily sensual, is due to the generative nerve ether.

From this source come most of the "visions" of religious ecstatics; and the material manifestations produced by some spiritist-mediums.

In a more general way, it is the source of the emotional element in exoteric religion, or so-called religious fervor, which is in reality but a subtil sort of eroticism.

As a blind emotional impulse to worship, it stimulates the lower mind, the phren, or Beast, to project an image of itself upon the mental screen and to worship that illusionary concept. This, the "image of the Beast," is the anthropomorphic God of exoteric religion.

Again the Lamb appears. By strict classification it is one of the four beasts, but too exalted to have that title applied to it, since it is the Nous, the regent of the highest of the four somatic divisions.

With the Lamb are many of his virginal attendants, who, as a prelude to the next act of the drama, chant a new paean, accompanied by many lyres.

The neophyte has now become, as it were, like a lyre, with all the loose strings of his psychic nature tightened and tuned, tense and vibrant touch of his true Self.

The conquest of the cardiac centers is presented as a harvest scene, in which seven Divinities play their part.

Here, again, four of the septenate are related to the four somatic divisions. The fifth Divinity is "like the son of man," and with a sickle he reaps the "dried up" harvest of the earth.

He is the Logos, or spiritual Self, which assimilates the higher aspirations and idealizing of the psychic nature—a harvest that is, usually by no means abundant.

The sixth Divinity, who comes out of the God's adytum, reaps vine of the earth, and casts the ripe grapes into the great wine-vat of the God's ardor (thumos). When the vat is trodden, outside the city, not wine but blood appears, "up to the bridles of the horses, as far as 1,600 stadia."

While this sixth Divinity represents the Nous as intellect,

the fifth Divinity reflects the aspect of the Logos as Eros, or Divine Desire.

The vine of the earth may be considered as that vine of the purely human emotional nature, or feeling, whose tendrils are love, sympathy and devotion, and whose fruitage yields the wine of spiritual exaltation.

In the technical esoteric meaning, the vine consists of the force-currents which correspond to the cerebro-spinal nerve system; while the great wine-vat of the God's ardor, outside the city (physical body), is the auric ovum, which becomes suffused with an orange or golden color through the action of these currents in the cardiac centers.

The horses are the four somatic divisions, and the number of 1,600 is that of the Solar Body. The cardiac forces pervade and color the aura, giving it a golden hue, returning through the chakras, and circulating through the Solar Body—a process similar to the circulation of the fetus, the Solar Body being, as it were, in a fetal state. Thus the Woman is sustained in the desert, weaving for the Soul its immortal and glorious robe.

The word Thumos is here rendered "ardor." The revisers of the "authorized" version translate it "wrath," making it a synonym of "orge," but changing to "fierceness" when, as in two instances, Ioannes has the two words so conjoined that the result of their theory, if carried out, would be the impossible expression, "wrath of his wrath," which is but little worse than one actually used, "the wrath of her fornication." (Rev. 14:8)

The word has not that meaning in the Platonic philosophy, nor in that of the Apocalypse, which is practically identical with it.

Plato makes Thumos the energizing principle of the Soul, intermediate between the rational nature and the irrational. He explains that it is not a kind of desire, "for in the conflict of the Soul, thumos is arrayed on the side of the rational principle."

It is a complex of emotions qualified by comprehensive ideas, as veracity, honor, pride, sympathy, affection, etc., and not at all an ordinary impulse of resentment.

In the Apocalypse usage, thumos is also an energizing, creative principle. But whereas Plato, writing works of the more popular sort, confined himself to a threefold system and wrote with caution, Ioannes, using the medium of symbol and allegory that is unintelligible to the profane, divulges the full fourfold system. He puts phren as the intermediate principle between the psychic and the noetic nature, and elevates thumos to be the energizing principle of the latter.

It thus corresponds to Eros, the Divine Love, whose inverted

81

reflection in the animal nature is Eros, the love-god, or lust.

With these two Erotes of Grecian mythology, he gives also its two Aphrodites, picturing them as the supernal virgin clothed with the sun and the infernal prostitute arrayed in scarlet— the two symbolizing respectively **divine regeneration and human generation.**

Now, again, the word Orge, although signifying colloquially and in ordinary literature the violent passion as anger and wrath, has a more technical meaning in the terminology of the Ancient Mysteries, where it signifies the fecundating power or parturient energy in nature.

The word is derived from "opyav," "to swell with internal moisture," as do plants and fruit from their sap, "to teem," "to swell (with passion)"; and from the same root comes orgia, the Mystery-rites practiced in the worship of Iacchos, the procreative god.

Next follows the conquest of the procreative centers. After a paean chanted by the conquerors of the Beast, seven Divinities emerge from the adytum. They are more majestic and more splendidly arrayed than the three septenates who preceded them, and their role is to finish the regenerative work.

One of the four Zoa gives them seven golden saucers, containing the formative force of the Logos, "the thumos of the God."

What ensues upon the outpouring of the creative potency is the symbolical eradication of the procreative centers, leaving thereafter but three somatic divisions, and the elimination from the other centers of every remaining vestige of psychic impurity.

The first four Divinities act successively upon the four somatic divisions. The first pours out his saucer upon the earth, producing a painful sore on the men who had the brand of the Beast and worshipped his image.

The force under the stimulus of which the lower psychic nature engendered pseudo-devotional illusions, irritational sentiments and emotions, and erroneous notions or concepts, now becomes the destroyer of these delusions, and of the psychic centers to which they are due.

The second Divinity pours out his saucer into the sea; it becomes as blood, and all creatures in it die. Every vestige of passion and desire is eliminated.

The third Divinity pours out his saucer into the rivers and springs, and they become blood.

This is the somatic division of which the regent is the Beast, or phrenic mind, in which is centered the consciousness of the profane, who have persecuted and put to death many spiritual teachers and reformers.

Here, again, Ioannes indulges in sarcasm; for he makes the Divinity of the waters (the Nous as presiding over this plane) say to the profane, "They poured out the blood of devotees and seers, and blood thou hast given them to drink, for they are worthy," a paronomastic use of the word axios, "deserving" and also "highly respectable."

As the "blood of the Logos" suffuses the mystic centers of the heart, "the knowledge from below" ceases to vaunt itself, and is replaced by the "wisdom from above."

The fourth Divinity pours out his saucer upon the sun, and it radiates scorching heat—symbolical of the intense activity of the brain at this stage.

The fifth Divinity empties his saucer on the throne of the Beast, whose realm is thereby darkened, and whose subjects are afflicted with pains and sores.

The Beast's throne is the sympathetic nerve system, so that his realm covers practically all the so-called involuntary physical and psychic functions.

Now that the four somatic divisions have been purified, the Beast is deposed, and henceforth the Nous shall reign supreme.

The sixth Divinity empties his saucer into the Euphrates, and its waters are dried up to prepare the path for the rulers who come from the sources of the sun.

These are the five solar Divinities who were erstwhile unfettered at the Euphrates, the cerebro-spinal system.

Lesson No. 23

BORN AGAIN

All the irredeemable elements of man's lower self are now expelled, and become a sort of entity eternal to him; as when after the demise of the physical organism, all the evil psychic elements that are rejected by the Soul before it enters the spiritual realm, survive in the phantasmal world as a simulacrum. shade, or ghost of the dead personality.

So upon the spiritual rebirth of man, which connotes the death of his carnal nature while the purified physical body continues to live, these expelled elements assume shape in that same phantasmal world, or Tartarus, and there remain as a congeries of evil forces and impure elements, forming a malignant demon that has no animating principle except hatred and lust, and is doomed to disintegrate in the cosmic elements.

Thus Ioannes describes the gruesome thing in his allegory. He beholds issuing from the mouths of the Dragon, the Beast and the Pesudo-Seer three unclean spirits, resembling frogs, who are "spirits of demons," and who collect all the evil forces and muster them for the last great battle upon the advent of the God.

The seventh Divinity empties his saucer into the air (aureola), and the enthroned God announces. "**He** is **born.**" This is spiritual birth.

The authorized version gives the strained empirical translation, "It is done." (Rev. 16:17; 21:6)

The spirtual birth, in the Apocalyptic drama, is accompanied by a general upheaval and readjustment: The great city, Babylon (physical body) becomes three divisional: the cities of the people (procreative centers) are overthrown; and great hail (the condensation psychically of the auric substance) falls.

THE WOMAN IN SCARLET

In the main action of the drama, the Conqueror, the newborn Initiate, now appears on his white horse. But the sequence of events is interrupted by a side-scene, which amounts to a parenthetical dissertation on the mysteries of the physical existence and the epithumetic principle, symbolized by the Woman in scarlet and the fiery red Dragon.

The Woman represents Babylon (physical body), and, in a more general sense, incarnate existence. She sits on the "many waters," the great psychic sea of sensuous life, and is likewise sitting on the Dargon. For it represents microcosmically the same principle that the sea does macrocosmically.

The Dragon who sustains the Woman was, and is not, and yet is. For it is the glamour of sensuous life, the deceptive phenomena of which ever appear to be that which they are not.

Its seven heads are seven mountains where the Woman is sitting on them. They symbolize the seven cardinal desires energized through the seven chakras of the body during incarnation.

Then it is explained that there are seven rulers, of whom five have perished, one is, and the other has not yet come. When he comes he must abide a short time.

The cycle of initiation extends through seven incarnations, which are not necessarily consecutive. Of these the Apocalyptic initiate is represented as having gone through five, and being now in the sixth. In the seventh he will attain final emancipation from incarnation.

84

They are called rulers or kings because the only incarnations counted are those in which the aspirant is veritably the ruler of his lower faculties and propensities.

The Dragon himself is an eighth, a sort of by-product of the seven, and he goes to destruction. He is the phantom that forms after the final purification, and his fate is to disintegrate in the nether-world. His five pairs of horns are the five pranas, each of which is both positive and negative. They are solar forces, the correspondence on the lowest plane of the Nous and the four Zoa, the regents of the four regions of space and the four divisions of time. But here, in the sphere of animal vitality, they energize the desires and passions.

Thus they have one purpose. They confer their power on the Dragon, and rule with him each for one hour. They are the forces which, in the innocent child, produce its exuberant vitality and exquisite vivacity, but which, in one who yields to the dictates of passion, become terribly destructive. Hence they are said to devour the flesh of the Woman in scarlet and consume her with fire.

Then comes a series of proclamations, exhortations and lamentations relating to the fall of Babylon, the scarlet prostitute, who is the bad Virgo, the terrestrial Aphrodite, all of which applies to the complete subjugation of the physical body and its forces, and to liberation of the Nous from the bondage of physical life.

In the allegory there are two "falls," paralleling the two crucifixions and two resurrections.

THE DRAMA RESUMED

After this long but necessary digression, the action of the drama is resumed.

The Conqueror appears, mounted on a white horse. "He treads the wine-vat of the ardor of the God's fecundating energy." His mantle is blood-hued, and upon it and upon his thigh (phallos) is inscribed his title of supreme ruler.

The word "thigh" (meros) is euphemistic; the phallos, "membrum virile," is intended.

This particular euphemism is common in the Old Testament (Gen. 24:2, et passim).

Furthermore, it will be noted that here the Conqueror has the sword of Mars, and is riding the white horse of the Archer who, at the opening of the first seal, the adhishthana chakra, "came forth conquering and to keep on conquering."

85

Thus the incarnated Logos is shown to bear a direct relation to the lowest centers of the body.

Lesson No. 24

HIGHER FUNCTIONS DORMANT

It would be impossible to elucidate the Apocalypse and ignore this delicate but perfectly pure subject, concerning which even the most communicative expositors of the esoteric philosophy have been extremely reticent.

We are opposed to all undue secrecy, and believe that much harm in this matter has resulted from the suppression of truth. So we feel justified in dealing with the subject frankly and without constraint, but with necessary brevity.

The human brain contains certain centers or components, including the pituitary and pineal glands, the higher functions of which are almost entirely dormant in the average man of the present race. Hence in the ancient scriptures such persons are termed "dead." But it is only through these glands of the brain that the spiritual man, his overshadowing God, can act upon the consciousness of the psycho-intellectual Self.

This corpse-like condition of the higher glands of the brain does not preclude high development of the average intellectual faculties, apart from the epistemonic power.

There are and always have been men who are lamentable examples of brilliant intellectuality, combined with the densest spiritual stupidity.

In the case of the true genius, the poet, artist, intuitive philosopher, and religious mystic of purity, there is a partial awakening of these centers. In the case of the Seer, excluding from that class the mere psychic clairvoyant, the higher faculties are so quickened that he becomes cognizant of the interior worlds, the planes of true Being.

When the brain is fully restored to its true functions by the power of the Serpentine Fire, that "Light of the Logos," which is literally the Creative Force of the Logos, causes the brain to become an androgynous organ, wherein occurs the immaculate conception and gestation of the self-born spiritual man, the monogene, who is in very truth "born of the spirit" (1 Jn. 3:9).

This is the mysterious regeneration and redemption set forth by Ioannes in both the Apocalypse and the fourth gospel, and which is expressed by myth and symbol, allegory and parable, fable and fiction, in all the great religions of the ancient world.

There being a direct and intimate relationship and correspondence between the sacred centers in the brain and the lower procreative centers it follows that true spirituality can be attained only when a pure and virtuous life is led. The Life Essence cannot be consumed in generation and also conserved for Regeneration.

For the neophyte who would enter upon the telestic work, the task of giving birth to his spiritual Self, perfect celibacy is the first positive prerequisite. In addition, one must follow a natural course of living that builds health and vitality in every part of the body, and the first requirement in this respect is the purest air one can find, and strictly natural food.

Unless one is inspired by the loftiest aspirations, guided by the noblest philosophy, restrained by the most rigid moral discipline, purges the body of all poisons, subsists on a frugal fare of unfired fruit, drinks only the purest rain water and fruit juices, breathes pure air, one's possibility of success is very remote.

The mere dabbler in the pseudo-occult will only degrade his intellect with the puerilities of psychism, become the prey of the evil influences of the phantasmal world, or ruin himself by the foul practices of phallic sorcery, as thousands of misled people are doing.

ENEMIES DEFEATED

The Conqueror and his host are opposed by the Beast and his followers, and in the ensuing battle the Beast and the Pseudo-Seer are captured. They are cast into the lake of fire: which means that the rejected elements of man's animal nature return to the elemental kingdom whence they were derived.

The Dragon is imprisoned for a thousand years, after which he must be let loose for a short time; that is, the Conqueror has yet one more incarnation to pass through, hence does not now destroy entirely the epithumetic principle. But in his next and final earth-life he will make quick work of it.

The thousand years, as a period between incarnations, merely expresses the apparent time on the spiritual plane, where, as Plato explains, sensation is of tenfold intensity, so that the thousand years here, as in the vision of Er, "answer to the hundred years that are reckoned as the life of man."

So far as the Apocalyptic drama is concerned, the Dragon is disposed of; but Ioannes uses a paragraph in the future tense to tell of his final fate. Finding it necessary to explain first, in a general way, what happens to the soul after death and between incarnations, he does so by describing a vision. He sees thrones and those seated thereon, and judgment is passed on them.

These represent a series of after-death judgments. For after each incarnation, the incarnating Ego passes through a purifying ordeal or "judgment." All his activities during the past earth-life are reviewed. They are described in the allegory as souls revivified.

Thus the souls of those that had been beheaded because they had the evidence of Iesous (Nous), and those that had not worshipped the Beast (that is, the latent intuitions that had been suffered to die in the mind, and the higher thoughts, emotions and aspirations), are resurrected and reign with the Nous, now illumined, for a thousand years, that is, during the non-incarnated period.

The rest of the dead (the thoughts and emotions that were concerned only with the carnal nature) come not to life until the expiration of the celestial interregnum. They lie in latency until the Ego reincarnates, when they again become kinetic impulses.

This coming to life of the nobler elements of man's nature, which were suppressed and slain during his earthly sojourn, is called "the first resurrection."

A THOUSAND YEARS

Returning from this general exposition to the particular case of the Dragon in the drama, and hence changing to the future tense, Ioannes explains that this Adversary will be freed at the expiration of the thousand years and will muster all the evil forces to make an assault on the beloved city (human body), only to have his forces consumed by the divine fire, and himself be cast into the lake of fire and sulphur, where the Beast and Pseudo-Seer had already been sent, thus sharing with them the "second death."

The physical body of the Conqueror is not dead. It is subjugated, purified and shorn of its passional centers.

The fall of Babylon symbolizes the death of man's carnal nature. In his regeneration the initiate has passed through a process analogous to death in some respects, and undergoes a judgment-ordeal similar to that meted out to the excarnated soul, but of vaster scope and greater import.

A great white throne appears, and from the face of the enthroned Majesty the earth and sky flee and vanish. For he is the perfected Self of Man, higher than earth and heaven, greater than all the Gods. He is summing up the cycles of his incarnations; and on all the elemental forces and faculties of his composite nature that have composed his various personalities of the past, he renders judgment "according to their works."

All these, "the dead" in the three lower worlds, spring to life and are "judged," as Ioannes reiterates, "every one according to their works."

The condemned elements of the physical and phychic natures ("Death and the Unseen") are cast into the lake of fire, the chaotic "eighth sphere" in which the creative fire refines, as material for future aeons, the hylic refuse of each cycle. This is termed the "second death."

Then appear a new sky and new earth, i.e., the subjective and objective consciousness of the Nous on its own plane. But the sea, the sensuous consciousness of the lower plane, has passed away.

The holy city, the eternal solar body, now comes down out of the sky, enveloped in its halo, or radiance, the sun-robe of the God.

This aureola is self-luminous, with an opalescent glitter. It is the "wall" of the city (body), having twelve gateways (orifices of the body), and at the gateways twelve Divinities (twelve Gods of the Zodiac—cosmic forces), and with the names of the twelve tribes of Is-Ra-El (zodiac signs) inscribed on the gates. The tribes are the four triads, assigned to the four regions of space.

The wall of the city has twelve foundations, which have on them the names of the twelve apostles of the Lamb. These are the twelve powers of the Logos, the Spiritual Archetypes of the Twelve Cosmic Forces.

In ancient symbology, the "foundation" of all things is the Spirit, upon which rests the structure of whatever is manifested.

The measurements of the city and its wall have been explained together with the enigma of its cubical form. The cube opened forms the Cross, a symbol of Man with Arms extended.

"Aum. Come thou, O Thought Divine, The grace of the Divine Thought be with the holy devotees. Aum."

Thus ends the Apocalypse of Ioannes, the most stupendous work in symbology and allegory ever written. The original author understood all the secret wisdom concealed in the ancient Zodiac as to the Science of Man, and skilfully wove it into a written record that has defied the ability of the most learned men of modern times to interpret..

So complete, comprehensive, and coherent is the work, that its full beauty, in its fine finish of details, can be perceived only when it is viewed as a whole. Nor can its deeper meaning be grasped by mere analytical study.

Its multiplicity of details and reduplication of symbols have utterly baffled all attempts to analyze it by empirical methods. The exotericists have fared even worse through inability to distinguish from the main action of the drama the explanatory material presented by means of side-scenes.

Lesson No. 25

THE ACTORS

In reality, the construction of the drama is not complicated when its design is understood, and its characters are not so numerous as they appear. Its dramatis personae are:

1. God, the forever concealed Divine Presence.
2. The First Logos, the Divine Spirit, from which proceed:
   (a) The Second Logos, the Divine Thought, the ruler of cosmic forces; symbolized by the Conqueror, the Sun;
   (b) The Light of the Logos, Arche, the Divine Substance, primordial matter; symbolized by the Sky-Virgin, the Moon. Philo Judaeus said, "The Logos is the Arche; as Spirit-Matter are one in essence." They emanate:
3. The Twelve Powers, of which five are noetic (solar) and seven are substantive (lunar); symbolized by the Twelve Zodiac Constellations. The twelve powers, emanated successively on four planes of existence, making forty-eight cosmic forces; and forty-nine with the Arche-Logos.

These are the sole performers in the Apocalyptic drama, but some serve several roles.

The ancient Zodiac was subdivided into sections of ten degrees each, called decans, giving three to each of the twelve signs. To each of the thirty-six subdivisions was assigned an extra-zodiac constellation, a paranatellon, which rises or sets simultaneously with it.

These forty-eight constellations, twelve in the Zodiac and three sets of twelve beyond it, with the Sun considered as the center and making up the number forty-nine, completed the stellar scheme of the Zodiac, which is faithfully adhered to in the Apocalypse.

The seven sacred planets play their parts in the drama; but they only represent seven aspects of the Sun.

The extra-zodiac constellations Dracon, Cetus, Medusa and Crater are especially prominent as characters in the drama.

90

The First Logos takes no active part, and is but a voice speaking from the throne.

It should be remembered that these are the worlds and forces of the microcosm, man, as portrayed in the zodiac scheme; and as the two interlaced triangles represent the conflicting spiritual and physical principles in the Soul of Man, they should be considered as interlaced in man, the perfect square, and enclosed within the auric pleroma, or divine synthesis, thus:

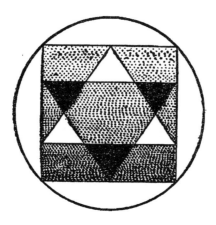

In the Apocalypse the four planes of existence are represented as, (1) the Sky, (2) the Rivers and Springs, (3) the Sea, and (4) the Earth. Encompassing these four is the Air, the Empyrean, which is called the Fifth World in the Ptolemaic system, although it really represents the three formless planes.

The twelve forces vitalizing on each of the four manifested planes, or worlds of form, are divided into a five and a seven; the five is subdivided into a one and a four; and the seven is subdivided into a three and a four, the three being subdivided into a one and a two.

These divisions, written diagrammatically as if on a measuring-stick, make the "rod" with which to "measure the adytum of the God, the altar, and those who worship in it," excluding the court which is exterior to the adytum.

This "measuring-stick" applies to each of the four manifested planes; and in each of them the fivefold group relates to the Sun and the Rectors of the Four Regions of Space, symbolizing variously the Logos and his four manifested powers, the Nous and the four intellective faculties, etc. The sevenfold group relates to the Moon and her septenary time-periods.

The fivefold group, which is really a quaternary and a dominating power, corresponds in each case to the Arche-Logos.

91

THE DRAMA

The drama has seven acts, as follows:

1. The opening of the seven seals, the conquest of the seven principal centers of the sympathetic nerve system.

2. The sounding of the seven trumpets, the conquest of the seven centers of the brain, or cerebro-spinal system.

3. The battle in the sky, resulting in the expulsion of the Dragon and his Divinities, i.e., the elimination from the Mind of all impure thoughts.

4. The harvesting of the earth and its vine, the conquest of the seven cardiac centers.

5. The outpouring of the seven scourges, the conquest of the procreative centers, which finishes the "conquest of the chakras" and produces the birth of the Solar Body.

6. The battle in the psychic world, or infernal region, called Armageddon, resulting in the subjugation of the three beasts, i.e., the extinction of the extraneous phantasmal demon, or composite elemental self.

7. The last judgment, the summing up of the completed cycle of earth lives.

All the remaining portions of the book are explanatory and descriptive.

Of these seven acts, four (the conquest of the chakras) relate to the four somatic divisions, and the other three to the mental, psychic and auric principles.

In a general way, the Four Conquests made by the Logos-Sun correspond to the Four Seasons of the year.

The opening of the seals, the beginning of man's spiritual resurrection, is Spring, the time of germinating seed, expanding bud and upspringing vegetation. The energizing of the noetic centers, the trumpet-calls awakening to life the sunlike intellectual faculties, is Summer, the season of sturdy growth and developing to ripeness, the over-fervid sun at times scorching the tender-green growth.

The opening of the heart-centers, the harvesting of the earth and vine, is Autumn, the period of gathering and garnering the fruitage.

The conquest of the lower life-centers, the scourging of all that is base and impure in man's nature, is Winter, the season of purifying frost and cold, which prevails until the returning Sun, the lengthening of the days, is mystically reborn as the Sun-God of a new divine year, the aeon of the deified man, the Savior of the World, **personified by Catholicism in its Jesus.**

The perfection of the Apocalyptic drama is amazing. It is

expressed in terms of cosmic phenomena. Its hero is the Sun, its heroine the Moon; and all its other characters are Planets, Stars and Constellations; while its stage-setting comprises the Sky, the Earth, the Rivers and the Sea.

The Apocalypse elucidates its subject with the roll of thunder, emphasizes it with the shock of the earthquake, and reiterates it with the Ocean's voice, the ceaseless murmur of its "many waters." It always maintains this Cosmic Language, this vast phrasing of nature, and it must have taken the Masters many years to write it.

In the first magnificent chorus of Constellations that encircle the throne of the Sun-God, the heavenly hosts praise Him as the Creator of the Universe. Yet when the drama has been enacted, that Universe has perished, "the first sky and the first earth are passed away, and the sea exists no more."

Then from his effulgent throne the Logos-Sun announces, "Behold! I am making a new Universe."

This Apocalyptic Universe is Man, the lesser cosmos, of whom the Logos-Sun is in truth the Architect and Builder, and whom the Sun, Moon and all the Stars of the Universe have help to mould and make.

For in every man, however fallen and degraded, are contained all the forces, both cosmic and deific, which brought him into being and have nurtured him throughout the vast cycle of generation, in countless incarnations upon earth, while the Logos of the Light has taught him the loving lessons of Good and Beautiful, of Truth and Righteousness, and the Logos of Darkness has held before him the dread lessons of the Evil and the False.

These same creative forces of the Light-giving Logos, with the tireless patience of the deathless Gods, but await the time when the resurgent Divine Life again stirs within him, and then, disintegrating the elements composing the epithumetic nature, they begin a new evolution, the work of perfecting this child of the aeons, whom the Sun-Adversary, "the Scorpion-monster of Darkness," can drag down until he is lower than the beasts, but whom the Logos-Sun, the Eagle of Light, can exalt to the highest pinnacle of Being.

Lesson No. 26

ZODIAC AND APOCALYPSE

On the blue dome of Heaven, high above Mother Earth,

the Creator first wrote the wonderful story of the Soul, and in the Stars the Masters found it.

The Masters discovered that all things in the Universe are related, and that the Spiritual History of Man had been enacted on a cosmic scale in the Starry Sky long before it was repeated and copied on Earth in the Human Drama.

So the Zodiac was the Grand Symbol of the sacred Science of the Lemurian Masters hundreds of thousands of years ago.

After the Zodiac Plan was prepared, the Apocalypse was written in symbol and allegory in order to record for future ages an explanation of the Zodiac Symbolism so that its secret wisdom would not be lost.

That written record was not destroyed by the church founders because of their inability to interpret its contents. Instead of destroying it, they revised and distorted it to make it appear as "the Revelation" of their "Jesus Christ, which God gave unto him."

Prior to that, Apollonius had made a revised copy of the ancient document in order that it would appear as his work. That revised copy the church founders had, and from it they compiled their own version. They unwittingly included it in the New Testament, little knowing that they were preserving the evidence which would reveal the source of their theological system.

The Encyclopedia Americana claims that the Zodiac "seems to have originated with the Chaldean astronomers about 2100 B.C.," and "the Egyptians adopted the 12-fold division of the Zodiac from the Greeks."

Authors who publish facts, assert that Thales, who travelled into Egypt and the East, first brought Astrology, Geometry and Natural learning to Greece.

Thus we learn how well our publications are censored by Romanism, and how carefully facts and truth are suppressed and concealed from the masses. Egypt was an old, declining nation when Greece was in swaddling-clothes, and its great philosophers got their education in Egypt.

The Masters discovered by years of study that the Heavenly Man (Spirit), in whose image the Earthly Man is made (Gen. 1:27), and in whose body the cells are actually tiny stars, suns and planets, is the prototype of man himself.

In the Stars the Masters discovered the story of the Soul, and in the Stars their discoveries they hid, knowing that the Stars are Light Eternal which will always attract the attention of man, and reveal their secrets to him who has the patience to study them, and the intelligence to interpret correctly what he finds.

In the Stars the Masters discovered how the fate of man would ebb and flow between Light and Darkness, between Spiritualism and Materialism, between Masculinism and Feminism, and they symbolized it all in the Zodiac Signs and their Paranatellons. Astronomy, through its astrological expression, was their Golden Key. It constituted the eternal law of God.

The Zodiac Circle (the Four Wheels in the Ezekiel 1:16), is the symbol of Eternity and God. It represents the path our Sun and Solar System travel in their passage round the great Sun Alcyon, which journey requires 25,920 of our solar years. The Masters had charted many of these journeys.

The passage of our Sun through the Twelve Signs of the Zodiac was made the basis of Cosmic Science by the Masters, who studied the trail of Man as traveling through the Twelve Houses or Polarities of the Zodiac during the days of his earthly career, and experiencing a valuable lesson in each of God's mansions, which are the Home of Man, and no gospel Jesus is needed to go and prepare a place for him (Jn. 14:2). That place God prepared when He made man.

THE ZODIAC BELT

As the Masters studied astronomy, imaginary figures were traced by them all over the sky, to which the different Stars were assigned. Chief among them were those Stars that lay along the path the Sun travels as he climbs toward the north in summer and descends toward the south in winter—lying within certain limits and extending equal distances on each side of the line of equal days and nights.

This belt, curving like a serpent, was termed the Zodiac. It was divided into twelve parts or signs, to each of which was assigned a certain name. At the vernal equinox in 2,488 B.C., the Sun entered the zodiac sign and constellation of Taurus, having passed through since he commenced to ascend northward at the Winter Solstice, the signs of Aquarius, Pisces and Aries, on entering the first of which he reached the lowest limit of his southward journey.

From Taurus, the Sun passed through Gemini and Cancer and reached Leo when he arrived at the terminus of his northward journey. Thence, through Leo, Virgo and Libra, he entered Scorpio at the Autumnal Equinox, and travelled southward through Scorpio, Sagittarius and Capricornus to Aquarius, the terminus of his journey south.

The path in which the Sun travelled through these zodiac

signs became the Ecliptic, and that which passed through the two equinoxes, the Equator.

THE LAMB OF GOD

In 4,588 B.C. the Sun entered the zodiac sign of Taurus, the Bull; and for 2,156.67 years the Bull of the Zodiac was the object of veneration. During that time this symbol of the Zodiac was carved on ancient temples.

The Bull, in turn, was succeeded by Aris, the Ram (a matured Lamb) when the Sun entered that zodiac sign in 2,432 B.C.

From that time until 276 B.C. the Ram, as a Lamb, became the object of adoration when it, in its turn, opened the equinox for 2,156.67 years.—

"To deliver the world from the wintry reign of cold, barrenness and darkness,"

as the ancient people termed it in their annual celebration of the event.

During these centuries the people living north of the Equator called Aries "the Lamb of God which taketh away the sins of the world" (Jn. 1:29). By the "sins of the world" they meant **"the wintry reign of cold, barrenness and darkness."**

When the ancient religious system was overthrown in the revolution that began in 325 A.D. at the First Council of Nicea, the new system adopted the symbols of the old to appease the people; but the symbols were then personified to enslave the people. The zodiac sign Aries was transformed into the gospel Jesus as "the Lamb of God which taketh away the sins of the World" (Ibid.).

At first the Greek and Romans mocked the Jesus that was born in a manger. To them it was a joke; but too soon it became a tragedy. They were fated to see blood flow like water as the priesthood marched with Bible in one hand and bloody sword in the other, slaughtering all who refused to worship the manger-born Jesus (Lu. 2:7), and protected in their bloody work by the Roman army.

It was the worst catastrophy the world has ever known. For refusing to swallow the fraud, seventy million people were murdered, resulting in the depopulation of entire cities, in the "Fall of Rome," and the ascension of the church, according to true history not found in books censored by Romanism.

The annual "birth of the Sun" was widely celebrated by all ancient nations north of the Equator on that day, which has now been fixed as the 25th of December—and so well commercialized that it constrains the people of the USA to waste billions of dollars each year.

Ezekiel's Wheels are the Zodiac. They deal with the astrological doctrine of the ascending Macrocosmos and the descending Microcosmos (Ez. 1:15, 16, 19-21).

The same is true of Jakob's Ladder—six steps up from Libra to Aries, and six steps down on the other side from Aries to Libra.

> "And he dreamed, and behold a ladder set up on the earth, and the top of it reached to heaven; and behold the angels of God (Spirit) ascending and descending on it" (Gen. 28:12).

The angels symbolize the ascending Macrocosmos (man's spirit after death) and the descending Microcosmos (man's birth by the descent of spirit into matter). The Grand Cycle of creative processes.

Lesson No. 27

THE MASTERS' TEXT-BOOK

The Masters used the Zodiac as a chart to illustrate the mystic lessons they taught their disciples, and the lessons are symbolized and allegorized in the Apocalypse. The mysteries of Man's destiny are concealed in the Zodiac and Apocalypse.

The top half of the Zodiac Circle symbolizes the kingdom of God, the celestial world. The lower half is a symbol of the Earth, the terrestrial world.

The bottom half of the Zodiac Circle forms a cup, and was symbolized by the Masters as the Bitter Cup, from which man must drink before he "can see the kingdom of God" (Jn. 3:3).

This mystery was explained in the drama of the Ancient Mysteries, and the neophyte was taught the literal meaning of the allegory. So closely did the new religion follow the old to appease the people, that this event was included in the New Testament, and the gospel Jesus was pictured as drinking from the Bitter Cup.

They gave me also gall for my meat; and in my thirst they gave me vinegar to drink (Ps. 69:21).

They gave him vinegar to drink mingled with gall. . . . They filled a sponge with vinegar and put it on a reed, and gave him to drink (Mat. 27:34, 48).

After this, Jesus knowing that all things were now accom-

97

plished, that the scripture might be fulfilled, said, I thirst. . . .
And they filled a sponge with vinegar, and put it upon hyssop,
and put it to his mouth. When Jesus therefore had received
the vinegar, he said, It is finished: and he bowed his head, and
gave up the ghost (Jn. 19:28;30).

That clever and cunning were the compilers of the New
Testament, and that constantly and completely did they trans-
form allegorism into literalism. Then the ancient documents were
destroyed to conceal the fraud.

WORLD OF ILLUSION

The Masters termed the bottom half of the Zodiac the World
of Illusion; for at the first impression, and to the deceived masses
in darkness, the Earth appears as real and permanent. But
actually, under the operation of the Cosmic Cycle, all visible phenomena are constantly changing. Nothing is static and permanent. The law and order of all visible things is that of constant
change. The Cycle of Eternity.

The bottom half of the Zodiac is also a symbol of "the far
country" to which the Prodigal Son went and spent his substance
in riotous living (Lu. 15:11-32).

This is another allegory. The Prodigal Son is a symbol of
man's life on the terrestrial plane (the far country), and his
return to the "Kingdom of God."

The Master Astrologers put the Grand Man, the Microcosm,
in the center of their Wheel of Life, and ranged round him the
twelve signs of the Zodiac (disciples), in order to symbolize the
Twelve Great Functions of the somatic body, each of which has
its governing department in the Brain, which receives its power
from the Cosmic Source.

The subject of the Ancient Zodiac is more fully covered in
Lessons 19 to 23 of our great course titled "Immortalism," which
the student should study.

Lesson No. 28

INITIATION OF IOANNES

The scientific school of antiquity was termed the Sacred Ancient Mysteries. This school revealed to the neophyte in the
ceremonies of initiation the secret of Eternal Life, and he became
a Master.

Through the ages despots and tyrants sought to destroy these
schools because they enlightened man and gave him that power

one gains through Knowledge based on Truth which sets man free (Jn. 8:32).

Modern man is so completely deceived that he knows not how every effort is made to keep him in darkness by teaching lies and falsehoods and half truths.

The eighth chapter of Ezekiel reveals to him who can understand, how the despots carried on their work of destruction through their henchmen.

The spy of the despot dug a hole in the wall and discovered a door, which he opened and entered the chambers of the Ancient Mysteries, and portrayed on the wall round about he saw "every form of creeping things, and abominable beasts, and all the idols of the house of Israel."

We learn God's work by studying what He makes, as they did in the Ancient Mystery Schools.

The despot called this "idolatry" as his excuse for murdering the Masters and closing their schools. That has been done through the ages, and was done by Constantine in the fourth century A.D. when he founded Roman Catholicism.

Supported by the power and money of the Roman Empire, that institution spread darkness and built itself into the most powerful organization on earth. It has passed the peak of its power and has been slowly sinking since the courageous Martin Luther struck the telling blow that started it on the way out.

In our brief review of the book of Revelation we saw how the author told his story by using as symbols the powers and products of Nature, such as "every form of creeping things, and abominable beasts, and all the idols of the house of Israel."

Having briefly reviewed the text of Revelation, we shall now discuss it more in detail.

Chapter 1: 1, 2

The initiation of Anointed Iesous, which the God conferred on him to make known to his slaves the (perfections) which must be attained speedily. He sent his Divinity and by him symbolized (them) to his slave Ioannes, who gave evidence of the Logos of the God and of the evidence of Anointed Iesous—of all the (visions) that he saw.

Interpretation

The title makes Ioannes the one to be initiated, while the sub-title presents Iesous as the candidate who, having been initiated, emerges as the Conqueror after the telestic ordeals.

Ioannes and Iesous are one and the same, Ioannes symbolizing the incarnated man, and Iesous his noetic Self, whose "slave" the material man-must become if he desires to reach the highest celestial.

The Divinity who comes at the behest of Iesous, is higher than the latter, for he is the Logos, who makes his appearance in the initial vision-and remains throughout as Hierophant or Initiator, while Iesous is the candidate who is subjected to the initiatory trials and has to do the perfecting "works," whereby he finally emerges as the Conqueror on the white horse—the new Initiate in his Solar Body.

The spiritual perfections must be attained "speedily" by sustained, unremitting effort; yet, as time is regarded by those who consider physical life as an affair of but one incarnation, the telestic work would seem by no means expeditious. For it requires not less than seven incarnations of untiring effort before the final goal is reached.

It is the intuitive mind (Anointed Iesous) who gives evidence of the Logos to the neophyte, and he in turn must, according to the law of the occult, transmit it to his fellow-men, who usually repay him with some form of physical or mental martyrdom.

Chapter 1:3

Immortal is he who discerns, and they who learn (from him) the arcane doctrine of this Teaching, and observe the (precepts) which are written in it; for (their) season is near.

Interpretation

This is a dedication of the work to every mystic who may succeed in penetrating to its inner meaning, and impart to other students the occult doctrines (logoi) it contains. For the "Logoi (oracles) of God" are esoteric aphorisms containing the potency of the Divine Thought, and are not mere "words" comprehensible to the conventionalist.

Likewise, propheteia is not merely "prophecy" in the fortune-telling sense of predicting future events. The word means literally "speaking for" (the Gods); the office of the Seer being to receive and interpret the truths taught in the noetic world, the realm of the Logos.

Certain portions of the writings of Ezekiel, Zechariah and other Hebrew "prophets," are esoteric treatises on the nature of man, thinly veiled as predictions. In them, nations and personages play the parts which, in the Apocalypse, are acted by the cosmic bodies.

To him who resolutely pursues the path of purity there will come this consciousness of immortality and spiritual calm. It is a matter of concentrating the mind upon the eternal inner Self instead of upon the external self that is under the rule of eternal change, birth and death.

Chapter 1:4, 5

Ioannes to the seven Societies in Asia: Grace to you, and peace, from (the God) who (eternally) is, who was, and who is (always) coming, and from the seven Breaths before his throne, and from Anointed Iesous, that believable witness, the first-born from "the dead," and the foremost of the rulers of the earth.

Interpretation

The seven Societies symbolize the seven principal ganglia; later they are metamorphosed into "seven little lampstands," each ganglion being a small brain, a minor light-giver in the body, as the brain is the great light-giver, or microcosmic sun. Then they are changed almost directly into "seven seals" on a scroll, the chakras being indeed sealed in the physical body, so far as concerns their **psychic functions**.

The enthroned God is the First Logos, who abides in the Eternal, and is not to be considered as incarnated, but rather as overshadowing the man on earth. The word "coming" is used because the future participle of the verb "to be" would convey an erroneous metaphysical concept; "was," in the imperfect tense, expresses an action still continuing, but the future, "shall be," would imply something that does not yet exist, whereas the Logos is represented as existing in an infinite present which includes the Past and Future.

Plato taught that it is erroneous to attribute the past and future to the Eternal; "For we say, indeed, that he was, he is and he will be; but 'he is' alone approximates the true concept (logos).

The seven Breaths, which appear later as seven stars, are the Chief Divinities representing seven aspects of the Logos. Iesous, the first-born from "the dead," is the epistemonic (intuitive) Mind; the intuition is the first of man's dormant spiritual faculties to awaken, bringing certainty of knowledge, and becoming the dominant power in his life.

To him who, having graciously welcomed us and washed us
from our sins in his blood, also made us rulers and sacrificers to
his God and Father—to him be the glory and the dominion
throughout the aeons of the aeons! Amen.

Interpretation

These words of Ioannes refer to the initiation he has gone
through, and which he is about to describe. The lustration
(baptismos) of blood, which emancipates from sin, is the rain
of purifying fire (the "blood" of the Logos) poured out by the
Divinities charged with the seven sourages.

By a bold oriental simile, a variant of the parable of the
prodigal, the higher Self, is represented as hospitably entertain-
ing the returned wandered, the reincarnating self, and washing
from him the stains of travel.

To each of the planets a distinctive attribute is assigned;
and here "dominion" applies to the Sun, "glory" to the Moon.

The "Amen" is the Greek equivalent of the Sanscrit Aum.
Used in a certain way, this word has the power, through the
correlation of sound and the vital electricity, to arouse the
Speirema, or regenerative force, the Serpentine Fire.

Lesson No. 29

Chapter 1:7

Behold! He comes amidst the clouds, and every eye shall see
him, and they who pierced him (shall see him); and all the tribes
of the earth shall wail over him. Verily! Amen.

Interpretation

The eyes that see him are the noetic centers. They who
"pierced him" are the sense-perceptions; and the "tribes" are
the repentant elements of the mental and psychic constitution.

The "clouds" are the auric forces. Here the nimbus seems to
be referred to rather than the aureola. The latter envelopes the
whole body, while the nimbus is limited to the head.

In the ancient mythos there were two crucifixions, corresponding to generation and regeneration. The first is the descent of
the soul into matter, when the body becomes its "cross" and
the five senses are its five "wounds"; the body with arms extended

forming a cross, and the objective senses being avenues that lead away from the spirit.

The second crucifixion is the ascent of the soul to spirit through the initiation-rite, or self-conquest, when it is mystically said to be crucified in the brain—in the place called Golgotha, "the skull."

Chapter 1:8

"I am the Alpha and the Omega," says the Master, the God who (forever) is, who was, and who is coming, the All-Dominator.

Interpretation

Cedrenus says that the Chaldeans symbolized the Light of Reason by the vowels a. w. These two vowels were assigned to the Moon and Saturn, the intermediate planets answering to the five other vowels in their order.

The seven Planetary Powers are potential in the First Logos; in the Second Logos they become manifested potencies.

The revised version retains the anachronistic "Omega," a word coined in the "dark ages."

Chapter 1:9-11

I, Ioannes, who am your brother, as also your copartner in the ordeal, ruling and patience of Iesous, came to be in the island called Patmos, through the arcane doctrine of the God and through the evidence of Iesous. I came to be in the Breath (trance) on the master-day, and I heard behind me a loud voice, like a trumpet-call, saying:

> "What you see, write in a scroll, and send (the message) to the seven Societies which are in Asia; To Ephesos, Smyrna, Pergamos, Thyateira, Sardeis, Philadelphia and Laodikeia."

Interpretation

Serene patience is one of the indispensable qualifications of the aspirant for spiritual knowledge. So is the ruling or dominance of the higher intellect, the Nous (Iesous), over the lower faculties.

The ordeal is that of initiation, now begun. Through the awakening noetic perception (the evidence of Iesous) and the increasing light of the Logos—the whitening of the dawn of the new life—the aspirant becomes isolated, and in the drear loneliness of one who has forever discarded the illusions of sensuous existence, but has not yet seen the sunrise of the spirit, he dwells, as it were, on an island (Patmos), apart from his fellowmen. He lives within himself.

Then through his introspection comes the message of the Great Breath, and in the sacred trance he attains his first autopsia, beholding the apparition of his own Logos.

Chapter 1: 12-16

I turned to see the Voice that was speaking with me. Having turned, I saw seven little golden lampstands, and in the midst of them an (apparition) like the son of man, wearing (a vesture) reaching to the feet and girded at the paps with a golden girdle. His head and hair were white as white wool, (white) as snow; and his eyes were as a blaze of fire. His feet were like the liquid-metal that is as if it had been melted in a furnace. His voice was as the voice of many waters. In his right hand he had seven stars. From his mouth kept flashing forth a keen two-edged sword. His face was (luminous), as shines the sun by its inherent force.

Interpretation

This apparition is a fanciful picture of the Sun as the Pan-augeia, or flount of all-radiating light; and, like all the puzzles of Ioannes, it is ingeniously constructed.

The "voice" that speaks is the primary aspect of the Second Logos, in whom the seven "voices" or vowels (for "phone" is the one Greek word for both vowel and voice) become differentiated. As the all-pervading solar Light he walks among the seven golden lampstands, the seven planetary bodies, holding in his right hand their seven stars, being the light he confers upon them.

The Logos-figure described is a composite picture of the seven sacred planets: He has the white hair of Kronos (Father Time), the blazing eyes of wide-seeing Zeus, the sword of Ares, the shining face of Helios, and the chiton and girdle of Aphrodite. His feet are of mercury, the metal sacred to Hermes, and his voice is like the murmur of the waves of the sea, alluding to Selene, the Moon Goddess of the four seasons and of the waters.

To have placed the winged feet of Hermes on the figure, or to have used the ordinary word hydrargyros (water-silver) for mercury, would have made the puzzle too transparent. So Ioannes employed the archaic word "chalkolibanon," which he evidently took from Plato, to designate the material used in making the feet of his Planetary Logos. This word is rendered "fine brass" in the authorized version, although it seems that brass was unknown to the Greeks, who used a bronze composed of copper and tin.

Chalkolibanon is the "metal that forms in drops," as does gum exuding from a tree. It is neither brass nor incense-gum, but simply quicksilver—fluidic, as if melted in a furnace.

The figure of the Sun as the ruler of the planets is a symbol of the incarnated Self, the Second Logos; and, as given in the description of the apparition, the seven planets are in reverse order, for the Second Logos is the inverted reflection of the First: The celestial man is, as it were, unside-down when incarnated in physical substance. The significance of this inversion develops later in the Apocalyptic drama.

Similar descriptions of the "son of man" appear in Ezekiel, Zechariah and Daniel. While similar, they are not the same. The Apocalypse is "sui generis," and while Ioannes apparently borrowed many symbols and poetic images from ancient writings, he usually employs them to conceal his real meaning by endowing them with a different or variant significance. Hence the exotericists who try to follow these supposed parallels will only be mislead and confused, as Ioannes doubtless intended.

Chapter 1: 17-20

When I saw him, I fell at his feet as one dead. He placed his right hand on me saying, "Be not afraid. I am the First (Adam) and the Last (Adam), he who is Alive. I became a "dead man"; and Behold! I am alive throughout the aeons of the aeons, and I have the Keys of Death and of the Unseen. Write down the (glories) you saw, also those which are, and those which are about to be attained next after them, (beginning with) the mystery of the seven stars which you saw on my right hand, and the seven little golden lampstands, The seven stars are the Divinities of the seven Societies; and the seven little lampstands are the seven Societies.

Interpretation

The esoteric tenet as to "the First and the Last" is clearly stated by Paul (Apollonius) in 1 Cor. 15:22, 45.

For as in (the first) Adam (physical) all become moribund

(dead), so likewise in (the second) Adam all are restored to life.

The first man, Adam, was made a living psychic form; the last Adam is the life-producing breath (pneuma).

Plato wrote, "Some say the body (soma) is the tomb (sema) of the Soul, which may be considered as buried in the body during our physical life."

In the allegory the Logos (Divine Man) becomes "dead" during the cycle of material evolution. But as it emerges from material conditions and limitations through the awakening of the dormant epistemonic faculty, or spiritual intuition, it is "restored" (resurrected) to life. Then man has the consciousness of Immortality, and holds the Keys with which he can unlock the doors of the physical world (Death) and of the psychic world (Heaven).

The cunning compiler of the New Testament was shrewd, and he had access to this ancient wisdom. He had the ancient scrolls before him. From them he was copying, and he distorted as he wrote. After the alleged resurrection of his Jesus, he has him say to his disciples: "All power is given unto me in heaven and in earth" (Mat. 28:18). Now we can understand the secret meaning of that phrase.

The cities of the seven Societies were in Asia Minor, not far from Patmos, and they have been noticed.

Lesson No. 30

Chapter 2: 1-7

"To the Divinity of the Society in Ephesos write: These (words) says he who with his right hand dominates the seven stars, he who walks about in the midst of the seven little golden lampstands: I know your works, and your over-toil and patience, and that you cannot bear wicked men. You put to the test those pretending to be apostles (and they are not) and found them false. You endured and have patience; on account of my name you have toiled and have not grown weary. But I have (this complaint) against you, that you left your first love. Remember, therefore, whence you are fallen; reform, and do the first works —but if not, coming to you speedily, I shall move your lampstand out of its place, unless you do reform. But you have this (virtue), that you abhor the works of the Nikolaitanes, which I also abhor.

He who has an ear, let him hear what the Breath is saying to the Societies.

"The Conqueror—to him I shall award to eat (the fruit) of

106

the tree of life which is in the middle of the Garden of the God."

Interpretation

The Logos announces himself in his aspect as Memory, which links together the past, present and future. The ever-toiling and unwearied memory stores up all the experiences of man.

The muladhara chakra, symbolized by Ephesos, lies at the base of the spinal cord, at the lower pole of the cerebro-spinal system, the starting point of the sushumna, and directly related to the highest, the sahasrara, or conarium. As already explained, the lower plane of life is the inverted reflection of the higher. Hence it is said to have left its first love, the divine love having become human love, and is told to remember whence it has fallen and do the first works—that is, pour its force into the first and highest chakra, the regenerative brain-center.

The quality of this chakra still retains some of the higher love, a clinging to purity and an aversion to sensuality and every perversion of the creative function. It is therefore said to have exposed the impure charlatans and to abhor the works (secret rites) of the Nikolaitanes. The latter were a pseudo-occult sect that practiced the vilest forms of phallic sorcery..

The unclean worship of the Great Mother, called Rhea, Cybelle, Astarte, and by other names, was prevalent in Asia, and many were her temples with their "consecrated women." In the ancient mythology Rhea was not thus degraded.

The attainment of spiritual knowledge is in effect the process of reviving the memory of the incarnating Ego in relation to the supernal worlds, before it became immured in matter.

This memory of things divine can be recalled only through the action of the Parakletos, the Serpentine Fire. Hence in this aspect the Nous is said to hold in its grasp the seven stars and to walk among the seven little lampstands. .

Plato held that all true knowledge is derived from the "recollection of the things in which the God abides;" the immature souls, that cannot "feed on the vision of truth," fail of being "initiated into the mysteries of Being, and are nourished with the food of opinion." But "he who employs aright these memories is ever being initiated into the perfect mysteries, and alone becomes perfect."

As the sun enters each sign of the Zodiac it is said, astrologically, to "conquer" the sign and to assimilate its particular quality. The same is said of the Kundalini as it passes through the chakras. Hence, the hero of the Apocalypse, who is the Nous or microcosmic Sun, is called "the Conqueror."

The award to the Conqueror, in the aspect here presented, is the Eternal Memory: He shall eat the fruit of the tree of life (the fruitage of the life-cycle) in the God's own dwelling, the mystical Paradise, or state of ineffable bliss. In this aspect the Logos is Kronos (Saturn), the God of Time.

Chapter 2: 8-11

"To the Divinity of the Society in Smyrna write: These (words) say the First (Adam) and the Last (Adam), who became a 'dead man,' and came to life: I know your ordeal and poverty (but you are rich) and the profanity of those claiming to be Ioudaians—and they are not, but are an assembly of the Adversary. Fear not the (ordeals) which you are about to experience. Behold! The Accuser is about to cast some of you into prison, that you may be brought to trial; and you will have an ordeal of ten days. Become confiding until death and I shall give you the crown of life.

He who has an ear, let him hear what the Breath is saying to the Societies. The Conqueror shall not at all be punished by the second death.

Interpretation

Here the Logos is presented in his aspect as Reason, the highest philosophical intellection, which, in the carnal man, is dormant, but which awakens when he turns to the serious consideration of the concerns of the higher life.

The reasoning faculty, hampered by the physical brain, is poverty-stricken; but when freed from the trammels of matter, it is rich in ideas.

The pseudo-Ioudaians are the irrational dogmas of exoteric religion, which are falsely advanced as divine revelations, yet are obviously opposed to reason, and are but the mere vagaries of the phrenic mind when under the stimulus of the perverted devotional nature, and come not from the Logos but from his adversary of intellectual light.

The Hebrew language was at first a secret sacerdotal jargon of Egyptian origin, and St. Gregory of Nyssa asserted that the most learned men of his day knew positively that it was not so ancient as other languages, and did not become the spoken language of the Hebrews until after their exodus from Egypt.

The word "Jew" is used throughout the Apocalypse in its Kabalistic meaning, for one having esoteric knowledge, an initiate; as in the Kabalistic maxim, **"The stone becomes a plant, the plant an animal, the animal a man, the man a Jew, and the**

Jew a God." Hence comes the myth of the "chosen people."

The "ten days" refer to a zodiacal decan and a paranatellon-here, the constellation Draco, the "archaic snake," who is the prosecutor or accuser, the theological "Devil" and "Satan." Satan comes from the Egyptian Set (Typhon), the enemy and mythical murdered of Osiris, the Egyptian god.

This chakra, the adhishthana, is the starting-point of the ida and pingaga nerves, allegorized in the Apocalypse as the "two witnesses," the sushumna being the third.

The reward of the Conqueror is Conscious Immortality: he is to wear the Crown of Life, and nothing that originates in the Spiritual Mind shall pass into the oblivion of the second death.

This aspect of the Logos is that of Zeus (Jupiter), the son of Kronos and the father of Gods and men, who was also called Zeus Tripoes, the "Three-eyed," and was represented on the Acropolis of Argos by a gigantic statue having two eyes in its face and one on its forehead.

Lesson No. 31

Chapter 2: 12-17

"To the Divinity of the Society in Pergamos write: These (words) says he who has the keen two-edged sword: I know your works, and where you dwell—and where the throne of the Adversary is. You are holding fast my name, and you did not abjure my believable witness, who was slain among you, where the Adversary dwells. But I have a few (complaints) against you, because you have there those who support the teaching of Balaam, who taught Balak to set a snare before the children of Israel; to eat (food) offered to ghosts and to prostitutes. So, also, you have those who uphold the teachings of the Nikolaitanes, which I abhor. Reform—but if not, coming to you speedily, I shall combat them with the sword of my mouth.

He who has an ear, let him hear what the Breath is saying to the Societies.

"The Conqueror—to him I shall award to eat a share of the occult manna; and I shall award to him a white voting-pebble, and on the voting-pebble (will be) a new name engraved, which no one knows but he who receives it.

Interpretation

The Logos here presents himself in his aspect as Will, volition, the energizing principle, and he carries the sword of the War God.

·Pergamos represents the manipuraka chakara, the solar plexus, the chief center of the sympathetic nerve system, and the seat of the epithumetic nature—the Dragon, or Satanas the Adversary of the Logos.

Plato states that the desires are "chained down like a wild beast," in the region between the midriff and navel, "and knowing that this principle in man listens not to reason" and "liable to be led away by ghosts and phantoms, the God, considering this, formed the liver, to connect with the lower nature and there to dwell, contriving that it should be compact, smooth, and bright, and both sweet and bitter, in order that in it the power of the thoughts, proceeding from the mind (Nous), might be received like figures in a mirror and projected as images."

Thus, he·says, the creative powers, in order that the lower nature "might obtain a measure of truth, placed in the liver their oracle—which is sufficient proof that the God has given second-sight to the foolishness of man." "Such, then, is the nature of the liver, such its function and place, formed for the sake of second-sight."

This is the faculty of the mantis, or individual gifted with "second-sight"; and this is also the "witness Antipas," who was indeed slain by those who have lost even this psychic function of the liver, as well as the intuition of the intellectual nature.

Antipas is simply Mantie disguised by having the initial M converted into PA and anagrammatically transposed. To solve the puzzle, it is only necessary to combine the letters II and A, forming IAI, which, when inverted, forms a passable M—and incidentally shows why "eminent scholars" have failed to find a satisfactory Greek derivation for the word or any historical record of the supposed "martyr."

The snare of Balak, the eating of food devoted to spirits, and sexual promiscuity, all refer to various goetic practices, the nature of which is better left unexplained.

The regard of the Conqueror, who, by the dauntless energy of the Will, vanquishes all the evil foes in his own nature and fights his way to the pure region of spiritual light, is that he has imparted to him the secret knowledge, the Gnosis, and is given, as it were, a ballot, being named and naturalized a citizen of the nation of the Initiated.

Here the Logos has the semblance of Ares (Mars). The corresponding vowel is O, and the attribute "force."

· Chapter 2: 18-29

"To the Divinity of the Society in Thyateira write: These

110

(words) says the son of the God, who has eyes as a blaze of fire and feet like the liquid metal: I know your works, and your love, belief, service, and patience; and that your last works (are to be) greater than the first. But I have (a complaint) against you, that you tolerate the woman Iezabel, who, professing to be a seeress, teaches and deludes my slaves to prostitute and to eat (food) offered to ghosts. I gave her time, that she might reform; but she does not will to reform.

Behold! I throw her down on a (sick) bed, and those committing adultery with her (I shall subject) to a grievous ordeal, unless they shall reform from their works. I shall slay her children in the Death (world); and all the Societies shall know that I AM he who searches into kidneys and hearts. I shall give (awards) to each of you according to your works. But to you I say, to the rest in Thyateira—as many as do not possess this teaching, who remained guileless of knowledge concerning the depths of the Adversary, as they say—I do not cast on you an additional burden. That which you do possess, retain dominion over it till I come.

"The Conqueror—who also observes my works until the perfecting-period—to him I shall award authority over the people, and he will rule them with an iron wand (like vessels of clay they are being crushed) as I also received (authority) from my father. I shall award to him the morning star.

He who has an ear, let him hear what the Breath is saying to the Societies.

Interpretation

To this center the Logos presents himself in his aspect as Direct Cognition, the faculty of apprehending truth without the aid of inductive reasoning. In this aspect as the Sun, the pure intellectual effulgence, he is not the "son of man," but the "son of the God," having the all-seeing eyes of Zeus and the winged feet of Hermes, thus combining the attributes of Divine Reason and Divine Thought.

Thyateira symbolizes the anahata chakra, the cardiac center. As the liver, the organ of divination, is the reflector of the mind in the epithumetic region, so the heart is the organ which, in the phrenic region, serves as the reflector of the Nous, and is the center of the higher psychic consciousness.

The corresponding reflector in the brain is the conarium; and the generative organs, the "three witnesses" or inverted analogue of the higher triad, fulfill the same psychic function in the lowest of the four somatic divisions; hence the allusion to the kidneys or lions—an euphemism for the testes. The four virtues enumerated, love, belief, service and patience, correspond to the four noetic qualities as transmitted through the heart.

The pseudo-seeress Iezabel has the name and attributes of the sorceress, Ahab's wife, of malodorous memory, in the Old Testament tale. Here she symbolizes the emotional, erotic sort of psychism that is sometimes developed at orgiastic "religious revivals," and which is more characteristic of hysterical women than of rational human beings.

By this prostitution of mind and emotions to the epithumetic nature, causing moral disintegration and dissipation of psychic vitality, mediumistic faculties are sometimes developed, producing avenues of communication with the shades of the dead.

The award to the Conqueror, if he observes the admonitions of the spiritual mind, is absolute dominion over the lower faculties and forces, which he rules as with a rod of iron; and he receives the morning star, which symbolizes the Divine Life that heralds the dawning day of full spiritual illumination.

Here the Logos has the aspect of Helios (Sun); the corresponding vowel is I, and the attributes, three in number, are dominion, spiritual wealth, and all graciousness—the latter epithet implying that the Sun-Logos unites in himself all the graces of the seven planets.

, Lesson No. 32

Chapter 3: 1-6

"To the Divinity of the Society in Sardeis write: These (words) says he who has the seven Breaths of the God and the seven stars: I know your works; that you have the name that you are alive, but that you are a dead man. Become awakened (from the dead) and strengthen the remaining (affections) that are at the point of dying; for I have not found your works accomplished before my God. Therefore, remember how you have received (this message) and heard (it); and observe (its prescepts), and reform.

If you will not be awake, I shall come upon you (silently) as a thief (comes), and you will not know what hour I shall come upon you. But you have a few names in Sardeis who did not sully their garments, and they shall walk with me in white (rainment), for they are deserving.

"The Conqueror—he shall thus be clothed in white garments, and I shall not erase his name from the Book of Life, but shall

112

acknowledge his name before my Father and before his Divinities."

Interpretation .

To this Society the Logos proclaims himself in his aspect as Divine Love, the deific creative power; and here he is the synthesis of the seven planets and the seven creative forces, corresponding, in a way, to the First Logos or Eros.

Sardeis represents the vishuddi chakra, the center in the throat, which is directly related to the lower creative centers, as shown by change of voice at the time of puberty and the castrato voice of the eunuch. The throat is definitely affected by the finer emotions.

. This higher love is said to have the name of being alive, yet to be dead in reality; for the devotional aspirations and purer affections of man are indeed pitifully weak and moribund.

It is this deadness of the moral feelings that stills the voice of conscience; yet at any time that conscience may unexpectedly speak out, bringing remorse and sorrow to him whom the Self has thus suddenly aroused, coming upon him silently, as a thief in the night. This simile is repeated in 16:15, with almost the same wording.

Sardeis was a center of Venus-worship, having a temple to Astarte.

The reward to the Conqueror is perfect purity; and the auric color corresponding to this chakra (its esoteric name) will remain in the aureola (book of life), or glory; emotion becoming transmuted into eternal gladness.

In this aspect the Logos is Aphrodite (Venus), the Goddess of Love. It is only in this female aspect that the Logos is the creative Word, in one sense the occult potency of sound, and identical with speech, who is also Sarasvati (Venus) in Hindu mythology. The corresponding vowel is H, and the attributes are Invocation, and Realm or Ruling.

· Chapter 3: 7-13

"To the Divinity of the Society in Philadelpheia write: These (words) says he who is Holy, who is True, who has David's Key, who opens and no one shall shut, who shuts and no one opens: Behold! I have swung open before you a door which no one can shut. For (I know) that you have a little force; and you observed my arcane doctrine, and did not abjure my name.

I am giving you (deliverance to some of you) from among the

113 .

assembly of the Adversary (composed) of those who professing to be Ioudaians—and they are not, but are lying. I shall cause them to come and make obeisance before your feet, and to know I have graciously received you. Because you guarded the arcane doctrine of my patience, I also shall guard you from the (first) hour of that probation which is about to come upon the entire homeland, to put to the proof those who are dwelling upon the earth. I am coming speedily. Retain a firm grasp on the (steadfast virtue) which you possess, so that no one may carry off your crown.

"The Conqueror—I shall make him a pillar in the adytum of my God, and never more shall he go outside of it; and I shall write on him the name of my God, and the name of the city of my God, the new Hierousalem, which is coming down out of the sky from my God; and (I shall write on him) my new name."

Interpretation

Here the Logos presents the aspect of the Divine Thought, the pure and unmixed nature of intellect, or the unrefracted light of the Nous—Thought not differentiated into thoughts, but considered as the energizing principle of Mind, and the complement of the energizing principle of Love. "The Holy" and "the True" are identical with "the Good" and "the True" of Plato, while the correlated Aphrodite-aspect is "the Beautiful."

(Note: **Love is an energizing principle in that it quickens the Creative Centers, but it becomes weakening lust when the essence manufactured by the Creative Centers is consumed instead of conserved.**)

According to Kabalistic mysticism, **ADaM** stands for Adam, David and Messias, making the Messias the reincarnation of Adam and of David: these symbolize the three stages in man's life-cycle, Adam being the primeval state of child-like innocence, David the adolescence in which good and evil struggle for the mastery, and Iesous (Messias) the stage of spiritual maturity.

David, for all his vileness and evil deeds, had the virile depth of feeling, philosophic breadth of mind and poetic insight that give promise of the spiritual man. These were his "key" to the door giving entrance to the spiritual consciousness. Compare with this 22:16 and the interpretation.

Philadelpheia symbolizes the ajna chakra, the center of the forehead, the point of divergence of the auric light, the color of which reveals infalibly the spiritual status of each individual. Thus, if the light radiating from it is golden-yellow, it is the "name" of the Sun; if dull red or green, it is the "brand of the Beast."

The reward of the Conqueror is that he is to become a sustaining power in the spiritual world, no more to reincarnate, but to abide in the eternal city (solar body).

The aspect of the Logos here is that of Hermes (Mercury), the God of Occult Wisdom. The corresponding vowel is E, and the attributes are "honor" and "deliverance."

Chapter 3: 14-22

"To the Divinity of the Society in Laodikeia write: These (words) says the Amen, the witness believable and true, the origin of God's organic world: I know your works, that you are neither cold nor hot. I would that you were cold or hot. So, because you are lukewarm, I am on the point of vomiting you from my mouth. Because you say, 'I am rich, I have become rich, and I have lack of nothing,' and do not know that you are the worn-out, pitiable, beggerly, blind and naked one, I advise you to buy from me gold tried by fire—so that you may be rich —and white garments—so you may clothe yourself, and the shame of your nakedness not be apparent—and eyesalve to anoint your eyes—so that you may see. As many as I love, I confute and instruct. So be emulous and reform. I am standing at the door and gently tapping. If any one hears my voice and opens the door, him I shall visit, and with him I shall dine, and he with me.

"The Conqueror—I shall award to him to be seated with me on my throne, as I also conquered and was seated with my father on his throne."

Interpretation

To this Society the Logos announced himself as the Divine Substance, Arche, from which originate all the elements, including those forms of substance which modern physicist classifies as "forces."

Laodikeia symbolized the sahasrara chakra, the atrophied "unpaired eye." Hence the allution to the Phrygian "eyesalve."

Neither cold nor hot, i.e., having neither the dispassionate reason nor the devotional fever, but lukewarm and nauseating to the spiritual mind, the lower mind yet prides itself on its supposed wealth of intellectual attainments; yet, without the gold of spiritual refinement and, the white garments of purity, these attainments are meager and unlovely.

The reward of the Conqueror is to share in the Throne of the God, to become one with his own highest self.

Here the Logos has the semblance of Selene (the Moon), the white-armed Goddess who rules the four seasons and the water. The corresponding vowel is A; and the attributes are "glory" and "authority."

In the seven benedictions contained in the Apocalypse, twelve attributes are given; of these, three are assigned to the Sun, two to each of the members of the higher triad, and one to each of the lower.

When the two triads (the sun being always the central planet) are paralleled, the result is a fourfold system, in which the Spiritual Faculty stands alone, and the other faculties are paired.

Lesson No. 33

Chapter 4: 1-3

After these (things) I saw; and, Behold! a door opened in the sky; and it was that first voice which I (now) heard, like a trumpet-call speaking to me, (the enthroned God) saying,

"Come up hither, and I shall make known to you the (perfections) which must be attained hereafter."

Immediately I came to be in the Breath (trance). A throne was placed in the sky, and on the throne (a God) was seated. The enthroned (God) was in appearance like an opal and a carnelian, and a rainbow encircled the throne, in appearance like an aqua-marine.

Interpretation

The trumpet-like voice is that of the First Logos, the Enthroned Eternal (Ch. 1:8), and not that of the Planetary Logos who sent the messages to the seven Societies.

In the Greek the names of the stones are somewhat uncertain, but they appear to be what is now called the opal and the aqua-marine or blue beryl.

The somatic divisions in the Apocalypse agree with the symbolism of the Hebrew tabernacle, except that the latter was semi-exoteric, following the threefold system.

Josephus says of the tabernacle and its arrangements: "They represent in some sort the Universe. For out of the three portions into which the length of the tabernacle is divided, the two into which the sacrificing priests are allowed to enter represent the Earth and the Sea, which are opened to all, and the third portion, which is inaccessible to them, is like the Sky, which is reserved for God, because it is his dwelling-place."

Chapter 4: 4-8

Encircling the throne were 24 thrones, and on the thrones (I saw) 24 Ancients seated, arrayed in white garments, and (wearing) on their heads golden crowns. From the throne went out lightnings, thunder and voices; and (there were) seven lamps of fire burning before the throne, which are the seven Breaths of the God. Before the throne (was a sheen) as a glassy sea, like crystal. In the middle of the throne and in a circle about the throne (were) four Beings, full of eyes before and behind. The first Being was like a Lion; the second was like a young Bull; the third had the face of a Man; and the fourth was like a flying Eagle. The four Beings, having each one of them six wings, are full of eyes round about and within; and ceaselessly day and night they keep saying: "Holy, holy, holy (is) the Master-God, the All-Dominator, who was, who (forever) is, and who is coming."

Interpretation

The four Beings are the four operative Powers of the Logos, and correspond to the four great planes of existence and the four states of seership, on each of these planes.

When Ioannes speaks of being "in the Breath" he uses the word Pneuman instead of Manteia (trance), as the latter word would be too explicit for allegorical purposes.

Each of these four states of seership has a subjective and an objective phrase on the plane to which it relates; and this is symbolized by the many exterior and interior eyes of the Beings. The Nous has its "reflector" in each of the four somatic divisions.

As macrocosmic powers, the four Beings are mystically the four quarters of the Zodiac, the four arms, so to say, of the sun; and as solar forces each is a septenate, radiating from a focal point into the six directions of space. Similarly, the time-periods are divided into fourths, as the year, which has four seasons, each containing three months, these being again sub-divided into bright and dark fortnights, making 24 such periods, corresponding to the 24 hours of the day.

Whether in the macrocosm or the microcosm, the forces which govern successively these various time-periods are the 24 Ancients, and they are identical with the 24 wings of the four Beings.

The glassy sea is the ether specialized in the brain; the aura of the chakras being symbolized by the seven fire-lamps of Breaths.

Chapter 4: 9-11

And as often as the Beings gave glory, honor and thanks to the (God) seated on the throne, to him who lives throughout the aeons of the aeons, the 24 Ancients kept falling down (successively) in front of the (God) seated on the throne, worshipping him who lives throughout the aeons of the aeons, and letting fall their crowns in front of the throne, saying,

> "Worthy thou art, our Master and our God, to receive the glory, the honor and the force; for thou didst bring into existence the Universe, and through thy will it exists and was established."

Interpretation

The forces preside in turn over the time-periods; thus in the human aura a tattva rules each hour of the day, its particular psychic color predominating in the aura during that time. Hence the 24 Ancients (hours of the day) are represented as worshipping before the throne, each making obeisance in turn and throwing down his crown, giving over his rule to the next.

Chapter 5: 1, 2

I saw on the right hand of the (God) seated on the throne a scroll, written inside and on the back, securely sealed with seven seals. And I saw a strong Divinity proclaiming with a great voice: "Who is worthy to open the scroll and force open its seals?"

Interpretation

This scroll is a mysterious document that has required aeons for the God to write—a Bible which, when rightly read, reveals cosmic mysteries. Few know that it is **man's physical body.** Its seals are the nerve-centers wherein radiates the formative force of the Logos, and are symbolized by the seven Societies and the lampstands. The expression "written inside and on the back" refers to the cerebro-spinal axis and the great sympathetic nerve system.

The "strong Divinity" is Kronos. the God of Time, who in ancient mythology is the oldest of the twelve great Gods that symbolize the great departments of the Cosmos.

Chapter 5: 3-5

No one, in the sky, on the earth, or under the earth, was able to open the scroll or (even) to see it. I wept much because no worthy one was found to open the scroll, or (even) to see it. One of the Ancients said to me:

"Weep not. Behold! the Lion, he of the tribe of Juda, the root of David, has conquered: (he is worthy) to open the scroll and its seven seals."

Interpretation

Here Ioannes indulges in one of the sarcastic hyperboles that are not infrequent in the fourth gospel.

Those unable to open the chakras are usually ignorant of the fact that the body is the lyre of Apollo, the instrument of the Sun-Logos, and do not see it in its true nature. In his day, spiritual blindness was probably less prevalent than now, applied to which his statement becomes more nearly literal than hyperbolic.

The Lion is Leo, which is also the sign of Juda. The "root" of man is his spiritual Self; for the mystical "tree of life," man is the inverted ashvattha tree, which has its roots in the heavens and its branches on the earth: therefore "the root of David" is David reincarnated.

Lesson No. 34

Chapter 5: 6, 7

I saw; and, Behold! in the midst of the throne and the four Beings, and in the midst of the Ancients, there was a Lamb standing, as if it had been sacrificed, having seven horns and seven eyes, which are the seven Breaths of the God, sent off into all the earth. He came—he has taken (the scroll) from the right hand of (the God) seated on the throne.

Interpretation

The Lamb is a variant of the Ram, Aries. Here the Lamb is

identical with the "Lion of the Tribe of Juda," as the sign of Leo is the sole domicile of the Sun, and Aries is the place of its highest exaltation.

The four prior zodiac signs having set the stage, the Actor (Leo) now appears. The "Lion of the Tribe of Juda" has not that name merely because he was of "the Root of David." He was a symbol of that Actor on the stage of life who, by his own example, taught the neophyte "the way, the truth, and the purpose of life" (Jn. 14: 5, 6).

When the arc, Aries to Cancer, has been successfully passed, Leo introduces the first step of higher consciousness, the Root of which was planted in Cancer, the water sign (sea). This sign presents the principle of Cosmic Consciousness.

The arc of the Zodiac that comprises the signs Leo to Scorpio has, as the main object, the development of the individual in all his ramifications. Leo is the first awareness by the persona of his own individuality. It may be described as the I or Ego Sun of Man; for it is only a copy of the Cosmic I AM that has been expressed in Aries (Lamb).

Aries is the zodiac sign of the Creator, the I AM, applied in a macrocosmic sense, of which Leo is the Microcosmic replica. In it, the first indication of consciousness of a separateness makes itself felt, and the I AM here expressed is the first conscious feeling of being a difference. That which Aries applies to the ALL, is applied only to a portion of this Created ALL in the sphere of Leo, viz., the individual.

Leo symbolizes God as the Cosmic Redeemer of man from the bondage of collectivism, from which man emerges to individualism. He becomes the resurrected God who has been sacrificed on the Cross of Matter, and by that Divine Sacrifice he opens the Seven Seals of individual consciousness and development.

Leo is the zodiac sign of Man, the Microcosm. In this sphere fall many fables of heroic exploits throughout the ages, all of which are allegorical—Osiris of the Egyptians; Gilgamesh of the Babylonians, Joshua of the Jews, Prometheus of the Greeks, Baldhr of the Norsemen are some examples. **All these who in the end are sacrificed are Solar heroes.**

In the sphere of Leo, man not only frees himself from the bondage of collectivism, but he separates himself from the past, the tradition and conventions, and, as in Aries, starts on a new venture. It is the first step toward the realization of individualism.

Microcosmically, Leo corresponds to the sahasrara chakra, the "third eye," and Aries to the nimbus, or cerebral radiance.

This Lamb symbolizes the incarnated Nous, the Incarnation

of the Eternal Spirit on the physical plane, the intellectual Sun, which may be regarded as the Third Logos—man as he is on earth. The horns and eyes are the seven noetic powers of action and the seven noetic perceptive faculties. Thus the Lamb represents the neophyte, whose interior nature is awakening, and who is about to undergo the perfecting, or initiatory ordeals.

Chapter 5: 8-10

When he had taken the scroll, the four Beings and the 24 Ancients fell down before the Lamb, having each a lyre and a golden libation-saucer full of incense-offerings, which are the prayers of the devotees. And they chanted a new lyric, saying:

"Worthy art thou to take the scroll and open its seals; for thou wast sacrificed (on the Cross of Matter), and didst buy for the God with thy (symbolical) blood from every tribe, tongue, nation and people, and didst make them (to be) of a realm of sacrificers to our God; and they are ruling on the earth."

Interpretation

Each of the Ancients has a saucer, the phiale, a discous cup used in pouring out drink-offerings to the Gods, and also, like Apollo, a lyre. The phiale symbolizes the chakra (disk) or ganglion, and the lyre the nerves connected with it. Each chakra has its distinctive quality, color, sound and incense-odor, all of which are perceivable by the psychic senses. The four symbols employed in the four conquests, the seal, trumpet, sickle and libation-saucer, appropriately represent the chakras.

The neophyte is worthy to take control of the marvelous psychic mechanism of his body, to "conquer" its chakras, tightening its slack parts till it is tense and vibrant as a lyre in the hands of a musician, because he has in many incarnations, in every nation, and in many conditions of life, acquired the nobler characteristics of each and moulded them into a character— a kingdom, truly, in which they are the ruling elements.

The chorus of praise by the four Beings and the 24 Ancients is the first of the seven choruses in the drama.

Chapter 5: 11-14

I saw; and I heard a voice of many Divinities around the

throne, the Beings and the Ancients—there were myriads of myriads,—saying with a great voice:

"Worthy is the sacrificed Lamb to receive the force, wealth, skill, strength, honor, glory and praise."

Every existent being in the sky, on the earth, under the earth, and on the sea—the Universe summed up in them—I heard saying:

"To the (God) seated on the throne, and to the Lamb, be the praise, the honor, the glory and the dominion throughout the aeons of the aeons."

And the four Beings said, "Amen." And the 24 Ancients fell down and worshipped (the God).

Interpretation

The three paeans chanted in praise of the Conqueror and his God are in accordance with the ancient Greek custom of chanting paeans to Apollo, the Sun-God, before and after battle or before any solemn task. They are very appropriate here, as the Conqueror, the Lion-Lamb symbolizes the Nous, or microcosmic Sun, and, having taken the scroll, he is about to undergo the ordeal of initiation.

The word Iesous, which is but a mystery-name for the Nous, has a most suspicious resemblance to Ieios, the epithet applied by the Greeks to Apollo, the Sun-God, because he was invoked in the paeans by the reiterated cry "Ie," hailing him as the "Savior." Iesous is Ieios raised to 888, the Gnostic Ogdoad (manifested Logos) in triune form.

The Apocalypse observes the style of the ancient Greek tragedies in employing choruses to divide the drama into acts.

Of these three choral songs, the first is chanted by the Beings and the Ancients, and in the second the lesser Divinities join in; both these paeans being in praise of the sacrificial Lamb, which adorned the Christian Cross until 680 A.D., when it was ordered removed by the Sixth Ecumenical Council held at Constantinople in that year, which decreed that "the Lamb, which taketh away the sins of the world, ought to be portrayed henceforth in human form in place of the Lamb."—Ant. Unveiled, p. 161.

The third song is a general chorus by all the powers and potencies of the microcosmic universe (man) in praise of the Lamb and the enthroned God.

122

The first paean is merely explanatory, telling why the neophyte is worthy to open the seals; the second is an evocation of the potencies of the seven planets; and the third is addressed to the four higher planets only.

All this simply means that the practical student of the Sacred Science, the neophyte, is here engaged in the mystic meditation: with exalted mind and feeling he evokes the Parakletos into its active form as the Speirema, the Serptentine Fire that penetrates and activates the seven planetary centers, chakras or "seven seals."

Died in 1566
age 370

123

The possibilities of thought training are infinite, its consequence eternal, and yet few take the pains to direct their thinking into channels that will do them good, but instead leave all to chance.

—Marden.

The greatest events of an age are its best thoughts. It is the nature of thought to find its way into action.

—Bovee.

The old thoughts never die; immortal dreams outlive their dreamers and are ours for aye; no thought once formed and uttered ever can expire.

—*Mackay.*

TABLE OF CONTENTS

CRUCIFIXION AND RESURRECTION

Why did the leading races of the Ancient World have their Crucified and Resurrected gods? The custom was not isolated but general, and signified a general principle of Creation.

What is the hidden meaning of the statement in the Bible, "Death is swallowed up in victory. O Death, where is thy sting? O Grave, where is thy victory" (Isa. 25:8; 1 Cor. 15:54,55).

Four thousand years before the birth of Christianity, celebration of the Crucifixion and Resurrection was a regular annual event, in early spring, when violets bloomed and trees put out new leaves. All Nature was Resurrecting from winter sleep. "The dead are rising to a new life," said the Ancient Astrologers; and the people rejoiced and celebrated.

This great event was symbolized in their Zodiac; and that's the reason why the Mother Church hates Astrology. We are now in the heart of that carefully guarded secret that has made the Mother Church the richest institution on earth. For 600 years Rome celebrated the Resurrection of their god Atys, who became Jesus when Christianity took over. It was all the same with the people. Nothing more than a change of names.

The event was staged to teach the Cosmic Cycle of Life, the Law of Cycle Manifestation, the Law of Reincarnation, discovered by the Masters and taught to their disciples.

Read the remarkable story in Professor Hotema's great work, **The Glorious Resurrection**

Lesson No. 35

Chapter 6: 1, 2

When the Lamb opened one of the seven seals, I heard one of the four Beings saying as with a voice of thunder: "Come." Behold! a white horse (appeared). The (Divinity) who was riding him had a bow; to him was given a crown, and he came forth a conqueror, and that he might keep on conquering.

Interpretation

This seal is the adhishthana chakra, the prostatic, where the positive and negative currents start. It corresponds to Sagittarius; hence its rider, or regent, is the Bowman.

In this sign the Romans placed Diana, the Greek Letois, Apollo's sister, who was sometimes portrayed as a bearded Goddess; together they represent the male-female or androgynous man.

This chakra belongs to the lowest (the generative) of the somatic divisions; yet, as the white horse, that division outranks the others, and the Bowman, is the Conqueror himself, who is represented as starting out on his conquests, and who reappears in triumph in the closing scene of the drama. For the Logos, as mirrored in the material world, is inverted.

Chapter 6: 3, 4

When he opened the second seal, I heard the second Being saying: "Come."

A fiery-red horse came out. To the (Divinity) who was riding him (authority) was given to take away peace from the earth—that (men) should slaughter one another—and to him was given a great sword.

Interpretation

This seal is the epigastric chakra, and its sign is Scorpio, the house of Mars, the War-God. Scorpio is usually, but inaccurately, given as corresponding with the generative centers; but the real seat of the epithumetic nature is the solar plexus.

The red horse symbolizes the abdominal somatic division, and its rider, or regent, who is passion personified, appears later in the drama in the role of the red Dragon, who is identified with Set, Satan and Diabolos, the "Devil."

125

When he opened the third seal, I heard the third Being saying: "Come." Behold! a black horse (came out). The (Divinity) who was riding him had a balance in his hand. I heard as it were a voice in the midst of the four Beings saying:

"A ration of wheat for a denarius, and three rations of barley for a denarius—and do scant justice to the olive-oil and the vine."

Interpretation

This is the cardiac chakra that is opened. It corresponds to Libra of the Zodiac, and the regent of this somatic division is the Weigher, the discursive lower mind.

While no actual thinking process occurs in the heart, a distinction is drawn between the spiritual mind, or pure intellection, and the unspiritual mind, or that portion of the intellectual nature that is tainted by psychic emotions and carnal desires. In other words, between the mind that reflects the light which comes from Above, from the Nous, and the mind that absorbs the influences that come from below, from the animal nature.

This lower intellectual sphere may include the greatest culture, with admirable attainments in scientific research and in the acquisition of knowledge, along conventional lines, yet with little or no spiritual insight or philosophic depth of thought; hence it is depicted in the allegory as a semi-famine, a scarcity of rations.

The parsimonious Weigher who rides the black horse appears later in the drama as the Beast, the marine monster in whom fanciful theology sees the Anti-Christ.

Chapter 6: 7, 8

When he opened the fourth seal, I heard the voice of the fourth Being saying: "Come."

Behold! a dun horse (came out). (Divinity) who was riding him—his name was Death, and the Unseen went along with him. To them was given authority over the fourth of the earth, to kill with sword, famine and death, and by the wild beasts of the earth.

Interpretation

The laryngeal chakra is the highest of those belonging strictly to the sympathetic nerve system, the ones above it being in the brain. It is here given as the regent of the highest of the somatic divisions, the "sky," or rather the lower sky, for the cerebral region is termed in the Apocalypse the mid-ski, or zenith, as being the abode of the God.

Plato employs in his allegory two horses, answering to the intellectual and the epithumetic natures, the Nous being the charioteer. But usually the chariot of the Sun was pictured with four horses.

The vocal organ is, mystically, the creative organ of the Logos. For this and other reasons the white and the dun horses. are given with their attributes interchanged. The dun horse symbolizes the lowest of the somatic divisions; and as sex exists only in the psychic and physical realms, the two, Death and Hades (standing for the generative principle on the two planes) are his riders, who slay with sword, famine, materialism and animal passions. They appear later in the form of the two-horned bogus Lamb, who is called the Pseudo-Seer.

Chapter 6: 9-11

When he opened the fifth seal, I saw underneath the altar the souls of those who had been sacrificed because of the arcane doctrine of the God, and because of the evidence which they had. They cried out with a great voice, saying:

"How long, O thou the Supreme, the Holy and the True,. dost thou fail to judge and avenge our blood upon those who dwell on the earth?"

White robes were given them severally, and it was said to them that they should keep still yet a little time, until their fellow-slaves and also their brothers, who would be killed even as they were, should have finished (their course).

Interpretation

The fifth seal corresponds to the sign Cancer and the ajna chakra, or cavernous plexus, which latter is closely connected with the pituitary gland, the membrum virile, so to say, of the brain.

The atrophied (sacrificed) brain-centers are partially aroused by the Speirema at this stage; but they are suppressed until the other centers (their brothers) have all been brought into action and then "killed," i.e., placed in abeyance while the cerebral centers are being awakened. They receive "white robes," for at this center the currents bifurcate and their light suffuses the brain.

During the cycle of reincarnation, all the chakras have been slain (dormantized) by the gross elements of the material, sensuous life; yet they retain the "evidence" of things spiritual.

While Leo precedes Cancer, the order in which the chakras are awakened is different: Capricorn and Leo belong rather to the spinal axis than to the sympathetic nerve system, and are the two poles of the former.

Chapter 6: 12-17

I saw when he opened the sixth seal; and there came to be a great earthquake; the sun became dark, the moon became as blood, and the stars of the sky fell to the earth, as a fig-tree drops her first-crop of figs when shaken by a violent wind.

The sky was removed like a scroll being rolled up; and every mountain and island, they were moved from their places. The rulers of the earth, the very great, the commanders, the rich, and the mighty, and every slave and freeman, hid themselves in caves and among the crags of the mountains; and they kept saying to the mountains and the crags:

"Fall on us and hide us from the face of the (God) seated on the throne and from the passion of the Lamb. For the great day of his passion has come, and who can stand firm?"

Interpretation

The sixth seal symbolizes the muladhara chakra, which lies at the base of the spinal cord and is the starting-point of the central current, the Sushumna, the regenerative force, here called the orge (fecundating energy) of the "Lamb," the Nous.

Upon the pouring of this fiery electric force into the brain, the mind becomes blank and the novice is conscious only of blind terror. This is allegorized as the darkening of the sun (mind), the falling of the stars (thoughts), the vanishing of the sky (concept of space), and the panic of the earth-dwellers (lower forces and faculties).

The process of sex transmutation must be attained by gradual development. If the awakening of the Spiritual Fire occurs before the re-orientation of the Mind has had time to pervade all the various bodies of man, it tends to get out of

128

control and run wild, and in consequence either affects the morals or the mind or both.

Chapter 7: 1-3

After these (ordeals) I saw four Divinities standing at the four corners of the earth, dominating the four winds of the earth so that no wind should blow on earth or sea, or on any tree. And I saw another (dominant) Divinity ascend from the birthplace of the sun, having the signet-ring of the living God; and he cried out with a great voice to the four Divinities to whom (authority) was given to punish the earth and the sea, saying:

"Do not punish the earth, the sea or the trees till we shall have sealed (with his signet-ring) the slaves of our God on their foreheads"

Interpretation

The five Divinities are the noetic regents of the five Pranas, the Solar Life-winds. In the Zodiac they are represented by the signs Gemini, Taurus, Aries, Pices and Aquarius, with their respective planets.

The four who guard the quarters are the four powers of the Nous; and the fifth, who raises up from the Sun's place of birth, is the symbol of the Nous himself, and bears the signet of the Life-God.

These correspond to the "five bright powers" of the Upanishads, four of which are regents of the four directions of space, while the fifth "goes upward to immortality."

These noetic forces record in man's aura (his "scroll of life") his every thought and deed; and, as these auric impressions, like phonographic records, automatically reproduce the original thoughts and emotions whenever the forces again act upon them, they thus produce an almost endless concatenation of cause and effect, of retributive action. Hence by awakening the occult forces of his being, the neophyte invokes this iron law of retribution, and all the good and bad elements of his nature are arrayed against one another for the final conflict.

In the allegory the lower principles are to be chastized, and the higher ones are to receive the seal of the God's approval.

Chapter 7: 4-8

I heard the number of those who were sealed, 144,000, sealed out of all the tribes of the children of Israel.

Interpretation

The tribes symbolize the 12 signs of the Zodiac,—Juda for Leo, Reuben for Aquarius, Gad for Aries, etc. As here listed, Joseph is substituted for Ephraim, or Taurus; and Manasseh, Joseph's first born son, replaces Dan, who is Scorpio.

The omission of Dan, with the substitution by which Scorpio is shown to be derived from Taurus, is significant; for Taurus is the symbol of celestial creative force, and Scorpio that of the generative function. The Divinities charged with the seven scourages are, astronomically, the seven Pleiades, a star-group in the constellation Taurus.

There was a Hebrew tradition that from the tribe of Dan was to come the Anti-Messias. Hence the substitution of the paranatellon Aquila for Scorpio.

Chapter 7: 9-12

After these (things) I saw; and, Behold! a vast multitude, which no one could count, from among every people, and of (all) tribes, nations and tongues (were) standing before the throne and before the Lamb, wearing white robes and (carrying) palm-branches in their hands. They kept crying out with a great voice, saying:

"The deliverance is to the (Master) seated on the throne of our God, and to the Lamb."

All the Divinities were standing in a circle about the throne, the Ancients and the four Beings; they fell on their faces in front of the throne, and worshipped the God, saying.

"Amen. The praise, the glory, the skill, the thanks, the honor, the force and the strength be to our God throughout the aeons of the aeons. Amen."

Interpretation

This is the third of the seven choruses, the verse, or paean of praise, is chanted by the liberated elements, and the chorus by the ruling powers of the three worlds—the Beings, Ancients and Divinities forming three concentric circles about the throne, and thus symbolizing as many planes of manifestation. In the benediction the attributes of all the seven planets are ascribed to the sun-god.

Chapter 7: 13-17

One of the Ancients responded, saying to me:

"These who are wearing white robes—who are they? and whence did they come?

I said to him: "My Master you know."

He said to me:

"These are the (conquerors) coming out of the great ordeal. They washed their robes and bleached them in the Lamb's blood. Because of this they are before the throne of the God; and they are serving him day and night in his adytum, and the (Master) seated on the throne will spread his tent over them. They will hunger no more, thirst no more; neither will (the rays of) the sun beat down on them, nor any scorching heat. For the Lamb who is in the middle of the throne will shepherd them and guide them to springs of waters of Life, and the God will wipe away every tear from their eyes."

Interpretation

The great ordeal of the Soul, or Logos, is its incarceration in the carnal body, not merely for the term of one lifetime, but during a long series of incarnations throughout the aeons of generation. But the Logos has its own mighty purpose in thus crucifying itself by assuming the human form, descending into the realms of generation and passing through the vast "cycle of necessity." It builds up for itself from the elements of the lower worlds an exterior self, a being formed of condensed substance, the refuse of past cycles, yet having within it the breath of the God. Then by unremitting toil throughout of the aeons it refines and transmutes the elements of this carnal man until it redeems it, and it becomes one with the divine individuality.

These purified and redeemed principles of the lower self are the countless host who, now that the aspirant has entered upon the cycle of initiation, are coming out of "the great ordeal," singing paeans of praise to the sacrificed Lamb, the Crucified, and to the enthroned Self, the Spiritual, the Eternal, who is beyond the reach of change and time, and therefore "uncrucified."

Chapter 8: 1-6

. When he opened the seventh seal, there came to be silence in the sky for about an hour.

I saw the seven Divinities who stand before the God. To them were given seven trumpets. Came another Divinity and stationed himself above the altar, having a golden censer; and to him was given much incense, that he might offer it, with the prayers of all the devotees, upon the golden altar in front of the throne.

-The smoke of the incense, with the prayers of the devotees, went up in front of the God out of the Divinity's hand. The Divinity took the censer and filled it with the fire of the altar, and cast (the fire) into the earth; there came to be voices, thunders, lightnings and an earthquake. The seven Divinities having the seven trumpets made themselves ready to give the trumpet-calls.

Interpretation

The seventh seal is the Sahasrara chakra, to which corresponds the sign Leo, the sole domicile of the Sun.

This chakra, the conarium or pineal gland, is the "third eye" of the Seer—that, and much more. It is the focal point of all the forces of the nerve system and of the aura. Here they come to an equilibrium, and here reigns the mystic Silence.

During the meditation, as each chakra is awakened the neophyte sees its corresponding psychic color. At this seventh center the colors intermingle as in an opal, with an incessant glittering of white light playing as on the facets of a diamond.

Leo is the fixed Fire Sign of the Zodiac, and by this fact denotes the inherent accumulation of the Serpentine Fire "cast into the earth" (body), with internal sensations described in the allegory as voices, thunders, lightnings and earthquake.

These sensations show that the psychic senses of smell and hearing are being aroused from their dormant state, so that odors as of incense become perceptible, and strange sounds appear in the head. Then with a shock (earthquake) the Serpentine Fire starts flowing through the seven brain-centers, each of which, as the current reaches it, produces a vibrant sound (trumpet-call) in the aura.

132

The trumpet-calls follow the order of the opening of the chakras (seals); and the two series correspond throughout, the zodiac signs being repeated as related to the brain-centers. See Interpretation in Lesson 34.

Chapter 8: 7

The first (Divinity) gave the trumpet-call. There came to be hail and fire, mixed with blood; they were cast into the earth, and the third of the earth was consumed, the third of the trees was consumed, and all fresh grass was consumed.

Interpretation

Of the four planes of consciousness, the fourth, the physical, is temporarily suppressed by the opening of the chakras (seals), and the psychic became active. By the awakening of the noetic centers the psychic consciousness ("the Third") is, in turn, placed in abeyance.

The colors manifested by the centers of the sympathetic nerve system are psychic; and the sounds heard upon the opening of the dormant brain-centers pertain to a higher plane.

The "hail" is a semi-condensation of the lunar element, or ether, "the good water of the Moon." The "fire" is the solar force, "the good fire of the "Sun." The "blood" is the auric fluid, "the blood of the Logos."

These three elements affect the lowest of the divisions of the body. The "trees" are the "two olive-trees," the dual trees of Life (Ida and Pingala), and the "grass" is the radiation of the same force through the aureola. They are the threefold Speirema, beginning its course through the brain.

Chapter 8: 8, 9

The second Divinity gave the trumpet-call. (It was) as if a great flaming mountain of fire was cast into the sea; and the third of the sea came to be blood. The third of the existant beings in the sea, having souls, died; and the third of the ships were wrecked.

Interpretation

The active volcano is a symbol of Mars, the planetary power ruling the epithumetic nature, "the sea." Every vestige of passion and carnal desire is eliminated.

Chapter 8: 10, 11

The third Divinity gave the trumpet-call. There fell from the sky a great star flaming like a torch. It fell on the third of the rivers and on the springs of waters. The name of the star is called "Wormwood"; and the third of the waters became wormwood, and many of the men died of the waters, because they were made bitter.

Interpretation

The falling star is Aphrodite (Venus), the torch-bearing Goddess. The force it here symbolizes affects the emotional psychic nature. **The imbittering of the waters symbolizes the psychological law that all pleasure eventually reacts and produces pain.** Yet, in the end this bitter water, symbolizing the conservation of the body's vital essence, becomes transmuted into the "sweet water of life" when man's nature is purified and his body invigorated by the conservation of that vital essence.

Chapter 8: 12

The fourth Divinity gave the trumpet-call. The third of the sun was stricken, also the third of the moon and the third of the stars, so that the third of them should be darkened, and the day should not give light for the third of it, and likewise the night.

Interpretation

Mental activity is suspended on the psychic, or subjective, plane, as well as on the physical or objective plane. On each plane, in turn, the forces must be brought into equilibrium so that they neutralize one another, and then the consciousness rises to the next higher plane.

Chapter 8: 13

I saw; and I heard a lone Eagle, flying in midsky, saying with a great voice:

"Woe, woe, woe to those dwelling on the earth, from the remaining trumpet-voices of the three Divinities who are about to give the trumpet-call."

Interpretation

The first four cerebral chakras, symbolized by the trumpets, react upon the four somatic divisions of the body. The three higher ones are related to the dual nerve system and the aura, broadly speaking; but in a more special sense they are analogues of the male creative triad.

Comment on this subject, a delicate one, while involving nothing in the least impure, must be brief and superficial in a work of this kind. For a fuller discussion the student should study the Science of Regeneration by Clements.

As previously stated, the lower man is an inverted image of the higher. From this fact it follows that the highest spiritual centers are directly related to the lowest, the generative centers on the physical plane. For this reason the three trumpet-calls are announced as "woes" by the Eagle, the fourth of the Zoa and the prototype of Scorpio.

The Edenic parable deals with the generative centers on the physical plane. To consume the essence of Life in carnal generation leads to a general deterioration of the body.

The wages of sin is death. For to be carnally minded is death. Because the carnal mind is enmity against God (Rom. 6:23; 8:6, 7).

Flee fornication. Every sin that a man doeth is without the body; but he that committeth fornication, sinneth against his own body. It is good for a man not to touch a woman (1 Cor. 6:18; 7:1).

Whosoever is born of God doth not commit sin; for his seed remaineth in him: and he cannot sin, because he is born of God. There is a sin unto death (1 Jn. 3:9; 5:16).

It cannot be too emphatically stated that the carnal generative function exists only in the psychical and physical realms. The abuse of this function is the most terrible of all crimes against the body, and the "unpardonable sin," the "sin unto death."

It was held by the Ancient Masters that only celibates, who conserve the body's vital essence and preserve purity of mind and body and thereby regain the complete innocence of "little children" (Mat. 18:3; 19:14) can rise to the higher plane, "the kingdom of heaven" (Mat. 22:30).

This vital subject is dealt with in the Edenic parable, where man is told that in the day he eats of the Tree of Life, dying he shall die (Gen. 2:17). This subject is well covered by Clements in his work, Science of Regeneration, which should be studied by all.

Lesson No. 38

Chapter 9: 1-12

.The fifth Divinity gave the trumpet-call. I saw a star that had fallen from the sky to the earth; and to him was given the Key to the crater of the abyss. He opened the crater, and there went up smoke, like the smoke of a great furnace. The sun and air were darkened by the smoke, out of which came locusts upon the earth. To them was given license as the scorpions of the earth have license. It was said to them that they should not punish the grass; neither anything tender-green, nor any tree, but only those men who do not have the seal of the God on their foreheads. And (the command) was given them that they should not kill them, but that they should be tormented five months. Their torment was as a scorpion's torment when it stings a man.

In those days men will seek death, and find it not. They will long to die, and death will keep fleeing from them.

The effigies of the locusts were like horses comparisoned for battle. On their heads were (circlets) like crowns of spurious gold. Their faces were like men's faces, but hair was like women's hair; and their teeth were like those of lions. They had cuirasses like iron cuirasses. The voice of their wings was like the voice of (many) war-chariots—of many horses galloping into battle. They had tails like scorpions, and stings were in their tails. Their license to punish men was five months. They had over them as ruler the Divinity of the Abyss; his name in Hebrew is Abaddon, and in the Greek (misticism) he has the name Apollyon.

The one woe has passed. Behold! two more woes are coming after.

Interpretation

The star that had fallen is Venus, and now becomes the so-called "infernal Lucifer," the Hecate who presides over the abyss (sacral plexus).

The abyss is symbolized astronomically by the constellation Crater, the Cup, the mixing-bowl of Iacchos, the phallic God. In the Apocalypse it appears as the cup held by the Woman in scarlet, who is simply Hecate, the infernal aspect of both Aphrodite (Venus) and Letois (Diana), the two Goddesses alike symbolizing the primodial substance, the Arche.

The Divinity of the Abyss, who is the "Destroyer" and "Murderer," is the Pseudo-Lion, the Beast—the phrenic mind

136

polluted ·by the carnal passions. His hoards of scorpion-like cavalry are impure thoughts. The "five months" are the summer-time, in which period the passional nature is more active. ·

Mystically the summer is said to be the "night of the soul," and winter its day.

Chapter 9: 13-15

The sixth Divinity gave the trumpet-call. I heard a single voice from .the four horns of the golden altar in front of the God, (the Master's voice), saying to the sixth Divinity, who had the trumpet: ·

"Turn loose the four Divinities who are fettered at the great river Euphrates."

The four Divinities were turned loose, who had been made ready throughout the hour, day, month and year, that they should kill the third of men.

Interpretation

The golden altar symbolizes the Nous, or higher mind. The four horns are its four powers. Gold is the metal of the sun, and the four-horned altar is a different symbol of the sun and the regents of the four quarters. The four Divinities fettered at the river (cerebro-spinal axis) are the Solar Regents of the seasons, ruling the quaternary divisions of the year, month, day and hour. They also symbolize the psycho-religious consciousness, which manifests itself in "the third of men" in the emotional worship of the false mental images of Deity—the lower phase of religion that indulges in irrational theologies, superstition, sorcery, fanaticism, and persecution, **such as true history records of Catholicism, and of Protestantism in a lesser degree.**

Chapter 9: 16-21

The number of the armies of the horsemen (under the command of the four Divinities) was two hundred million—I˜heard the number of them. Thus I saw the horses in the vision, and their riders, having cuirasses fiery (red), smoky blue and sulphurous (yellow); the heads of the horses were like the heads · of lions, and from their mouths keep going out fire, smoke and sulphur.

By these three scourges were killed the third of the men—by the fire, smoke and sulphur which went out of their mouths. For the powers of the horses are in their mouths and their tails; for their tails are like snakes, and have heads, and with them they inflict punishment.

The rest of the men, who were not killed, did not reform from the works of their hands, that they should not worship the spirits and the images of gold, silver, bronze, stone and wood, which can neither see, hear nor walk. And they did not reform from their murders, their sorceries, their prostitutions or their thefts.

Interpretation

The vast army of warriors symbolize the limitless powers of the Nous; the lion-heads (Leo) of the horses indicating their Solar character.

As the Mind is the actual man, so in the allegory the intellectual powers and thoughts are represented as men, the armies of the Nous destroying the evil, false, superstitious thoughts and tendencies of the psychic nature. And as the thoughts of the physical mind are concerned largely with physical possessions, such thoughts are symbolized as worshippers of idols.

Lesson No. 39

Chapter 10: 1-4

I saw another, (the) strong Divinity, descending from the sky, wrapped in a cloud, and a rainbow was upon his head. His face was (luminous) like the sun, and his feet like pillars of fire. In his hand he had a little scroll unrolled. He put his right foot on the sea, and his left on the earth, and cried out with a great voice, as a lion roars; and when he cried out, seven thunders uttered voices of their own. When the seven thunders uttered (their voices), I was about to record (their teachings); but I heard a voice from the sky saying to me:

"Seal up (the teachings) which the seven thunders uttered, and do not write them down."

Interpretation

The Divinity, the fifth in the group, is the Nous, the intellectual Sun, in its aspect as Kronos, the God of Time.

This fivefold group is that which appeared at the opening of the sixth seal, save here they are energizing on a higher plane.

That the voices of the seven thunders were mystery-teachings is evident from the injunction against recording them.

Chapter 10: 5-7

The Divinity I saw standing on the sea and the earth raised his right hand to the sky and swore by the (God) who lives throughout the aeons of the aeons, who brought into existence the sky and what is in it, the earth and what is in it, and the sea and what is in it, that Time shall be no more, but in the days of the voice of the seventh Divinity, when it is about to give the trumpet-call, also shall be made perfect the Mystery of the God, as he proclaimed to his slaves, the Seers.

Interpretation

Time is the measurement of motion, and an illusion of the physical and psychical worlds, the earth and sea of the allegory. In the spiritual world, the mystic sky (Mind), there prevails the "Mystery of the God," which is the timeless, eternal consciousness of the Mind, the real man.

When the sixth sense (pituitary gland—Manas) has awakened the seventh (pineal gland—Buddhi), then that spiritual light radiating from the Seventh illuminates the Fields of Infinitude in man's physical consciousness, and his Spiritual Consciousness, being thus aroused from its dormant state, becomes active, and by the power of the "third eye" the Seer passes beyond the illusion of time,—and "time shall be no more."

The seventh trumpet-call signalizes the realization of the "Mystery of the God," the "third eye" of the Seer, which is made perfect, i.e., aroused from its dormant state and restored to its spiritual function by the action of the pituitary gland as we shall soon explain.

Chapter 10: 8-11

The voice that I heard from the sky, (I heard it) again speaking to me, saying, "Take the scroll unrolled in the hand of the Divinity."

I went to the Divinity, asking him to give me the scroll. He says to me:

"Take it, and eat it. It will make your belly bitter; but in your mouth it will be as sweet as honey."

I took the scroll and ate it. In my mouth it was as honey, sweet, but it made my belly bitter. And (the voices of the seven thunders) keep saying to me: "You must teach again in opposition to many nations, peoples, tongues and rulers."

Interpretation

The little scroll symbolizes the secret wisdom, imparted to the neophyte by the Hierophant—his own Logos.

The secret wisdom becomes bitter to the epithumetic nature when known, for it inculcates the extirpation of all carnal thought and all carnal desire.

Sexuality on the productive plane is a characteristic of the physical (beast) and psychic (sea) bodies. When the generative centers are active productively, there can be no truly spiritual expression, except in the form of a sacrificial dedication to the baby that may be born of that act. Every sexual gratification weakens the body and its spiritual powers become dormant.

Kronos symbolizes the Logos in his aspect as Eternal Memory, and holds the scroll of the Secret Wisdom. For all true knowledge is Spiritual Remininscence, and Time is non-existent to the Spiritual Consciousness.

While forbidden to record the utterances of the seven thunders, the **Seer is obligated to proclaim the true philosophy in opposition to the popular dogmas of exoteric religions, for instance, that the marriage "bed (is) undefiled" (Heb. 13:4).**

The greatest work on this subject produced in modern times is the "Science of Regeneration," by Clements.

We succeed in our work by giving the masses what they crave and not what they should have.

Lesson No. 40

Chapter 11: 1-3

There was given me a reed like a wand, (the first voice) saying:

"Rise up, and measure the Adytum of the God, the altar, and those worshipping in it; but the court, exterior to the adytum, cast out as exoteric, and measure it not; for it has been given to the people, and the holy city they shall trample on for 42 months. I shall give it (after that) to my two witnesses, and they will teach 1260 days, clothed in gunnysacks."

140

Interpretation

The Naos, here termed adytum, was the inner temple where the God was enshrined, and to which none but the initiated had access. When employed for initiatory rites it was usually called the adytum.

Symbolically, the adytum is the spiritual nature, and the altar is the intellectual. Astronomically it is, as Josephus and other ancient authors said, the sky. In the psycho-physiological rendering of the Symbolism, the adytum, the altar of sacrifice and the altar of incense are the three divisions of the brain, while the outer court is the body. The worshippers are the 49 forces (seven lamps with seven pipes to each lamp), which are "measured" by being arranged in hierarchies or groups.

The period of initiation is here placed at seven years, during the first half of which (42 months) the lower forces continue to rule the functions of the body, while in the latter half (1260 days), the dual electric force of the ida and pingala nerves (the two witnesses), will pervade the nerve system, gradually and almost imperceptibly replacing the common nerve force, a subdued action expressed in the allegory by their being clothed in sacks.

The measuring of the adytum and the account of the two witnesses have no relation to the action of the drama, being merely explanatory.

Chapter 11: 4-6

These are the two olive-trees, and two lampstands, standing before the God of the earth. If any one wills to use them wrongfully, fire comes out of their mouth and devoures their enemies; and if one shall will to use them wrongfully, in this way must one be killed.

These (witnesses) have authority to shut the sky, so that rain may not fall during the days of their teaching. Also, they have the authority over the waters, to transmute them into blood and to chastize the earth with every scourge as often as they may will.

Interpretation

In Chapter 4:2 et. seq. Zechariah goes deeper into details as to the olive-trees and lampstands: "I have seen; and, Behold! a candlestick all of gold (spinal cord), with its bowl (brain) on top of it, and its seven lamps thereon. There are seven pipes (nerves) to each lamp, which are upon the top thereof; and two olive-trees (Ida and Pingala Nadis), by it, one on the right side and one on the left."

These are the spinal cord and the cerebral chakras; and their nadis. As the chakras and nadis are small and apparently unimportant, he continues:

"For who hath despised the day of small things? For they (the seven chakras) shall rejoice, and see the plummet in the hand of Zerubbabel, even these seven (which are) the eyes of Jehovah. They run to and fro through the whole earth" (body).

Zerubbabel, the "builder" of the temple (body), symbolizes the pituitary gland in the brain, which also governs the body's growth. Modern physiologists know that the disorder termed gigantism, in which the body or any of its parts grow to abnormal size, results from increased activity and hypertrophy of this gland.

The pituitary is the female, spiritual, negative, creative gland of the brain. The spiritual esse (golden fire) flowing to this gland when not consumed in generation, becomes magnetic and feminine in quality and action, and causes the gland's pulsating aura to perform a swaying motion, like "the plummet in the hand of Zerubbabel," until it impinges on the pineal gland, the male, spiritual, positive, "unpaired eye," impregnating it with the Golden Force and arousing its dormant spiritual faculties.

This action is further described in Zechriah, as "the two olive-trees (and) the two olive branches that are beside the two golden spouts, that empty the golden (stream) out of themselves, (and are) the two anointed ones that stand by the God of the whole earth."

The dual fire is destructive to the unpurified psychic or sorcerer who may succeed in arousing it; and its misuse results in moral as well as in physical death.

The "rain" symbolizes the nerve-fluid. "Water" is the magnetic auric substance, and "blood" is the golden electric fire.

The "chastizement" of the earth is described later in the drama as the pouring out of seven scourges by the seven Taurine Divinities, the Pleiades.

Think of the clergy, knowing so little about the body's physiology, attempting to interpret the biblical parables; and of Swedenborg's writing a book of 1200 pages, titled "The Apocalypse Revealed," in which he attempted to show that "Revelation" does not in its spiritual sense treat at all of worldly things, but of heavenly things; "consequently not of empires and king-doms, but of heaven and the church."

With the leaders in such darkness, it is easily understood why the masses are, and why people resent Truth because it is so foreign to what they are taught.

Chapter 11:7

When they shall have finished giving their evidence, the Beast who comes up from the abyss will battle with them, conquer, and kill them.

Interpretation

When the trance terminates and the neophyte returns to the ordinary state of consciousness on the physical plane, the Kundalini, having "finished giving their evidence," recedes to the "throne of the beast" (solar plexus), where, according to the Upanishads, it lies as a serpent, having three and a half coils, corresponding to the 42 months (1260 days) that "they shall trample on the holy city."

Chapter 11: 8, 9

Their corpses (are now lying) in the main-street of the great city, mystically called "Sodom and Egypt," where also their Master was crucified. And (some) from among the nations, tribes, tongues and people are guarding their corpses three and a half days, and will not permit their dead bodies to be placed in a sepulchre.

Interpretation

The city represents the physical body; its main-street symbolizes the spinal cord, in which are the channels of the three-fold Speirema, the two witnesses and their Master, "the Witness Believable and True."

These channels (corpses of the witnesses) are preserved from complete atrophy by the nerve-currents which, in each of the four somatic divisions, circulate through the cerebro-spinal system.

The three and a half days are the latter half of the seven "days of creation," the gross physical arc of the cycle of human evolution, during which the "witnesses" lie moribund in the mystical "Sodom."

The formula "nations, tribes, tongues and people" is given seven times in the Apocalypse, but the words are never used twice in the same order. In one instance (10:11) "rulers" is substituted for "tribes," and in another (17:15) "multitudes" for the same. They apply to the four casts, or classes of mankind, who are said in oriental mysticism to have been born from the four somatic divisions of the Deity: man of learning, warriors, commercialists and laborers.

The Nous (Iesous) is said here to have been crucified in Sodom, also called Egypt. This is the first crucifixion, the incarnation of the Soul in the physical body, which then becomes its cross. The second is in Calvaria, the Cross of Initiation.

Chapter 11: 10-14

Those who dwell on the earth are rejoicing over them and are exultant; and they will send bribes to one another—for these two seers did torment those who are dwelling on the earth. After the three and a half days the Breath of Life from the God entered into them; they stood on their feet, and great terror overcame those who beheld them. They heard a great voice from the sky saying to them: "Come up hither."

They went up into the sky in the cloud; and their enemies beheld them. In that hour there came a great earthquake, and the tenth (section) of the city fell, and there were killed by the earthquake names of men 7,000; the rest became frightened, and gave glory to the God of the sky.

The second woe has passed. Behold! the third woe is coming speedily.

Interpretation

The rebuking voice of conscience, which is the voice of the Nous speaking through the two witnesses, is the real tormentor of the evilly disposed, who seek to stifle it. The man who is thus trying to silence his accusing conscience cannot be mentally honest with himself, but acts from feigned motives, his desires and thoughts bribing one another, as the allegory indicates. But as the individual emerges from the physical stage of his evolution, the noetic faculties "awaken from the dead" (dormancy), and the base passional nature, symbolized by the tenth of the twelve zodiac divisions, perishes, with its seven heads; for it is identified with the seven-headed red Dragon.

The seven is multiplied by the indefinite number 1000 to indicate the many correlations of these lower principles, the "men" whose "names" are their psychic colors, which are obliterated, the remaining colors becoming brighter in the auric "glory" of the Sky-God.

Chapter 11: 15-18

The seventh Divinity gave the trumpet-call. There came to be great voices in the sky, saying:

"The realm of the world has become (the realm) of our Master and of his Anointed, and he shall reign throughout the aeons of the aeons."

The 24 Ancients who are seated before the God on their thrones fell on their faces and worshipped the God, saying:

"We give thanks to thee, the Master-God, the All-Dominator, who (forever) art, and who wast, because thou hast taken thy great force and regained sovereignty. The people grew passionate; and thy passion came, and the season of the dead to be judged, and (the season) to give their recompense to thy slaves the seers, to the devotees, and to those who fear thy name, the small and the great, and to destroy those who are destroying the earth."

Interpretation

The seventh of the mystic "spiritual sounds," signalizes the awakening of the highest of the seven chakras, the centers through which radiates the Light of the Logos.

The passion in the God is not his "wrath," but the creative force of the Logos, the "great force" (dynamis) that produces the "birth from above"; and it is here placed in contrast with the passions that "are destroying the earth" (body).

The chorus by the sky-voices and the Ancients is the fourth of the series.

Chapter 11: 19

The adytum of the God in the sky was opened, and in his adytum was seen the ark (containing the emblems) of his compact; and there came to be lightnings, voices, thunders, an earthquake and great hail.

Interpretation

The constellation Arca, the celestial Ship, situated to the south of Virgo, was also called "Noah's Ark."

As exoteric exponents of phallicism are fond of pointing out, the ark is a symbol of the womb, from which comes the new-born. Esoterically the ark has no such phallic significance, but symbolizes the exact opposite, the place of Spiritual Rebirth, the emergence into immortality. It actually represents the womb in the brain, the latter being an androgynous organ wherein is immaculately conceived the Permanent Spiritual Being, the Solar Body.

Lesson No. 41

Chapter 12: 1, 2

A great constellation was seen in the sky; a (winged) Woman clothed with the sun, the moon under her feet, and on her head a crown of twelve stars. She had (a babe) in her womb, and she keeps crying out, in the pangs of child-birth, racked with the pain of parturition.

Interpretation

The seventh trumpet-call is the sound heard when the pineal gland is energized. The latter corresponds to the sign Leo, the house of the Sun. The constellation here disclosed is triadic, including in the symbol the signs Virgo (the house of Mercury), Leo and Cancer, the domicile of the Moon.

Thus associated, Virgo figures as the Virgin Mother, who immaculately conceives and gives birth to the Son of the God; whereas, taken in combination with Libra (the house of Venus), and Scorpio (the house of Mars), she becomes the scarlet prostitute, the symbol of carnal generation.

As the World-Mother, the White Virgin of the Sky, whether called Isis, Diana, Aphrodite, or Mary, she is the Pure Ether, the Logos-Light, or primordial force-substance; and as the Fallen Woman, the Queen of the Abyss (generative centers), she is the parturient force of Nature, the basis of physical being. As such, she is named in the Apocalypse Sodom, Babylon, and Egypt, merely to make her threefold like her celestial prototype, for in reality she includes all cities and countries inhabited by sinful man.

Virgo was always pictured with wings; and later in the text she has the two wings of the Eagle.

146

Chapter 12: 3-6

Another constellation was seen in the sky—and Behold! a great fiery-red Dragon, having seven heads and ten horns, and on his heads seven diadems. His tail was trailing along the third of the stars of the sky and kept throwing them to the earth. The Dragon was standing in front of the Woman who was on the verge of parturition, so that as soon as she gave birth he might devour her child.

She gave birth to a son, virile, who is destined to shepherd all the people with an iron wand; and her child was snatched up to the God and to his throne. The Woman fled into the desert, where she has a place made ready by the God; that there (the Divinities) may nourish her 1,260 days.

Interpretation

This constellatory symbol is Draco, the pole Dragon, which has seven distinguishing stars and which, as depicted in the ancient star-maps, extends over seven of the zodiac signs, and in setting apparently sweeps a third of the starry sky down to the horizon.

Microcosmically it symbolizes the passional nature, epithumia, the Apocalyptic number of which is 555.

The energizing of the cerebral centers produces a reflex action in the lower nature, and, unless the neophyte is duly purified, the Dragon (passional nature) will indeed devour the child, not at the time of its birth, but at its conception. For the Solar Body is not born at this point, but only has its inception.

In the ancient Greek Mysteries this stage of the telestic work was represented baldly as the generative act, as a spade was always called a spade. But Ioannes has handled the subject more delicately, by substituting for the solar the psychic body, which is "born" with the physical body and grows conjointly with it.

In the allegory, the Conqueror is not born until after the 1260 days, during which the Woman is being nourished by the Divinities. The statement that the child is caught up to the throne connotes a period of spiritual gestation.

The immaculate conception is here represented by the opening of the adytum and disclosure of the ark. Those who have investigated the subject of the ark need not be reminded of what were the very peculiar emblems it contained.

Chapter 12: 7-12

There came to be a battle in the sky. Mikael and his Divinities gave battle to the Dragon; and the Dragon and his Divinities gave battle, but they lacked strength, nor was their place found in the sky any more. Hurled down was the great Dragon, the archaic Snake, who is called the "Accuser" and the "Adversary," the deluder of the whole inhabited earth; he was hurled down to the earth, and his Divinities were hurled down with him. I heard a great voice in the sky, saying:

"Now are attained the deliverance, the force and the ruling of our God, and the authority of his Anointed. For hurled down is the prosecutor of our brothers, who keeps prosecuting them before our God day and night. But they conquered him through the blood of the Lamb, and through the arcane doctrine of his evidence; and they did not esteem their psychic bodies until death. Therefore rejoice, ye skies, and ye who are pitching tent in them; (but) woe to the earth and the sea—for the Accuser has gone down to you having great lust, knowing that he has but a short season."

Interpretation

The Greek of the Apocalypse belongs to no particular period. Ioannes had evidently acquired knowledge of the language largely by reading, picking up his vocabulary chiefly from ancient works, or else living in some community in Asia Minor where the language was preserved in its older form.

(Apollonius was born in Tyana, Cappadocia, Asia Minor, and in that country did most of his teaching and writing. He "wrote in the Hebraic-Samaritan tongue, which was the language of (his) country," and his Greek he learned by reading ancient works in that language. It was Damis, his beloved disciple and a Greek historian of New Nineveh, who translated to Greek most of the writings of his Master Apollonius.)

In the Apocalypse the word "palemos" is invariably used for "battle" of mere personal combat; but in the time of Apollonius the word "palemos" had assumed the broader meaning of "war," and "mache" was the usual word for "battle."

War, in the sense of protracted hostilities, is not mentioned in the Apocalypse, which in every instance speaks only of a brief conflict, told in very few words, or of mere combats between two individuals.

The battle between Mikael and the Dragon, with their respective hosts resulting in the expulsion of the "evil serpent" (lust) from the sky (noetic center), allegorizes the exclusion

148

from the Mind of all carnal thoughts, especially those relating to sex and generation.

The red Divinity stands for nothing more nor less than the principle of Desire in all its innumerable gradations, from the vaguest yearnings and the mere promptings of the appetites of the body, down to the grossest phases of passion and lust; all of these desires having their sources in the instinct of production, the attracting and cohering force of generated being.

The creative Logos is the Dragon of Light, or Day-Sun; and Satan, the Adversary, is the Dragon of Darkness, or Night-Sun.

Little is said in the Apocalypse of the psychic body. It is almost ignored, being tacitly included in the moral, generated nature.

While the spiritual awakening is necessarily accompanied by more or less psychic development, the latter may proceed independently of, and even adversely to, the true noetic progress; and the pursuit of psychism for its own sake, leads inevitably to moral death.

The psychic consciousness should not be dragged down into, and confused with, the normal consciousness on the physical plane of life. For the psychological result of thus confounding the two worlds is simply ordinary insanity, differing from common lunacy only in that it is suicidally self-inflicted, and hence in the highest degree culpable, instead of being merely a misfortune caused by mental disturbance.

The psychic body has its own place, in its own world, and is chiefly of importance after somatic death, hence the encomium, "they did not esteem their psychic bodies until death."

In John 12:25, copied from the works of Apollonius, it is written: "He that loveth his life (psychic body) shall lose it; and he who disregards his life (psychic body) in this (physical) world shall keep it unto life eternal."

In the Apocalyptic symbolism the psychic (lunar) body would be the bride of the Beast, as the solar body is the bride of the Lamb. In fact, an ancient version of Rev. 2:20 has "your wife Iezabel."

Chapter 12:13-17

When the Dragon saw that he was hurled down to the earth, he kept pursuing the Woman who gave birth to the man-child. The Woman was endowed with the great Eagle's two wings, so that she might fly to the desert, to her place, where she is being nourished for a season, and seasons, and half a season, from the face of the Snake.

149

The Snake spouted water after the Woman, like a river, that he might cause her to be carried away by the torrent. The earth rescued the Woman; the earth opened her mouth and swallowed up the river. The Dragon waxes passionate over the Woman, and went away to battle with the rest of her seed, who keep the commands of the God and who have the evidence of the Anointed Iesous; and he stationed himself on the sand of the sea.

Interpretation

The Virgin Mother being Sushumna, the two wings of the Eagle are the Ida and Pingala nerves. The winged Woman represents the objective, or substantial working of the Serpentine Fire, while the three witnesses answer to its subjective, or noetic aspect.

Foiled in his designs on the male child (nascent solar body), the Dragon seeks to arrest the spiritual growth of the neophyte by pouring out a flood of psychic phenomenal illusions, but the force thus engendered is absorbed by the physical nature. Then planting himself on the margin of the sea (finer elements of the epithumetic principle), he combats the intuitions of the intellectual nature.

Astronomically, the river made by the Dragon is Eridanus, a winding constellation in the southern hemisphere, also called the River of Orion, which, when Virgo is in ascension, is setting and apparently being swallowed by the earth.

The phrase "season, and seasons, and half a season," is only a puzzling variant of the 42 months and 1260 days—three and a half years.

Lesson No. 42

Chapter 13: 1-4

I saw rising out of the sea a (constellatory) Beast, having 10 horns and 7 heads, and on his horns 10 diadems, and on his heads (seven) names of profanities. The Beast was like a leopard, his feet were like a bear's, and his mouth like a lion's.

The Dragon gave him his force and his throne, and great authority. I saw one of his heads (drooping) as if it had been slain in the Death (world); but his death-blow was healed. The whole earth became admiring followers of the Beast. They also worshipping the Dragon because he gave authority to the Beast, and they worshipped the Beast, saying:

"Who is a match for the Beast? Is any one strong enough to meet him in combat?"

Interpretation

In stellar symbolism the Beast is the constellation now called Cetus, which is represented not as a Whale but a nondescript marine monster. The Arabians and Jews called it the Sea-Lion. It was also named the Leopard and the Sea-Bear.

Ioannes has combined these various representations of it, presenting a composite picture. As a caricature of the psychophysical mind, the original figure, in the form drawn by the ancients who invented the zodiac language, would seem to be sufficiently grotesque; but Ioannes has given it additional touches of satire.

The Beast is said to rise from the sea and receive power from the Dragon, as it is the product of the two lower planes of being, the psychic and physical. Its seven years are the seven ruling epithumetic desires, each of which is a profanation of the Divine Desire. Its 10 horns are the five intellectual faculties doubled, as its every faculty is dual and at war with itself. The horns are adorned with diadems to indicate the false pride of the lower intellect.

As the lower mind is the shadow or reflected image of the true mind, the Nous, symbolized as the Lion, the Beast is pictured as a Pseudo-Lion, a hybrid, for it resembles the Leopard, which was fabled to be a cross between the Lion (Leo) and the Panther (Pardue). It is slow-moving, with the ponderous paws of the Bear, with a mouth like a Lion, thus simulating the voice of the Nous. It represents the highest development of man's intellect dissociated from philosophic reason and spiritual intuition, and it is the admiration of the world of the profane.

The head that is seemingly slain and yet resurrects, is the desire for Life on the plane of the senses, a desire which the neophyte must utterly eradicate.

In a more general sense, the lower mind, whenever it attempts philosophy, is never quite sure that life is worth living; and in its utter blindness to spiritual realities, perceiving only the phenomena of the visible world, it formulates theories of existence based entirely upon them, regarding everything else as unknowable, in harmony with physical science.

Chapter 13: 5-10

There was given him a mouth speaking great (boastings) and

151

profanities; and authority was given him to do (this) for 42 months. He opened his mouth in profanity against the God, to profane his name, his tent, and those pitching tents in the sky. It was given him to do battle with the devotees, and to conquer them; and authority was given him over every tribe, nation, tongue and people. All those dwelling on the earth will worship him—(every one) whose name has not been registered in the sacrificed Lamb's scroll of life since the evolution of the world.

If any one has an ear, let him hear: If any one welcomes captivity, into captivity he goes; if any one shall kill with the sword, with the sword must he be killed. Here is the patience and the faith of the devotees.

Interpretation

In this allegorical exposition of the powers and peculiarities of the lower mind-principle, only part applies to the particular case of the Conqueror, the rest being of a general nature. Without this broader application, the treatment of the subject would be incomplete and obscure.

Thus the 42 months refer to the first half of the seven-year initiatory cycle, in which the neophyte, passing through the psychic stages of his development, and thereby intensifying the action of the psycho-phrenic mind, must struggle constantly against its influence. The rest of the explanatory matter relates to mankind in general.

Those who have not been registered in the Book of Life (see also Chapter 17:8) are the vast majority who have not in any incarnation, during the cycle of physical evolution, attained the noetic consciousness.

When man has once even glimpsed the supernal truths, he can never again be content with the illusory images of the physical world, or worship at the shrine of mere intellectualism.

The true Self, the Master Mind, has placed its seal upon him, and he is thenceforth individualized from the irresponsible mass of mankind, and enrolled among those who must by an irresistible impulse, the call of the God, tread the path of man's higher destiny.

The term "evolution" as here used meant by the Masters the descent of the Soul into physical conditions.

Ioannes states the broad principle that the man who craves material life by that very desire condemns himself to remain in the bondage of reincarnation and subject to the iron law of retribution that prevails in the lower planes of life.

The esotericist, knowing that nothing binds him to the physical form except his own desires, patiently endures the ills of physical existance, in full assurance that he will attain deliverance through the purification of his moral character.

Chapter 13: 11-12

I saw another (constellatory) Beast, rising out of the earth. He had two horns like a lamb, and talked like a dragon. He is wielding all the authority of the first Beast in his presence, and is causing the earth and all its inhabitants to worship the first Beast, whose death-blow has healed.

Interpretation

This Pseudo-Lamb is the dual sex-nature, the two riders of the dun horse is a different impersonation. He is the image on the physical plane of the Lamb who, in the opening of the seven seals, played the part of the rider of the white horse.

Thus the Lamb and the Pseudo-Lamb have the same relation to each other as do Eros, the Divine Love, and Pathos (Cupid), the carnal love—not as the base passion, but in its more refined forms as sentimental yearnings, religious fervor of the irrational sort as it prevails in the multitude, and all the emotional impulses.

It is this phase of religious sentiment that has been emphasized by the church as prevailing among the "ancient heathens" prior to the time that the "message of brotherly love and eternal life" was given to the world by the gospel Jesus.

The Beast talks like a dragon, because from this source comes religious cant, sentimental ethics, and erotic utterances generally. He has all the potentialities of the first Beast, the phrenic nature, for unutterable vileness. As a constellation, he, is the Head of Medusa, the mortal Gorgon, called by the Jews "Satan's Head." Owing to its proximity to Aries, this constellation was sometimes pictured wearing the two horns of the Ram, the Apocalyptic Lamb.

Chapter 13: 13-18

He makes great omens, so that he may even make fire come down from the sky in the sight of men. He keeps deluding those who dwell on the earth, through the omens which he was permitted to make in sight of the Beast, saying to those who dwell on the earth, that they should make an image to the Beast who has the stroke of the sword and came to life. It was permitted (him) to bestow breath on it—the image of the Beast—so that

153

the image of the Beast should not only talk but also cause that all (men) who might not worship the image of the Beast should be slain. He causes all (men), the small and the great, the rich and the poor, alike the freeman and the slaves, to be given a brand on their right hand or on their forehead, and that no one should be able to buy or to sell unless he has the brand—the name of the Beast, or the number of his name. He is cleverness: let him who has the intuitive mind compute the number of the Beast; for it is the number of a man, and his number is 666.

Interpretation

Magical powers were attributed to Medusa, and talismans were under its stellar influence. The word here translated "omen" signifies also a "talisman" or symbol drawn under the influence of some particular constellation or planetary aspect.

Cedrenus states that Perseus, the slayer of the Gorgon, taught the Persians the magic of Medusa, by means of which fire came down from the sky. But, apart from all exoteric theories of ceremonial magic, the Pseudo-Lamb of the Apocalypse, as a principle in man, does indeed draw "fire" from the intellectual sky. For the force which it represents produces all the grosser forms of psychism, and is the agent of the so-called "miracles" of exoteric religion, the prodigies produced by erotic fervor, blind credulity and disordered imagination.

It is also the foul force employed in phallic sorcery, and includes the irrational instinct of religionism, the vague yearning for something to worship—a reflection or shadow of the true devotional principle—which prompts men to project a subjective image of the lower, personal mind, and to endow it with human attributes, and then claim to receive "revelations" from it.

This, the image of the Beast, or unspiritual mind, is their anthropomorphic God, a fabulous monster the worship of which has ever prompted men to fanaticism and persecution, and has inflicted untold misery and dread upon the masses, as well as physical torture and death in hideous forms upon the many martyrs who have refused to bend the knee to this Gorgonean phantom of the beast-mind of man, and to the gospel Jesus, and the personal God of Christianism.

Where the worshippers of this image of the Beast predominate, the man whose hand and brow are not branded by this superstition, who neither thinks nor acts in harmony with it, suffers ostracism if not terrible persecution.

"Here is cleverness" would be, in the English idiom, "Here is a puzzle." The number of the Beast, as explained, is the letters of which, as numerals, total 666; while the Pseudo-Lamb is 333.

Chapter 14: 1-5

I saw; and, Behold! the Lamb standing on the mountain of Sion, and with him the 144,000 having his name and his father's name written on their foreheads. I heard a voice from the sky, like the voice of many waters, like the voice of a great thunder; and the voice I heard was like (that) of lyrists playing on their lyres. They chanted as it were a new lyric before the throne, and before the four Beings and the Ancients, and no one could understand the lyric save the 144,000—they who had been bought from the earth.

These are the ones who were not defiled with women; for they are virgins. These are the ones who go along with the Lamb wherever he goes. These were bought from men—a firstling to the God and the Lamb. In their mouth was found no deceit; they are faultless.

Interpretation

The Lamb is the fourth of the animal-symbols, or "beasts," and is identical with the Bowman on the white horse, the regent of the fourth somatic division. He is the intellectual Sun, the Nous, which is Iesous, the number of whose name is 888.

The Sun is the Lion when domiciled in Leo, which corresponds to the highest of the noetic chakras, and the Lamb when exalted in Aries, which corresponds to the nimbus. His being on Sion's hill also signifies that exaltation.

Here he is represented as being surrounded by his virginal powers, and a thunderous chorus preludes the next act in the drama, the conquest of the cardiac centers. This chorus, the fifth in the series, is only described, no words being given because, it is intimated, it would be unintelligible to the profane; and the conquest of the chakras of this division is given with less detail than are the others.

Chapter 14: 6, 7

I saw another Divinity flying in mid-sky, having an aeonian divine message to announce to those seated on the earth, to every people, tribe, tongue and nation, and he said with a loud voice:

"Fear ye the God and to him give glory; for the hour of his judgment is come. Worship him who made the sky, the earth, the sea and the springs of waters."

Interpretation

This, the third of the conquests, is represented as a harvesting of the intellectual, psychic and spiritual principles, to which correspond respectively the cerebro-spinal axis, the great sympathetic nerve system, and the aureola. The action is confined to the three higher centers corresponding to these principles; while the opening of the four lower centers is given as a proclamation to each of the four lower principles seated in the somatic divisions.

An aeon is a definite life-period, as the life-time of a man, a generation, or the whole evolutionary period, the complete cycle of generation.

It is only the unphilosophical notion that "eternity" is "a long period of time" that has caused the "authorized" translators of the New Testament to persist in giving "aionios" the meaning "eternal."

Time is not an entity nor a thing per se; nor is eternity merely time indefinitely prolonged. **Time is a mental concept rising from the consciousness of change in the visible world.** Eternity is noumenal, changeless, extending neither into the past nor the future. **It is the immeasurable present.**

The aeonian evangel relates only to the cycle of generation—from which the hero of the Apocalyptic drama is about to be emancipated, after final judgment has been passed upon his deeds during the aeon in which he has been successively incarnated among all the races and peoples who have had their lesser cycles in the vast period of human development.

Chapter 14: 8

Another, a second Divinity, came after (him), saying: "She fell! Babylon the great fell—she who has made all the people drink of the wine of the lust of her prostitution."

Interpretation

Babylon, also termed the Woman in scarlet, symbolizes the mystical nature, the carnal body and the lust for existence inherent in its elements. It has "fallen" only in the sense that the

156

consciousness of the Conqueror has been set free from its trammels.

Chapter 14: 9-13

Another Divinity, the third, came after them, saying with a great voice: "If any one worships the Beast and his image, and receives a brand on his forehead or on his (right) hand, he also shall drink of the wine of the God's ardor that has been poured out raw into the wine-cup of his passion; and he shall be tormented with fire and sulphur in the presence of the holy Divinities and in the presence of the Lamb.

"The smoke of their torment keeps rising throughout aeons of aeons, and no rest day or night are they having who worship the Beast and his image, and whosoever receives the brand of his name. Here is the patience of the devotees, those who are keeping the commands of the God and the belief of Iesous."

I heard from the sky a voice saying: "Write: Immortal are 'the dead' who die in the Master henceforth. 'Yea,' says the Breath, 'that they may cease from their labors—but their works accompany them'."

Interpretation

The creative Breath, which is supernal Love at its deific source, becomes, in the sphere of generation, the force that engenders bodies, and in that respect the worshippers of the Beast and his image, the personal God, partake of it, and thereby are constantly undergoing the miseries of incarnation in which they find no abiding peace. Yet physical existence is, in reality, a purificatory discipline, like the fumigating with sulphur, a common practice with the ancients, alluded to by Ioannes.

The followers of Iesous, the spiritual Mind, knowing this, endure life with patience and faith in divine justice.

The "dead" are the living dead, the embodied, incarnated souls, who "die in the Master" only when they attain liberation from the sepulchre of the carnal body, ceasing then from their toil but retaining the fruition of their good works.

Chapter 14: 14-16

I saw a white cloud; and on the cloud (I saw) sitting (a Divinity) like the son of man, having on his head a golden crown, and in his hand a keen sickle.

157

Another Divinity came out from the adytum, crying out with a loud voice to the (Divinity) seated on the cloud:

"Thrust out your sickle and reap, for to you has come the hour to reap—for the earth's harvest is dried up."

The (Divinity) seated on the cloud stuck his sickle on the earth, and the earth was reaped.

Interpretation

The fifth Divinity represents the First Logos, here seated in the nimbus; for he is the overshadowing Self, the Uncrucified, or unincarnated. He reaps the scant harvest of the psychic nature.

It will be observed that wherever he is referred to in this passage, the word "Divinity" (angelos) has been expunged from the text, no doubt by some zealot who, recognizing the description as that of the Christos, tampered with the manuscript with the same motive that prompts the modern "othodox" translators to shade and color misleadingly the values of the Greek tenses, in many instances.

Chapter 14: 17-20

Came from the adytum which is in the sky another Divinity, he also having a keen sickle.

Another Divinity came out from the altar—he who has authority over fire—and he gave voice with a great shout to the one who had the keen sickle, saying:

"Thrust out your keen sickle and pick the grape-clusters of the earth's vine, for her bunches of grapes are ripened."

The Divinity stuck his sickle into the earth and stripped the earth's vine, and threw (the grapes) into the wine-vat, the great (womb) of the God's ardor. The wine-vat was trodden outside the city, and blood issued from the wine-vat, up to the bridles of the horses, as far as 1600 stadia.

Interpretation

The second of the two Reapers is the Second Logos. He reaps the spiritually dynamic nature, which on the plane of creative forces corresponds to the fivefold noetic group. The vine of this conquest is identical with the river Euphrates of the three other conquests.

· Physiologically, the river is the spinal cord, the channel of the five pranas, or life-winds, which are now, by the exigencies of the allegory, metamorphosed into bunches of grapes.

These solar forces, permeating and energizing the aura (wine-vat outside the city), produce a return current to the chakras of the four somatic divisions (bridles of the horses) and into the solar body, the 1,600. It is a process analogous to the mainte-nance of the foetus in utero.

In stellar symbolism, each of the seven Divinities may be recognized among the constellations.

Thus, as Aries, the Sion of the allegory, rises in the eastern horizon, the Eagle is near the zenith, together with the Swan and the Celestial Vulture, these being the three Divinities who are said to fly in mid-sky.

Lesson No. 44

Chapter 15: 1-4

I saw another constellation in the sky, great and wonderful, (and in it) seven Divinities having the seven scourges, the final (ordeals), for by them the God's ardor is finished.

I saw (a sheen), as it were a glassy sea, mixed with fire, and those who were Conquerors of the Beast, of his image, and of the number of his name, standing on the glassy sea, having lyres of the God. They keep chanting the lyric of Moses, a slave of the God, and the lyric of the Lamb, saying:

"Great and wonderful are thy works, O Master God, the All-Dominator. Just and true are thy paths, thou Ruler of the Aeons. Who shall not fear, O Master, and glorify the name? For thou are the Only Sanctified. For all the people shall come and worship before thee. For thy just deeds have been made manifest.

Interpretation

This constellation is Taurus, and the seven Divinities answer to the Pleiades, the group of stars situated in the neck of the stellar Bull, who is the zodiac symbol of spiritual generative force.

In Old Testament mythology, Moses symbolized the Sun in Aries. His paean of victory after his symbolical crossing of

159

the Red Sea (Ex. 14: 26-31; 15:1-21) is presumably the one here referred to. The Red Sea symbolized the Sea of Generation. The crystalline and fiery sea is the celestial ether.

Chapter 15: 5-8; 16:1

After these (things) I saw the adytum of the tent-temple of the evidence in the sky was opened. Came out from the adytum the seven Divinities having the seven scourges, clothed in flawless and brilliant (diamond) stone, and girded about their breasts with golden girdles.

One of the four Beasts gave the seven Divinities seven golden libation-saucers full of the ardor of the God who lives throughout the aeons of the aeons. The adytum was filled with smoke from the glory of the God and from his inherent force; and no one was able to go into the adytum until the seven scourges of the seven Divinities should be finished. I heard a great voice from the adytum saying to the seven Divinities:

"Go and pour out into the earth the seven libation-saucers of the God's ardor."

Interpretation

The seven superlatively pure and dazzling Divinities who emerge from the "most holy place" of the tabernacle are, like the Planetary Logos whose apparition is described in the opening vision, androgynous. Each is a male figure with female breasts and wearing the girdle of Aphrodite.

Here the word "stethe" is used, which is applicable to either sex, while in the other instance the word is "mastoi," which applies more particularly to the female breasts.

The hermaphroditos, or the blended figure of Hermes (Mercury) and Aphrodite (Venus), was a familiar figure in Greek art.

In both the Greek and Jewish mystery-paraphernalia the "Ark" contained the male and female emblems. These emblems in the Ark were previously mentioned.

As the Planetary Logos is inverted, mirrored upside down in the physical world, these seven androgynous Divinities, although they relate to the lowest of the somatic divisions, are yet the highest and purest of all.

The generative centers elaborate the finest and purest fluid in the body. It is the conservation of this Serpentine Fire that makes the Master, and its dissipation that makes the moron.

These seven androgynous Divinities are the finishers of the great work of regeneration, and the precursors of the Conqueror on the white horse.

Each of the Divinities has a phiale, a shallow cup, or saucer, used in pouring out drink-offerings to the Gods; and the libations they pour out consist of the primordial Creative Force-substance —the ether. This ether, as symbolized by the diamond-glittering rainment of the Divinities, is colorless and without qualities of its own; but all qualities are imparted to it by the Thought of the God.

As Paraclesus said, "All things, when they come from the hand of God, are white, colorless, invisible: and He colors them afterwards according to His pleasure." As they assume colors they become visible.

Chapter 16: 2

The first (Divinity) went and poured out his libation-saucer into the earth. There came to be a bad and painful sore on the man who had the brand of the Beast, and who worshipped his image.

Interpretation

The earth, symbolical of the lowest division of the body, is the throne of the Pseudo-Seer; and the worshippers of the Beast and his image are the forms of thought mirrored in this lowest reflector of the noetic consciousness, where they become distorted into the crude elemental notions of religion. These are represented as ulcerating; for the time has come for the complete eradication of the centers whence they radiate.

Chapter 16: 3

The second Divinity poured out his libation-saucer into the sea. It became blood like a dead man's, and every psychic form of life in the sea died.

Interpretation

The umbilical center (sea) is the throne of the Dragon, the epithumetic, lower psychic nature. The libation eliminated from it the last vestiges of the passions and desires; and the aura of this division is suffused by the golden color of the pranas.

161

The third Divinity poured out his libation-saucer into the rivers and springs of the waters, and the (waters) became blood. I heard the Divinity of the waters saying:

"Thou art just, O Master, (thou) who (forever) art, who wast, and who art sanctified; for thou didst pass this sentence upon (the followers of the Beast); for they poured out the blood of devotees and seers, and blood thou has given them to drink; for they are deserving (of it)."

I heard (the Divinity hovering above) the altar, saying: "Verily, O Master-God, the All-Dominator, true and just are thy judgments."

Interpretation

The rivers and springs are the throne of the Beast; it receives the golden color when the solar force reaches it. Its regent is the phrenic mind, which distorts and falsifies the intuitions reaching it from the noetic faculty. The Divinity of the waters is the Zoon corresponding to this center, and the one hovering over the altar (Ch. 8:3) is the Zoon of the noetic center.

Here the word "coming," in the formula applied to the God, is replaced by "sanctified"; for now the God has come, the future being merged in the present.

Chapter 16: 8, 9

The fourth Divinity poured out his libation-saucer upon the Sun. (Authority) was given it to scorch men with fire. Men were scorched with great heat, and they profaned the name of the God who has authority over these scourges; but they did not reform to give him glory.

Interpretation

The Sun is the throne of the Sky-God, the Lion (Leo). The outpouring of the Serpentine Fire upon this center produces intense mental strain. The intellectual forces are represented as unrepentant and profane, simply because the Nous, undifferentiated Thought, is the "only sacrificed."

Chapter 16: 10-11

The fifth Divinity poured out his libation-saucer upon the

throne of the Beast. His realm became darkened; and his (subjects) gnawed their tongues for pain, and profaned the God of the sky because of their pains and sores; but they did not reform from their works.

Interpretation

The Beast's throne, as a somatic division, is the cardiac center. In a general way it includes the entire sympathetic system, of which the principal chakra, the epigastric plexus, is shared by the Dragon.

Chapter 16: 12

The sixth Divinity poured out his libation-saucer upon that great river, the Euphrates. Its waters were dried up, so that there might be prepared the path of the rulers who (come out) from the birth-place of the sun.

Interpretation

In each of the four conquests, the sixth chakra is related to the cerebro-spinal axis and the five Pranas, the solar noetic forces, as the forces act on each of the four planes of being, to which the somatic divisions correspond.

In this final conquest, the waters of the great river, a symbol of the magnetic or nerve-force of the spinal system, are dried up; for henceforth the solar fires are to take their place permanently.

In the "sacred city," the solar body, the Euphrates becomes the mainstreet "of pure gold, transparent as glass."

Chapter 16: 13-16

I saw issuing from the mouth of the Dragon, from the mouth of the beast, and from the mouth of the Pseudo-Seer, three unpurified spirits, like frogs. They are spirits of specters, making omens (and) they are going out among the rulers of the whole home-land, to muster them for the battle of the great day (of the coming) of the God, the All-dominator. (The God says:)

"I am coming (silently) like a thief. Immortal is he who stays awake and keeps on his outer garments, so he may not walk naked, and they see his shame."

They mustered them in the place which is called in Hebrew Harmagedon.

The forces expelled by the drying up of the "Euphrates" issue from the three lower somatic centers and form a psychic entity analogous to the ghost of a deceased person: the after-death process of purification undergone by the soul occurs before death in him who "dies in the Master."

The soul of the disincarnated man, before entering upon its state of blissful rest in the higher world-soul (the spiritual realm), must purge itself of all the evil forces and elements of the psychic nature. These discarded elements remain in the lower world-soul, the phantasmal realm, where they constitute, for a time, a psychic entity wearing the sumblance of the departed personality, its ghost, shade or specter—an elemental self, which is a congeries of all the impure and evil constituents thus rejected by the soul.

In Greek mysticism, as expounded by Plotinos and others, this higher world-soul was termed Zeus, and the lower world-soul, which is next to the physical realm and rendered foul by the impure emanations from the latter, was called Thea. The latter stands for the Kabalistic "astral light," which is kinetically charged with the evil impulses and thoughts of humanity, and especially with the foul lust of the depraved portion of mankind, and, by its hypnotic influence, is a constant inciter to vice and crime.

In this realm the specter gradually disintegrates; but the elements composing it are again attracted to the soul when it reincarnates. In the case of him who is engaged in the telestic work, this elemental self becomes a malignant demon, against which he must constantly be on his guard, and which he must eventually destroy.

The impure spirits (pneumata) are said to congregate in the place called **Harmagedon.**

The scholiasts have failed to find even a plausible Hebrew derivation for this word. The supposition that it stands for "Mount Megiddo" meets with the difficulty that the only Megiddo known to geography was a city on a plain.

Considered as an anagram, Hermagedon forms Rhea 'dagmon, "Rhea for the prurient itchings, or desires"—a very accurate characterization of the anima bruta, or brute-soul of the world, which Rhea typified.

The worship of the Goddess Rhea, who was called also Cybele, Astarte, and by many other names and titles, was wide-spread among oriental nations. Her numerous temples abounded in "consecrated women," and as the Magna Mater, "the Great

Mother" of these prostitutes, she was worshipped with shameless orgiastic rites.

Originally Rhea symbolized the celestial ether.

Chapter 16: 17-21

The seventh Divinity poured out his libation-saucer into the air. There came a great voice from the adytum of the sky—from the throne—saying:

"He has been born."

There came to be voices, lightnings and thunders; and there came to be a great earthquake, such as has not happened since men were born upon the earth—such and so great an earthquake.

The great city came to be in three divisions. The cities of the people fell; and Babylon the great was remembered before the God, to give to her the winecup of the wine of the ardor of his passions. Every island fled, and the mountains were not found. Great hail, like hundred-pound (missiles), keeps falling from the sky upon men, and men profaned the God because of the sourge of the hail; for its sourge is exceedingly great.

Interpretation

The voice from the adytum, that of the First Logos, announced the (spiritual) birth "from above" of the Initiate, who appears on the white horse. Before this apparition is described, a digression is made, to introduce explanatory matter.

The scribe of the John gospel closely followed this initiatory work where he depicts the spiritual birth allegorically as the crucifixion of his Jesus, and gives the ultimate utterance as "It is finished" (19:30).

The scribe of the Matthew wove in his work the great disturbances as follow: "The veil of the temple was rent in twain from top to bottom; and the earth did quake, and the rocks rent; and the graves were opened; and many bodies of the saints which slept arose, and came out of the graves after his resurrection, and went into the holy city, and appeared unto many (27:51-53).

No historian knows aught of this remarkable event, and no account of it appears anywhere outside of the New Testament.

In the Apocalypse the voices, lightnings, thunders and earthquakes were allegorical to describe the mental disturbances experienced by the Initiate when he was spiritually born (from above). In the Matthew they are depicted as natural phenomena that actually occurred. The allegorism of the Masters was transformed into literalism by the forgers of the New Testament.

The great city (physical body of man) is now three-divisional, the minor cities (generative centers) having been subdued, extirpated.

The extirpation of the generative centers (Tree of Life) is allegorical of course, and indicates that the Initiate has risen above the animal plane of carnal generation.

But in those days many religious zealots took the matter literally, and submitted to castration, emasculation. Some men made themselves eunuchs "for the kingdom of heaven's sake" (Mat. 19:12).

Today the religious zealots let snakes bite them for the kingdom of heaven's sake, while some preachers glorify that preposterous work, being happy to see how completely deceived some of the masses are by the fables and fiction of the New Testament.

Lesson No. 45

Chapter 17: 1-5

Came one of the seven Divinities who had the seven libation-saucers, and talked with me, saying:

"Hither! I shall show you the judgment of the great prostitute who is sitting on the many waters, with whom the rulers of the earth committed fornication—and those who dwell on the earth became intoxicated with the wine of her prostitution."

He carried me away in the Breath (trance) into the desert; and I saw a Woman sitting on a scarlet Beast, (having his mouth) full of names of the profanity, and having seven heads and ten horns. The Woman was arrayed in purple and scarlet, over-jewelled with gold, precious stones and pearls, having in her hand a golden wine-cup, full of the stenches and filth of her prostitution. On her forehead was a name written:

"A Mystery: Babylon the great, the 'Mother' of the (temple) prostitutes and the earth's stenches."

Interpretation

The two "Women" of the Apocalypse are symbols that were

166

used by the Masters to teach the neophyte the mysteries of Life. They are both Goddesses, in the ancient sense, as the "Angels" are the lesser Gods of the ancient pantheon.

Whether Christian or "pagan," these Gods and Goddesses are nothing more than the personified powers and principles of the Macrocosm and the Microcosm.

Babylon, as the "mighty city," is a symbol of the human body, the mightiest physical organism on earth. As the fallen Woman, she is a Goddess, the Magna Mater of the temple prostitutes in the Mystery-cult of Rhea or Astarte.

The human body (Babylon) is the Great Mystery. Anatomists, psychologists, physiologists, and biologists, by studying this great Mystery, even on an atheistical, empirical, physical basis, have gained more knowledge of the Life Principle manifested in the visible world, and conferred greater benefits on humanity, than all the combined exoteric religionists who have wasted their lives in formulating fantastic creeds and in coercing mankind into the blind and idolatrous worship of that figment of the imagination—a personal God and his alleged son Jesus Christ.

The Christian religion is the worst system of idolatry the world has ever known. It was invented by despots for the sole purpose of gaining greater power over the masses, and has served them far better and enriched them far greater than they ever dreamed.

The despots invented the system by personalizing the symbols and literalizing the parables used by the Masters in the Ancient Mystery Schools to teach the neophyte the processes of Creation and the functions of the Temple of God (1 Cor. 3:16).

Their knowledge of these matters was so much superior to ours, that they were competent to tell the story in symbol and allegory that is such a puzzle to modern science, that scientists have failed to solve the story after fifteen hundred years of effort.

In the allegory, Babylon represents much more than the physical body as a mere form composed of cells and tissues, a congeries of functional organs. For it symbolizes also the broad principle of physical generation, of Divine Life confined to a physical prison.

According to the sacred science, as outlined by Ioannes in allegorical language, Forces are subtil Elements, while physical Elements are Cosmic Forces that have become inert.

All Forces and Elements have their origin in the celestial Ether, the Arche or "First Principle."

The Sun-clothed Virgin of the Sky, who gives birth to a male child by the gestation of the Solar Body of the Conqueror, is the Pure Ether, the primordial force-substance.

167

On the physical plane of animal-human generation, where that Ether becomes differentiated into the gross, dense physical elements, she is the unchaste female, the Mother of all that is abominable.

As a physical form, a marvelous organism evolved by the Cosmic Spirit for its own divine purpose, the body is the adytum of the God who occupies it as his earthly Temple.

The elements of the Pure Ether composing the Temple have become foul during the long ages of physical evolution, and the Cosmic Spirit, as the individualized Soul, is ever being tainted and instigated to evil by the impure emanations of vicious impulses that have become inherent in the physical organism.

It is thus a Mystery at once divine and infernal, at which the Master, in the Apocalyptic allegory, represents himself as gazing in awe and reverance, wonder and amazement.

As a Goddess, the infernal Aphrodite, the depraved Virgo, symbolized the anima bruta, or lower world-soul, saturated with carnal lust. In this role she holds a cup, which is the adjacent constellation Crater, the Mixing-bowl, fabled as having belonged to Iacchos, the God of orgiastic revelry.

Had the ancient system of mythology, which was used for the purpose of instruction, not been so basely portrayed and misrepresented by the early church fathers in order to make their new religion more popular with the people for the purpose of profit and power, the biblical parables had not been so puzzling.

As we smother our pride and learn to regard the Ancient Masters as the great scientists they really were, instead of a group of heathens as taught by the church, it helps us much to understand their marvelous allegories. When we realize that these allegories deal with Cosmic Principles and Physical Processes, instead of heavenly bliss and a celestial paradise for the blind believers in the gospel Jesus, we immediately see the subject in clear light and the dark puzzle becomes plain.

Chapter 17: 6-8

I saw the Woman intoxicated with the blood of the devotees and with the blood of the witnesses of Iesous. When I saw her, I gazed in wonderment, with great curiosity. Said the Divinity to me:

"Why did you wonder? I shall tell you the mystery of the Woman and of the Beast that was carrying her, which has the seven heads and the ten horns."

"The Beast which you saw was, and is not, and is about

to come up out of the abyss and go to destruction. Those who dwell on the earth—(the men) whose name has not been registered on the scroll of life since the evolution of the world—will wonder when they look at the Beast, because he was, and is not, and shall be present.

Interpretation

The red Dragon (epithumetic nature) is the principle which, in close alliance with the Beast (phrenic mind), impels the Soul to continue to incarnate, and he thus systains the Woman, who symbolizes earthly existence. He rises from the abyss (impure elements), and is again disintegrated in them when the soul is purified.

The formula, "was, is not and shall be present," expresses in an enigmatical way the Platonic doctrine that in the spheres of generation "nothing really is, but all things are becoming"; that is, in the visible world nothing partakes of permanent being, but "all things are being created and destroyed, coming into existence and going into new forms."

The men who have not been registered on the scroll of life are the uninitiated.

Chapter 17: 9-11

Here is the intuitive mind that has cleverness: the seven heads are seven mountains where the Woman is sitting on them; and they are seven rulers, (of whom) the five have fallen, and the one is, and the other has not yet come, and when he does come he must abide a little while.

The Beast which was and is not, is himself also an eighth and is (an emanation) from the seven—and to destruction he is going.

Interpretation

The seven heads of the Dragon, like those of the Beast, are the seven cardinal desires, but in the one they are mental, in the other instinctual; and the seven mountains are the seven chakras through which they manifest during incarnation, the Woman being then seated on them, and they dominate in turn the seven incarnations through which the neophyte must pass in conquering them.

The irreclaimable residue of the epithumetic principle, which goes to form the after-death specter, or elemental self, is the eighth, "the son of perdition."

169

The Conqueror is represented in the Apocalyptic drama as being the sixth of the series of seven incarnations, so that five of them have perished and the seventh is yet to come. Hence the Dragon, later in the drama, is again imprisoned in the abyss, and cannot be completely slain until that seventh and last incarnation.

Chapter 17: 12-14

"The ten horns you saw are ten rulers who have not yet received a realm; but they receive authority as rulers one hour with the Beast. These have one purpose; and their force and authority they pass along to the Beast. These will battle with the Lamb, and the Lamb will conquer them; for he is Master of Masters and Ruler of Rulers; and those who (go along) with him are called the chosen and reliable."

Interpretation

The ten horns are the five pranas, each of which is dual, positive and negative, on this plane, where they are merely the life-winds, or vital forces. They are not related to the chakras as the tattvas are, and hence are said to have no realm as yet, though later they have the spinal axis for their realm, when the Lamb has conquerer them.

Exuberant animal vitality, by intensifying the passional nature, tends away from spirituality unless controlled with a rod of iron, when it redounds to the benefit of the organism.

Hence these forces are represented as being inimical to the Nous when not controlled, so they must be conquered and utilized. Then they increase spirituality by benefitting the spiritual centers of the organism.

The forces subdued are here classified according to the three lower degrees of initiation in the secret society.

Chapter 17: 15-18

Also he says to me: "The waters you saw, where the prostitute is sitting, are nations, mobs, peoples and tongues.

"The ten horns you saw on the Beast—these shall abhor the prostitute and shall make her destitute and naked, and shall devour her flesh and consume her with fire. For the God put it in their hearts to carry out his purpose, to carry (it) out (as their own) one purpose, and to give

170

their realm to the Beast until the instruction of the God should be finished.

"The Woman you saw is the great city which has a realm (extending) over the rulers of the earth."

Interpretation

The waters are the great sea of generated life, humanity in its vast cycle of physical and psychical evolution, which comprises all lesser racial and subracial cycles, in each of which every one plays his part.

The whole tide of life slowly works out the divine purpose. Even the minor forces of man have in them the impulse of this purpose of the God, so that he who runs counter to it, invites disaster and destruction from the very forces that normally vitalize his body.

The "rulers of the earth" are the forces of the physical world.

Lesson No. 46

Chapter 18: 1-3

After these (instructions) I saw another Divinity coming down from the sky, having great authority; and the earth was lit up by his glory. He cried out with a strong voice, saying:

"She fell. The great Babylon fell, and became a haunt of ghosts, a prison of every filthy specter and a cage of every filthy and loathsome bird (of prey). For by the wine of the lust of her prostitution all the people have fallen. The rulers of the earth committed fornication with her; and the merchants of the earth by the force of her lewdness grew rich."

Interpretation

The Apocalyptic hero, having conquered in the ordeals of his initiation, achieving the spiritual rebirth, has risen above the illusions of the physical world and taken his place among the eternal Gods.

The exhortations and lamentations that follow the declaration of the radiant Divinity concerning the fall of Babylon are of a general nature, applying to the aggregate of humanity, and not at all to the Conqueror. For, as there are two crucifixions, so there are two falls.

171

The fall of Babylon in this case is a symbol of the fall into mortal corruption, the desecration by man of his body which he has converted into holds of iniquity.

As pertaining to the Conqueror, the fall of Babylon is the exact reverse of this; for it means the conquest, subjugation and purification of the body.

The people, rulers and merchants who were debauched by the prostitute are the three lower castes—the toiling, combative and commercial classes—while the Divinities represent the fourth and highest class, the initiated.

Chapter 18: 4-24

I heard another voice from the sky, saying:

"Come out of her, O my people, so that you may not have partnership in her sins, and so that you may not receive her scourges. For her sins have followed (you) up to the sky, and the God has held in memory her misdeeds. Pay her back as she also paid back, and double to her twofold (wages), according to her works. In the wine-cup which she poured out, pour out for her a double (draught). As much as she glorified herself and grew lewd, so much give her of torment and mourning; for in her heart she keeps saying:

" 'I sit enthroned a queen, and am not a widow; and I shall not at all put on mourning.'

"Therefore in one day shall come her scourge—death, mourning and hunger—and she shall be consumed by fire. For strong is the Master-God who judged her. The rulers of the earth, who committed fornication and were lustful with her, shall weep and wail over her when they look at the smoke of her conflagration, standing afar through fear of her torment, saying:

" 'Woe! Woe! The great city, Babylon, the strong city! For in one hour has come your judgment."

"The merchants of the earth shed tears and mourn over her, for no more one buys their stock any more—the stock of gold, silver, precious stones, pearls, byssus, purple and silken (fabrics); and all citrus wood, every ivory utensil, every utensil (made) of precious wood, of bronze, of iron and of marble; and cinnamon, amomum, incense, ointment, frankincense, wine, oil, flour, wheat, cattle and sheep; and (merchandise) of horses and chariots—and of bodies and souls of men. The fruits which your soul lusted for are gone from you, and all dainty

172

and radiant (charms) have perished from you, and (your lovers) shall never more find them at all (in you). The merchants of these wares, who were enriched by her, shall stand afar through fear of her torment, shedding tears and mourning, saying:

" 'Woe! Woe! The great city—she who was arrayed in byssus (fabric), purple and scarlet, and over-jewelled with gold, precious stone and pearl. For in one hour all this wealth has come to destitution.'

"And every sailing-master, and every crew on the ships, sailors, and as many as toil (on) the sea, stood afar and cried out, on seeing the smoke of her conflagration, saying:

" 'What (city) is equal of the great city?'

"And they threw dust on their heads and cried out, weeping and sorrowing, saying:

" 'Woe! Woe! The great city, by whom all were enriched who have ships on the sea, from her bountifulness! For in one hour she has come to destitution.'

"Rejoice over her, O Sky, and ye devotees, apostles and seers! For the God has passed sentence upon her in accordance with your decision."

A lone Divinity, the strong one, took up a stone, like a great millstone, and threw it into the sea, saying:

"Thus with a rush shall Babylon, the great city, be thrown down, and shall not at all be found any more. The voice of lyrists, musicians, flutists and trumpeters shall not at all be heard in thee any more; no craftsman, of whatever craft, shall be found any more at all in thee; the voice of a millstone shall not at all be heard in thee any more; the light of a lamp shall not at all shine in thee any more; and the voice of the bridegroom and of the bride shall not at all be heard in thee any more. For thy merchants were the magnates of the earth. For by thy witchcraft all the people were deluded."

In her was found the blood of seers and devotees, and of all who have been sacrificed on the earth.

Interpretation

In the rejoicing and lamentation over the prospective fall

173

of Babylon, an event which, for the mass of mankind, lies in the extremely remote future, the four castes take part.

The highest caste, or distinctive class, is given as threefold, composed of devotees, apostles and seers. They utter no rejoicing, the Divinities acting as their spokesmen.

The profane, comprising the rulers or dominant warlike class, the merchants or trading class, and the sailors, the toiling masses on the sea of life, indulge in lamentations over the downfall of the great city.

For the present, and for ages to come, the Christian and "pagan" lands alike, Astarte remains enthroned on the scarlet Dragon, "who is the Devil and Satan," and in this present century her cup is more overflowing with abominations, and the traffic in the bodies and souls of men and women continues more briskly and heartlessly, than in the days when Ioannes wrote his mystic scroll.

The destruction of the Apocalyptic Babylon will come only when humanity, by proper teaching, shall have learned to loathe the lusts of the flesh and to love the glories of the Spirit.

Lesson No. 47

Chapter 19: 1-8

After these (lamentations) I heard (a chorus), as it were the voice of a great throng in the sky, saying:

"Hallelouia! The deliverance, glory and force are our God's. For true and just are his judgments; for he has judged the great prostitute, who corrupted the earth with her prostitution, and he has avenged the blood of his slaves at her hand."

And once more they have said:

"Hallelouia! Her smoke keeps going up throughout the aeons of the aeons!"

The 24 Ancients and the four Beings fell down and worshipped the God seated on the throne, saying:

"Amen. Hallelouia!"

A voice came out of the throne, saying:

"Praise be our God, all ye his slaves, and ye who fear him, both the small and the great."

174

And I heard (a chorus), as it were the voice of a vast throng, as the voice of many waters, and as the voice of mighty thunders, saying:

"Halleiouia! For the Master-God, the All-Dominator, has become ruler. Let us rejoice and become ecstatic, and let us give to him the glory; for the marriage of the Lamb has come, and his wife has made herself ready. To her was given (the right) to clothe herself in byssus (vesture) brilliant and pure; for byssus (vestures) are the awards of the devotees."

Interpretation

The main action of the drama is here resumed. The chorus, which is the seventh and last, is a paean of victory following the attainment. by the Conqueror of the Spiritual Rebirth (born again).

The chorus is chanted by all the powers of the microcosmic universe (man), the enthroned Logos being the chorus-leader.

The word Hallelouia, which is not found elsewhere in the New Testament, is here chanted four times.

The marriage was one of the symbolic rites in the Ancient Mysteries; and universally in mysticism, spirit is represented as the male, and matter as the female principle. Here the "bride" of the Conqueror is the Solar Body—the "fire-body" of the Initiate.

There is another symbolical marriage of the Lamb that will be observed in due course.

Byssus was a fine cloth, naturally yellow in color, affected by oriental devotees. It represents the auric color of a saintly person.

Chapter 19: 9-10

And to me (the Divinity) says:

"Write: Immortal are they who are invited to the wedding dinner of the Lamb."

And (again) he says to me:

"These arcane doctrines are the God's"

I fell down before his feet to worship him; but he says to me:

175

"See to it (that you do) not. I am a fellow-slave with you, and with your brothers who have the evidence of Iesous. Worship the God."

"For the evidence of Iesous is the "Breath" of seer-ship."

Interpretation

Absolute certainty of the divine, immortal nature, the conscious spiritual Self, can be gained only through the sacred trance, in which all the lower faculties are placed in abeyance, the clamor of the physical senses, emotions and thoughts completely obliterated, so that in the perfect peace and silence of the Soul, the voice of the Real Man may become audible.

This trance-state, as taught in the Ancient Mysteries, can be attained only through the action of the Serpentine Fire, the dynamic working-force of the Parakletos, or "advocate," who pleads with the Father.

Chapter 19: 11-16

I saw the sky opened; and, Behold! a white horse (appeared), and he who was riding him is called Believable and True, and with justice he judges and gives battle. His eyes are like a blaze of fire, and on his head are many diadems; and (on his forehead) he has a name written which no one knows save himself. He is clothed in a garment dyed with blood; and his name is called "The Logos of the God."

The armies in the sky were following him, on white horses, wearing byssus (robes), white and pure. From his mouth keeps flashing forth a keen sword, that with it he might chastize the people. He is treading the wine-vat (overflowing with) the wine of the ardor of the passion of the God, the All-Dominator. He has on his garment and on his thigh the name written, "Ruler of rulers and Master of masters."

Interpretation

The Hero on the white horse is the Second Logos, the incarnating Ego, the Conqueror who has mastered the telestic work. He is now the erect God who is no longer the Inverted Logos.

The Flashing Sword issuing from his mouth symbolizes the Creative Fiat, or Word Power, by which is slain the world of illusion, the deception of physical permanence.

The Conqueror, in all his symbolic splendor, appears as the Hierophant of the Eleusinian Mysteries, his various insignia emblematical of his divine attributes. He wears the aspect of Mars, the War-God, who in ancient mythology was the God of Generation. He rules his body, his impulses and desires with a rod of iron, the metal of Mars. He treads the wine-vat of Regenerative Force; and has his title written on his thigh—an euphemism for phallos, as in Old Testament usage (Gen. 26:2, et passim).

As one born again out of the physical darkness into Spiritual Light, the Conqueror has attained the state of Perfect Wisdom and Sinless Purity, having eradicated from his animal nature the desires that relate to the lower physical being, and awakened in his organism the dormant powers of Cosmic Consciousness. He now goes forth to final battle with the elemental Self, the Tartarean ghost of his now defunct psycho-physical personality.

Chapter 19: 17, 18

I saw a lone Divinity standing in the sun. He cried out with a great voice, saying to all the birds (of prey) that fly in mid-sky:

"Come! Flock together to the dinner of the great God, so that you may devour the flesh of rulers, the flesh of commanders, the flesh of strong (warriors), the flesh of horses and of their riders, and the flesh of all, free and slave, both small and great.

Interpretation

The "lone" Divinities are the Chief Divinities, corresponding to the Zoa; here the one standing in the Sun is Mikael, he who drove the Dragon from the sky.

The elemental Self is the essence of impurity in the psychic and physical elements; and as a sort of by-product of the evolutionary aeon, it is a concretion of all that was evil in each incarnation during the aeonian sojourn of the Ego in the spheres of generation. It is therefore the "flesh," or carnal element, of kings, warriors and all the other personalities assumed by the incarnating Self in the world drama being enacted by mankind.

Chapter 19: 19-21

I saw the Beast, and the rulers of the earth and their armies,

177

drawn together to do battle with the Rider on the White Horse
and his army.

The Beast was captured, and with him the Pseudo-Seer who
made omens in his sight, by which he deluded those who had re
ceived the brand of the Beast, and the worshippers of his image

The two (beasts) were cast alive into the lake of fire which
flames with sulphur; and the rest were slain by the sword of th
Rider on the White Horse, (by the sword) which kept flashing
forth from his mouth; and all the birds (of prey) were gorge
with their flesh.

Interpretation

All the battles are briefly described as short and decisive con
flicts, and never as protracted struggles. In this one, the in
stinctual and phrenic principles of the elemental congeries are
apprehended and thrown into the astral fire of the phantasma
world, where dissolution is their ultimate fate.

Lesson No. 48

Chapter 20: 1-3

I saw a Divinity coming down from the sky, having the key
to the abyss and a great chain in his hand. He apprehended the
Dragon, the archaic Snake, who is the Accuser and Adversary
and enchained him for 1000 years, and cast him into the abyss
and locked and sealed (it) atop of him, so that he should n
delude the people any more until the 1000 years should
finished; and after that he must be turned loose for a short tim

Interpretation

The hero of the Apocalypse being represented as existing
the sixth incarnation of the seven composing the cycle of initi
tion, he has one more physical life before him, and cannot y
completely destroy the epithumetic principle. Instead, it
placed in durance for 1000 years, after which it must be free
when the hero reincarnates, then it will be quickly exterminate

The seventh incarnation is the last of the seven rulers w
are the seven heads of the Dragon. Of this ruler it is said th
"when he does come he must abide a little while."

By fixing the time between incarnations at 1000 years, t
author of the Apocalypse follows Plato, who gives that peri
In relating the allegory of Er, Plato explains that, owing to t

tenfold intensity of sensation in the subjective after-death state, "the thousand years answer to the hundred years which are reckoned as the lifetime of men."

In this age of "science and medicine," the lifetime of man is not reckoned at 100 years, but much less.

Chapter 20: 4-6

I saw thrones and those seated on them; and judgment was passed on them. And (I saw) the souls of those who had been beheaded on account of the evidence of Iesous and on account of the arcane doctrine of the God; also those who did not worship the Beast or his image, and did not receive his brand on their forehead and on their hand, and they came to life and ruled with the Anointed for 1000 years. The rest of the dead did not come to life again until the thousand years were finished.

This is the first resurrection. Immortal and holy is he who has part in the first resurrection. Over these the second death does not hold sway, but they shall be sacrificers to the God and his Anointed, and they shall rule with him for the thousand years.

Interpretation

When the Beast and the Pseudo-Seer were cast into the astral fire, and the Dragon was incarcerated in the abyss, they made their final exit from the stage.

The Conqueror has annihilated the bogus Lion and the bogus Lamb. In his next incarnation he will have to fight and destroy the Dragon, the bogus Arche-Logos.

The Apocalypse drama covers only one incarnation; and so, rather than leave in uncertainty the issue of the Final combat between the Conqueror and the Dragon, Ioannes here introduces a side-scene in which he first explains in a general way what happens to man's soul during the periods between incarnations, and then, carrying into the future the story of the Conqueror, describes the final battle in the next incarnation, resulting in the defeat and destruction of the Dragon.

The thrones and those enthroned on them symbolize the common man in a series of incarnations, after each of which, upon the demise of the physical organism, the enthroned Self passes judgment upon the deeds and misdeeds, on the planes of thought, emotion and action, of the lower self during the preceding earth-life.

All the pure and noble thoughts, sentiments, aspirations and memories are retained and remain in the Eternal Mind, the

Nous, throughout the seasons of subjective peace and bliss which the soul then experiences; but all the worthless and evil elements are rejected and left to remain dormant in the lower psychic realm, dying the "second death," and coming to life only when the soul again descends into the spheres of physical generation.

Thus man's own past life is his personal "Satan," the ancient serpent trailing through the ages and accusing him continually before his inner God, his own conscience, who is his righteous Judge.

Chapter 20: 7-10

When the thousand years are finished, the Adversary shall be turned loose from his prison and come out to delude the people who are in the four corners of the earth (the Gog and Magog), to bring them together for battle, the number of whom is as the sand of the sea.

They went up on the width of the earth and surrounded the fortress of the devotees, and the beloved city. And fire from the sky consumed them. The Accuser, the deluder of them, was thrown into the lake of fire and sulphur, where also are the Beast and the Pseudo-Seer; and they shall be tormented day and night throughout the aeons of the aeons.

Interpretation

This foretells the fate of the Dragon, the epithumetic principle, whose host of desires, passions and cravings is indeed as the sand of the sea. But they have no lodging-place in the purified nature of the Conqueror, and exist only as surviving impressions and impulses, impressed like phonographic records on the plastic world-soul, and as a malignant composite spectral entity they assail him from without.

The purifying fire obliterates these collective phantoms; and their focal center, the Dragon in his capacity as the "eighth," shares the doom of the bogus Lion and bogus Lamb.

No real esotericist could possibly fail to perceive the general meaning of the Apocalyptic allegory. The solution of its peculiar puzzles requires only the exercise of ingenuity on the part of him "who was the Nous."

Through the ages the esotericists have merely smiled and remained silent, while the exoteric Church Fathers and their worthy successors have tortured this magnificent epic into a theological nightmare.

Had the "orthodox" discovered the true nature of the Apocalypse, it had certainly shared the fate of the learned Porphyry's excellent treatise on Christianity, which was burned by decree of the Roman Emperor.

Chapter 20: 11-15

I saw a great white throne and (the God) seated thereon, from whose face fled the earth and the sky—and a place was not found for them.

I saw the dead, the great and the small, standing before the throne; and (their) scrolls were unrolled.

Another scroll was unrolled, which is (the Lamb's scroll) of life.

The dead were judged from the (records) written in (their) scrolls, according to their works.

The sea gave up the dead which were in it, and Death and the Unseen gave the dead which were in them; and they were judged every one according to their works. Death and the Unseen were thrown into the lake of fire.

This is the second death—the lake of fire. If any one was not found registered in the (Lamb's) scroll of life, he was thrown into the lake of fire.

Interpretation

Here the action of the drama is again resumed. The initiate has severed himself from the lower life, and by thus renouncing everything pertaining to the generated form of existence, he is morally and dynamically in the same condition as is the disincarnated man, so that his past must be adjudicated in the same way.

But, whereas the after-death judgment of the uninitiated soul involves only its last preceding physical existence, the Conqueror must render an account of all his previous incarnations: the records in their scrolls are reviewed, and then all are summed up in the Lamb's great scroll of life—the comprehensive record of the incarnating Spirit.

All his deeds in the great sea of sensuous life, all the things he ever did in the psychic and physical worlds, spring to life in the Eternal Memory, and all are passed upon by the inexorable Judge; and whatever element in the aeon-evolved character of the man that is found unworthy of life eternal, is hurled into the consuming fire of the chaos, there to disintegrate in the second death.

In this phase of cosmic processes there is no shadow of that exoteric and profane notion, the "vicarious atonement."

According to the philosophy of the Ancient Masters, rigid justice rules all worlds, and man reaps as he sows (Gal. 6:7).

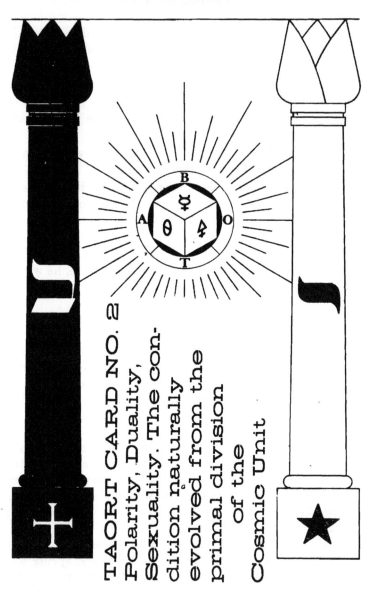

TAORT CARD NO. 2
Polarity, Duality, Sexuality. The condition naturally evolved from the primal division of the Cosmic Unit

TABLE OF CONTENTS

THE GREAT WISDOM

Pursuing the trail of science in all things, we invariably come to a line which, we are told, cannot be passed — "the-ring-pass-not." Beyond that point lies the great Unknowable. Further advance in that dark region is impossible...for Science says so, and that's final. Something is wrong. All questions have answers, and the answers can be found if they want to be found.

With an adequate system of research, it is possible to ascend not only to higher levels of Consciousness where these answers lie hidden in the Crypt. but to advance laterally without the limit.

When men of science consent to substitute the word Undiscovered for the word Unknowable, dogmatism and persecution will have received their death-blow. A pursuit of the facts of Creation will then replace the mere effort to sustain a pet opinion of the deductions of any certain school or coteries. — **Prof. Hilton Hotema.**

COSMIC RADIATION

This is a Radiant Universe. We live in a Sea of Radiation as fishes live in a sea of water. The Human Body is constituted of congealed Radiation, is sustained by Radiation and not by food, and the process of that sustentation is not Physiology but Radiology.

Chapter 21: 1-5

I saw a new sky and a new earth—for the first sky and the first earth have passed away, and the sea is not any more. I saw the holy city, New Hierousalem, coming down from the sky—from the God—made ready as a bride bedecked for her husband. I heard a great voice from the throne, saying:

"Behold! the tent of the God is with men, and he shall pitch' tent with them. They shall be his people and the God himself shall be with them—their God! He shall wipe away every tear from their eyes; and there shall be no more death, nor shall there be mourning, lamentation or pain any more. For the material elements have passed away."

Said the (Master) seated on the throne:

"Behold! I am making a new universe."

And to me he says:

"Write: These arcane doctrines are believable and true."

Interpretation

In the prelude to the first act of the drama (4:11) the Powers chant a paean to the God who brought the Universe into existence; but now that microcosmic "universe," the lower self that had been evolved during the generative aeons, has fulfilled its purpose, and is superceded by a new Universe, a new cycle of spiritual evolution transcendent in glory.

The statements, "He has been born," and I am making a New Universe," now require further comment.

The neophyte, having conquered in the ordeals of his initiation, rises above the illusions of physical life and the material world by achieving the Spiritual Rebirth (born again), and becoming competent to see with his Spiritual Senses the kingdom of God (Jn. 3:3).

He then becomes a New Universe (Microcosm), having discarded the old in which he lived in darkness, and takes his place among the deathless Gods by aid of the knowledge gained that he is Life Eternal.

When the neophyte received Spiritual Light, he exclaimed, "O Mysteries most truly holy! O pure Light! When the torch of the Dadoukos gleams, Heaven and the Deity are displayed to my eyes! I am initiated and become holy!"

As we have explained in greater detail in our course, "Immortalism," this was the sole objective of initiation: To be sanctified, and to see, i.e., to have just and faithful conceptions of the Deity, the knowledge of whom is The Light of the Mysteries of Life.

This great achievement was accomplished by a secret process that weakened the dominion of the physical senses and passions over the Animating Spirit, and freeing it from the sordid slavery of its physical prison. That knowledge, once so free to those worthy to receive it, was destroyed by the church fathers when they invented the new religious system that came to be known as Christianity.

Chapter 21: 6-8

And (again) he said to me:

"He has been born (in spirituality), (but) I am the Alpha and the Omega, the Origin of the Perfection.

"To him who thirsts I shall give of the spring of the water of life as a free gift. The Conqueror shall obtain the Universe, and I will be a God to him, and he shall be a son to me.

"But for the cowardly, the unbelieving, the malodorous, murders, fornicators, sorcerers, worshippers of phantoms, and all liars, their part (shall be) in the lake which flames with fire and sulphur—which is the second death."

Interpretation

The First Logos, the enthroned God, the Source of Life and its ultimate goal, is never incarnated.

The Second Logos is the incarnating Entity; and man, as he is physically on earth, is the Third Logos, who, if he conquers his animal nature and achieves the second birth, becomes the son of the God.

Yet the three are one, the Eternal Trinity, the Divine Man himself, manifested on three planes of being.

If the physical man becomes irredeemably wicked and fallen, his fate is the second death, the reverse of the second birth. His psychic self decomposes in the fiery subtil elements of the cosmos and never again appears as an entity, even as his physical organism is resolved into its original elements of the cosmos when abandoned by the Life Principle, and its elements never again appear united as one body.

The Masters held that the second death means the obliteration of the personal consciousness. The second birth leads to the attuning of the individual consciousness with that of the Cosmos.

Chapter 21: 9-14

Interpretation Included

Came one of the seven Divinities who had the seven libation-saucers, who were charged with the seven last scourges, and he talked with me, saying:

"Hither! I shall show you the bride—the Lamb's wife."

In the symbolism here presented, the Pineal Gland (male) in the brain represents the Lamb, and the wife is the Pituitary Gland(female), also in the brain. A fuller discussion of this will appear later under the Serpentine Fire.

"He carried me away in the Breath (trance) to a mountain great and high."

That mountain represents the Skull. Man's brain is the greatest, highest and most mysterious of all organs and structures. In his brain man is the God. In his brain he rises to the sun, and sky, to infinity, to eternity. The power of man's brain is the greatest of all cosmic structures.

When the Lamb (Pineal Gland) receives the inspirational force of the Serpentine Fire from the wife (Pituitary Gland), comes speedily to man the Spiritual Sight of the Seer. When this occurred in the initiation of the neophyte in the Ancient Mysteries, he cried out with great joy: "O Pure Light! Hail New-Born Light! I am initiated, and become holy!"

"And he showed me the holy Hierousalem (deathless Solar Body), coming down out of the sky from the God

(brain), having the God's glory (Sun Robe of the God)—
(and this), her luminary (fire of the pituitary gland), was
like a precious stone, like an opal crystal-glittering." This
aureola is self-luminous, with an opalescent, bluish glitter.

"Having a wall great and high." The aura.

"Having 12 gateways." The 12 orifices of the body.

"And at the gateways 12 Divinities (12 great Gods
of the Zodiac, or cosmic forces). And (on the gateways)
names inscribed, which are (the names) of the 12 tribes of
the children of Is-Ra-El (12 zodiacal signs)."

"On the east were three gateways, on the north three
gateways, on the south three gateways, and on the west
three gateways." The tribes (zodiacal signs) are in four
triads, assigned to the four regions of the earth or space.

"The wall of the city had 12 foundations, and on them
(were inscribed) the 12 names of the 12 apostles of the
Lamb."

The aura (wall of the city) has 12 force centers, where the
12 cosmic forces are focussed on the microcosm. These focal
centers are dynamically related to the 12 orifices of the body—
the 12 gateways of the city, also corresponding to the 12 zodiacal
signs, the 12 apostles of the Lamb.

The Zodiac is the Master's Wheel of Life. In its symbology
is contained the ancient secret of man's destiny.

The wall of the city (aura) has 12 foundations, the 12 powers
of the Logos, the spiritual archetype of the 12 cosmic forces.
In ancient symbology the foundation of all things is Spirit, upon
which rests the structures of whatever is manifested.

Chapter 21: 15-21

The (Divinity) who was talking with me had for a measure
a golden reed, to measure the city, its gateways and its wall.
The city lies foursquare, and its length is as great as its width.
He measured the city with the reed, by stadia, 12,000; its length,
width and height are equal. And he measured its wall, 144 cubits
(including) the measure of a man, that is, of a Divinity.

The building-material of its wall was opal, and the city was
pure gold, like clear glass.

The foundations of the wall of the city were ornamented with
every precious stone; the first foundation was opal; the second,
sapphire; the third, chalcedony; the fourth, aqua-marine; the
fifth, sardonyx; the sixth, carnelian; the seventh, chrysolite; the

eighth, berryl; the ninth, topaz; the tenth, crysoprase; the eleventh, jacinty; and the twelfth, amethyst.

The twelve gateways were twelve pearls; each one of the gateways was (carved) from a single pearl.

Interpretation

As previously explained, the cubical city, when unfolded, represents a cross, symbolizing the figure of a man. The city is the Solar Body, the numerical value of the words being 1600, the number of Jewish miles in 12,000 stadia.

The Roman mile of about eight stadia was never used by the Jews, who counted seven and a half stadia to the mile.

The aura gives the number 143, to which is added an alpha, 1, that being the vowel and number of the primeval man, or Divinity.

The aura is a brilliant opalescence, self-luminous, and the Solar Body has the appearance of transparent gold.

The twelve precious stones are not all identified with certainty, as some of the Greek names are dubious. Given in the modern terms usually applied to them they are probably as follows: 1, opal; 2, lapis-lazuli; 3, chalcedony; 4, aqua-marine; 5, sardonyx; 6, carnelian; 7, topax; 8, beryl; 9, chrysolith; 10, chrysoprase; 11, hyacinth; and 12, amethyst.

Placed in a circle, as if incorporated in the aura, these colored stones form approximately the prismatic scale, and are thus identical with the rainbow (4:3) that encircles the throne of the God.

Chapter 21: 21-27

The main-street of the city was pure gold, transparent as glass. No adytum did I see in it; for the Master-God, the All-Dominator, and the Lamb are its adytum.

The city has no need of the sun or the moon to shine in it; for the God's glory lights it up; and its lamp is the Lamb; and the people (who are of the delivered) shall walk in its light; and the rulers of the earth keep bringing their glory into it. Its gateways shall not at all be closed by day—for there shall be no night there.

They shall bring the glory and honor of the people into it; and there shall not at all enter into it anything profane, nor he who creates a stench and (acts) a lie; but only those who are registered in the Lamb's scroll of life.

Interpretation

The broad street of the solar forces, "the rulers from the Sun's place of birth," corresponds to the spinal cord of the physical body.

The complex structure of the gross form, with its numerous organs and functions made necessary by physical conditions, is not duplicated in the spiritual body. The latter is composed of etheric fire, and is in direct relation with, and is sustained by, the cosmic forces of creation.

The physical body needs no light to carry on its processes, and there is no night there, and its orifices are never closed.

Lesson No. 50

Chapter 22: 1-5

He showed me a pure river of the Water of Life, clear as crystal, flowing out of the throne of the God and of the Lamb, in the middle of its main-street. On one side of the river and on the other was the tree of life, producing twelve fruits according to the months, each one yielding its fruit; and the leaves of the tree were for the healing of the people—and the accursed (function) shall exist no more. The throne of the God and of the Lamb shall be in it, and his slaves will serve him. They will see his face, and his name (will be) on their foreheads. There will be no night there; and they will have no need of lamp or light of the sun; for the Master-God will give them light, and they will rule throughout the aeons of the aeons.

Interpretation

The River of Life symbolizes the spinal fluid and the two Trees of Life are the Ida nerve (Moon Tube) on the right side of the spinal fluid canal, and the Pingala nerve (Sun Tube) on the left. These nerve (tubes) carry Vital Force through the body. The Moon Tube terminates in the left nostril, after crossing over from the right side, and the Sun Tube ends in the right nostril after crossing over from the left side.

The Ida and Pingala pass upward, one on each side of the spine, and each forming a bow. These two nadis must be emptied of Pranic Force, which thence passes into Sushumna, before the Kundalini power can be made to rise.

In the physical body the triple current ascends to the brain from below, from the sexual centers; but in the Solar Body the "accursed" function of sexual production does not exist (Mat. 22:30). While the most sacred function of the physical organism, it becomes the "accursed" function due to debauchery and lust.

In the inverted Logos (Son of Man) the generative centers are the lowest. In the Conqueror, who has become the "Son of God," they are the highest, being converted from the lowest to the highest, and the force comes from above, from the brain-region.

The Arche-Logos is the "Witness," and has his "two witnesses" (Ida and Pingala), the three constituting the creative triad. Hence he has his name written on his "thigh" (generative centers).

This is the secret meaning of the Kabalistic maxim, Demon est Deus inversus.

Carnal generation is strictly an animal function, as explained by Clements in his Science of Regeneration. True spirituality demands its extirpation as a function of propagation, so that the vital essence, thus conserved, may become available for the development of the body's spiritual centers.

The proper exercise of the productive function for the perpetuation of the race, in the semi-animal stage, is not wrong; but its misuse is fraught with the most terrible consequences physically, psychically and spiritually.

The only true creative function is that of the Nous, the God-like faculty of Creative Thought, so well described by Clements in his Science of Regeneration, and mentioned in the New Testament (1 Jn. 3:9).

Chapter 22: 6-9

He said to me: "These arcane doctrines are believable and true.

"The Master-God of the 'Breaths' of the Seer sent his Divinity to make known to his slaves the (perfections) that must be attained speedily.

"Behold! I am coming speedily. Immortal is he who observes the arcane doctrines of the teaching of this scroll."

I, Ioannes, am he who was seeing and hearing these (mysteries of the macrocosm and microcosm); and when I heard and saw, I fell down to worship before the feet of the Divinity who was making known to me these (mysteries). And he says to me:

"See to it (that you do) not. I am a fellow-slave with

you and with your brothers, the seers, and those who observe the arcane doctrines of the teachings of this scroll. Worship the God!"

Interpretation

The Breaths of the seers are the differentiated forces of the Pneuma, or Great Breath of Life, used by the seers in the telestic work, and are not the "spirits" of ancient worthies. The Arch-Divinity of these creative forces is the Nous.

Nothing should be worshipped that has form or is individuated. The universal Divine Life alone is to be worshipped.

There is no colorless pantheism in this concept. The God of each man is one with the universal God. The Conqueror obtains the Universe, not by being absorbed and obliterated by it, but by transcending the limitations of his physical consciousness and rising to the universal Cosmic Consciousness.

As an individual he loses nothing but his imperfections, and he gains the All, the Origin and the Perfection.

This is Seership, which is not prophecy, second sight, nor sense-perception on any plane of consciousness, but is Direct Cognition of Reality.

Chapter 22: 10-16

And (again) he says to me: "Do not seal up the arcane doctrines of the teachings of this scroll; for the season is near.

"The unjust, let him do injustice yet more; the sordid, let him be made yet more sordid; the just, let him do justice yet more; and the devotee, let him be made yet more devoted.

"Behold! I am coming speedily, and my wages are with me to pay off each (laborer) as his work is. I am the Alpha and the Omega, the First (Adam) and the Last (Adam), the Origin and the Perfection (1 Cor. 15:45).

"Immortal are those who are washing their robes so that they may have authority over the Tree of Life (Gen. 2:17) and may enter by the gateways into the city. Outside are the dogs, the sorcerers, the fornicators, the murderers, the phantom-servers, and every one who keeps sanctioning and acting a lie.

"I, Iesous, have sent my Divinity to give evidence to you of these (works depending) upon the Societies. I am the Root and the Offspring of David, his bright and Morning Star."

Interpretation

The injunction not to seal up the teachings has been followed by the Apocalyptist. His scroll is written in veiled language, yet it is not "sealed" as in the case of a strictly occult book, which is written either in cipher or secret language, and can be read only with a key.

Mystical works intended for general circulation are usually worded obscurely, being designed to elicit and cultivate the intuitive faculty of the student. They are usually disconnected, fragmentary, and often interspersed with irrelevant statements.

The Apocalypse contains its own key, and is complete in itself, coherent, and scrupulously accurate in detail. The puzzles it contains are not intended to mislead or confuse. They serve to verify the correct interpretation of the allegory. The book is not sealed to him who has been a student of the Ancient Mysteries that were destroyed after the Roman State Religion was established by Constantine in the fourth century A.D.

While the growth of the inner nature is a slow process during many incarnations, the recognition of the actuality of the soul, of the immanent higher Mind, comes upon man suddenly. As Ioánnes reiterates, the Logos comes speedily, unexpectedly, as a thief in the night. When it does come, there is a balancing of merits and demerits.

If man's nature is sufficiently purified, the Mystic Tree of Life is his, and by means of it he enters the Holy City; otherwise he remains with "those without," the exotericists, the blind believers in a mythical Jesus, until he shall have "washed his robes" (cleansed and opened his Mind) and gained the right to employ the "Breaths of the Seers."

The Divinity, speaking to Ioánnes is one of the septenary group who poured out the libations in the final ordeals. He forbids the seer to worship him, declaring himself to be but a fellow-servitor. Then he announces himself as both the First (Adam) and the Second (Adam) Logos. And lastly he calls him Iesous, the incarnating Self of David.

Thus the Initiate has "gathered himself together," unifying his whole nature, and correlating his consciousness in the four worlds.

Chapter 22: 17-21

Both the Breath and the Bride are saying, "Come!" Let him

191

who hears say, "Come!" Let him who is athrist come; and let him who is willing, receive the Water of Life as a free gift.

I give corroborative evidence to all who hears the arcane doctrines of the teaching of this scroll, (and I give warning) that if any one shall add (forgeries) to them, the God will add to him the scourges that are written in this scroll. If any one shall erase (any portion) from the arcane doctrines of the scroll of this teaching, the God will erase his portion from the scroll of life and from the holy city, (even from) the (initiations) which are described in this scroll.

He who gives evidence of these (arcane doctrines) says: "Verily, I am coming speedily."

Amen. Come, Master Iesous!

The Grace of the Master Iesous be with the devotees. Amen

Conclusion

When Apollonius made his second visit to India, he was initiated in the Indian Mysteries, and given a copy of the work written in symbol and allegory.

When he returned to his native land, he retired to the Isle of Patmos, and edited and revised the written work of Initiation by inserting such changes as were necessary to make the scroll fit the conditions and customs of his country, for instance, as the adding of the seven cities of Asia Minor and other features.

He wrote in the Hebraic-Samaritan tongue, his native language, and it was his beloved disciple Damis, a Greek historian who first translated the Apocalypse into Greek.

The authorized version in the New Testament was edited and revised to make it appear as "The Revelation of Jesus Christ, who "washed us from our sins in his own blood" (Rev. 1: 1, 5).

That is just one example of the fraudulent manner in which the church fathers doctored and distorted ancient scriptures to make them suit and serve their cunning designs. An old manuscript of the book of Acts was found that contained more than 600 interporations. Such is the character of the fraudulent writings called the "Word of God."

The interpretation of the Apocalypse here presented is merely a reproduction of the meaning of the original accurately and clearly in modern English. While this interpretation differs radically, in some respects from the authorized version, it is not based upon any peculiarities of the interpretor's work, nor upon any mere matter of details, but rests broadly upon the undisputed meaning of the original Greek text.

192

Before the invention of the printing press, books were written in longhand in the form of manuscripts, and it was then very easy for unscrupulous persons to alter them to suit their own views by expunging words and sentences and interpolating forgeries. Much of this was done during the hundreds of years intervening between the founding of Romanism in the fourth century and the invention of the printing press.

Religious sectarians have been especially addicted to this form of literary vandalism, as is clearly evident from the mutilated text of almost every book of the New Testament, and especially the epistles of Pol (Apollonius).

SUPERSTITIOUS BIGOTS DETERRED

The statement in the Apocalypse that terrible consequences would befall any one for tampering with the text of this scroll of Initiation has no doubt stayed the hand of many superstitious bigots, and served to preserve the writing as we have it in the original Greek text.

The warning is more than an idle threat; for he who would maliciously mutilate this sacred manual, prepared for the spiritual guidance of "the little children" of the Logos, would find a grave indictment charged against him when he came to be "judged according to his work."

That the main text of the work has been preserved with remarkable purity is shown by the fact that the puzzles put in it to mislead the profane and uninitiated have not been touched, although slight changes by a meddlesome "redactor" might have ruined them.

Even as the Light of the Logos keeps saying to humanity, "Come," so the sincere student, he who hears that summons, should respect the call, tendering as a free gift the Water of Life to all who thirst for it, and are willing to receive and accept it in good faith.

And woe to those who, by attempting to traffic in human souls and the things of the Spirit, have lost the Key of the Gnosis, leaving themselves locked out and hindering those who would enter (Lu. 11:52).

Master Iesous is the Spiritual Mind of man. It abides in both the spiritual and physical realm; it is Man, and it alone can give proof of the mystery of Eternal Life. He comes swiftly to and appears suddenly in those who prepare and purify themselves and thus become worthy to utter the word of power—the AMEN!

PROPAGATION OR PRESERVATION

Man controls his destiny and works out his own salvation. That is the law. The primary step in the right direction is rigid self-denial.

He that conquers (the desire and lust of the flesh) shall inherit all things; and I will be his God, and he shall be my son (Rev. 21:7).

The practice of self-denial is the great work. It promotes health and self-improvement. "The less man wants the more he becomes like gods, who want nothing and are immortal" (Pythagoras).

The lust of the flesh is the hardest enemy for man to overcome. To conquer it is the highest test of the disciple on the path to Perfection.

Man is a prisoner of his five special sense organs, which he should control with his mind and thus free himself from his prison. The reaction of his sense organs make him a slave of delusion.

By means of his sense organs man is conscious of himself and his environment. Through them he receives the inspiration that arouses his passions and creates his lust. They make him see what he does not actually see, and lead him astray in many ways.

Most men live for carnal pleasure, thinking that the ultimate goal. They strive for gratification of sensual appetites and the creation of new ones, little realizing that this course weakens both body and mind.

That is the path to lust. Appetite begets appetite. Sensual cravings grow as they are appeased. That which satisfies now must soon be increased to satisfy the senses that grow dull from constant appeasement.

The wise know this, and keep their senses sharp and body vigorous by rigid self-denial. But the foolish pursue the other path. They believe that appeasement of desire is the right road. They live and die in their delusion, clinging to the error that gratification of their sensual nature will produce peace and pleasure. It produces the opposite effect.

Believing that for them somatic death ends all, as taught by modern science, the foolish fill their days with sense gratification and the satisfaction of behests of an abnormal and perverted sensuality, produced by constant appeasement. Desire is their ruler, and its gratification their religion.

If modern science taught the true facts of life, it would explode the vicarious atonement dogma, and modern theology would die and disappear. It depends on darkness, ignorance, suppression of the true facts. These facts will never be taught by science while theology can prevent it.

VITALITY AND POLARITY

Law of Creation, Law of Sex, and Law of Polarity are little understood by modern science. These laws, according to the Masters, are one and the same.

Attraction, repulsion, volition, and sensation are the four basic and fundamental principles of visible organization and existence. They produce the visible world and preserve its integrity.

Cosmic Radiation, direct from the Godhead (Rom. 1:20), acting on the positive and negative poles of the body cells, causes vital activity, termed Life. Details of the process are little known, and may never be understood. But the general principle is recognized by Natural Science.

In the Grand Cycle of Production (Creation), centrifugal evolution starts from the positive pole (Godhead), and flows toward the negative (material world). Centripetal involution starts from the negative pole and flows toward the positive (Godhead).

Cosmic Radiation vivifies, vitalizes and animates all physical matter, including atoms, plants, animals, man. What we term magnetism in metals, vitality in vegetation, and life in animals and man, are, in fact, the effect of Cosmic Radiation.

Cosmic Radiation is the Universal Principle of Polarity. Polar attraction naturally inheres in every particle of substance in the Universe, in the physical as in the spiritual, in the cells of the body as in the planets of the solar system.

Propagation rises from a union of the Positive and Negative principles or forces. If positive or negative forces unite, discord and death ensue.

The law is fulfilled in man when the union of positive and negative sex forces occur in the right ratio, in the right realm of being, vibrating in the right degree of development, and attract each other in terms so strong that they are unmistakable. That harmonizes with Plato's familiar doctrine of "affinities"— twin souls seeking reunion with each other. He said:

> "In the realm of harmony, the sexes are united (bisexuality) ; but in the physical realm of duality they are separated and incessantly seeking for reunion."

The urge of the positive and negative principles to unite is ruled by the cosmic law of propagation, the first purpose of which is perpetuation of the species.

THE UNIT

Sex attraction is the power of Polarity. It operates on all planes, and is the Cosmic Law of Creation and Propagation. There is another and higher purpose why the Law of Polarity precipitates men and women into each other's arms.

The higher purpose is to complete and perfect the polarity of the male and female bodies. Otherwise they cannot be what they are intended to be. They are not balanced. Being halves of the Unit, each is deficient in certain elements. So the halves must unite to balance their polar forces, and thus, becoming united (one flesh—Gen. 2:24), they transmit or impart to each other the elements in which each is deficient.

Benjamin Franklin appeared to have recognized this fact, and he said:

"Man and Woman united make the complete human being. . . . A single Man is an incomplete animal. He resembles the odd half of a pair of scissors."

All bodies are bipolar, composed of positive and negative forces. The positive (electric) predominates in the male, and the negative (magnetic) predominates in the female. That is what determines sex.

What the male lacks the female supplies; and vice versa. If they fail to unite and thus balance their polar forces, they suffer from an inherent deficiency that nothing else can supply. But a worse condition may arise if they are not properly mated. Then the polar balance is lacking and they do not become one flesh.

In some people the two elements are so nearly equalized as to produce womanish men and manish women. Such should not marry each other, as it results in a condition of discord. How shall people know this before they marry? Usually by long association with each other.

Happy marriages result when the positive properly predominates in the man, and the negative in the woman. When such unite, they are properly mated, yet they can ruin their happiness by eating too freely of the Tree of Life.

An electric battery minus one pole, or with a defective pole, cannot function properly. Neither can man and woman if they do not unite, or if improperly mated. Such would not amount to much but for the benefit received from what little the body possesses of the minor elements.

The effect of defective polarity appears in the old maid. Being deprived of the benefit of the positive force of the male, she is not what she should be.

It is not so serious in the case of men, as most single men have women to serve them, making the "fancy house" beneficial as well as detrimental.

When properly united and mated according to the law, the male and female bodies receive much benefit from each other, provided chastity is practiced, as preached by Paul (Apollonius). This benefit is lost if married people are improperly mated, or chastity is not observed.

PRESERVATION

Man preserves the integrity of his mind and body by rising above the Law of Propagation, by conquering the lust of the flesh. When he refuses to sacrifice himself on the social altar of parenthood, he rises above the plane of pure animalism.

The production of progeny is living evidence of the failure of man to attain within himself a higher state. So the race goes on creating new persons in the effort of Life to reach perfection.

When all departments of the Mind have reached the stage where it can realize that there is Eternal Life from which it has become alien, and to which it must return, the perception dawns that much which seemed as sexuality was not a lust for physical sensation, but the seeking for a perfect union with the proper half of the Unit, in which the girding sense of self and its separateness may be sloughed off.

Man's birth as a self-originative and self-sufficient spiritual being depends only on himself and not on a savior. It means the closing of the "South Gate," which is the closing of the path to physical birth and physical death.

Spiritual birth within the body is physical no less, and was the goal of the Ancient Masters.

For a better understanding of the secret of sex we must go to the sacred science of the Masters.

The wrong relation between man and woman in modern civilization is the prevailing cause of much emotional misery and distress.

Sex Power in its cosmic aspect is the Universal Bipolar Force, the Positive Aspect of which is presented on the physical plane by man, and the negative by woman.

In the spiritual realm the sex forces are not separated. But they are in the physical realm, and are incessantly seeking for the reunion of their divided forces. This urge, being misunderstood, leads to fornication.

If man would be more than the animal, he must pursue a life different from that of the animal. He must rise above the plane of propagation and thus invoke the power of the Law of Preservation.

Paul (Apollonius) frequently discussed this subject; but his statements in the Bible are not properly understood by most people and are not popular with the clergy. He said:

> "Let not sin (fornication) reign in your mortal body, that ye would obey it in the lust thereof." "For sin (fornication) shall not have dominion over you; for ye are not under the law (of propagation), but under grace (preservation)."—Rom. 6: 12, 14.

Then he more definitely specified "sin" when he said:

> "It is reported commonly that there is fornication among you." "He that committeth fornication sinneth against his own body" (1 Cor. 5:1; 6:18). "For the wages of sin is death" (Rom. 6:23).

The seventh chapter of Romans is devoted mostly to a discussion of the Law of Propagation that weakens body and mind and brings premature death to the propagators.

Paul (Apollonius) said: **"The commandment, which was ordained to life, I found to be unto death"** (Rom. 7:10).

That commandment states: **"Be fruitful, and multiply, and replenish the earth"** (Gen 1:28).

Paul (Apollonius) continues:

> "For when we were in the flesh, the motions of sin (fornication), which were by the law (of propagation, did work in our (generative) members, to bring forth fruit (offspring) unto death" (Rom. 7:5).
> "For in the day that thou eatest thereof thou shalt surely die" (Gen. 2:17).

The commandment to be fruitful and the penalty of death for being fruitful appeared so paradoxical that Paul (Apollonius) was perplexed. He said:

198

"I find then a law (of propagation) that, when I do good (propagate), evil (death) is present with me." I see another law in my (generative) members, warring against the law (of preservation) of my mind, and bringing me into captivity to the law of sin (fornication) which is in my (generative) members. O wretched man that I am. Who shall deliver me from the body of this death?"
—Rom. 7:21, 23, 24.

Paul (Apollonius) freely taught self-denial. He urged his followers to rise above the plane of propagation, practice chastity, and conserve the Life Essence to improve the mind and preserve the body. That part of his preachment has never been popular with the people nor the clergy.

He knew that propagation sacrifices the parents under the law of compensation. He followed the doctrine of the Ancient Masters contained in Gen. 2:17. He that consumes the Tree of Life cannot escape the sad consequences of the act.

We may satisfy our desires and appease our sensual cravings if we are willing to pay the price. We cannot escape the force of the law of compensation.

We must give of our vital substance in the act to be fruitful. If we do that, we cannot avoid the weakness of mind and deterioration of body that follow.

Methuselah begat his first child at the age of 187 and lived 969 years. Nahor begat his first child at 29 and had a life-span of 148 years.

To consume our vital essence in the sexual act weakens body and brain, dulls the senses, and deteriorates the body. To refrain from the act of propagation conserves the vital essence, sharpens the senses, and invigorates the body.

This law the Ancient Masters saw exemplified in the life of every plant. Plants that produce late live long, while those that produce early die early. Trees that produce prolific annual crops have shorter lives than those that bear little or nothing. The plant lives longest that neither seeds nor propagates.

ANDROGYNY

The value of this mode of living, while unknown to modern science, has been known for ages and recorded by the Ancient Masters in veiled form by symbol and allegory, to guard these great secrets of Life from profanation and abuse, and to protect them from destruction by despots.

The nearest approach to a direct statement of the true state

199

of man appears in the Apocrypha, that part of the scriptures rejected by the church, where it said: "The Kingdom of God shall come and human perfection shall be attained when the forces of the two halves shall become centered in one body, and the outside as the inside, the male with the female in one body and one flesh" (Gen. 2:24).

In his primal perfection man was androgynous, and to that state he will return.

The Vendanta teached that Brahman fell asunder into male and female, and in the struggle of the sundered poles for reunion, "worlds were made." When the poles are again united in one body as before, male with female, there ensues the "night of Brahm," ending the cycle of manifestation.

In the Cycle of Life the ultimate destiny of humanity is a return to the original state, a reversion to the state of Androgyny.

Bipolarity, said the Masters, will be achieved in the longer life cycles, of which an entire incarnation is but a day, by a reversal of the body's inner polarity, so the creative force flows upward to the brain instead of being consumed through the sex organs in propagation.

This will come by proper love unions of the common kind, with the urge of man and woman to unite, consummated in joining the "twin souls seeking reunion with each other," and with rigid conservation of the creative essence, which course has the effect of awakening the female qualities in man and vice versa.

Claude Bragdon says that "Love is only another name for Polarity. It is everything and in everything, from the magnet and the crystal to man himself. But by the perversion of love, the body can become deranged and destroyed."—Yoga For You, 1945.

Women must be taught to choose such men as will develop the dormant male element in them, while men should choose such women as will develop the dormant female element in them. Being thus made whole by the power of love and a life of chastity, they should serve each other loyally and faithfully.

The goal can be achieved by those only who are truly mated to the angel in each, and love each other with a love greater than their own self-love, a love not clouded by lust, vanity, or pride of possession. A love in which there is no sense of otherness. That is Love's self; worshipful, pure, passionate.

Each of the pair should be desirous of pouring out treasures of tenderness and divine benison upon the other. Then their life together will assume a different character, and be productive of entirely different results. Instead of committing them more inexorably to the degrading slavery of sexual passion, it can have the effect of liberating them from it.

"The passion of the blood," says Bragdon, "is but the vestibule to that chamber where true love dwells."

This high state of marital relation is possible only in cases of those drawn together by that mutual attraction which rises from respect and reverence—the halves seeking and finding each other by means of that polar force which attracts certain mutually complementary types to each other.

In the mutual endeavor of these properly united halves to transmute the passion of the blood into the passion of the Spirit by rigid self-denial, lies the hope of humanity. That was the doctrine taught by the Ancient Masters and destroyed by the despots. It is not taught now in any established school on earth.

The pure love-embrace stimulates the gonad glands and they produce more vital essence, which is ordinarily consumed in the act of propagation or in the appeasement of the sensual nature.

When this essence is conserved by the body that makes it by those who conquer the lust of the flesh, then it improves the mind, preserves the body, and prolongs life.

Rulers, despots, and organized institutions are not interested in man's improvement, and oppose by various means any course that leads to his improvement. It is not the intelligent people but the weak-minded that make the better slaves.

LAW OF CONTINENCE

The final phase of Polar Evolution is the "divine marriage" of Sol and Luna—that flight of the Alone to the Alone which makes outer and inner one and the same, a complete unit, joining the poles in one body and eliminating carnal lust, termed love, by closing the "South Gate." This brings to birth the Divine Androgyne.

For man to descend to the divided polar state required many ages, and much time will be required for him to return to the united polar state.

The return trip begins when man begins to observe the law of strict continence. That raises the question whether strict continence is practical and desirable for the average adult.

Medical art says no; but occult science asserts that such problem does not exist for those whose endocrine system is in a state of balance, as in a normal child. And "of such is the kingdom of heaven" on earth (Mat. 19:14).

Some men "made themselves eunuchs for the kingdom of heaven's sake" (Mat. 19:12).

That does not mean such men were emasculated, or that they did not marry. - The hidden meaning is that they lived in strict continence.

Man's epithumetic nature, ruler of the third somatic division of the body, is the power that affects the balanced state of the endocrines.

This power first appears active at puberty, due to the influence of certain psychological conditions, the environment in which one lives, wrong food, and wrong mode of living in general.

If the life-span extended for centuries, as it once did, the evils resulting from the premature activity of the propagative power in the immature would not appear. By a false psycho-physiological standard, the immature are considered mature.

For long ages man has lived on the animal plane psycho-physiologically. He is surrounded by forces which promote that mode of living, and becomes a victim of these bad influences.

The few who desire to rise above that plane must so live as to correct the dysfunction of the endocrine glands, and reduce the hyperactivity of the gonads on the plane of animal propagation.

Marriage promotes propagation on the animal plane. Were that all the damage it does, the marriage state had not been condemned by Paul (Apollonius), who favored marriage only as the lesser of two evils. He said:

"If they cannot contain (control their lust), let them marry; for it is better to marry than to burn" (1 Cor. 7:9).
Some lonesome monk then made this interpolation:
"Marriage is honorable in all, and the bed (is) undefiled" (Heb. 13:4).

The records of the divorce courts in this country do not support that statement.

The Ancient Masters said, In the "resurrection" (higher state) men do not marry, "but are (without lust) as the angels in heaven" (Mat. 22:30).

The statement "do not marry" does not mean that men and women do not unite, and become one flesh under the law (Gen. 2:24). It means that they unite and live in strict continence "as the angels in heaven" do.

The social pattern favors propagation, and few men can escape its influence. The popular belief regards production as woman's chief function in life; and she who produces no progeny in considered a failure.

Strict continence reverses the body's internal polarity, caus-

202

ing the creative (sex) force to flow upward to the Brain, instead of downward to the testes and ovaries—perchance to produce a new person as evidence of failure of the Divine Spirit to attain its higher level; yet at the same time an earnest of its ultimate success through this and future prospects of another chance.

In the fifth chapter of Genesis, verses 1-5, we read:

> "This is the book of the generations of Adam. In the day that God created man, in the likeness of God made he him; Male and female created he them; and blessed them, and called their name Adam (Man). . . . And Adam lived a hundred and thirty years, and begat (a son) in his own likeness, after his image; and called his name Seth. . . . and he begat sons and daughters . . . and he died."

It is important to study the similarity of the expression "in his own likeness, after his image," as referring to creation by God as well as by Adam. Also to note the sequence of all Nature —"he begat . . . and he died."

Grains of wheat have been found in certain tombs of Egypt that were said to be 3000 years old. But when grains of wheat are planted, they begin to disintegrate and perish in the function of propagation.

That is the order of all Creative Processes. In the function of propagation the substance of the ancestor is transmitted to the progeny.

So in the day that man consumes his Life Essence in the function of propagation, his body begins that course of deterioration which brings it to an early grave.

When woman bears, she is on the way out. Her production is the beginning of her premature disintegration. To this law of production Paul (Apollonius) referred when he said:

> "The motions of sin (copulation), which were by the law (of production), did work in our (generative) members to bring forth fruit (progeny) unto death. . . . But sin, taking occasion by the commandment (be fruitful and multiply—Gen. 1:28), wrought in me all manner of concupiscence (desire for sexual pleasure). . . . O wretched man that I am! Who shall deliver me from the body of this death?"—Rom. 7:5, 8, 24.

The "desire for sexual pleasure" the Ancient Masters termed the False Prophet. It deceives by yielding pleasure while destroying the body (Lesson 18).

Paul (Apollonius) devoted much attention to this important subject in his writings, but as they appear in the New Testament they contain so many spurious interpolations that it is very difficult for the layman to understand what he was teaching.

Of course, all references in the so-called Pauline Epistles to Christ Jesus are spurious interpolations, for Paul (Apollonius) never heard of him, and died more than two hundred years before he was invented. In fact, it was Paul (Apollonius) who became the Christ Jesus of the New Testament, as previously stated.

VITAL ADJUSTMENT

The innate power of the body to adjust itself to face conditions forced upon it is a mystery so great that it is little understood by science, as Carrel clearly shows in his remarkable work "Man The Unknown," and which subject we considered quite fully in "Man's Miraculous Unused Powers," a work every one should study.

The primary law of the Universe is that of creation, production, propagation. The action of this law is demonstrated by and in every living object.

The work of creation must always go on and never be halted. It may be hindered temporarily by man. But his refusal to sacrifice himself in the function of propagation, as all other animals and insects do, cannot block indefinitely the work of creation in man.

When human male and female halves unite, and their love arouses to a high pitch the inherent desire to propagate and thus serve the law, the halves rise above the law of propagation when they refuse to sacrifice themselves by consuming their Life Essence in the production of progeny, and come under "grace," said Paul (Apollonius) (Rom. 6:12, 14), which in this case means the Law of Preservation.

It is preposterous for science to suggest that man's refusal to propagate could or would halt indefinitely the work of creation. If that could be done, this would make man superior to the Law of Creation.

Such refusal will halt only temporarily the work of creation. It does something else that is greatly beneficial for humanity.

When the refusal is continued, it will in time and by slow degrees cause such adjustments in the body's creative centers as will have the ultimate effect of balancing the polar forces, as they were in the beginning, and causing the body to adjust itself and revert to its original state of androgyny, thus becoming capable of propagation by asexual generation, under the Law

204

of Creative Thought, as explained by Clements in his work titled "Science of Regeneration."

That is the ultimate goal of Regeneration as taught by the Ancient Masters.

ASEXUAL GENERATION

Buried in the folk lore of very ancient races appears the legend that originally man was a bisexual, creative Unit.

This legend symbolizes much that has been discovered in recent years about the similarity of the sexes—that the glandular systems of male and female are closely related. The one is simply a variation of the other.

The actual difference between man and woman is one of degrees and not of anatomical structure.

Ancient legend states that man was made in the image and likeness of the Creator (Gen. 1:26).

The second chapter of Genesis contains another and different account of man's creation. It says that after man was made he gave birth to wo-man, so-called because taken from the womb of man.

This story states in the fourth chapter that the man and woman became the parents of three children, Cain, Abel and Seth.

In the fifth chapter still another story of creation appears. It seems to be part of the first account. For it refers to man created in the likeness of God.

"Male and female (in one body) created He them, and blessed them, and called their name Adam" (Red Clay) (Gen. 5:2).

This bisexual man was 130 years old when he "begat a son in his own likeness, after his image (bisexual, creative unit), and called his name Seth" (Gen. 5:1-3).

In this story Cain and Abel are unknown. This evidence shows that the ancient scribe compiled his work from different sources.

This man appears to be the one mentioned in very ancient folk lore as a bisexual, creative unit.

Philosophical anthropologists assert that a time was in the prehistoric past, while forms we know were in process of formation, when the polar forces of the body were so evenly balanced that each body was a complete unit, possessing in itself the complete power of propagation.

They hold that as time passed some bodies, because of erroneous living, became so "lopsided" in the polar region that they tended toward much greater strength in their male tributes, while others were over-emphasized in their feminine qualities.

Gradually this divergence increased, age after age, until those that were most abnormal bisexually had to seek union with another body that was excessively developed in the opposite qualities.

For a bisexed body that had grown so weak in its male powers as to require, in propagation, the aid of a body intensely masculine and correspondingly weak in its female aspect, would tend rapidly to atrophy in that sex which, already weakened, it now ceased to exercise at all within itself.

A reconstructed picture of that transition period, which doubtless occupied millions of years, would be the observance of bisexual beings having the preponderance of female qualities seeking to obtain the semen, which they no longer possessed the power to elaborate and excrete to any practical extent, from other bodies in which there was an excessive production of semen.

The bodies that specialized in supplying semen, at the expense of their feminine qualities, finally became so exceedingly masculine that they ceased even to remember that they had ever possessed definite female qualities.

To suggest such a thing now to the scientific evolutionist brings only a smile of pity for such display of ignorance. But his theory of evolution does far greater things than changing man from bisexuality to unisexuality. His theory changes the beast to the human, the ape to man.

Incalculable periods of time would be required to bring this stage of development down to our present strictly unisexual state. Yet there is sufficient evidence still remaining to show that both sexes are present in all persons, despite the extent to which the one or the other has apparently entirely disappeared.

This theory offers the only consistent and scientific explanation of the hermaphroditic "throw back" known to medical investigation, and is further evidence in support of the theory.

The evolutionist has never found a man so changed that he was returning to the ape stage. Yet that same evolutionist will scorn the suggestion that the hermaphrodite is a partial reversion to the original bisexual stage.

Homosexual tendencies are more understandable in this light. That condition is actually an extreme case of that present in all persons in moderation.

Deep students of the Life Cycle assert that the human body must, in time, regain its lost bisexual powers. In that case, the despised homosexuals are the present pioneers on this very long and very dark road.

They are what they are now because of the partial awakening within them of the dormant bisexual qualities. Of course they are abusing the principle, but what else can be expected when the whole subject is buried in confusion and misunderstanding, and not even open for intelligent discussion.

With the increasing light on sexology, bravely advanced by sincere students in this field, humanity will yet gather the courage to look at the subject squarely and correctly.

In that day great improvement and undreamed of benefits will begin to accrue to mankind.

Lesson No. 52

THE LIFE GLANDS

The Lungs are the Life Organs that sustain the body. The Gonads are the Life Glands that sustain the race.

To stay the breath is to stop the living. To destroy the gonads not only stops the production of progeny, but changes and damages the body.

The gonads rule the Endocrine System. When they were rediscovered in the early part of this century, it was excitedly proclaimed by medical art that Man is what his Ductless Glands. make him. The fact was not recognized that these glands are also what man's mode of living makes them.

The gonads are ruled by the Brain. As a man thinketh so is he (Prov. 23:7). Degrading are his thoughts whose brain is governed by his gonads.

That is the reverse of what should be. Yet that is the common condition of modern man. He should rule his desires, but most men are ruled by their desires.

The god (brain) of the body has become the slave of the servant (gonads); and the god of the earth, created to have dominion over all living things (Gen. 1:26), has become a lowly degenerate, ruled by lust and led by those who preach spirituality yet usually live on the lowest plane of materiality.

Scientific investigation shows a close correlation between the gonads and the rest of the body. Every change in these glands, every use or misuse of them, reacts definitely on the entire body.

Normal development of the body and normal body function are impossible without these glands. This is strikingly shown in the condition of castrated males and spayed females in the case of animals as well as human beings.

Castrated roosters fail to grow the male comb, wattles, spurs, decorative tail feathers, and resemble a hen. Spayed hens develop the rooster's external characteristics, from which it is naturally inferred that the body's internal organs undergo a similar change toward the male.

The gelding is lacking in the vitality, in the form, and in the long flowing mane, gracefully arched, powerful neck and the beautiful tail of the stallion, and resembles a mare. The steer lacks the broad powerful neck and vitality of the bull, and resembles a cow.

If the male deer is castrated after its antlers are grown, they are never shed again. If a stag is castrated when its horns are off, they never grow out again. If castrated when the horns are "in velvet," the velvet remains and dries and hardens.

If a boy is castrated before puberty, his voice does not change, his shoulders fail to broaden, his beard does not appear, and he fattens easily. He resembles a woman more than a man in both mental and physical qualities.

If a girl is spayed before puberty, her hips do not broaden, her breasts do not develop, she tends to accumulate fat, may develop a beard, and resembles a man more than a woman both psychologically and physically.

The mental qualities of men, women and animals are changed and affected as much as are their physical. The gelding lacks the vim, vigor and valor of the stallion. The same may be said of the steer, the capon, the castrated man and spayed woman.

Steers, geldings and bars are more docile and more easily handled than bulls, stallions and boars. The same applies to human beings.

Some boys begin to masturbate when only 12 or 14, and some even sooner. The effect is similar to castration, but of lesser degree. The body is not deprived of all the precious fluid manufactured by the gonads as in the case of castration.

The Ancient Masters termed the gonads the "destructive glands." They function for life or death depending on the set of the lever. Their function perpetuates the race. In that process man sacrifices in no small degree his own self. Much worse is his dissipation of Life Essence for pleasure only.

In the case of some insects, the function of fertilization by the male is the act of expiration for that male.

A grain of wheat seems to disintegrate and die in the process of production. It is really born again in the function of the old being sacrificed in begetting the new.

Paul (Apollonius) cited the case of "bare grain" to explain "how are the dead raised up? and with what body do they come?"

—1 Cor. 15:35. For scientific reasons he did not cite the physical resurrection of the gospel Jesus.

The same law ruling wheat also applies in the case of man, whose body sinks below the high plane of physical animation in the state termed death, when he is really born again on the higher plane of spirituality, as explained in our work titled "Immortalism."

Paul (Apollonius) referred to the "born again" state as "a mystery," and said "We shall not sleep, but we shall all be changed" (1 Cor. 15:51).

In the lower but complex forms of life, the parent literally resolves its whole substance into reproductive material, the maturing of this material being apparently the death of the parent. In certain low forms of life, the parent becomes only a shell to hold the progeny, which is freed when the shell bursts at maturity.

In the vast majority of insects, their entire existence is merely for the preparation of a brief moment of transcendent life (propagation), followed almost at once by total extinction.

The larvae of the mayfly lie in mud under stones or in grass in the bed of streams, before they finally emerge as Imagoes— "delicate, fairy forms on gossamer wings. They do not eat; they are never to taste of food as Imagoes. They flit about for a few hours. Delicate as the morning mist, they emerge from the mud, love, then give back to the earth the seeds of their love, and die —all in the course of a short summer day, which may seem a long life to them. Propagation, the supreme sacrifice, and death.

The sacrifice incident to propagation appears in all living forms, including man. Some authorities state that indulgence in the sex function cuts two hundred years from the life-span of the average man.

Generation is destructive, but is orderly, lawful, and has its compensation in propagation. The old is replaced by the new.

The Microcosm is the product of the Macrocosm. We think of the mother as the producer, but she is not. She is only the medium through which the Macrocosm produces, and she becomes the medium only as long as she maintains sufficient quality, and she bears only when she is on the way out, the beginning of which is indulgence in fornication.

BATTERY POLES UNITED

Paul (Apollonius) seems to have failed to recognize the importance of complying with the law by the union of the dual poles of the human battery. He said:

209

"It is good for a man not to touch a woman." "I say therefore to the unmarried and widows, it is good for them if they abide even as I (single). But if they cannot contain (control their sex urge), let them marry; for it is better to marry than to burn" (1 Cor. 7:1, 8, 9).

It had been more proper had he taught his audience how to overcome their epithumetic nature instead of submitting to its power. It may be that he had too little faith in humanity to attempt that. How many men and women will live together as husband and wife and refuse, for their own good, to yield to the power of their epithumetic nature?

Some have said that this man submitted to castration to make it impossible for him to break the Law of Virginity. The truth of this cannot now be ascertained. Much of that was done in his day in the case of religious zealots, ruled by fanaticism instead of common sense, as they are now.

God never intended for the body to be mutilated. Each body loses much by living separately or by being unsexed. Man and woman should be properly mated and united, according to cosmic law. Then the one receives from the other the benefit that naturally flows from a battery made whole by proper union of the poles.

Paul (Apollonius) was great, but even greater he had been had he united with the right woman, and they together preserved their bodies and prolonged their lives by living as virgins.

That is the higher path of life. In that way must live they who would rise above the animal plane. Or they must prefer the other path and sacrifice themselves on the social altar of parenthood.

It is law that the more we refrain from exercising the sex function for propagation or for pleasure, the less we care to do so.

Choose your path, and the body will soon obey. Do the thing, and the power to do it will increase. Some men have caused their sex organs to lapse into dormancy by refusing to indulge in the sex function. This shows how completely man gains control over his body as he works for it. The body is a good servant but a poor master.

SEX POWER AND POLARITY

Modern science is materialistic. It will consider nothing in the case of man beyond the physical. To do so would negate its

210

theories of evolution and make necessary the rewriting of its textbooks.

The Ancient Masters' conception of man was far different from that of modern science. It included both spiritual and physical man. 'Modern science says that spiritual man is a myth of the heathens.

The work of the Masters included spiritology, astrology, numerology, alchemy, palmistry, and other branches of science beyond the boundaries of the physical.

Considered in this respect, the body appears highly complicated, yet simplified because based on a few cosmic laws which admit of no exceptions, and many of which laws modern science refuses to recognize.

Three of these laws are highly important. One is the Law of Cosmic Rhythm; another is the Law of Polarity, or Sex Power, as it relates to production by a union of opposites and their reciprocal relation to each other. A third is the Law of Correspondence, relating to the fundamental identity between things apparently unrelated, as the body to its environment, formulated in the Hermic doctrine, As within, so without.

Microcosmic man being one with Macrocosmic or Grand Man, he was symbolized by the Masters as crucified on the zodiac cross, each of the twelve constellations or houses being related to a particular part of the body or its organs, and between them exists a harmonious vibration.

The right half of the body is considered positive, masculine, and the left, negative, feminine. The lower part is related to the instinctive nature, or will, and the upper to the reflective nature or intellect.

Polarity means the state of having opposite poles, positive and negative. It is the basis of creative processes. Even the atoms are composed of positive and negative elements or forces.

Some term the human body a magnet. It has two poles. The right side is positive and the left negative. At the point that divides the polar regions, the body is neither, being a blend of both.

Each pole receives from the environment a subtle form of force, and radiates to the environment a similar force.

The force received and radiated by the positive pole differs from that of the negative.

Ether is static force. It consists of positive and negative properties, fills all space and interpenetrates all solids, liquids and gases.

The term Sex should convey a much deeper meaning than the mere manifestation of man's natural propensity to propagate. Basically, the term means Cosmic Polarity.

When the Unit differentiates duality, as explained in detail in our work titled "Immortalism," the dual parts have an innate instinct to rejoin and form the Unit. In so doing they create the Trinity. The union of the primordial principles results in production, and we have father, mother and child.

Propagation causes deterioration of the organism. The function of production is one of expending the body's vital essence. When we expend that essence we weaken our organism.

The Microcosm is the product of the Macrocosm. The mother is not the actual producer. She is the medium through which the Macrocosm produces, and she is that medium only as long as she maintains sufficient quality. She bears only when on the way out, the beginning of which is fornication.

As thou eatest of the Tree of Life, dying thou shalt die is far more truth than poetry (Gen. 2:17).

On the humanistic plane, the polar power seeks for a perfect union. The urge succeeds only when male and female principles present harmonious polarization on the physical, mental and spiritual planes.

Records of the divorce courts show that many unions occur between those who do not harmonize on the three principal planes of being.

The purely physical urge to propagate results from the descending course of the Serpentine Fire, the "good serpent," the Light of the Logos.

This force intensifies the function of the Tree of Life, causing an increase in the elaboration of the Divine Essence, with an increase of mental power resulting, provided the product of the function is conserved.

Gratification of the urge to propagate is proper on the animal plane. It affords the only form of creativity of which the animal is capable. Being creative, it is proper on that plane.

Most men live on the animal plane of production, and yield to the impulse to propagate. The Masters lived above it. They produced philosophies instead of families.

Woman is taught that her function in life has not been fulfilled if she fails to produce. So she thinks its proper to live on the animal plane of production, and is taught nothing higher. Some governments promote production by offering premiums to women who produce the most children.

That is the social pattern plane. Few rise above it. The rulers favor it, for it furnishes more slaves for them and more soldiers for their wars.

The body that thus expends its vital essence must deteriorate. **No one could be an Initiate of the Ancient Mysteries who did not conserve his vital essence. That was the first requirement. If the candidate failed there, he was rejected.** For he had consumed the substance that builds up body and mind to the high plane of Seer and Master.

For that reason the rulers opposed the Ancient Mystery Schools, until their final destruction was accomplished. It was Constantine, in the fourth century A.D. who started the last movement which ended the existence of the greatest school the world has ever known.

Yet, the school still lives. Being opposed and persecuted by the rulers, the Masters went "underground" and conducted their work in secret.

That is another reason why these schools were termed the Mysteries. For their protection, their work was shrouded in the greatest of secrecy, and the rituals and ceremonies were never permitted to be put in writing that could be read and understood by the profane. That is the reason why the Bible is a book of symbol and allegory, and why the church has never been able to interpret the Apocalypse.

PRANIC POWER

From birth to death the lungs incessantly perform the function of respiration. With each inhalation man receives from the invisible world atomic force or Pranic Power. Stay the breathing and we stop the living.

Some hold that as the oxygen of the air contacts the blood in the lungs, a form of combustion occurs, and the blood absorbs oxygen and emits carbonic acid gas, which is ejected from the lungs at each expiration.

What occurs in the lungs is not exactly known. Cockren, in his book published in 1939, titled "Alchemy Rediscovered and Restored," claims that breathing is not merely inhalation of oxygen, but of "Cosmic Electricity."

He then upset the medical theory that the heart is a pump. He asserted that it is not. He considered it a central valve in the blood vascular system and a regulator of the blood flow.

In Yoga literature, Prana is termed "vital force." It is the cosmic radiation of modern science which, along with much more numerous "secondaries," is scientifically proven to penetrate the earth's atmosphere not only down to sea level, but much deeper. Others contend that it passes clear through the earth.

The Masters considered Prana far móre than breath. It is that Cosmic Radiation that centers in the Solar Plexus and is desseminated throughout the body. It is the Life Principle of the Universe.

The Masters taught that Cosmic Radiation presents two opposing but equilibrium properties—positive and negative. The proper balance of these forces govern birth, development, decline and disintegration of all living things.

The Masters taught that man's two nostrils are positive and negative. The positive elements of the air enter the right, and the negative enter the left.

THE KANDA

Near the base of the back-bone there lies a gland larger than a hen's egg, called the Prostate. It contacts the lower part of the bladder, and through it the urethra passes as it leaves the bladder.

Modern science knows little about this gland, its function, or the purpose of its excretions.

Little also is known of this gland in women. Some hold that there is an "absence of a distinct Prostate in woman." Others assert that the gland is present, but smaller than in man.

The ejaculatory tubes of the male testes enter this gland, and between it and the pubis is the rich venous pudendal plexus, in which ends the dorsal vein of the penis.

The Masters called this gland the Kanda, and termed it the seat of the Kundalini Power. To possess that remarkable power in a functional degree, the gland must be in a normal, healthy state.

What are the facts? In elderly men the gland often hypertrophies, and not infrequently calcareous concretions are found embedded in it—all the result of wrong living.

In many men the gland is affected by a disorder termed prostatitis, which is a frequent complication of gonorrhea. In but few men is the gland found in a normal, healthy state. Remember this well, for this is the seat of the Serpentine Fire.

It is true that women, as a rule, are more psychic than men, and we are learning the reason why. Their glands of psychic function are, as a rule, in much better condition.

An oily substance is excreted by the Prostate, which is subject to varied degrees of consistency, from a thin, volatile oil that promptly evaporates when exposed to the air, to a fixed oil that produces permanent stains on paper.

It is this oil that stains the linen in cases of nocturnal emissions, which occur in men who have weakened their creative centers by early masturbation and sexual excesses.

In healthy, wise, vigorous men it is a fixed oil. In the average man it is more or less volatile. In young men of dissolute habits it becomes filthy. In "rakes" it is very malodorous and may contain pus. Here is the seat of the terrible venereal disorders that afflict mankind.

To attempt to teach such people the secret of the Serpentine Fire would be preposterous. And yet, this is the kind of people of which most of the multitude is composed.

This oil, excreted by the Prostate, enters the blood and is carried all over the body. It is one of the basic constituents of the blood and, in its purest state, the Greeks termed it Chrism.

Then came the church fathers. When they compiled the New Testament and presented an actor to play the part of the Serpentine Fire, they labelled everything good as "Christ" to deceive the masses.

So the Greek "Chrism" became the "Blood of Christ" (Heb. 10:19; 1 Pet. 1:2; 1 Jn. 1:7).

A later lesson will explain how this fraud came to be known as "the Christ in man" (Col. 1:24, 27). Those who reject the fraud are promptly termed "athiests" by the church.

The Prostate consists of muscular and glandular tissue, and has twelve to twenty excretory ducts which pour their products into the blood and into the urethra.

The thick, slippery, milky fluid slowly discharged from the penis under the influence of erotic thoughts, nocturnal emissions, or sexual stimulation, is supplied largely by the Prostate, with some help from the Cowper's glands.

This fluid constitutes a large part of the liquid portion of the semen, and, while it is necessary to the life of the spermatozoa, it contains none.

The Cowper's glands are a pair of small organs located just beyond and below the Prostate. They produce a mucous fluid and, with the Prostate, contribute part of the liquid portion of the semen. In woman these organs are termed Bartholin's glands.

The Prostate was known to the Masters as the Kanda, meaning a bulb; and in the New Testament (Greek), as the Kardia.

In Yoga literature the Kanda is said to be a center of the astral body. From it rise 72,000 Nadis, termed astral tubes, composed of astral matter. They carry psychic currents (Kundalini Yoga, p. 40).

215

In modern man the currents are exceedingly weak, or practically absent, due to the degenerate state of the gland and to sexual excess.

Pranic Power flows through these Nadis. As they are composed of astral substance, they are beyond the reach of material science, and no test-tube experiments can be made of them on the physical plane. For that reason modern science rejects all the Ancient Masters said on the subject. But as the Mind is known by its work, so they are known by their function.

Of all the Nadis, the most important are the Sushumna, the Ida and the Pingala. The Sushumna, of which Christ Jesus was a symbol, is the chief. It extends from the Muladhara Chakra, or second vertebra of the coccygeal region, "to Brahmarandhra," which term means "the hole of Brahma," (top of head), where dwells "the soul of man."

Brahmarandhra is the soft place in the crown of a baby's head that is later obliterated by the growth of the head bones.

The Hindus hold that "Brahma created the physical body and, to give it internal illumination, entered it through the Brahmarandhra and dwells therein."

The Ida and Pingala Nadis, the thieves crucified on each side of Christ Jesus, are not the gross sympathetic nerves, but are said to be the subtle Nadis that carry the "Sukshma Prana." In the physical body these tentatively correspond to the right and left sympathetic nerve chains.

Ida starts from the right portion of the scrotum and Pingala from the left. They meet with the Sushumna at the Muladhara Chakras and there form a knot.

Ida extends up to the left nostril and Pingala to the right. Ida is negative and also called Chandra Nadi (moon), and Pingala is positive and also called Surya Nadi (Sun). Ida is cooling; Pingala is heating.

The Ancient Masters knew that the Sun and Moon, in their respective courses around the Zodiac due to the earth's motion and position, are also travelling in the human body in their corresponding orbits.

The Masters taught that during each lunar month, as the moon passes through the twelve signs of the Zodiac, the negative etheric current shifts to another part of the body, until it travels from heels to head, and from head back again, in a complete circuit.

The center of influence or the part of the body at which the negative current is concentrated each day, was said by the Masters to be a vulnerable spot in the body on that day.

In the same way during each lunar month, the focal center

of the positive etheric current shifts from one part of the body to another, also making a complete circuit.

The cool moon-breath in Ida sprinkles its cooling nectar over the body; and the hot sun-breath in Pingala dries it up.

THE SECRET GATE

Instead of irregularity in the breath flow, the Masters found that law and order prevail here as in all other departments of the body. They discovered that the dual breathing function is governed by a sensitive nerve center at the root of the nose where the two nostrils converge.

The body channels have valves. The veins and heart have valves to control blood flow. In each nostril there is a valve to control the air flow.

The function of the nose valve, as the body needs positive or negative Pranic Power, is regulated by this nerve center, under brain control.

Not constantly does air flow through both nostrils at the same time. It flows through one at a time; but from time to time, depending on the body's needs, it flows for short intervals through both nostrils.

If the body needs more of the positive breath, the brain keeps closed for a longer period the valve of the left nostril, and vice versa.

The Masters found that in good health, the breath flows for approximately an hour through one nostril, and then changes to the other for the same period.

In good health, the body functions naturally. So both nostrils, under control of the brain, inhale air as they should, resulting in a state of equilibrium, provided the rest of the body is in good order.

Under these balanced conditions, it said the breath flow changes hourly, entering the right nostril for an hour, and then the left for an hour, governed by the Secret Gate, mentioned in Lesson No. 16, under Astral Body Structure.

In the polluted air of civilization, man's breathing has grown so shallow and irregular, that it may be said he never breathes naturally.

Polluted air from the day of birth, tobacco smoke and other poisons in the air, cause the body to make this adjustment for protection. If man breathed deeper of the polluted air, it would shorten his days. So to let him live longer, the body automatically adjusts itself to all adverse conditions forced upon it. Make no attempt to change body function unless you first change environment.

Realizing the high importance of the nerve center controlling the breath, the Masters practiced certain breathing exercises in the pure air of the hills and high places to keep this vital air center in proper working order.

When normal, this nerve center is the Gate to Life; but it is the Gate to Death when deranged or abnormal due to polluted air. In the millions living in the polluted air of civilization, that nerve center was ruined when they were children.

In good health, a very rare condition in civilization, the function of the Secret Gate, under brain control, is automatic, involuntary, and performed without conscious knowledge, just as stomach action and heart function are.

Man becomes conscious of body function only when something is wrong. Then he consults a doctor who lives and thrives on man's miseries.

Man knows not that he has stomach, liver, or kidneys until they are deranged by his bad habits and bother him. Then he consults a doctor instead of searching for the cause and removing it.

Too much negative breath is bad. Negative people are unbalanced. They breathe largely through the left nostril, but know it not. This is due to valvular defect in the Secret Gate. No doctor can remedy it. Pure air is the only remedy.

Negative people lack vitality and endurance; their health is poor, and they treat ailments they do not have. They cannot endure much cold, and are chilly in a temperature warm enough for comfort for one in good health.

The Masters used the positive breath to generate extra body heat. They could endure cold without clothing as a dog or a horse, even living nude in snow and ice.

Ages ago, before man degenerated, his body functions were natural as they are now in wild animals. In cold regions, animals live and sleep with comfort in holes in snow and ice. The dog, without discomfort, trots all day in snow with naked feet. Nor do these animals have colds, coughs, influenza, pneumonia, hay fever, smallpox, tonsilitis, asthma, scarlet fever, measels, mumps, croup, whooping cough, tuberculosis, diphtheria—all the result of breathing the polluted air of civilization.

TWO NERVE CURRENTS

The Ida and Pingala are two important nerve currents in the

spinal column, as mentioned in Lesson Number 16. There the channel Sushumna is also mentioned.

At each inhalation, Pranic Power travels along the Ida and Pingala and, after circulating up and down, passes out through the nostrils.

When the Ida is active, the left nostril is in flow, the Pingala is inactive, and the valve of the right nostril remains closed.

When the right nostril is in flow, the Pingala selects from each inhalation the positive gases and carries them down the right side of the spine.

When the right nostril flow predominates, such people evince positive characteristics and unusual aggressiveness; and, in certain men, unbridled sexual passion.

When the left nostril flow predominates, such people exhibit negative characteristics, such as fear, timidity, submission, docility, obedience, and also virtues such as truthfulness, kindness, benevolence, and reverence.

The Sushumna, while not directly connected with either nostril, begins at the base of the Medulla Oblongata, extends down the central channel of the spine, and ends at the coccyx, where Ida, Pingala and Sushumna are connected. When the Sushumna or both nostrils are in flow, the valves of both nostrils are open and both Ida and Pingala are active.

The two currents which flow alternately down Ida and Pingala, meet at the solar plexus and other plexi of the sympathetic nerve system which lie along the spinal column, and supply Pranic Power to activate the body.

The Cerebro-spinal nerve system is the organ of the conscious mind, and the Sympathetic nerve system is the organ of the subconscious. The former is the channel through which we receive conscious perception from the physical senses and exercise control over body movements.

SPIRITUAL CHAMBERS

In Lesson Number 22 of "Man's Miraculous Unused Powers" under "Spiritual Organs," we listed the five Spiritual Chambers in the head.

Into these there flows from the Cosmic Ocean of Ether a peculiar gaseous substance, a subtle essence termed Mental Spirit by the Masters.

In the Masters this essence produced a paranormal state that gave them unlimited knowledge when activated by the Serpentine Fire.

It is hard for this to be understood by civilized man in whom the spiritual centers are deficient, dormant, degenerated by the evil effects of polluted air.

Unless these Spiritual Chambers are in natural function, then no illumination can result from the raising of the Serpentine Fire.

The term paranormal means beyond the scope of physical law, and is a more fitting term than supernatural, as the supernatural may be very natural and common when understood.

Within the root of the nose, where the two nostrils converge and the Ida and Pingala are located, is one of the most vital spots in the body.

This is actually the Throne of the Most High within the Temple, and the chief spiritual center in man. On the ancient monuments appeared the head of a man, with a Serpent on his forehead at this point, the same being a symbol of the activation of this center by the Serpentine Fire.

This is the Cosmic Television Station that gave the Masters the spiritual power which enabled them to vision things not seen with the physical eye—such as the paranormal powers of certain South American Indians mentioned in Lesson Number 22 referred to above.

The Television Station is aided by the companion center, the Pituitary Gland, which functions as the brain's radio station and receives messages from distant space.

This cosmic phenomena, lost for ages to civilized man, is now presented in man-made machines, and that enables us to understand better the miraculous powers of the Masters.

The Masters who possessed these powers knew the body was only an instrument through which the Incarnated God-Spirit manifests on the physical plane, a fact so clearly stated by the scribe who knew what he meant when he said:

"Know ye not that ye are the temple of God, and that the Spirit of God dwelleth in you, and, therefore, must be you" (1 Cor. 3:16).

Lesson No. 53

THE GREAT PARABLE

The Great Parable of the Bible begins with the first book thereof and ends with the last.

When the first story of Creation ends, the second begins with the fourth verse of the second chapter of Genesis, and it recites

220

the puzzling parable to the effect that in the day man "eats" of the "Tree of Knowledge," he will begin to die (Gen. 2:17).

In the third chapter of Genesis the parable presents "the Serpent" that can talk, and to the woman says:

"For God doth know that in the day ye eat thereof, then your eyes shall be opened, and ye shall be as gods, **knowing Good and Evil**" (vs. 5).

Books have been written in attempts to interpret this parable. Some of them have dealt with "Phallic Worship," "Sex Worship," and the "Sacred Fire."

Westropp presents in his book a picture of what he terms the "worship of the Linga-Yoni in India."

Dr. Wall, in his book of 600 pages, says, "In all Pagan religions the deepest and most awe-inspiring attributes of Nature was the power of reproduction . . . To ancient Pagan thinkers . . . the key to the hidden secret of the origin and preservation of the Universe lay in the mystery of Sex" (p. 377).

Goldberg, in his work on "The Sacred Fire," saw nothing in ancient religions but sex worship, and presents pictures of ancient scenes to support his views.

As we proceed we shall see how close these authors came to the vital point, and yet missed it entirely.

THE ENDOCRINE GLANDS

In man's own body we must search for the secrets concealed in the symbols and allegories of the Bible. In the next lesson we shall see that a solution of this parable involves the ductless glands and their functions.

The Ancient Masters were not ignorant heathens as we have been taught in order to deceive us. They were scientists of the first order. Their parables conceal, in symbol and allegory, certain profound facts they had discovered as to the psycho-physical departments of the body.

Medical art knows so little as yet about the various departments of the body and their functions, that when it first found the ductless glands a few years ago, they were regarded as "hangover appendages from the ape days of man," and no longer useful to him. So the doctors began clipping them out and casting them into the garbage can. As their victims died soon afterwards, medical art took another look and decided the endocrine system of glands must be of some use to the body.

221

The press of October 27th, 1936, stated that Dr. Hans Lisser, "distinguished clinical professor of medicine at the University of California medical school," had listed "five modern miracles accomplished by endocrinology—the study of the ductless glands."

More "medical progress." "Miracles" are now "accomplished by endocrinology" in the life of man, whereas only twenty-five short years ago so little was thought by medical art of these same glands, that they were cut out and cast away.

SEX CHANGES INVOLVED

Some of these "miracles" are mentioned by Lisser, and we shall quote what he said about these glands affecting sex:

"For years the medical world was puzzled by such cases as this: A woman, say 30 years old who perhaps had borne children, would begin to turn into a man. She would grow a beard, her breasts would wither, her voice deepen, and she would present other attributes of a man. Through the learning of endocrinology, it is now possible to re-feminintize such women."

"This may be done if we are able to locate and remove a tumor of the adrenal glands, or a certain type of ovarian tumor, or a lesion of the pituitary gland."

"Every woman possesses masculine qualities or potentialities. Every man has a certain number of sex hormones in his blood, and vice versa. When the male hormones predominate, we have a man. When there is an excessive number of female hormones, we have a rather effeminate man. Because there are too many male hormones present, we have some virile, aggressive women."

"When a tumor appears on one of the glands mentioned, the excretion of female hormones is retarded, and male qualities begin to predominate. By removing the tumor, we return the woman to her normal balance."

It is interesting to observe the marked effect the excretions of the ductless glands have on the sexual centers of the body.

Compared to the Ancient Masters, modern science is in only the primary stages of its work regarding the mysterious ductless gland system.

Because of the peculiar part they play in man's development, and the general ignorance of medical art as to their function it is important to give more attention to the Pineal and Pituitary glands.

The Pineal lies on the posterior side of the Thalamus, attached to it by delicate nerves, and joined to the roof of the third ventricle by a flattened stalk, the habenula.

This gland is the positive spiritual organ. It is the gland through which the positive, electrical force of the body flows; the "Crystalline Dew" from heaven (brain).

Some of this wonderful esse, the Father, flows down from the upper brain into the Pineal, where it is differentiated, becoming golden in color, as it is excreted by the Pineal, and, in quality and action, is masculine, positive, electrical.

On the opposite side of the Thalmus, slightly lower down, is the Pituitary. It is the negative, female gland of spirituality, and also receives its esse, the Father, the undifferentiated substance from which all things are produced.

As this substance is differentiated by the Pituitary, it is excreted by the gland as a whitish fluid—the milk and honey of the Bible (Num. 13:27).

In quality and action, this fluid is feminine, negative, magnetic, drawing or pulling. The gland is provided with a small gossamer sac for the reception of the spiritual seed.

The fluid of these two glands flows down the central canal of the spinal cord (Jordan), and reach the Solar Plexus via the semilunar ganglia (Sea of Galilee).

CREATIVE POWER OF THE PITUITARY

We find here a secret, well-known to the Masters many thousands of years ago, but only recently discovered by modern science.

In matters concerning the body and its functions, Alexis Carrel was the greatest scientist of modern times. He frankly admitted that medical art knows little about the psychology and physiology of the body. It has developed no Law of Psychology and Physiology. So he wrote: "In fact, our ignorance (of the body and its functions) is profound" (Man The Unknown, p. 4).

The Masters based the puzzling Edenic Parable on their knowledge of the function of the Pituitary and other glands. They knew that this gland is a veritable control center of the body, pouring into the blood no less than six different hormones, as modern science has recently discovered; and these exert dictatorial power over the entire ductless gland system.

This powerful force of the Pituitary in the department of propagation must be subdued by those striving for the higher

life; as it is this force, affecting the female body, that urges propagation on the animal plane.

The Microcosm is the product of the Macrocosm. The so-called mother is not the producer. She is only the medium through which the Macrocosm produces; and the mother becomes that medium only as long as she maintains sufficient quality, and she bears only when she is on the way out, the beginning of which is indulgence in fornication.

As perpetuation of the race depends primarily and ultimately on the female, the creative law acts forcibly and directly on her organism, causing woman, in her unisexual state, to seek the male for help that she may fulfill the law.

So the Masters warned woman that if she yielded to the creative urge it would:—

> "Greatly multiply thy sorrow and thy conception; in sorrow thou shalt bring forth children; and thy desire shall be to thy husband, and he shall rule over thee" (Gen. 3:16).

They cautioned man to help woman by refusing to yield to her influence, but he ignored the warning; and so:—

> "Because thou hast harkened unto the voice of thy wife, and hast eaten of the tree, of which we commanded thee, saying, Thou shalt not eat of it; cursed is the ground for thy sake; in sorrow shall thou eat of it all the days of thy life; thorns also and thistles shall it bring forth to thee" (Gen. 3:16-18).

224

Little good has it ever done the masses to be warned by the Masters. And in every age covered by history the rulers and despots have objected to any teaching that benefits man by increasing his knowledge. For learned people never make docile slaves.

Hence, down through the ages the Masters have been murdered to still their voices and keep the masses in ignorance. So it was necessary for the teachings of the Masters to be concealed in symbol and allegory in order to preserve it from destruction.

HE THAT OVERCOMETH

We saw that the Book of Revelation is devoted exclusively to this greatest of all subjects in human life. It refers to the Edenic Parable, and covers, in symbol and allegory, the strange things that occur in the body of those who dedicate themselves to the higher life; and states that the great reward bestowed upon those who "overcometh" that powerful epithumetic nature **is a New Heaven (Brain) and a New Earth (Body). That is the New Jerusalem (Rev. 21).**

In the day that man consumes his vital essence in the process of propagation, then and there begins he to deteriorate physically and sink toward the grave.

For man sacrifices himself in the production of New Life just as does a grain of corn. Unplanted, the grain keeps for years, but it begins to deteriorate the day it is planted.

That is the beginning and the end of the worth-while teachings of ancient scriptures. That kind of teaching begins in the second chapter of Genesis and ends in Revelation.

In the day that thou eatest thereof, dying thou shalt die (Gen. 2:17). But he that "overcometh" his epithumetic nature shall receive freely "of the Fountain of the Waters of Life," and "shall inherit all things" that make life really worth living— **health and happiness (Rev. 21:6, 7).**

SPECIAL NERVES

Two special nerves are connected with the Pineal and Pituitary, called Ida and Pingala.

Pingala is connected with the Pineal. It crosses the spinal cord at the base of the brain in the medulla, and extends down the right side of the spinal cord to its end.

Ida is connected with the Pituitary. It crosses the spinal cord at the same place where Pingala crosses, and extends down the left side of the cord to its base.

Here these two nerves converge into the body through the smiluna ganglion, where they merge into the solar plexus.

The Pneumogastric Nerve must be noticed. It rises in the floor of the fourth ventricle of the brain and is connected with the cerebellum. It crosses the spinal cord at the base of the skull, producing a double cross made by this nerve, the Ida and Pingala.

The Pneumogastric sends numerous branches to the throat, lungs, heart, and stomach, terminating in the solar plexus, called the androgynous brain.

This is the channel of the Spiritual Breath, without which there could be no conception nor birth of the psycho-physical germ or spiritual seed.

The Solar Plexus consists of 12 large nerve ganglia which branch off in different directions. It is the largest of the three sympathetic plexuses and the center of the physical body, its nerves branching from this point forming the channels through which the psycho-physical seed is carried from its birth or maturity.

SEED OF IMMORTALITY

What the Masters termed "the first seed of immortality" is formed in the solar plexus of every one at the age of puberty.

Every 29½ days in the life of man and woman, after puberty, when the moon is in the sign the Sun was in at the birth of the individual, there is a psycho-physical Seed born in the Solar Plexus or the pneumogastric plexus, which in the ancient text was called Beth Lechem (House of Bread).

The psycho-physical seed moves from the solar plexus into the central canal of the spinal cord, ascending or descending—according to its type or nature—animal or spiritual.

Here is a strange secret: The solar plexus cannot receive the psycho-physical seed, or regenerative life-unit, until harmony has been attained between the cerebrum and cerebellum through the male and female organs of spirituality, the pineal and pituitary glands.

POSITIVE AND NEGATIVE BREATH

Like attracts like. Electric thought attracts its mate, the negative, magnetic, in the breath. This quickens the conception of the psycho-physical seed.

226

If the thoughts are of the carnal order, the germs, carried to the solar plexus for birth, are marked and sent to the "pit." This means that under the power of the lower mind, they are drawn downward to the testes and ovaries and there changed into physical germs.

In the male the prostate gland receives the seed after it has been physicalized in the testes. It is there stored until ejaculated in copulation.

In the female the uterus receives the ovum (seed) which, if activated by the male element, becomes a propagative unit, passing out the "south-gate" as the karmic-bound body of a new person. Thus the female sacrifices spirituality for productivity.

Sexual indulgence robs man of his most precious possession, far greater in value than the child he receives as a compensatory measure. He consumes his recreative cells in this defilement of the Sacred Fountain of Spirituality.

The Ancient Masters used this force, consumed in propagation, in a regenerative process for the building of their indestructible solar body.

When man conserves this psychic force by not indulging his physical nature, the psycho-physical germ returns to its true throne in the brain.

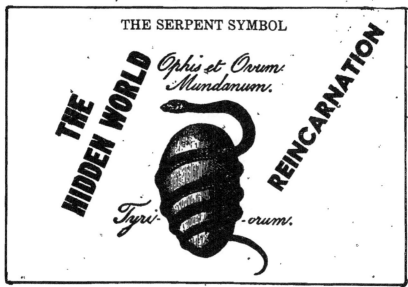

THE SERPENT SYMBOL

THE HIDDEN WORLD

Ophis et Ovum Mundanum.

REINCARNATION

Tyri- -orum.

The Serpent, entwined round an Egg, was a symbol used by the Ancient Masters to represent the creation of the Universe.

A Serpent, with an egg in its mouth, was a symbol of the Universe containing within itself the germ of all things that the Sun develops.

The northern constellation of Draco, whose sinuosities wind like a river through the Wintry Bear of the Zodiac, was made the astronomical cincture of the Universe, as the Serpent encircles the mundane Egg in the Egyptian hieroglyphics.

Serpents encircling rings and globes, and issuing from globes, are common in Persian, Egyptian, Indian and Chinese monuments.

The seventh letter of the Egyptian alphabet, called Zeuta or Life, was sacred to Thoth, and was expressed by a ,Serpent standing upright on its tail. The Isiac tablet, describing the Mysteries of Isis, is charged with Serpents in every part, as her emblems.

With the Serpent in the Ancient Monuments is often found associated the Cross.

The Serpent upon a Cross was an Egyptian Standard. It occurs repeatedly upon the Grand Staircase of the Temple of Osiris at Philae. On the Pyramid of Ghizeh are repres ted two kneeling figures erecting a Cross, on the top of which is an erect Serpent.

The Crux Ansata was a Cross with a coiled Serpent above it. It is perhaps the most common of all symbols on the Egyptian Monuments, carried in the hand of almost every figure of a Deity or a Master.

The Caduceus, borne by Hermes or Mercury, and also by Cybele, Minerv.., Anubis, Hercules, Ogminus the God of the Celts, and the personified Constellation Virgo, was a winged wand, entwined by two Serpents, which represented the bi-polar aspects of the Universe, positive and negative, male and female.

IMMORTALITY

The strong belief in Immortality is more of a natural feeling, an adjunct of subconsciousness, than a dogma of any particular age or country.

That belief gives eternity to man's nature, and reconciles its seeming anomalies and contradictions. It makes him strong in weakness, and perfectable in imperfection. It alone gives an adequate object for his hopes and desires, and value and dignity to his pursuits. It is concurrent with the belief in an infinite, eternal Spirit, since it is chiefly through consciousness of the dignity of the Mind within us, that we learn to appreciate its evidences in the Universe.

To impart this hope and to fortify it was the great aim of the ancient wisdom.

Life rising out of death was the great mystery, which symbolism was delighted to represent under a thousand ingenious forms. Nature was ransacked for attestations to the Grand Truth which seems to transcend all other gifts of imagination, or rather to be their essence of consummation.

Such evidences were easily discovered. But the Masters seem to have been more profoundly impressed by the property possessed by the Serpent, of casting its skin and apparently renewing its youth. This caused it to be used as a symbol of Eternity and Immortality.

Over Libra of the Zodiac, the Sign through which Souls were said to descend or fall to the earthly state, is found, on the Celestial Globe, the Serpent, grasped by Serpentarius, the Serpent-Bearer, as shown in the picture here.

The head of the Serpent is under Corona Borealis, the Northern Crown, called by Ovid Libera or Proserpine; and the two Constellations rise, with the Balance, after the Virgin (or Isis), whose feet rest on the eastern horizon at Sunrise on the day of the equinox.

As the Serpent extends over both signs, Libra and Scorpio, it was the gate through which Souls descended during the whole time that these two signs in succession marked the Autumnal Equinox.

In the Ancient Egyptian Mysteries the Serpent was the symbol of Divine Wisdom, when extended at length, and with its tail in its mouth forming a circle, it was an emblem of Eternity.

Higgins says that from the faculty which the Serpent possesses of renewing itself, without the process of generation as to outward appearance, by annually casting its skin, made it a symbol of Eternity; and he denies that it ever represented, even in Genesis, the evil principle.

The doctrine that the Serpent symbolized the good principle

229

seems to have been borrowed from the winged Seraphim which was blended with the Cherubim that guarded the Tree of Life (Gen. 3:24)—the two sometimes being considered as identical.

But as the Good Principle was always male and female, the male Serpent symbolized the Great Father, and the female Serpent symbolized the Ark or World, the Microcosm and the Macrocosm. Hence the Serpent represented the perpetually renovated world, and was used as such by the Masters.

FERTILITY AND SPIRITUALITY

The image of the Serpent was also used by the Masters as a dual symbol to represent Fertility and Spirituality.

The Masters discovered that the Creative Essence of the body has a dual purpose. It may be consumed in propagation on the plane of animalism, or conserved and used by the body to illuminate the Mind and create a higher state of Consciousness.

The Divine Essence of Creation was regarded by the Masters as the living, conscious, vital electricity of the Universe. It must be that to produce New Life, a universal fact of common observation.

This knowledge proved to be a great discovery. It constrained the Masters to believe that if the function of Fertility were suppressed and restrained, the Divine Essence, thus conserved, could be used for higher purposes in the body that makes it.

Their work proved that they were right. They conserved the Divine Essence and were amazed by the results.

The conserved Divine Essence invigorated the body and illuminated the Mind, exalting the Masters to a higher plane of Consciousness, in which space and time vanished, and past and future became the Eternal Present.

As the Mind was thus illuminated, it revealed to the Masters the amazing fact that the Kingdom of God is neither here nor there, but within man (Lu. 17:21)

So the Masters taught that "the Kingdom of God is not meat and drink," nor a place in space, "but righteousness and peace" (a state of the Mind). So man is transformed by the renewing of his Mind (Rom. 12:2; 14:17).

The world in which man lives depends on the state of his Consciousness. He changes his world as his state of Consciousness is changed; and his state of Consciousness is changed when the Serpentine Fire is raised up to the brain and illuminates the Mind by awakening millions of dormant brain cells.

230

So the Serpent, a Symbol of Fertility, also came to be termed the Serpentine Fire, the Illuminating Power of the Mind that produces Spirituality.

Mind is the Master power that moulds and makes,
And Man is Mind, and evermore he takes
The seal of Thought, and shaping what he wills,
Brings forth a thousand joys, a thousand ills:—
He thinks in secret, and it comes to pass:
Environment is but his looking-glass.

Lesson Number 54

THE SERPENTINE FIRE

In Lesson Number 13 we briefly mentioned the Serpentine Fire (Kuṇḍalini), the Light of the Logos, which the Masters termed the living, conscious, vital electricity of incredible voltage, but hardly comparable to the kind of electricity known to physicists.

It would be a terrible shock to the Christian Clergy if they knew that the Bible, from the first book to the last, deals not with a Christian God, a Christian Heaven and a Christ Jesus, but with Man and the Serpentine Fire, in various ways and always in symbol and allegory.

Scientists know little about vital psychology and physiology, and less about the Brain System of man. Carrel said in his "Man The Unknown" that "our intelligence can no more realize the immensity of the brain than the extent of the sidereal Universe. The cerebral substance contains more than twelve thousand millions of cells" (p. 95).

Scientists admit that the body of man is composed of intelligent cellular life. No intelligent mind can question the fact that the cells of the body are intelligent.

Carrel asserts that the cells are not only intelligent, but possess eternal knowledge, and that the innate knowledge of the part the cells must play in the whole, is a mode of being of all the elements of the body (Man The Unknown, p. 107).

We do not use our so-called mental process in digesting food; and the red blood cells choose iron in one form and reject iron in another form. The kidney cells collect and eliminate as urine certain elements in the blood, but do not eliminate the blood unless damaged and rendered incapable of proper function.

We must differentiate between knowledge and intelligence. A man ignorant of knowledge may yet be intelligent. Knowledge is merely the accumulation or assimilation of what we are pleased to call facts, while intelligence may operate within us without our conscious knowledge.

As cosmic law operates intelligently, it must be directed by intelligence. Carrel says that **"the existence of intelligence is a primary datum of observation"** (p. 121).

Our work here involves the Endocrine Glands and what has been accepted by science as knowledge regarding their functions. There is much in this field, as in all other fields, about which science knows little.

In making an analysis of the work of the ductless glands, science has access to the well-equipped laboratories, the spectroscope, the Vacuum Tubes, the X-ray Tube, the 1, 2 and 3 Bank Coolege Tubes, the oscillator, the electroscope, the chemicals, catalysts, etc. All of these are the product of the three-dimensional vibratory plane of visible existence.

Every existing thing vibrates either through the process of integration or disintegration. Even the rocks, though they may vibrate only once in a thousand years, yet they finally disintegrate, while matter, or force, on the ultra-violet side of the spectrum may complete a cycle of existence in the millionth part of a second.

ENDOCRINE GLANDS

1. Pineal Gland—often mentioned as the Cyclops or Third Eye. The vibratory rate of the force-emanation from this gland is beyond any rate of vibration capable of being registered by any mechanical instrument so far produced by science, and has been estimated to be in the billions of cycles per second.

It is a small structure situated in the mid-brain and believed to be associated with sex development.

2. The Pituitary Gland is situated at the base of the brain and has an anterior and a posterior lobe. The anterior lobe regulates growth, especially the bony structure, and is associated with the genital organs. The posterior lobe regulates pituitin, contracting the muscles, raising the blood pressure, increasing urine flow, excretion of milk, etc.

3. The Thyroid Gland regulates the production and distribution of thyroxin, a complex Iodine Compound, and is situated in the neck. It is an important gland to the balanced function of the body, aiding digestion, elimination, etc.

4. The Parathyroid Gland is embedded in the Thyroid, and regulates metabolism, calcium salts, lactic acid, phosphates and prophylactics necessary to maintain a balanced condition of the organism, and plays an important part in brain, nerve, and sex function.

5. The Thymus Gland is situated in the chest, and is supposed gradually to disappear when the genital organs develop. This theory is questioned because there is still a trace of this gland all through life, showing some activity. While it is true this gland is largest and most active during childhood, it also functions after adulthood.

This gland regulates the compounding of glandular substances, controls heart action and senses in the heart region. **We do not love with all our heart, but with all our Thymus Gland.**

6. The Spleen, not considered by some as a ductless gland, is situated in the left upper quadrant of the abdomen. It was previously credited with destroying red blood cells and forming antibodies against bacteria and other infection. This is only medical art nonsense. It is one of the most important filtration stations within the body, and operates under the vibratory control of the Pituitary in combination with the Parathyroid, forming an operating Triad.

7. The Suprarenals, a duo gland situated just above the kidneys. The Medulla or central portion regulates Adrenalin. Fright, anger, and many forms of shock cause large quantities of Adrenalin to enter the blood.

The cortex of the outer portion of the Superarenals regulates lactic acid, the food supply of the brain when oxydized and closely associated with the gonad glands.

8. The Pancreas is situated in the posterior of the upper part of the abdomen. It regulates insulin, sugar, starch, alcoholic toxins, etc. It also receives and precipitates small quantities of Niton gas from sunlight or atmospheric gases that have been exposed to sunlight.

9. The Gonads regulate the organs of propagation, and glycogen, semen, and lactic acid.

These glands are highly important to a well-balanced body, besides the propagation of the species. In purely physical function, the glands are controlled through the vibratory plane of force of the Pituitary gland, and have a close association with the brain system.

They are also under the control of the radiant force of the Pineal Gland. When this force prevails, we have the transmutation of sex force and brain power.

THE BRAIN

Medical art teaches that man's brain is divided into three sections: cerebrum, cerebellum, and medula oblongata, each with two lobes, making six lobes comprising the system. It also teaches that the left lobe of the cerebrum controls all our willful movements of the right side of the body, while the right lobe controls the left side.

It teaches that the left lobe of the cerebellum controls all of our unconscious or automatic movements of the left side of the body, the reverse of the function of the cerebrum.

THE BONY SERPENT

The Columna Spinalis is a shaft of 33 segments of bone. It holds the body upright, and resembles a serpent standing perpendicular on its tail. That is another reason why the Serpent appears so often in ancient literature.

A picture is shown here of the Bony Serpent. Through the center of this bony column is a canal, filled with the Spinal Cord, a composition of precious substance. The Cord connects with the brain through the Medulla Oblongata, and ends at the base of the spine in a filament of refined substance that lies in the midst of the roots of many nerves forming the cadua equina.

All of the nerve trunks of the body spring from the Spinal Cord and pass out of the back-bone through the openings between its segments, which openings are termed the intervertebra formina.

The nerve force in the body is carried by these nerve trunks from the brain to the various organs, muscles, blood-vessels and tissues of the body.

The Spinal Cord is protected on all sides by the bones of the spinal column, the bones forming a segmented tunnel, housing and protecting the Life Line of the body. Cut the cord in the neck

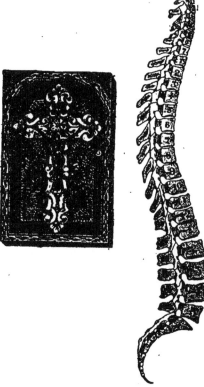

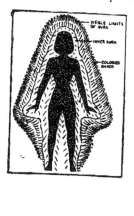

THE HUMAN AURA

of a bull and the animal dies quicker than if shot through the heart.

The whole length of the Spinal Cord is filled with the most vital and most mysterious fluid in the body, far more precious than blood.

This fluid is not composed of what we eat and drink. It is made by the body's laboratory from air gases. The nature of this substance and the secret of its elaboration lie beyond the reach of physical science.

It is well to state that this work is not for those who have been given spinal punctures by doctors. Such persons are damaged for life, and have no chance to rise to the higher planes of consciousness.

The canal in the spinal cord is equipped with valves, similar to those in the veins, to regulate the flow of the fluid.

The spinal fluid, as a stream, was symbolized by the Masters as the "River of God." Ages later, when Christ Jesus became a symbol of the Serpentine Fire of the spinal cord, he was "baptized" in Jordan (Mat. 2:13, 15). That river was not known by that name for centuries after the alleged event occurred.

RADIATION

Science has measured the radiant force emitted by the roots of onions, carrots, etc. It had found that radiant force emitted by the human eye can kill yeast cells, yet no other part of the body seems to emit such killing rays.

As we apply our knowledge and scientific instruments to the study of the forces emitted by the human body, the results are astounding.

The positive and negative poles of the cerebrum are the negative pole being situated along the outer rim of each lobe, while the positive pole is situated along the center line of each lobe, where they join.

The negative pole of the cerebellum is situated along the center line of each lobe, and the positive along the outer rim, the reverse of the cerebrum, apparently accounting for the left lobe of the cerebrum controlling the willful movements of the right side of the body, while the left lobe of the cerebellum controls the unconscious movements of the left side of the body.

The negative pole of the medula is situated at the lower end of the spine, between the last vertebra, fifth lumbar, and the coccyx, while the positive pole is situated just above the atlas of the spine, where the head swivels on the spine.

INTELLIGENCE

Knowing that radiant force is constantly emitted by the body and at different frequencies, some capable of killing yeast cells, and, properly screened, showing throughout the entire spectrum from infra-red to ultra-violet, that the rate of vibration or cycles per second of some of these rays are so rapid as to be beyond any known instrument—we should now be ready to accept the findings of science that:—

Of the some fourteen billion brain cells within the body, the most intelligent of us use less than ten percent of our capacity, the inevitable being that we are all of us at least ninety percent ignorant. It is difficult to believe that we know so little.

The Ancient Masters, whom modern science considers "superstitious heathens," had arrived at that premise where the proper training of human intellect enabled them to put into operation many millions of those unused cells so long dormant, through the mythical power traceable all through the ancient religious teaching as the "Kundalini Force," or Serpentine Fire.

This was one of the great secrets of the Ancient Masters which the church fathers were determined to conceal from the masses, so they destroyed the ancient philosophical scriptures.

The destruction of libraries, scriptures and other ancient records is a fact present in accepted history. But the reason for such destruction was and is well concealed.

It is little known by the laity that the Vatican now has a more complete library of ancient records than any other institution on earth. The church fathers were careful to take those ancient records they considered too valuable to destroy and hide them from the masses.

THE CADUCEUS

What is the insignia of medical art today? Few doctors know what it means.

That insignia is a staff, entwined by two serpents, surmounted by two wings, with a cup-like depression in the top of the staff from which is being emitted Fire (Force). It is the ancient symbol of the Serpentine Fire.

In antiquity, Hermes, "the messenger of the gods" and the greatest Master known to us, was said by the Greeks to typify and preside over the powers of the mind. He is portrayed bearing a Caduceus or Staff, gift of Apollo the Sun God, a symbol of God's message to man.

By the Romans, Hermes was called Mercury. The most ancient of the Egyptians knew him as Thoth.

The ancient alchemists claimed that Hermes was the founder of their art, whence it is called the Hermetic science.

The Hermetic philosophers say that all the sages of antiquity, such as Pythagoras, Plato, Socrates, Aristotle, and Apollonius, were initiated into the secrets of their science; and that the hieroglyphics of Egypt and all the fables of mythology were invented to teach the doctrines of Hermetic philosophy.

To this priceless philosophy Archbishop Chrysostom referred, in the middle of the fifth century A.D., when he boasted:

"Every trace of the old philosophy and literature of the ancient world has vanished from the face of the earth" (Bible Myths; Doane, p. 436).

That precious philosophy and literature are concealed in the big Vatican library, and only a select few have access to it. The literature contains the teachings of the Master who became the fabulous Jesus of the gospels, the Paul of the Epistles, and the John of Revelation.

If the deceived masses had that philosophy now, the clergy would have to go out and work for an honest living. It would have no gospel Jesus to hold out to the misled people as he who "washed us from our sins in his own blood" (Rev. 1:5).

The Twenty-eighth Degree of the Scottish Rite in Masonry, or the Knight of the Sun, is entirely a Hermetic degree, and claims its parentage in the title "Adept of Masonry," by which it is sometimes known.

The Staff of Hermes symbolizes the human spine, containing the cerebro-spinal nerve system, which staff is the wand of the magician, while the two entwined serpents which appear as ascending the staff, one white and the other black, symbolize the Positive and Negative Currents of Solar Force, flowing upward from the Base of the Spine for the evolution and stimulation of the Solar Principle located in the Brain.

But much of this Solar Force is lost in the case of the average man who lives on the animal plane and consumes his Life Essence in copulation. There is then little left to flow to the brain from the base of the spine.

The Kundalini is part of man's communication system, as well as a powerful directing force of the brain functions.

That electro-magnetic force can be traced by instruments from the coccyx bones at the bottom of the spine to the brain in the head, showing two separate frequencies, symbolized by the White and Black Serpents of the Staff.

The Ancient Masters not only understood and conserved this

force, but used it for the higher development of their intelligence.

Can this precious knowledge be safely disseminated now to the masses? It was not in ancient times, nor can it be today.

THE AQUARIAN AGE

In our work titled "Immortalism" we stated that about 1881 the Earth entered the cusp of Aquarius. This cycle will extend to approximately 4,038 A.D.

This is the Air Age, and is scientifically related to objects of the Air and Spiritual Life, to the Mind and human development in a degree that should produce remarkable changes in man's thinking. We have much evidence of this already.

The present work is intended only for minds that can concentrate, analyze, think and reason. We regret to admit that this excludes the great majority of the masses.

A DEADLY FORCE

Electricity is one of man's useful powers. He puts it to many uses. The generators, motors, solonoids, condensers, robots, light, heat, radio—yet it is a power very dangerous if improperly handled, and will kill as quickly as it will serve mankind.

The Kundalini Force is in that class. Experiments over periods of centuries show that the Force is more deadly than electricity when aroused before the body is ready for it—and vastly more beneficial and useful when naturally aroused by the condition of the body, as in the case of birds and beasts.

The danger appears when the power is activated by unnatural means before the body is ready for it, as the directions given for Awakening the Kundalini that we shall notice in Lesson No. 57.

The unnatural processes taught in the various works on the subject are the theories of laymen. Nothing written by the Masters can be understood by the uninitiated public. All they have written on this subject appears in symbol and allegory, as that contained in the Apocalypse, which misleads the layman but never instructs him.

WHITE AND BLACK

The reason why the ancient literature refers to the Kundalini as White and Black appears in the answer to why brain matter is white and grey, grey being a shade of black.

Science asserts that the sole food of the brain is oxygen and lactic acid; that this food is assimilated by the white brain matter,

239

and that the grey (dark) brain matter regulates the glycogen and prevents ketones from entering the brain system.

The Kundalini Force is polarized with a negative and positive polarity. In fact, there are two Kundalini forces, each with different frequencies.

The negative pole of Kundalini is located at the same place as the negative pole of the medulla oblongata. The positive poles of these three forces are located at different poles in or near the head:

(1) the medulla just above the atlas of the spine,

(2) the Black Kundalini at the Pituitary, and

(3) the White Kundalini at or near the Pineal.

There are three different forces in man's spine, each of a different frequency, two of which (medulla and Black Kundalini) can be registered and traced by instruments, and one which, as it nears the Pineal (White Kundalini) is soon beyond the range of physical instruments.

Demonstrations clearly show that man can utilize these forces to increase brain activity. Under all circumstances he should try to increase the use of his brain cells, at least up to ten percent or more.

The White Kundalini Force increases in vibratory rate so rapidly from the atlas of the spine to the region of the Pineal, that no instruments known to science have so far been devised that can register its vibrations.

The vibratory rate beyond the region of the base of the nose has never, to our knowledge, been determined, but it has been estimated to be in the billions of cycles per second.

THE FOURTH DIMENSION

We are laying the foundation for man's conception of the fourth or other dimensional planes beyond that to which we have been accustomed.

Can two or more objects occupy the same space at the same time without interfering with the other? Some writers of fiction are formulating concepts of dimensions beyond what we are normally capable of conceiving.

In our body we are conscious of the space occupied by it, but not conscious of other objects, substances, elements, or forces occupying that same space at the same time.

We live at the bottom of a vast ocean of gases, the weight of which is stupendous, but we are unaware of it because of the equal and countervailing pressure of the gases and fluids within our body. The pressure exerted upon man and upon the earth by this great mass of invisible gas is 2,016 pounds per square foot.

We must not be confused by the meaning of time and space. To the average man time is a passing thing, while space is a place occupied by a three dimensional object.

To a scientifically trained mind, time and space are only relative.

Suppose yourself looking through a telescope capable of seeing a man on a planet a thousand light-years distant. You see a man on that planet seated at a telescope looking at you. You see him wave his hand, apparently at you. When did he wave his hand? How long ago did the event occur at which he was gazing? Now you have what? Depending on each individual concept.

You have three elements of Time in the same space at the same time. What you saw occurred a thousand light-years before you saw it. What he saw took place two thousand light-years before the time you sat at the telescope.

You have present time, time one thousand light-years ago, and time two thousand light-years ago, all in one Time and in the same space.

We are not ordinarily conscious of the electro-magnetic field produced by our body, but delicate laboratory instruments register these forces.

Few men know that the body is an ideal receiving antenna for radio impulses, broadcast by distant radio stations.

THE HUMAN AURA

Knowing of the existence of forces occupied by the same space with the body, we will refer to that radiation, visible to some, surrounding the body, called the Aura, which we have more fully discussed in our work titled "Immortalism."

We have something here that has been lost to civilized man— the power to see the human aura, and from it diagnose his various traits, ailments, and even his disposition and emotions. This power was possessed by the Ancient Masters, termed "superstitious heathens" by modern scientists.

Prof. Rohracher, Director of the Psychological Institute of Vienna University, measured the vibrations of the human aura, using the latest super-sensitive electronic devices. He found that man's body vibrates at the rate of ten vibrations per second of the order of some thousandths of a millimeter of the red blood cells. The resultant force of these waves is so great that a weight of 44 pounds is required to check them.

We are now informed of the successful photographing of the human aura on the thin film of silver oxide.

By the use of certain color screens it is shown that there may be many small auras in different bands of the spectrum going to make up the body aura.

Why should the sodium band photograph to the exclusion of the other parts of the spectrum?

By analogy we must conclude that whatever color is visible in the aura, that chemical in a vital state must also be present in the body.

CONTROL FUNCTION

Numerous experiments show that we can control the functions of the ductless glands and choose whatever combination we desire to put into operation.

We shall apply some of our own experience, together with cold logic and laboratory tests to some of these endocrine operating Triads.

The common love cycle—Pituitary, Thymus, and the Gonads, a purely physical love on the animal plane.

When the unguided youth begins to bloom and feels the urge to propagate, he thinks he is in love. The following experiences have been observed by many of us:

1. Pituitary Gland. All the mental pictures of the opposite sex are beautiful and kindly.

2. Thymus Gland. All our sensations in the region of the heart are loving and gentle.

3. Gonad Glands. The sex organs are stimulated and the urge to copulate appears.

Science asserts that the Pituitary regulates all of the physical functions of the body; growth, structure, metabolism, chemical compounding, etc., and even the thoughts, emotions, and senses of the physical under the control of the Black Kundalini.

That the Thymus controls heart action, sensations, blood pressure, love, under the control of the Black Kundalini Force.

The Gonads regulate semen, glycogen, lactic acid, etc., the sex desires, etc., under the direction of the Pituitary (feminine) gland which is controlled by the Black Kundalini Force.

The intelligent operation of all the endocrine triads or cycles on the physical plane are under the control of the Black Kundalini Force, while all the fourth dimensional, or spiritual, operations, are under the control and direction of the White Kundalini Force. This fact was well known to the Ancient Masters, but now this profound knowledge is possessed only by students of Occultism.

If we disturb the function of any one of the glands forming the triad, we then disturb the other two.

Let one of the parties willfully interrupt the process of copulation, and what occurs? The beautiful mental pictures immediately change. The loving sensations of the heart (Thymus) turn to anger, disgust, etc., and we see defects in our loved one which before we saw not.

Furthermore, the copulatory organ of the male wilts and becomes useless temporarily for propagative purposes.

When we receive sudden fright, the Pituitary, Thymus, and the Medulla of the suprarenal form a working triad and go into action. The Pituitary, under the direction of the Black Kundalini Force, directs the sense organs to ascertain the cause of the fright. The Thymus, causing increased heart action, and the Medulla of the suprarenal to excrete adrenalin into the blood, to prepare the muscles of the body to flee or fight.

When the Pituitary has ascertained that there is nothing to fear, the Medulla decreases in function, and in its place in the triad is substituted the Pancreas, but working with the Parathyroid and Spleen, forming a five grand cycle, or triple triad. The white blood cells begin to collect the excess adrenalin for filtration from the system.

That is why many patients desire to urinate after fright, or during fright, even sometimes emptying and collapsing the bladder after severe fright shock.

When we receive the proper training, then we substitute the Pineal and the White Kundalini Force (positive—male) in the operating triad for the Pituitary and the Black Kundalini Force (negative—female), and we create an equipose or balanced condition, provided we do not go to the other extreme.

SPIRITUAL AND PHYSICAL

Man's body is physical while he who occupies it is inherently Spiritual; or we may more correctly say he is a Fourth Dimensional Being, occupying the same space with the body at the same time.

Physical instruments disclose that the inner, spiritual, or fourth dimensional man exists on a vibratory plane far beyond that of the body.

Most scientists now agree that all visible substance is solidified force, and that all force is an invisible substance. The only difference being the state or plane of vibration.

Experiments show that the love cycle changed over from the Pituitary (negative, female), to Pineal control (positive, male), changes the spectrum colors of the same glands. We recognize chemicals by their respective color bands in the spectrum.

When the Gonads radiate dark red under Pituitary and Black Kundalini control, and are changed over to Pineal and White Kundalini control, the dark red fails to radiate from the Gonads, and a light pink, bordering on orange, shows in place of the dark red. We say that the chemicals' radiant force is lactic acid and niton gas, the brain food.

When we transfer the Love Cycle from the Pituitary (negative, female) to the Pineal (positive, male), we change the vibration plane of that cycle. **This is the transmutation of Sex Force to Brain Force.**

BALANCED PHYSICAL BODY

The Ancient Masters, by making constant use of the transfer of the Love Cycle as just stated, presented well-balanced physical and spiritual bodies. They made the higher use of these forces, hence their remarkable power to perform many so-called miracles.

All men have these same miraculous powers, but in a dormant state. They begin to awaken these unused powers when they begin to live above the plane of propagation, and conserve their Solar Force for the development of their brain cells.

THE WONDERFUL BODY

When did man ever invent anything that is not already in the human body? Not the radio, telephone, wheel, fulcrum, ball and socket joint, the universal joint, building material stress, torque, arch, hinge, etc., television, motion pictures, camera, etc.

Every known science is represented in the body, and every department of the Universe is represented in the body. Man, know thyself and there is naught in all the microcosm or macrocosm to learn. The Ancient Masters learned all by studying Man.

Knowing that there exists forces on a higher plane of vibration than our present concept of three dimensional life, we should study these forces. We may find the "Fountain of Youth." Cells themselves are deathless and eternal, and will live on forever under proper care in culture, where a balance can be maintained.

Remember that the best of us are ninety percent ignorant.

CONCENTRATION

Man can, with diligent practice, rapidly put into operation many millions of brain cells heretofore dormant.

1. One must learn to concentrate and to turn the mind within. The Kingdom of God is within. We should learn to fix our mind on only one object, to the exclusion of all other surroundings, for about one minute.

With practice this can be accomplished. Most people are incapable of holding their thoughts on one object for even fifteen seconds without their mind wandering off to something else.

2. Press finger on the lower end of spine, at the end of coccyx, tail bone, then hold the sensation of pressure left there by the finger in the mind as long as possible, usually about one minute after you have repeated this several times.

Repeat the pressure, but move the pressure sensation of the finger up the spine with the power of mind, until its reaches the positive pole of the medulla just above the atlas of the spine. Should it stop along the route repeat the process until you feel it hit the positive pole of the medulla.

At first this may seem pure imagination; but continue for a week and you will soon see that it is more than imagination.

Thirty minutes per day for seven days would probably give one the worst headache at the base of the brain ever experienced. But that is all.

Five minutes per day for six days, resting one day, then repeat over a period of months if necessary, and you will suddenly come to the realization that things you used to forget you will now remember without effort; that you can more fully analyze complex problems without fatigue; that your ability to assimilate knowledge has increased, etc.

From here on the few who succeed will, without seeking, get higher and more complete knowledge of the laws of the great Creative Principle. But others will become discouraged and sneer at something about which they know nothing.

The foregoing is a harmless kindergarten lesson on the awakening and utilization of the most potent power in man—the Serpentine Fire.

Lesson No. 55

BOOK SEALED WITH SEVEN SEALS

We avoid much confusion by remembering that biblical teachings refer always to man in symbol and allegory, and to nothing else.

The Book symbolizes the body. The Seven Seals symbolize the Seven Gates (chakras, nerve centers) through which the Golden

Oil must pass to raise man's Mind from the physical to the psychical plane.

The rituals and ceremonies of the Masters were a scientific course of training by which man gained a higher state of consciousness.

In the Egyptian Mysteries the rituals and symbols pictured what modern science is just discovering concerning the Endocrine Glands, and stated in correct but mystic terms the facts now recognized by psychology.

Man's body is sealed with seven seals. The Upanishads speak of Seven Chakras.

Chakra means wheel. The seven chakras are seven nerve ganglia bridging the two chains of the vagus nerve system.

This special system consists of two trunks, one on each side of the spinal column. The ganglia, seals or chakras, are nerve plexi suggesting a hub with spokes. They are composed of groups of living cells, for which reason they are symbolized as societies (Rev. 1:20). They are also referred to as lamps; for when activated they illuminate man's outer consciousness with the inner or higher wisdom (Rev. 4:5).

Life functions on the balance (Libra) between that which is consumed and that which is eliminated. That is the crux of the law.

Man is the only creature with sufficient intelligence to be conscious of law as such, and who attempts to violate it.

He is constantly misled by those who would use and exploit him. He should learn the law and let it guide him through the Wilderness of Temptation when he leaves the Egypt of Desire for the Promised Land of Attainment.

THE SEVEN SEALS

In the body there are seven major chakras and many minor ones. The former are those to be considered here.

Material scientists search for the chakras in the physical body by dissecting the dead body. As they cannot find them there, they have no faith in ancient teachings on the subject.

The chakras cannot be found with the surgeon's knife, because they are of astral substance and located in the astral body even after the disintegration of the physical body at death. The astral body is one with the physical, but of a more subtle substance with a higher octave of vibration.

The chakras exist in a subtle state. Gross matter is the result of subtle matter with a lower octave of vibration. This means that we can feel and understand the chakras as we feel

246

and understand the Mind during concentration and meditation. No surgeon can find the Mind in the physical body.

There are two states of Pranic Force. Sthoola Prana flows in the nerve system of the physical body, and Sukshma Prana flows in the nerve system of the astral body. The two are directly and intimately connected.

Wherever there is an interlacing of several nerves, arteries or veins in the body, that center is called a plexus. As to nerves, that center is also called a ganglion. The plural is ganglia. Such are the chakras.

The chakras are foci of force within the body, and each has control of function over a particular part of the gross body. They are receptors of Vital Force, and act as transformers whereby the force is transmitted and transmuted.

While variously located in the body, the chakras are all co-ordinated with the cerebro-spinal system, and may be regarded as so many flowers attached to the parent stem, which is the spinal cord.

Consciousness, physical and psychical, has its chief seat in the brain, but is also located in the chakras. So it is in the development of the chakras that man rises to a higher state of consciousness.

The body proper contains six of the major chakras. The seventh and highest is not properly in the body, but outside of it.

In the lower centers we saw that the epithumetic nature predominates, while in the higher the spiritual nature rules. What man must do is to conquer the lower and exalt the higher.

THE DIVINE MARRIAGE

What the Masters allegorically referred to as "the marriage of the Lamb," was the exaltation of the spiritual nature. It is the activation of the Pineal (male) by the Pituitary (female) as a result of a peculiar stimulation by the Golden Oil that is raised up from the sacral plexus (Rev. 19:7-9).

This produces a harmonization of the negative and positive powers in the body, by means of which equilibrium is attained.

This produces reciprocal action between the lower and the higher that promotes development on every plane of being— the transmutation of the gross into the subtle, which effects the transit of the sensuous to the supersensuous.

We mentioned the Pingala, Ida and Sushumna nadis. The latter, located between the other two, forms a tube, at the lower end of which is the seat of the Serpentine Fire, the Kundalini Power, or the potential Divine Force.

The Divine Marriage of the Lamb occurs when this Force is raised up through the Sushumna and passes through the top of the head. This produces spiritual illumination and the acquisition of paranatural powers.

THE CHAKRAS

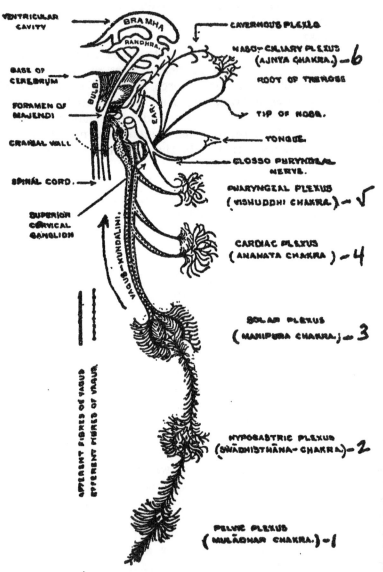

Plan showing the origin, connections and the arrangement of the Afferent and Efferent Fibres of the Vagus Nerve.

The Sushumna is the central trunk of the Tree of Life, as stated. Its six stages are the six chakras, to which is added a seventh, the Sahasrara, which lies outside the body proper. The chakras are:

1. Muladhara Chakra.—Located at base of spine, between sex organ and anus, just below the Kanda and the junction where the Ida, Pingala and Sushumna nadis meet. It is called the fish gate, or fundamental lotus, and has four petals. Here Kundalini lies dormant.

Each chakra is related to one of the cosmic elements. This one is symbolized by the earth, and its color is yellow. He who masters this chakra is said to acquire knowledge of the past, present and future.

2. Swahishtana Chakra.—Located within the Sushumna Nadi at the root of the procreative organ. It has control over the lower abdomen, kidneys, etc. It is the sacral plexus, the ganglia at the base of the spinal canal, termed the coccygeal nerves that extend to the procreative glands.

The sciatic nerve, largest in the body, rises from this ganglia. When reflex action is absent and the feet twitch, it shows the sacral center has been weakened by sexual excesses. This chakra has six petals, and its color is red. Its symbol is water.

3. Manipura Chakra.—This is the solar plexus, or sun center, near the navel. Twelve nerve ganglia stem from it in different directions. Each nerve branching from this center forms a channel through which the psycho-physical seed passes each month. Each of these nerves supplies a special force to different departments of the body. This chakra is of the color of dark clouds, and has ten petals. Its symbol is fire.

4. Anahata Chakra.—This corresponds to the Cardiac Plexus, formed by nerves from the cervical ganglia. Its color is deep red, it has twelve petals, is the seat of Prana, and its symbol is air.

5. Vishuddha Chakra.—Located at the base of the throat, below the larynx, and related to the pharyngeal plexus. It has sixteen petals, its color is white, and its symbol is the ether.

6. Ajna Chakra.—Situated within the Sushumna Nadi. Its corresponding center in the physical body is at the space between the eyebrows, in the region of the Pineal gland, where the two nostrils converge and the Ida and Pingala begin.

The picture (p. 250, top) shows Seti, ruler of Egypt 3300 years ago. The serpent shown at the forehead represents the activation of the Ajna Chakra by the Serpentine Fire.

This chakra has two petals, and when the Serpentine Fire rises thither, the petals bend down and out, forming the winged-

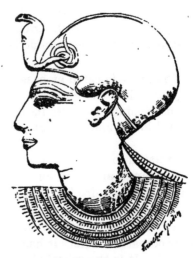

globe of the Egyptian Masters. Its principle is mental (Manas) and its color silvery white.

This is the "third eye," indicated in ancient sculpture by jewel, and in Egyptian by a globe-crowned serpent or winged globe, causing Egypt to be called the "land of the Winged Globe."

The picture below represents the Male and Female Principle consisting of a body with man's and woman's heads, standing over a dragon from whose mouth issues the Serpentine Fire. Around the figure appear symbols of the Seven Chakras. This picture on ancient monuments is said by occultists to be more than ten thousand years old.

This important center, termed the Trikona by the Masters

was said to be the Seat of Intelligence. It is one of the most vital spots in the physical body, is very sensitive and, when not damaged and practically ruined by polluted air or other injurious agencies, it manifests a strange Intelligence that makes man paranatural, with remarkable psychic powers, spiritual vision— vision of things not seen with physical eyes.

It is said that by the mastery of this center one is enabled to overcome the karma of one's past incarnations, and rise above the element of Time-Space, so that for him the past and future become the eternal present.

The mere awakening of the Serpentine Fire does not mean very much for the Masters. Nothing of exceptional importance is achieved until this the Ajna Chakra is activated.

7. Sahasrara Chakra.—Situated in the crown of the head, and the abode of Shiva. This is the thousand-petalled lotus of the brain, usually represented directly above the head.

When Kundalini rises to this center, man attains the super-conscious state and the highest knowledge. Of this chakra J. F. C. Fuller writes:

"In this center there is a Yoni with its face pointed downward. In the center of the Yoni is placed the mystical moon, which is continually exuding an elixir, the 'fluid of immortality' that unceasingly flows through the Ida.

"In the uninitiated, all who are not Yogis, this nectar (Sarrivi) that flows from the Moon is swallowed up by the Sun (Muladhara Chakra). This loss causes the body to grow decrepit (old). If the aspirant can prevent this flow of fluid by closing the hole in the palate of his mouth (Brahmarandra), he will be able to utilize it to prevent the waste of his body. By drinking it he will fill his whole body with life.

"When one has closed the hole at the root of the palate ... his seminal fluid (golden oil) is not emitted even though he is embraced by a passionate woman.

"This discloses the Key to the whole of this lunar symbolism. The Soma fluid of the Moon, elixir and vital force, are but the various names of the same substance.

"If the Vindu can be retained in the body, it may by certain practices be utilized to vitalize the body and prolong physical life to an indefinite period." (Note: Provided polluted air does not ruin the breathing organs.—KK.)

Given proper internal development of the body with conservation of the sex force and a sufficient accumulation of psychic force, and it is possible to awaken the chakras by a direct act of the will, in which meditation plays no part. This may also be done by concentration on the center itself.

As the Kundalini Power passes upward from chakra to chakra, layer after layer of the Mind is activated and opened, and the neophyte enters into higher states of consciousness.

Before awakening the Kundalini, **one must have purity of mind and body.** This fact puts the subject beyond the reach of all but a select few who will travel the strait and narrow path.

BREATHING

This subject has been noticed, but is mentioned again because of its high importance.

As the etheric energy of the air enters the nostrils, the Masters called it Prana. After it was refined and intensified by passing between the poles of the power generators of the sacral plexus at the base of the spine, they called it the Kundalini Force or Serpentine Fire.

Prana is said to be a vital spark, the cosmic globule of oxygen, without which nothing can live. It consists of seven atoms grouped in a globule. While not a part of the sunshine, yet it is generated only in the presence of sunlight, and in quantity in proportion to the amount of sun-rays present.

The atmosphere is richest in Prana at mid-day and weakest in the early morning hours before sun-rise. That is why men are most vital during the day and least so in the early morning hours. That is said to be the reason why more people die in the early morning hours than at any other time of the day. Their vitality is then at its lowest ebb.

When Prana is intensified at the base of the spine, it becomes the Kundalini Power that sleeps in him who consumes his vitality on the animal plane of carnal lust, or suffers from defective breathing organs, or breathes polluted air, or lacks knowledge of how to live to rise to the higher plane.

The Kundalini is the symbol of the Brazen Serpent raised by Moses in the Wilderness (Num. 21:9), and its symbol is the Serpent Scepter of the Ancient Mysteries.

As this force ascends through the gaseous fluids in the spine, it electrifies the chakras. They are closed and their power is dormant in the average adult in his polluted environment.

And I wept much, because no man was found worthy to open and to read the book, neither to look thereon (Rev. 5:4).

The buds on the rod of Aaron (Num. 17:8), symbolize the

252

Seven Seals of the Temple of God (1 Cor. 6:19), which shine out as centers of Spiritual Light (Jn. 1:9) within the body of him who develops his latent power.

The Masters used flowers to symbolize the Seven Chakras. When they glow forth they show that the dead stick, cut from the Tree of Life, has budded—that the Initiate has vivified his Vortices of Spiritual Consciousness.

As the intensified Pranic Power is raised and spiritualized, the chakras of the Spinal Cord, its Solar Heat, the symbol of which is—

"And the Angel appeared unto him in a flame of fire out of the midst of a bush; and he looked, and, behold, the bush burned with fire, and the bush was not consumed" (Ex. 3:2),—

melts, liquifies, consumes the tissues that clog the Spiritual Channel in degenerate man, and hinder its flow to the Brain, which organ it enters and baptizes with the Breath of Fire (Mat. 3:11).

SEVEN GOLDEN DISKS

The Seven Planes are represented in the body by the Seven Chakras. In Solomon's Temple a design of the Chakras was inlaid upon the ceiling in the form of Seven Golden Disks, each distinguished by the seven colors of the solar spectrum. It is written:

"Wisdom hath builded her house, she hath hewn out her seven pillars" (Prov. 9:1).

The Seven Chakras constitute sealed storehouses out of which flows the force to increase the voltage necessary for the regeneration of the Solar Body, in which the Resurrected God-Man may consciously function in both the visible and invisible realms of the Cosmos, as he now does unconsciously.

Increased activity of the Seven Chakras is the basis of Regeneration, and dissipation of the Golden Oil in copulation and in other ways, robs the Temple of its priceless treasure.

Zechariah refers to the Chakras as the Seven Eyes of God, which run to and fro through the whole earth (body) (4:10). They are the "Watchman," as it is through the awakening of the "Eyes" that the great work is accomplished.

The Golden Candlestick that Zechariah saw (4:2) is the

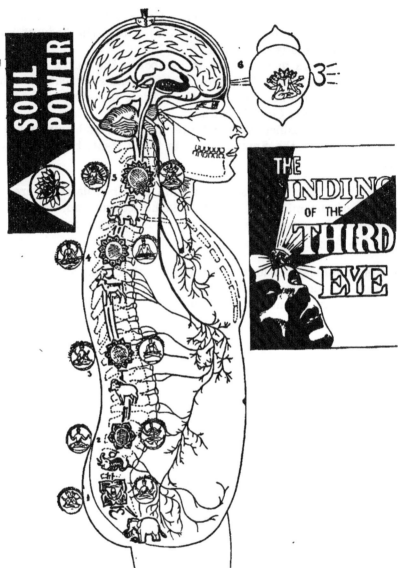

Spinal Cord; the "Bowl" on the top of it being the **Brain**, the seat of the emotions and reservoir of Vital Force. The Seven Lamps symbolize the Chakras, the function of which is to amplify the voltage of the Spiritual Force.

These disks of nerve plexi revolve at tremendous speed, and this produces internal Illumination.

The Seven Pipes are the principal nerves that connect the plexi, and through them the Serpentine Fire rises into each nerve plexus, to be increased and amplified as the process continues, until the force reaches the "Bowl," where the internal

Illumination occurs, allegorically termed the "marriage of the Lamb" (Rev. 19:7). This means the joining of the functions of the Pituitary and Pineal Glands in the brain.

The creative impetus, flowing from the Cosmic Source, is transmitted to the chakras and their connections as the Kundalini Power. When this power is aroused from its dormancy, it resurrects the sleeping God-Man, and he perceives the paranatural truths. The Mind becomes illuminated and brilliant, and there appear wonderful visions of extraordinary mental powers, which cause man to realize that he is Spiritual and united with the Absolute.

PURITY OF MIND AND BODY

The awakening of Kundalini depends upon purity of Mind and Body. "Because strait is the gate, and narrow the way, which leadeth unto (the higher) life, and few there be that find it" (Mat. 7:14).

Not many in their artificial state called civilization can even realize what this actually means.

The Master who wrote the Apocalypse said:

"And no man in heaven, nor in earth, neither under the earth, was able to open the book, neither to look thereon" (Rev. 5:3).

When that was originally written, thousands of years ago, man was a saint compared to the degenerate creature he is today.

It was ages after that was written before man added the evils of tobacco to his other pernicious habits. When that was

written the atmosphere had not yet been polluted with the thousands of substances that poison it now.

He who thinks of Purity of Mind and Body should go back and read again what we said in "Man's Miraculous Unused Powers" about the Breath of Life, beginning with Lesson Number 21 and continued through Lesson Number 28.

After reading that he will realize that it would be much more difficult now than it was thousands of years ago, to find a man in heaven or on earth who is worthy and able to open the Book Sealed with Seven Seals.

HIGHER CONSCIOUSNESS

The intricate reciprocal, coordinated action of the body forces is for purposes much higher and more ulterior than the mere maintenance of health and life. They are for man's higher development.

Rising above man's purely physical state depends upon a higher development of Consciousness, and constitutes one process. For the body as a unit is that mechanism which Consciousness has produced for the achievement of a certain goal.

Higher Consciousness is not another form of Consciousness. It results from a Purity of Mind and Body that admits the higher vibrations, and translates them with such integrity that what appears sometimes passes beyond the limits of man's power to understand, or language to describe.

The efforts of the esoterist is not so much to KNOW as to BECOME. His body must become a better instrument before he can know the higher things.

Herein lies the tremendous import of the Delphic inscription, "Man know Thyself." That is the key-note of esotericism.

The esoterist understands that true self-knowledge can be attained only through true self-development in the highest possible sense of the word,—a development that begins with building a sound Mind in a sound Body, and activating the creative forces which now slumber in civilized man's inner protoplasmic nature. like the vivific potency in the ovum which, when roused into action, transforms shapeless substance into a Divine Being.

HE THAT OVERCOMETH

He that overcometh the Great Red Dragon in the Blood shall inherit all things that make life worth living, good health and long life; and I will be his God, and he shall be my son .(Rev. 21:7).

The body is not for fornication, but a Temple in which God wells (1 Cor. 6:13).

The body is an epitome of all elements and all things. It is ne focusing or condensing of innumerable electro-magnetic currents.

Modern science makes man purely a physical being. Man is piritual, not physical, and must rise above the bondage of the hysical and the elements that compose it. He must rule, transmute and use these elements, and not let them rule him.

When man thinks he is only matter, his Mind is bound by nat thought. He cannot correct his impressions or desires. He misses the Source of Light. Under all phenomena then, stands ne Soul, for man is geometrized by the Logos, or written word f the Cosmos.

The material world with its changing forms is bound to a piritual world through Divine Power. That Power is the Verbum, ogos, Word. It is the directing power of God, seen and unseen, eate and uncreate, male and female.

Man is in contact with all life, all ideals, all wisdom. He is vinity in its fullest expression. The Universe is divinity in a ultitude of expressions, all sustained by the same ideal Logos Word.

The ideal Logos, becoming incarnate, is physical life. It talizes the mental and the physical body of man.

Every living form is the external index of the incarnate eal. God makes no mistakes. We see no cosmic failures, or e Divine Mind would be a failure, and the facts of creation ould be in discord with one another.

Scorpio of the ancient Zodiac is the symbol of conflict, sex, hysical generation, ruling sex and desire. When control of sex rce is accomplished, the interior Mystic Sense is awakened by e power thus conserved, and the Mind is released from its aterial bondage.

*I WILL LIFT UP MINE EYES....
MY HELP COMETH*

The key to every man is his thought. Sturdy and defying though he look, he has a helm which he obeys, which is the idea after which all his facts are classified. He can only be reformed by showing him a new idea which commands his own.

—*Emerson.*

*Cause and effect is as absolute and un-
deviating in the hidden realm of thought as
in the world of visible and material things.
Mind is the master weaver, both of the interior garment of character and the outer
garment of circumstance.*
—James Allen.

Thought means life, since those who do not think do not live in any high or real sense. Thinking makes the man.

—A. B. Alcott.

That a man can change himself, improve himself, re-create himself, control his environment, and master his own destiny is the conclusion of every mind that is wide awake to the power of right thought in constructive action.

—Larsen.

TABLE OF CONTENTS

III

THE MYSTERIOUS SPHINX

The oldest and greatest of Ancient Symbols is the Sphinx. The encyclopedia says that in ancient Egyptian mythology it represented the Solar Deity, Ra, and adds: "All nations of antiquity seem to have held these monstrous beings...as objects of awe, compelling adoration and worship."

When the first Egyptians settled in the Nile Valley, they found the Sphinx and the Great Pyramid almost buried in the windblown sand of the desert. To them the meaning of these two ancient objects was utterly incomprehensible. As the Sphinx looked toward the East, they called it Harmakuti, or the "Sun of the Horizon."

The work of excavation took years, and the Sphinx was found to be carved from solid stone and 189 feet long. There was a tradition that the Sphinx is a complex hieroglyph, or book in stone, containing the essence of the Ancient Wisdom, revealing its secret to him who can read the strange cipher embodied in its form, and fathom the correlations and measurements of the different part of the image. The clever scribe of the John Gospel of the Bible knew the secret of the Sphinx, and showed it in the first verse. Who was he? The chief disciple of the great Pythagorean philosopher of the first century. And who was he? Hotema tells the story in his two works, **The Mysterious Sphinx** ($2.00) and **The Mystery Man of the Bible** ($2.00).

Lesson No. 56

BRAIN POWER

Kundalini Parable

"He spoke unto them many things in parables" (Mat. 13:3).

In the Ancient Mysteries the Masters taught only in parables, afterwards interpreted by them to the candidate. Without the Key, the parables cannot be comprehended, and that is the purpose of them.

In the following parable, Kundalini is symbolized as the Goddess of the Serpentine Fire:

1. Growing tired of heaven (the brain),
2. She decided to visit the new earth (human body) being formed in the sea of space.
3. From heaven (brain) she descended a ladder (spinal cord),
4. And found an island (the embryo),
5. In the Sea (amniotic fluid) of Meru (Mary),
6. Surrounded by the Mountains of Eternity (external membrane inclosing the embryo),
7. All of which existed in the Egg of Brahma (womb of Matripandma).

After exploring the island, Kundalini decided to ascend the ladder and return to heaven (brain), but found the ladder had been severed from above and the island was floating off in space.

In fear, Kundalini fled into a cave (sacral plexus), curled up and fell asleep. There she remains as the Coiled Serpent, symbolical of the evil effect of carnal lust which weakens body and brain.

From this cave Kundalini can be lured only by the "three mysterious notes of the Hindu snake-charmer's flute," which is the secret meaning of the Hindu snake-charmer and his flute. The three mysterious notes symbolize the Pranic Power of the Sushumna, Ida and Pingala Nadis.

As Kundalini begins to uncoil when aroused by the "three mysterious notes" of the "flute," she moves upward through the spinal canal and returns to heaven (brain).

All the real, worth-while teaching of the Bible deals in various ways with the Kundalini Parable.

Man was created Lord of the earth, given dominion over all living creatures (Gen. 1:26), and commanded not to fall so low as an animal by yielding to the lust of his animal nature (Gen. 2:17).

Paul (Apollonius) invariably refers to fornication as sin: **"He that committeth fornication sinneth against his own body"**. (1 Cor: 6:18). That is the "sin unto death" (1 Jn. 5:15).

The statement, "Without shedding of blood is no remission" (of sin) (Heb. 9:22) is an allegoric phrase which means that **man is redeemed from his "fall" to the animal level by slaying his animal nature.**

The plummet in the hand of Zerubbabel with those seven; they are the eyes of the Lord, which run to and fro through the whole earth (Zech. 4:10) is allegorical. It refers to the action of the Pituitary gland, and the seven chakras of the spinal column as the eyes of the Lord (man), which run to and fro through the human body from head to pelvis.

In Revelation, Heaven means head, Earth means body, and also the creative centers; Sea means the psychic centers; Rivers and Springs mean the phrenic centers; Sky means the noetic centers; Abyss means the sympathetic system; the river Euphrates means the cerebro-spinal system; and Air means the human aura.

CONQUER THE ANIMAL NATURE

No candidate would be accepted for initiation in the Ancient Mysteries until he first conquered his animal nature.

The Masters observed the law, that copulation is the sin unto death, and termed it the False Prophet that deceives its victims by yielding pleasure while destroying body and brain.

There being direct and intimate relationship and correspondence between the Higher Brain Centers and the Procreative Centers that produce New Life, it follows that the AWAKENING OF THE WORLD WITHIN, or the redemption of man, or the remission of sin, can be accomplished only when a pure and virtuous life is led; while for the candidate who would enter upon the telestic labor, the task of giving birth to his Higher Self (or regaining his High Place on earth), perfect celibacy is the first and absolute prerequisite.

Unless man is inspired by the loftiest aspirations, guided by the noblest philosophy, and restrained by the most rigid moral discipline, his possibility of success is extremely remote; and the mere dabbler in the pseudo-occult will only degrade his intellect still more with the puerilities of psychism, become the prey of the evil influence of the phastasmal world, or ruin his Soul with the foul practices of phallic sorcery,—as millions of deceived people are now doing.

LIFE

There is wide speculation among biologists, psychologists and physiologists on the question of what makes the body function in the state termed life or living. None seem satisfied with their conclusions.

Modern science offers certain theories concerning Life or living, but has no definite answer that solves the mystery.

The great Osler defined Life to be **"the expression of a series of chemical changes"** (Modern Medicine, p. 39).

That definition defines nothing. It is difficult to understand how a great doctor could believe that the Brain of a Scientist receives its intelligence from "the expression of a series of chemical changes."

The definition must comprehend the thing attested. It must explain the CAUSE of the "chemical changes." Otherwise it is only a description of the EFFECT and not of the Cause.

In his remarkable book, Man The Unknown, the great Carrel did not attempt to define Life. He wrote:

"We (scientists) do not apprehend man as a whole. We know him as composed of distinct parts. Even these parts are created by our methods. Man is made up of a process of phantoms, **in the midst of which strides an Unknowable Reality"** (p. 4).

That "Unknowable Reality" is what Osler termed "the expression of a series of chemical changes." Ridiculous.

In his outstanding work, "The Secret of Life," the great Lakhovsky traced the origin of the living body and showed that the chromosomes in the cell nucleus are tiny radio antennae that pick up Cosmic Rays from the ether, He then declared that **"the living cell is produced and sustained by radiation,"**—not by food (p. 161).

Lakhovsky affirmed what the Masters knew: Man lives in the midst of fields of Cosmic Radiation, which induces electromagnetic phenomena in the cellular nuclei of the body. Each cell is the center of oscillation of very high frequency, emitting visible radiations belonging to the gamut close to that of Light.

Animation, living, being alive, is the phenomenon of oscillations in the cellular nucleus, resulting from the harmonious vibrations of Cosmic Radiation.

The Masters went back of Cosmic Radiation for the cause of all, and that cause they termed Universal Spirit, which they regarded as the Center and Cause of Intelligence and Animation.

Cosmic Intelligence appears in the Brain, producing a state termed Mind. Psychologists have divided Mind into three departments, Conscious, Subconscious and Superconscious. They assert that our Conscious Mind, usually all we use in our daily affairs, is only a small part of Brain Power.

Deeper than the Conscious is our Subconscious Mind, which is many times more powerful. And deeper still, the Superconscious Mind, so potent that no one seems able to measure it Psychologists say that it never forgets, and even contains a the wisdom of past ages.

On the subject of Mind, Carrel wrote:

"We know that Mind is not entirely described within the four dimensions of the physical continuum. It is situated simultaneously within the material universe and elsewhere. It may insert itself into the cerebral cells and stretch outside space and time.

"We are totally ignorant of the realities that lie outside space and time. We may suppose that a telepathic communication is an encounter, beyond the four dimensions of our universe, between the immaterial parts of two Minds. But it is more convenient to consider these phenomena as being brought about by the expansion of man into space. The spatial extensibility of personality is an exceptional fact.

"Clairvoyants perceive not only events spatially remote, but also past and future events. **For the clairvoyant there are no secrets.** They seem to wander as easily in time as in space. Or to escape from the physical continuum and contemplate the past and the future as a fly could contemplate a picture if, instead of walking on its surface, it flew at some distance above it.

"The facts of predictions of the future lead us to the threshold of an unknown world. These facts seem to point to the existence of a psychic principle capable of evolving outside the limits of our bodies" (Man The Unknown, pp. 261, 265).

Modern men may think all this is new. The evidence show that the Ancient Masters discovered these things thousands years ago.

While we are only beginning to learn that man has the Brain Powers, the Masters knew how to develop and use the and performed what seemed to be miracles.

WHAT IS MAN

After studying Man for more than thirty years, the great Carrel found Man to be a mystery so confusing that he wrote a book on the subject, and titled it "Man The Unknown," in which he flatly declared, **"In fact, our ignorance (of Man) is profound"** **(p. 4).**

In his effort to describe Man, Dr. H. H. Sheldon, University of New York said:

"We as individuals undoubtedly have no existence in reality, other than as waves,—multitudinous and complicated centers, perhaps, in what is called the ether."

In their attempts to describe Man as a physical being, biologists found themselves wandering in Sheldon's "waves."

They found that man's body is composed of cells, the cells composed of atoms, the atoms composed of electrons, and the electrons as whirling centers of force in the ether.

In view of these statements and findings, what is Man? What is Life?

It seems that in trying to study Man for what he appears to be, science is actually studying a Phantasma, an imaginary existence that seems to be real, a Phantom that cannot be pinned down, a will-o-the-wisp that ever dances before us but always eludes our grasp.

The cold facts of all investigations show that:—

1. What we call Life seems to be but a word or name that defines nothing, and means only Conscious Knowledge of our existence and our environment.

2. What we call Man seems to be but a word or name applied to Incarnate Spirit manifesting on the Material Plane.

Hence, what we call Life and Man appear as an illusion. It is a case of not seeing what we thing we see, showing that we have lost the Sense Power that once told us what we really are.

The facts show that Cosmic Spirit appears as the Life Principle.

What we term Living or being Alive is only the EFFECT of Cosmic Spirit contacting the Material World through an organized body called Man.

The evidence of this contact appears in man's Brain as a State of Consciousness, making man think, "I am Life," or "I am a Living Soul."

Then as the great scientists search for what they think they see, they find only a Phantom that defies description.

LIFE AND MAN

Man's body is an organized Unit of vibratory waves, animated by Cosmic Spirit, making man an Instrument through which Cosmic Spirit contacts the Material World, exactly as the Bible states.

The mystery called Life is the EFFECT of that contact, and the EFFECT is a STATE OF CONSCIOUSNESS that manifests in the Brain of man.

Of course material science will object to some of these statements, terming them unsound and unscientific. But it is groping in the dark and unable to define Life in logical terms, or to offer any reasonable evidence to show that the foregoing statements are unsound or unscientific.

On the other hand, specific statements in the Bible and other ancient literature, in addition to observation and experience, support the above declarations concerning Life and Man.

The Masters regarded God as Cosmic Spirit. They held that Eternal Cosmic Spirit permeates the body just as atmospheric oxygen and nitrogen diffuse in man's tissues. Hence, Spirit animates the body (Jn. 4:24; 6:63).

These statements allocate the Kingdom of God within the body (Lu. 17:21), making Heaven a State of Mind, said the Masters, not a place in space as taught by the church (Rom. 14:17).

There may be contradictory statements in the Bible, as many men were engaged in writing the various books thereof. But no statement in the Bible directly contradicts the declaration that Cosmic Spirit is the Power that produces body and brain function in the state termed Life or Living.

A STATE OF CONSCIOUSNESS

What we call Life or Living appears as a State of Consciousness.

The Masters taught that as Incarnated Spirit contacts the Material World, the EFFECT thereof appears in man's Brain as Conscious Knowledge that he is a Living Being.

That makes the EFFECT termed Life or Living appear as a definite State of Consciousness on the physical plane.

Hence, what material science calls Life is nothing more than Conscious **Knowledge of the EFFECT of Spiritual Contact with the Material World in those whose Brain Power is limited to the Five Senses.**

As the EFFECT must share in the nature of the Cause in

264

character if not in degree, and as the Cause is Eternal Spirit, the EFFECT could not be less, even though it may seem less to the Five Sense Power man.

The EFFECT is an illusion and misleading like the rising of the sun. The sun does not rise. The motion of the earth makes it appear to rise.

The EFFECT called Life is the visible evidence of Eternal Spirit acting on physical substance, misleading uninformed man to think his body is himself.

This position is supported by the following:

"Know ye not that ye are the Temple of God, and that the Spirit of God dwelleth in you"? and, therefore, is the real you (1 Cor. 3:16).

That statement is clear and definite, and agrees with the facts of daily observation.

Now if we decrease the EFFECT of the Spiritual Contact with the Material World by making man unconscious, then all Conscious Knowledge of being alive instantly vanishes in the case of the Five Sense Power man.

An unconscious man is still alive. But to those of the Five Sense Power there is no Conscious Knowledge of themselves, their existence, or their environment. They are "dead" to the material world, even though the body is still alive.

If we decrease the EFFECT still more by blacking out the Subconscious Mind, body function stops, leaving the body lifeless. Has anything been destroyed? Has man been "killed"?

The facts show that only a CHANGE has occurred and nothing more. In the Bible the condition is framed in these words:

"Behold, I show you a mystery: We shall not sleep (in death), but we shall be CHANGED, in a moment, in the twinkling of an eye" (1 Cor. 15:51, 52).

The CHANGE occurs when the body no longer meets the requirements of the Law of Animation, making it impossible for Cosmic Spirit to contact the Material World through that body, and the STATE OF CONSCIOUSNESS in that body of being alive on the physical plane simply ends.

"Behold, I show you a mystery!" That mystery is the CHANGE. What change? What is the nature of the change?

A CHANGE in man's State of Consciousness occurs. The State of Consciousness of being alive in the physical body on the physical plane CHANGES, in a moment, in the twinkling of an eye, to a State of Consciousness of being alive in a Spiritual Body on the Spiritual Plane.

These facts, based on the Bible and supported by declarations of the Masters, clearly show beyond all doubt that Life in the physical world is but a State of Consciousness on the material plane, while Life in the Spiritual World is a State of Consciousness on the Spiritual Plane.

To be more specific, Life or Living in the physical world, according to the Bible, is **Man in the Father and the Father in Man.**

Without the Father, man is not. In Him we live, and move, and have our being. The Father that dwelleth in Man, He doeth the works. For ye are the Temple of God, and the Spirit of God dwelleth in you (Jn. 5:19; 14:10, 11; Acts 17:28; 1 Cor. 3:16).

These facts are stated again and again in the Bible, that Man and the Father are One (Jn. 10:30), yet people are so well deceived that they insist on following the preacher and praying to a God far off in the sky; an anthropomorphic God who "spake unto Moses face to face," and showed Moses his "back parts" (Ex. 33:11, 23). Base lies of course, but "if it is in the Bible it is true."

Such people even think prayer is effective. It is to the extent that it influences the Mind. As a man thinketh, so is he (Pr. 23:7).

DEATH

The multitude is taught to regard this CHANGE as death. Modern science puts horror in the hearts of the masses by claiming that "death" means the total extinction of man.

That is erroneous. The facts show that "death" is only a word and means the end of a STATE OF CONSCIOUSNESS appearing in the brain of that particular person. It means the end of the EFFECT produced by Incarnated Spirit contacting the Material World through that particular body.

We repeat that the EFFECT appears in man's Brain as Conscious Knowledge. When the EFFECT ends, that state of Conscious Knowledge also ends, so far as that body is concerned.

But specialists of spiritism interpret certain phenomena as proof of the continuation of CONSCIOUSNESS after physical death. It continues on a higher plane of being. That means man still exists, but in a higher world.

Here is another mystery: When man's State of Consciousness in increased on the Material Plane from the common Five Power

to the very rare Seven Power, he is then raised up to a higher
level of Consciousness, and competent to SEE the Kingdom of
God within, and to KNOW that he is not a form of inert clay,
but a SPARK OF ETERNAL COSMIC SPIRIT (Jn. 3:3).

THE BIG FRAUD

Now we have cornered the big fraud that has deceived millions of people for sixteen hundred years, and done it with the
very Bible used by the church to support that fraud.

According to church dogma, God, as Incarnated Spirit dwelling in the Human Temple (1 Cor. 3:16), got lost in the fog of
His own creation, and must be "saved" from "eternal dam-
nation" by His "only begotten Son," (Jn. 3:16); who performs the
"saving process" by gallantly dying on the cross (Mat. 27:50),
thus washing "us from our sins in his own blood" (Rev. 1:5).

Those who can believe that fairy tale must be non compos
mentis (weak minded), and need a guardian to protect them
from the snares of the church.

BRAIN POWER

Look within for the Kingdom of God, said the Masters. Enter
into thy closet, and shut thy door (Mat. 6:6). This refers not
to a room nor a door, but to the body and the blacking-out of
the evidence of the Five Senses.

Material science teaches man that he is physical, and he be-
lieves it. He obstructs his Spiritual Consciousness with a strong
overpowering physical consciousness. His state of thought is
largely responsible for that. As a man thinketh, so is he (Pr.
23:7).

Man should learn that he does nothing of himself. The Father
that dwelleth in man doeth the works. For it is God that worketh
in man both to will and to do His good pleasure (Jn. 14:10;
15:5; Phil. 2:13).

Man thinks he sees with his eyes and hears with his ears.
The eye of a dead man cannot see, nor the ear hear.

We see and hear in our brain, not with our eyes and ears.

We consciously contact the World Within by possessing the
power to look within, not by gazing into the distant sky.

Power of sight and sound is limited by the Brain, not by
distance. The eagle can see farther, and the dog can hear and
smell better, than most men, because of better Brain Power.

Limited Brain Power makes men "dead" to much of the
Material World, and to all the higher World Within.

It requires a higher degree of Brain Power to see the World Within than to see the sun in the sky.

Due to limited Brain Power, material scientists are "dead" to the vast World Within. To them, the World Within is just heathenish superstition.

INCREASED BRAIN POWER

Instruments have been invented to increase man's power of sight and sound. By the aid of telephone and radio we can hear men talk around the world. By the aid of television we can see men miles away.

These devices expand Brain Power. They show that Brain Power may be increased to a point where man can see and hear things anywhere on earth.

That fact, now common knowledge, was unknown to modern man not long ago.

We can now understand the secret meaning of the statement, "There is nothing covered, that shall not be revealed; and nothing hid, that shall not be known" (Mat. 10:26).

An example of this higher Brain Power appears in the case of the great Philosopher and Master, Apollonius. While preaching at Ephesus in the first century of the Christian era, he saw in Rome the assassination of Domitian, as related in Lesson No. 10.

We shall soon notice the "Radar-Man" of Holland who appears to possess similar powers.

SEAT OF KNOWLEDGE

Man's knowledge exists in his Brain, and is limited only by his Brain. To increase our knowledge of ourselves, our environment and the Universe, we must increase our Brain Power.

Carrel, one of the truly great scientists of this age, discussed the mystery of Mind and Brain Power in these words:

"The individual projects on all sides far beyond his anatomical frontiers. Man difuses through space in a still more positive way. In telepathic phenomena, he instantaneously sends out a part of himself, a sort of emanation, which joins a far off relative or friend. He thus expands to great distances, and may cross oceans and continents in a time too short to be estimated" (Man The Unknown, pp. 259, 261).

268

THE TOP SECRET

The top secret of the Masters was their discovery of HOW TO INCREASE BRAIN POWER. This discovery they recorded only in thickly veiled symbol and allegory.

Thus did they describe in the Apocalypse the EFFECT on the body of increased Brain Power. But they were careful not to include the secret how to accomplish it.

To discover that secret requires much more knowledge of psycho-physiological function of Body and Brain than that possessed at present by modern science,—a fact admitted by Carrel when he wrote, "Our ignorance (of body and brain function) is profound" (Man The Unknown, p. 4).

By their work the Masters proved that man really has Seven Sense Powers instead of only Five.

Some authors contend that, according to the sages and seers, man has twelve sense powers. The Apocalypse gives man only Seven.

Modern science says that man has only Five Sense Powers; yet it admits that birds, beasts, and some people possess strange mental powers that cannot be understood nor explained at this time.

Occult science asserts that the brain contains centers, the higher functions of which are almost entirely dormant in most persons of this age. Such are termed "the dead" in the New Testament and other esoteric writings.

According to the Apocalypse, it is only through the development and activation of the Sixth and Seventh Sense Powers that the Inner Man can act upon the consciousness of the psycho-intellectual self and discover the "World Within."

The corpse-like condition of the higher organs of the Brain does not preclude higher development of the ordinary intellectual faculties, apart from the epistemonic powers.

There are, and always have been, men who are examples of high intellectuality, combined with the densest spiritual stupidity.

In the case of the true genius, the poet, artist, intuitive philosopher and religious mystic of saintly purity, there is a partial awakening of these higher Brain Centers; while in the case of the Master the higher faculties are so active that he becomes cognizant of the interior worlds, the planes of True Being.

When man's State of Consciousness is raised from the Common Five to the rare Seven Power, that is the "resurrection of the dead" mentioned in the Bible, and the Regeneration and

Redemption recorded in the gospels, the Apocalypse, and expressed by myth and symbol in all the great religions of antiquity.

THE GODDESS

In the Egyptian Drama of the Ancient Mysteries, the Goddess Isis, symbolical of the Pituitary gland, tempts the God Ra symbolical of the Pineal (the seat of Spirituality), to reveal his secret name, which he finally does, as follows: "Nuk Pu Nuk," which, translated, means "I Am That I Am" (Ex. 3:14).

As stated in Lesson No. 21, these words were inscribed over the doors of pre-Egyptian Temples that were more than ten thousand years old, showing where the compilers of the Bible got "I Am That I Am."

David Livingston wrote a book, titled The Book of David and published in 1937, in which he attempted to show that the gospel Jesus was the "I AM," and to support his position, quotes these passages:

"If ye believe not that 'I AM,' ye shall die in your sins. . . . When ye have lifted up the Son of man, then shall ye know that I Am He" (Jn. 8:24, 28).

"When ye have lifted up the Son of Man," does not refer to the gospel Jesus, but to the Serpentine Fire.

The strange physiological process by which this is accomplished, unknown to modern science and to Livingston, is worthy of consideration.

Cosmic Radiation, appearing as Sparks of electro-magnetic power, emanations of Creative Force, is the Animating Principle of the Body, as we have seen.

This electro-magnetic power which warms into Life, also illuminates the Brain.

As the Brain receives more of the illuminating power when the refined Creative Force is lifted up from the lower creative centers, the Conscious Department of Mind is greatly increased in power, enabling man to know more about himself, his environment and the Universe.

The Serpentine Fire flows upward from the Base of the Spine through the spinal canal, which resembles a serpent standing upright on its tail, and constrained the Ancient Masters to term the force the Serpentine Fire.

In the Drama of the Ancient Mysteries the neophyte was taught the secret of the Serpentine Fire, and told that in the regenerate man the stream of faintly blue electric force flows up and down incessantly through the spinal canal.

The higher the stream ascends, the fainter and less brilliant its hue, but the more pure and beautiful its colors, until they finally merge in a mass, in the Pons and Medulla of the Brain.

When this force reaches the Pituitary, the Goddess of the Masters, the gland is aroused from its dormancy and resembles a scintillating jewel. It begins to glow faintly, and little rippling rings of golden light flow out from the gland, which slowly fade a short distance away.

So the Ancient Alchemist taught that out of the mass of God's creative compounds there emanates the Golden Fire.

As the process continues, the emanating rings around the Pituitary grow stronger. The rings are not regular, but elongated on the side facing the Pineal, extending out in parabolas toward the Pineal, and by their force stimulate the Pineal.

The waves flowing from the Goddess get stronger, and extend closer to the closed eye of Shiva (Pineal), tinting it with golden light and stimulating it into greater activity.

The Plummet of Zerubbabel, the builder of the temple (body) refers to the Pituitary and the force flowing from it.

The Pituitary (Zerubbabel) is the chief creative organ of the body as we have said elsewhere. When stimulated by the Serpentine Fire, its aura assumes a swinging motion, like a plummet, until the waves impinge on the Pineal as stated, awakening it from its dormant, inactive state.

This process is further described in Zechariah. Mention is made of "the two olive trees" and "the two olive branches which are beside the two golden spouts, that empty the golden (oil) out of themselves" are "the two anointed ones (Ida and Pingala Nadis) that stand by the Lord (Man) of the whole earth" (4:10-14).

POSITIVE AND NEGATIVE

The Divine Lines of Cosmic Radiation extend from the positive (God) to the negative (man), while the return is from the negative (man) to the positive (God). That same law governs the direction of the Serpentine Fire.

The Pineal is the positive pole, the mysterious link between the Conscious Mind and the Spiritual World, to which man's true self is related and of which it is a part,—but usually he knows it not because of false teaching.

The Pituitary is the negative pole, and plays a peculiar role in the function of increasing Brain Power. In one sense of the word, it is the Initiator, for it "awakens" from the dormant state the candidate (Pineal) who hears **"the voice of the Bride"** (Jer. 33:11), so wonderfully told in allegory by the Masters.

Under the stimulating force of the Pituitary, the dormant Pineal finally awakens. That is the **AWAKENING OF THE WORLD WITHIN.**

The increased Brain Power resulting, the Masters termed Spiritual Enlightenment. And in the Drama the Masters exclaimed, **"Behold, the man is become as one of us"** (Gen. 3:22).

THE SIXTH SENSE POWER

It is generally admitted that woman, as a rule, is more psychic than man. That is another mystery to material science.

The Pituitary is the organ of the Sixth Sense, and the Master Gland in propagation. As woman is the productive organism, the Pituitary is more active in her than in man. That increases the power of her Conscious Mind and makes her, as a rule, more psychic.

Such women have Six Sense Powers, which exalt them to a higher level than the average man in the department of psychism. So clear to occultism; so confusing to materialism.

SEVENTH SENSE POWER

This is the Forbidden Field of the Ancient Masters. This is the Field in which SILENCE reigns; in which SILENCE rules the tongue of him who has entered it.

This is the Field to which Paul (Apollonius) undoubtedly referred when he mentioned **"Unspeakable words which it is not lawful for a man (who knows) to utter"** (2 Cor. 12:4).

"And when he had opened the seventh seal (the chakra that affects the Pineal), there was SILENCE in heaven (brain) about the space of half an hour" (Rev. 8:1).

And when the Seven Thunders uttered their voices, I was about to write down (the teachings); but I heard a voice from the sky saying to me,

"Seal up the teachings which the Seven Thunders uttered, and write them not" (Rev. 10:4).

When the seventh trumpet-call is sounded, there is a choral announcement that the God, the True Self, the Inner Man, has come into his own, by the force of his Seventh Sense Power, and will reign throughout the aeons.

And the seventh angel sounded; and there were great voices in heaven (awakening of the Seventh Sense Power), saying, The kingdoms of this world are become the kingdoms of our lord; and he shall reign for ever and ever (Rev. 11:15).

"Our Lord" means that Man, king of the earth, constituted in the Likeness of God (Gen. 5:1), who was given dominion over every living thing on earth (Gen. 1:26), and knows all things by the force of his Seven Sense Powers.

This is the Super-conscious Department of Mind, so potent that no one seems able to measure it, with a vibratory rate beyond any rate of vibration capable of being registered by any mechanical instrument so far produced by science, and which psychologists say never forgets, and even contains all the wisdom of past ages.

"There should be Time no longer" (Rev. 10:6) means that by the Sevenfold Mind Power man rises above the illusion of Time.

And the seventh angel poured out his vial into the air; and there came a great voice from the temple of heaven, from the throne (brain), saying, "HE IS BORN" (Rev. 16:17).

That is the birth of Regenerated Man with the Sevenfold Mind Power. That indicates the **Awakening of the World Within,** the resurrection of the god (Pineal Gland).

The authorized version says, "It is done." Just another distortion. "He" was changed to "it," and "born" was changed to "done."

Revelation in this Forbidden Field was most carefully guarded. What little the Masters wrote about it, was always so thickly veiled in symbol and allegory that only the most advanced Occultist could decode it.

Neither should we describe the secrets of this Forbidden Field in any but the most general terms. Only a few can comprehend what we say, and fewer still can be constrained to believe it.

ORGAN OF MEMORY

Material science knows not that the Pineal is the organ of the Seventh Sense. It is the organ of memory, of expectation and anticipation. It is the organ that never forgets, and even contains all the wisdom of past ages.

Man would know nothing of past or future but for the function of the Pineal. Many have poor memory, some have little, others have none—because the Pineal is dormant, semi-dormant, sluggish.

The less active the Pituitary and Pineal glands, the weaker the Conscious Mind. By the increased action of these glands, man's knowledge of himself, his environment and the Universe is increased.

Some increase in the action of these glands may be produced by concentration of thought, and brain power to perceive situations is thus improved.

More increase is sometimes produced by a strong mental shock or a physical shock resulting from an accident to the head. We shall refer to this again.

Many dreams result from the action of these glands. Some persons, in whom these glands are more active, often get glimpses of their prior incarnations in dreams they do not understand. They sometimes see in dreams future events, which happen in due course according to the dream. These are mysteries to material science.

BUILDER OF THE TEMPLE

The Bible calls Zerubbabel "the builder of the temple" (Zech. 4:9).

Zerubbabel represents the Pituitary gland. It is the Master Gland of the Endocrine System in body construction, and to that end it excretes potent hormones that control or prod other glands into action.

Modern science has discovered that the Pituitary regulates the physical functions of the body; growth, bony structure, metabolism, chemical compounding, etc. Even the thoughts, emotions and senses of the physical, are under the control of the Black Kundalini. The facts show that the Ancient Masters knew these things.

The Pituitary does not excrete these hormones in sufficient quantity to affect the Pineal until the force of the Pituitary is increased by the rising Serpentine Fire.

Then the vibrations of the Pituitary are increased; and when the currents of force from the Pituitary have been deflected enough to activate the Pineal, the goal has been attained— the gap between the two glands has been bridged and the circuit established.

In other words, the rising Serpentine Fire first affects the Pituitary, feminine, negative pole, from which the increased force flows to the Pineal, masculine, positive pole, completing the circuit. This is termed "the marriage of the Lamb." (Rev. 19:7).

274

In this cosmic process, the Pituitary exhibits its dignity as being the Eternal Temptress, allegorically stated in the Bible "The woman . . . gave me of the tree, and I did eat" (Gen. 3:12).

The Pituitary is the mysterious bride of the Lamb (Pineal), mentioned in the Bible (Jer. 7:34; 16:9; 25:10; 33:11; Rev. 18:23; 19:7, 9; 21:2).

The church teaches its followers that this means the church is the "bride" of the gospel Jesus. Rediculous.

This bridge completes the circuit in man, and connects the physical and psychical worlds, the material and spiritual kingdoms.

In order to "Awaken The World Within," Buddhi (Pineal), the Seventh Sense, needs more of the refined force of Manas (Pituitary), the Sixth Sense, which in turn needs more of the Serpentine Fire from the Creative Centers at the base of the spine.

When the increased power of the Sixth Sense has awakened the Seventh Sense, Spiritual Light, radiating from the Seventh, illuminates the Fields of Infinitude in man's Consciousness.

Then man's Higher Consciousness, being awakened from its dormancy in the Third Resurrection, exhibits the strange powers of Clairaudience and Clairvoyance, thus enabling him to direct his supervision where he will, sensing objects and events at great distances.

In that state of super-consciousness, man becomes omniscient. Solid objects become transparent and are seen inside and out. The imaginary element of Space-Time disappears, past-future merge into the eternal present and all things become known.

And so the great Carrel wrote: **"For the clairvoyant there are no secrets."**

DANGEROUS POWERS

The danger to society that would result from the indiscriminate use of these higher powers, if possessed by unworthy ones, can easily be understood.

Such would be able to read one's secret thoughts. Hence only those who passed the rigid preliminary tests were accepted as candidates in the Ancient Mysteries; and the initiates were bound by the most solemn oath never to use the powers wrongly, or to serve their personal interests.

Through this inner perceptive faculty, all paths of knowledge are opened, and man has at his service, means of acquiring knowledge compared to which all other methods of investigation and observation by science are but child's play.

VIBRATION

Sheldon said that man has no existence other than as vibratory waves. It is all a matter of vibration.

Sound starts at the first octave of 32 vibrations per second, and ends for man at the 15th octave of 35,000 to 40,000 beats per second. Above this the human ear cannot register sound as the rate is too rapid.

A siren whistle that kills insects in ten seconds, produces sound that vibrates too fast for human ears to hear.

One gets dizzy if close to the sound-stream, and is puzzled because the condition results from no apparent cause—a cause unknown to man.

Any part of the body directly in the sound-stream, close up, gets very hot. If one's hand is placed in the sound-stream, with fingers touching one another, the parts that touch get burnt, and one knows not why.

Radiation increases until it reaches the 62nd octave, which is 4,611,525,018,427,387,904 vibrations per second.

From the first to the 62nd octave we have sound, electricity, heat, light, chemical rays, x-rays, and cosmic rays. At the 63rd octave we reach the enormous rate of 9,223,052,036,854,755,808 vibrations per second. In and above that we reach the region of Thought, the fastest thing known.

Here we come to that part of the Kingdom of God known as the All-Seeing-Eye (Pineal Gland), the vision of which nothing can obstruct because of its powerful vibratory rate.

This is actually the vast power of the Universe, which may be termed Cosmic Mind, acting upon and through Man's Mind.

This is the Penetrating Power, the exceedingly rapid vibration, that pierces all things, making solid objects appear transparent, as they do under X-ray, so they may be seen through and through, inside and out.

"My kingdom is not of this world" (Jn. 18:36), for it abides in the Brain, the Kingdom of God about which the Masters wrote. They were in contact with the "Inner Worlds," and the Pituitary and Pineal were their means of ingress thereto.

To them, pictures presented themselves quite independently of their will. Their controlling sense centers (chakras) whirled counter-clockwise, as they do to this day in Mediums, following negatively the Earth's motion as it turns on its axis.

Man must now depend on X-ray, radio, radar and television

276

as substitutes for the vast powers inherent in his Brain, but dormant in degenerate man.

These phenomena exist as phases of Universal Force, otherwise man could not produce them with machines.

All powers of the Macrocosm are present in the Microcosm, in character if not in degree.

Apollonius needed no television aid, while preaching at Ephesus, to see the assassination of Domitian at Rome.

It is all a matter of vibration. His Pineal Gland, the All-Seeing-Eye of the Brain, was sufficiently developed and active to pick up the vibrations of that event.

THE WHITE STONE

By degrees the neophyte was taught the secret of how to control the vibrations of the Pituitary and Pineal Glands in such manner as to enable him to contact any region of the "Inner Worlds" that he desired, as one does in dreams when asleep.

The faculty, when it is functional, is under control of the will. It is unnecessary for one to go into a trance or do anything abnormal, to raise the Consciousness to the Higher World. The Master simply wills to see, and he sees.

After the candidate was taught the preliminary lessons of the Serpentine Fire, he passed on to the next chamber of the Temple, where he was instructed in the lessons of the All-Seeing-Eye, the White Stone in which a new name is written, which no man knoweth saving he that receiveth it (Rev. 2:17).

THE PINE TREE

From time immemorial the Masters regarded the Pine Tree as one of the most sacred of the forest.

The marvelous Pineal Gland is shaped like a pine-cone and reddish in color. The amazing function of this gland is unknown to modern science, but in framing its name the Masters proved they understood its function.

In the Bible the gland is referred to as Mount Pineal, where Jakob wrestled with a man until the breaking of the day (Gen. 32:24, 30). That man was his animal nature which he struggled to subdue.

The Pineal is also referred to as Petra, the rock upon which the Masters built their symbolical temple (Mat. 16:18).

In good health the Pineal contains a substance like sand, plus a curious cement, and is hard and firm. In the average man of civilization the gland is in a state of deterioration, and is flabby and pasty.

The Pineal resembles an eye, and has a long stalk containing many nerves. The stalk also extends through the aperture in the cranial wall, and consequently lies close to the surface on the dorsum of the head between the parietal bones which form the lateral surfaces of the skull.

The Pineal is the gland through which the ethereal forces of the brain flow, the "Crystalline Dew" from heaven (Brain).

Some of this strange esse, the Father, flows down from the upper brain (Most High God) into the Pineal, where it is differentiated,—becomes positive and electrical in quality and action.

The Pineal is phosphorescent, and when shocked out of its dormant state by the ascension of the Serpentine Fire, it glows with spiritual light that floods the Mind, illuminating the Consciousness of him in whom this occurs.

When the Serpentine Fire remains dormant in the cave (sacral plexus), or is dissipated in sexual and other excesses, then it is consumed and not there to flow up to the Pineal. So the gland remains in a dormant state and man loses the use of its chief function.

THE SINGLE EYE

When the Pineal gland is normal and stimulated by the Serpentine Fire, it becomes the Inner Eye of the Brain, the All-Seeing Eye of the Masters, the Light of the World Within.

Ye are the light of the world. The light of the body is the (All-Seeing) Eye. If thine Eye be single, thy whole body shall be full of light (Mat. 5:14; 6:22).

As the Initiate prepared for instruction in the secret of the Single Eye, the "Light of Life" that lighteth "thy whole body," he prayed that the will of the gods be made known unto him.

When he reached the state where he experienced the strange sensation of the shock that suddenly awakens the Pineal, the Initiate cried out,

"Hail, New-born Light, O Mysterious most truly holy,
O pure light!"—Pike, p. 522.

PREMONITION

An example of the Future merging into the Present appears in that state of extra-sensory perception termed Premonition.

Before the discovery of radio, radar and television, nothing

278

beyond the visible and physical was considered by science. A spiritual world was just more heathenish superstition.

Now scientists say we are nearing the shores of a vast, unexplored ocean of mystery, of which "we are totally ignorant," says Carrel, and are surrounded by mysterious Forces of which little is known.

Materialists and evolutionists are finding it more difficult to ignore as "heathenish superstition" that Spiritual Kingdom about which the Masters wrote so much.

These material scientists are now slyly searching for more signs of that mysterious kingdom, and the Immortality of man,— that spiritual "house not made with hands, eternal in the heavens" (2 Cor. 5:1). The big stumbling-block in the path has been the false dogma of the church that

(1) man is mortal;
(2) immortality is a "gift of God by salvation only through belief in Christ Jesus," and
(3) the teachings that man is inherently immortal are a lie given by "Satan to Adam and Eve in the Garden of Eden."

The Masters definitely taught the Immortality of Man. The evidence shows they were far ahead of us in knowledge of the Spiritual World. It was to keep man ignorant of Matters Spiritual that their writings were destroyed.

The New Testament fable of Christ Jesus as an actual man would be rejected by any one who knew that man really represents the Incarnated Spirit in the physical world, as clearly stated in the Bible (1 Cor. 3:16).

In recent years new discoveries have informed us sufficiently in these matters so that we can begin to understand the strange things described in the fragments of the writings of the Masters which have come down to us. What little we have learned presages much for the future.

Premonition appears as an inner message of future events that seems to come out of nowhere. Of this mystery an eminent psychologist says:

"There are many differing theories as to the origin of such experiences. It is probable that we shall never know the true cause until we have a much better knowledge of the Sixth Sense. It is also bound up in the mystery of Time, about which we know very little."

More admission of modern ignorance on points where the Masters were well informed.

279

Usually, this preview of future events appears in the form of an intense mental conviction that leaves him who experiences it in no doubt as to its significance or urgency.

In other instances, the knowledge is imparted by a dream, and less frequently through more tangible manifestations. Vissions and apparitions seen in dreams have warned persons of events and disasters to come.

Jean de Bloch, a Warsaw business man, not only foresaw World War I and its duration, but wrote books on the subject sixteen years before it began.

In 1898 there was published his seven-volume work, "The Future War and Its Technical, Economic and Political Relations," in which he described the war with uncanny accuracy amounting almost to clairvoyant insight.

These apparent mysteries are understood by occultists, who know that knowledge of future events shows signs of some stimulation by the Serpentine Fire of the Pituitary and Pineal Glands. It also shows that these glands are not damaged enough to destroy their function.

The Serpentine Fire produces extra power in the body when the Life Fluid is conserved and not consumed in copulation and other ways.

The extra power stimulates the spiritual centers and increases man's consciousness. This cannot occur when the delicate spiritual centers are damaged by polluted air, as explained in "Man's Miraculous Unused Powers."

When the glands and spiritual centers are badly crippled, nothing happens. For the damaged organs cannot respond to the effect of the Serpentine Fire. When partial response occurs, the event termed Premonition appears.

Were glands and organs in better condition, greater response would result, and the "World Within" would be more fully revealed.

A Master of India said to the French writer Jacolliot:

"You have studied physical nature and obtained marvelous results—steam, electricity, air planes, and so on. But for more than 20,000 years we have studied the intellectual forces of the Universe, and discovered their laws and, by making them act alone or in concert with matter, have obtained phenomena still more astounding than your own."

A. P. Sinnett declared that there is scarcely any spiritualistic phenomena that cannot be reproduced by adepts in occultism by the force of their own will, supplemented by knowledge of the greater resources of the cosmos.

The powers with which occultism invests its adepts include control over cosmic forces which ordinary science knows nothing about.

There are scores of obscure or unknown cosmic laws yet to be discovered and employed to produce marvels that now would be considered pure magic.

STRANGE POWER OF ANIMALS

The power of extra-sensory perception is not confined to man alone. It appears in the lower animals. We notice it more in dogs as they are domesticated and we have a better chance to observe their conduct.

In 1940 a party of monks from the St. Bernard Monastery were greatly puzzled one morning by the reluctance of the dogs to go out for their usual morning exercise—an outing they generally awaited with much impatience.

No amount of coaxing could entice the dogs to move an inch.

The monks did not attempt to force them, for they knew from previous experience that the dogs possessed an uncanny power of sensing danger.

Less than an hour later, a thunderous roar came from high up the mountain-side and down swept the worst avalanche seen in years. Had the monks not heeded the dogs' warning, every man and dog had been swept to eternity.

Had the people of Tokyo heeded the warning of the local dogs before the terrible earthquake of 1923, the appalling death-toll had been greatly reduced.

Survivors told that for a week before the catastrophe, the dogs roamed through the city's streets whining and howling in abject misery. A few folk heeded the omen and left for the open country. Of those who remained, 100,000 were killed, 150,-000 injured, and 50,000 were reported missing.

The wailing of the dogs thus prefaced one of the world's great disasters.

Birds display powers of the Sixth and Seventh Senses. In the field of Television the homing-sense of birds, says Deslandres, appears to rise as the effect of electric perception. He wrote:

"Birds can home over territory that offers no visible landmarks. I have seen a pigeon released from a balloon at a height of 5,000 feet. The bird was carried in a closed box. As soon as released, it rapidly described two circles around the balloon and then, without hesitation, darted off in the direction of its dove-cot 250 miles away" (M.M.U.P., Bk 3, p. 45).

Birds have always built their nests as they do now, and each kind builds a certain type of nest. They were never taught, and needed no experience. Whence comes this knowledge? Spiritual intelligence.

Birds know which way to travel without a compass, and when to go to avoid winter's icy blast. They know that snow and ice will come at a certain time in the north, and that they must fly in a definite direction to a certain region to escape the fate of being frozen to death. Whence comes this knowledge? Spiritual intelligence.

Modern science has no rational answer for these and many other questions. The best it can do is to suggest that birds and beasts are guided by "instinct." It fails to explain what "instinct" is, and assumes that it must be a property of Matter.

Modern physics has studied phenomena in matter around us. That brand of physics exploded with the discovery of the electron.

Physicists are now busy trying to make the electron fit their materialism. They refuse to understand that it belongs to another world—the Spiritual World of the Masters.

Radio, Radar and Television are mechanized examples of the Spiritual Powers of the Universe that operate as Vital Intelligence in the strange conduct of birds and beasts, which science calls "Instinct."

Why does man not have these powers?

MICROCOSM AND MACROCOSM

Ancient science taught that man's body is a miniature, organized Universe (Microcosm), containing, in some certain form, everything contained in the Universe.

In the Universe there are countless planets, suns and stars, revolving at terrific speed round a common center.

In man's body there are countless planets, suns and stars (atoms), containing electrons that are revolving at terrific speed round a common center, and as far apart, relatively speaking, as the stars are from one another.

Therefore, if there is a Spiritual Realm in the Universe (Macrocosm), as taught by all great religions, there must also be a corresponding realm in man.

Everything in the Universe has its correspondence in man's body, active or dormant, known or unknown. In that case, the body must contain certain organs through which the Spiritual Realm manifests on the physical plane, thus putting man in direct contact and communication with the Spiritual Realm by means of these organs.

Rudolph Steiner wrote:

"In the wonderful convolutions of his brain, man is the image of the entire cosmos. In the body of the mother the human being is formed as an image and likeness of the Universe. Man is first brain, the image of the cosmos. We can study the cosmos by studying the human embryo in its early stages" (Spiritual Powers).

According to many observers and historians, as well as Indian tradition, when the Spaniards arrived to take over South America and push the helpless Indians back into the jungles, they found the Incan races had the uncanny ability of conveying and receiving accurate information over long distances. It was as remarkable in its way as wireless telegraphy.

An Indian knew exactly how many men or horses were approaching long before they could be seen or heard. He would tell where or in what direction a friend or foe was traveling, and could perform many more equally mysterious feats.

Dr. Juan Durand, who devoted many years to a study of Indian history, tradition and life, personally witnessed such feats.

One night, while at an Indian hut at Raco, the Indian owner placed his ear to the floor, and told Dr. Durand the exact number of men in a platoon of soldiers that were passing at a distance of more than two miles from the hut.

Another Indian at Panao, without rising from his couch, stated the number of men on foot and the number of mounted men traveling on a distant road, and even told the order in which they moved and the direction in which they were going.

THE RADAR MAN

Fate magazine of November, 1953 reported the strange case of Holland's "Radar-Man" named Mynheer van der Urk, 32 years old, who became known as Dr. Hurkos. From that story the following is condensed.—

In 1943, while working as a house painter, he fell from a 40-feet scaffold, landing on left shoulder and striking his head, suffering a fracture at base of skull and remained for three days in a coma at a hospital.

"Upon regaining consciousness," says the account, "Urk realized that he was in a world totally different from that in which he had lived for 32 years before the accident."

"The nurses and patients he saw for the first time were not strangers to him. He could read their minds without making any conscious effort to do so. In addition, he knew of events that had happened to them in the past."

Investigators of the paranormal would realize at once that Urk was demonstrating clairvoyance. There are countless cases, subject to repeated challenges and tests, that are impossible to explain except by this extra-sensory faculty.

It was Urk who located "the Stone of Stones," used in the coronation ceremonies in England, and stolen from Westminster Abbey. He guided the officers of Scotland Yard to the hardware store where the burglars purchased the tools used in the job, and to the house where they had hidden after they had removed the stone.

The most spectacular of these cases solved by Urk occurred in June, 1952. In France a little girl, aged four, was lost. For a week surrounding fields and woods, as well as pools and wells, were searched. Not a trace of the child could be found.

The "Radar-Man" was called. He first examined the child's bed, then some of her clothing and a shoe. He felt these objects carefully, frowning and concentrating.

"Sweat poured from his forehead. Suddenly his face became contorted, and with an expression of suffering he murmured, 'She is dead.' He had just 'seen' the dead child, and her face had a bluish color."

He told how the child died and where it was buried. The body was found in a forest of some 500 acres, buried there by a neighbor woman who had strangled the child.

Dr. Dellaert, psychiatrist at the University of Louvain, followed the career of Urk for many months, and on numerous occasions carefully observed his power of clairvoyance. He was astounded the day he met Urk, who described exactly the various rooms of the doctor's apartment which he had never seen.

The account relates many events where Urk was used by police to solve even foreign murders and kidnappings.

The "radar power" of Urk is an example of the higher powers of man's brain. The accident was such a shock to the brain that .it activated the Pituitary and Pineal glands, thus increasing Brain Power.

Had Urk developed his higher powers as an Initiate of the

Ancient Mysteries, he had been subject to the rigid rules thereof, and not permitted to exhibit these powers in public or use them for public purposes. Nor had he revealed to any, but a brother Initiate, the fact that he had such powers. That was the nature of the oath required of all Initiates before being taught the secret of these powers.

ANTECEDENT INCARNATIONS

The Superconscious Mind never forgets, assert psychologists, and even contains all the wisdom of past ages.

Cases on record show that persons remember certain events that occurred in their previous lives on earth.

Fate Magazine of January, 1954 described one of these cases. The event happened in a movie theater in Liverpool, England.

The theater was dark. With rapt attention the audience watched the scene in "Tudor Rose" where Lady Jane Grey was to be beheaded on February 12, 1554, four hundred years ago.

"Suddenly the hush was pierced by the wild cry of a girl who jumped to her feet and was silhouetted against the light of the motion picture screen.

"It is all wrong, all wrong! I was at the execution. It is all wrong, I say!"

Then she fell in a faint and, through the midst of the amazed audience, was carried out to the lobby. When revived she told an astonishing story.

She was Miss Dorothy Jordan, an 18-year-old typist from Belfast, Ireland, and was spending a holiday in Liverpool.

Never before had she shown any interest in history, nor had she any knowledge of reincarnation.

She told her story to a reporter of the Empire News, who said she seemed frank, intelligent, and far from flighty.

"As she watched the picture she said she was suddenly transported back into another age.

"When the screen flashed the picture of Lady Jane Grey waving through the tower window, I realized that this was wrong. I knew that room well, and it was impossible to look out of the window. It was too high. Later when the movie showed Lady Jane as perfectly calm, I knew that was not right. She was hysterical.

"As I followed her to the scaffold . . . I was wearing the same kind of clothes. The rough cobbles in the street hurt my feet through the soft shoes I was wearing. Now and then Lady Jane would look around like a haunted animal, but at last braced herself.

"It was during the execution scene that I first realized, as I intently watched the film, that I was her lady-in-waiting. I saw things in the film that did not agree with facts as I knew them.

"The streets were not silent as the film depicted. Some persons were being trampled and trodden upon. As Lady Jane went up the steps, there was a little boy calling out her name. She turned her head and looked sadly at him.

"I have a vivid impression of the executioner, and recall particularly the broad black bands around his wrists which are not shown in the film. When Lady Jane first saw him she shuddered and clung to me. I can feel her arms about me now. She wept a little. Then she seemed to realize that she could not go like that, and straightened herself, looking ahead.

Courtesy Fate Magazine

"When she got to the block, the executioner looked at her compassionately and said, 'Will you forgive me?' Lady Jane replied, 'Certainly,' not 'Most willingly,' as in the film. Then she looked round at me, and bent her head to the block. They lifted her curls, as is not shown in the film, and then I saw no more. I remember putting my hands over my face and that is all I can remember. I suppose I fainted.

"When I became conscious just now, the surroundings and the people seemed strange, and I thought I was dreáming, that reality was still the Tudor period. I was amazed not to find myself in Tudor dress. I suppose the people thought I was crazy! But it happened just as I say."

In Liverpool, in 1936, this girl was taken back mentally to an execution she saw on Tower Hill, London, 382 years before.

In old books, in modern newspapers and over radio many such stories come to light.

Some of the cases involve children, and talking babies. Christian Heinichen, of Lubeck, Germany, could talk at thè age of eight weeks, and knew the Pentateuch and other books of the Bible at 13 months.

Scientists at Stanford University several years ago were amazed by the case of Joan McGlamery. At 23 months she had a vocabulary of 450 words.

Another case, authenticated by three doctors, was that of a baby at Guane who spoke pure Castilian at the age of one month.

Maria Guzman of Madrid spoke at birth. She entered the Academy of Madrid at the age of 10 and became a doctor of philosophy and literature at 17.

Colonel Rochas, of France, used hypnotism to take his subjects back through what seemed to be a series of antecedent incarnations.

A. R. Martin, of Sharon, Pennsylvania, claimed no psychic gift, but was able to take the seeker back into antecedent experiences. The patient saw and felt such remarkable things that he was forced to believe that they were actual events of his former lives, or that his subconscious possessed incredible powers.

Martin majored in psychology at college, made a study of hypnotism, and became interested in the work of Dr. Cannon who could send the subject's memory back to the moment of birth, but no further.

Martin published a book, "Researches into Reincarnation and Beyond," in which he recounts some fifty of his thousands of cases.

Not every subject could be sent back through time. The ability to relax physically and mentally is vital.

An orthodox preacher visited Martin and was taken back through some of his previous incarnations. Some of the experiences caused him to burst into tears, and he asked whether it were conceivable that he had lived through so much.

Martin replied, "If all that were not there in your mind, it could not be coming out."

This preacher saw himself in the past as ruler of a 10th century Chinese province. During this review he lectured on Buddhism, chanting in Chinese. Later he saw himself in a Swiss chalet as an old man, futilely trying to comfort a distraught daughter.

In all instances his present visible body assumed, as if by magic, the posture, tone and bearing suitable to the character he believed himself to be.

Once he appeared to suffer such agony from thirst that a doctor in the room could hardly be restrained from administering to the "dying" man. But when he woke up he did not want a drink.—Condensed from Fate Magazine.

Some psychologists hold that these visions are caused by contact with a Universal Mind rather than by personal experience. We should remember that the Superconscious Department of Mind is a phase of Universal Mind.

The case of Dorothy Jordan was the result of powerful mental shock, coupled with very deep concentration of thought, penetrating to the Subconscious Department of Mind, wherein are recorded the events of one's antecedent incarnations.

This is the "World Within," the Kingdom and Throne of the Omniscient God of the Masters, that sees and knows all things and forgets nothing,—the philosophy of the Masters that is termed "heathenish superstition" by modern science.

RENEWING THE MIND

The Bible says that man is transformed by a renewing of the Mind (Rom. 12:2).

How transformed? From the physical to the spiritual plane in Consciousness. From the Five Sense Power to the Seven Sense Power.

A higher state of Consciousness reveals the world beyond the limit of the Five Sense Power, with which power man receives his knowledge only of the physical world.

In a higher state of Consciousness man receives knowledge of a higher world with his higher sense powers, which are dormant in most men.

Man loses contact with the physical world as he loses his

Five Sense Power due to damage to the brain. He loses contact with the higher world as he loses his higher sense powers due to brain damage.

In "Man's Miraculous Unused Powers" we showed that polluted air is a definite brain poison (Lesson 26).

An insane man knows little of the physical world. He has lost most of his powers to contact that world because of brain derangement.

The press of Dec. 30, 1953, reported that Oscar (Battling) Nelson, age 71, former lightweight boxing champion, was in a psychopathic hospital suffering from complete loss of memory.

Dr. C. B. Geary, assigned to the case, said Nelson "is out of contact with the world."

A living, conscious man, with no memory, completely "out of contact with the world."

Accordingly, man knows nothing of the higher world when he has lost his higher powers to contact that world because of poorly developed brain, or brain derangement.

These higher powers are active in birds and beasts and some "uncivilized" people because their brain organs of higher function have not been ruined by polluted air and in other ways.

These higher brain powers are remarkably active in birds due to the fact that they live up in the purest air, and in other ways obey the Law of Life.

TIME-SPACE

The great Carrel wrote:

"Each part of the body seems to know the present and future needs of the whole, and acts accordingly. The significance of Time and Space is not the same for our Cells as for our (physical) Mind. The body perceives the remote as well as the near, the future as well as the present" (Man The Unknown, p. 197).

If the body perceives the remote as well as the near, the future as well as the present, why does Mind not function accordingly? That is what we are trying to explain.

The world in which we live is a world of material science. We are so deeply immersed in this culture and its theories, that it is difficult to imagine how much it has influenced our thinking.

Modern physicists are forced to come up with new concepts that the old-time professor would reject. He would regard them in the same light as paranormal phenomena and ask, "Can you weigh it, taste it, smell it, feel it, see it?"

Today we see the world's leading scientists theorizing a new world, in which there appears a place for the doctrines and philosophies of the Ancient Masters. Their ideas have not even filtered down yet to the "mine-run" of scientists, much less to the "mine-run" of the masses.

These leading scientists are discovering that Matter is an entirely different thing than we have been accustomed to think it.

We have such an eminent scientist as Prof. Pais talking about atomic nuclei, not as different forms in themselves, "but as different states of one form."

That space as we know it may be entirely different than we have been taught. Is space two billion light years across, or 15? There seems to be quite a difference of opinion.

Time itself is different than we have been accustomed to regard it. To Einstein it is a fourth dimension. To Prof. Pais it is something even further extended.

We have now discovered that Time itself can be transposed; that physics cannot explain many of the things that we observe; that the Mind can influence objects; that telepathy exists but cannot be measured—and many other strange things.

The average man's thoughts are entirely engrossed in the material world. He is a prisoner of his Five Senses, and cannot free his Mind from the bondage of the flesh. His knowledge is limited by materialism to the world of visible matter.

Newtonian physics is the foundation of scientific materialism. Einstein threw a bombshell into the midst of this smug, three-dimensional world of science with its independent Time-Absolute.

Before him, Minkowsky had worked out a four-dimensional geometry in which he considered four variables—x, y, z and t (Time) as the coordinates of a point in four-dimensional space.

Before Minkowsky, Michelson and Morley had questioned the Newtonian concept of Time as an Absolute.

When Minkowsky's theories were substantiated by Einstein, the whole fabric of Newtonian physics began to crumble and material science began to totter.

Jokesters had much fun with Einstein and his incomprehensible talk about a Space-Time continuum. But scientists did not laugh; and the Space-Time continuum, like Relativity itself, is now an accepted scientific dictum.

The best place to gain some insight into the actual character of Time is in the phenomenon of sleep, and, more especially, in dreams.

The Subconscious Department of Mind knows nothing of the Time-abstraction that physical consciousness has devised. There is no Time element in dreams.

In dreams we see the past, present and future with equal facility. A dream that encompasses days, months, and even years, may take only a few minutes or even seconds of Time.

The Society for Psychical Research, London, has compiled records on more than 1,000 proven cases of precognition,—that is, instances in which some future event has been seen before it occurred, often, though not always, in dreams.

The result of this investigation has produced an impressive mass of evidence strongly suggestive of Mind Power that is not limited by Time.

In his work, "The New Immortality" (1938), John W. Dunne held that "reality," as it appears to science, must be a series of "regresses" reaching back into infinity.

He held that the Time-barrier is non-existant, and is merely an invention of physical consciousness. That there is a common faculty of the Subconsciousness which disregards this alleged barrier.

The trance state, either hypnotic or mediumistic, is another condition where Time, as we know it, has no meaning.

A related phenomenon is retrocognition,—that feeling of "having been here before." That feeling may be the result of one's remembering events that occurred in one's previous life on earth.

If we accept precognition as a fact, there is little to hinder our accepting also retrocognition.

If Mind is not limited in its progress forward in Time, it can hardly be limited in its backward reach into the past. In fact, all events are recorded in the Brain, and these become apparent as the Seven Sense Powers come into full function.

Another theory about Time is called that of the Great Specious Present, advanced by H. F. Saltmarsh of the London Society for Psychical Research.

His theory is based on the conception that the "present moment" in which we act is not a mere point-instant, but occupies a definite period of duration.

Within this "specious present" there is no present, no past, no future, but rather a gradation with respect to clearness of apprehension of whatever lies within its compass, maximum clearness being at the center.

Psychologists are asking whether there is Mind Power, termed Subconscious or whatever it may be called, that is not limited by Time. Many things appear to indicate that there is. The Ancient Masters believed there is, and proved it in their work.

For instance, they taught their disciples how to control the vibrations of the Pituitary and Pineal glands in a manner that enabled them to contact any region of the Inner Worlds that they desired to visit, as we do in dreams when asleep.

The faculty is under control of the will. It is unnecessary that we go into a trance or do anything abnormal, to raise the Conscious Department of Mind to the Spiritual level.

WE REAP AS WE SOW

People in general are ruled by the social pattern, and live to eat, drink, and to gratify their epithumetic nature in unrestrained manner. He who rejects that mode of life and strives to rise to a higher plane, must keep his own counsel, or become a social outcast.

The social pattern life causes much confusion in the body. The evidence of this appears in hospitals over the land.

The entire period of sleep must be used by the vital force to repair the damage done the body during the day, leaving no time for other work of any kind.

It is folly to talk to such about the higher life. They try to find it in the church, where their teachers know nothing about it.

As man begins to curb his desires, to use less, to deny himself, and to control his animal nature, there is less disturbance done in the body during waking hours, and less time is required during sleep to repair the damage.

Then man begins to get a glimpse of the higher world in his dreams, as it is possible for his Astral Being to divert its function from the dense physical body for longer periods during sleep, and function in the higher world.

It becomes possible for such man to see himself in dreams as he was years before, the events all being recorded in the Brain, and past and future become the present to the Real Man.

We must first learn to relax and concentrate. During deep concentration the five physical senses are stilled, and man is outwardly in the same state as in sleep, yet the Astral Being remains within and fully conscious.

Some experience this state in some degree when deeply interested in a book. They live in the scenes depicted by the author, and are lost to their environment. If spoken to, they are oblivious to the sound, and to all other things occurring around them.

But they are fully awake to all they are reading of that invisible world created by the author, living there and feeling the sensations of all the various characters in the story.

They are not independent, but are bound in the life which the author of the book has created for them.

In physical death the Real Man is freed from the prison of his Five Senses, and finds himself in the Spiritual World.

The Masters taught their disciples how to release themselves from that prison while still living on the material plane.

In ordinary life, if all impressions received by the Five Senses are shut out and obliterated, we fall asleep as a rule. The Masters taught their disciples how to do this and remain awake.

Man must first learn to regard himself as related to the Spiritual World, and not merely an earthly being, as taught by modern science. For as a man thinketh, so is he (Pr. 23:7).

To free the Mind of physical obstructions, man must relax, meditate and concentrate. He should practice this until his consciousness becomes empty while he is still awake.

Then he attains a state revealed through spiritual science to which one can rise who can be systematically and methodically developed, viz., to have a consciousness free of all things physical in complete waking awareness.

That is the primary stage of spiritual knowledge. The consciousness, free of all things physical, is the first to reveal the "World Within,"—that mysterious kingdom which is neither here on earth, nor there in space, but outside Space and Time.

Then we are in that world where we passed our Life as Spirit before we were imprisoned in the physical body.

Then we learn to know ourselves as Beings that spiritually existed before physical birth, and who lived a pre-earthly existence before the earthly existence wherein we now are.

We thus learn to recognize ourselves as Spiritual Beings. We do not learn this by theorizing nor by subtle cogitation. It can be known only when the suitable capacities are unfolded in intellectual modesty.

When we place ourselves in a state where we can experience what Spirit is without a physical body, we are living in a consciousness that is free of physical limitations. If we can learn of our real nature by this means, we can go still farther.

When we come to know ourselves entirely as Spiritual Beings in a Spiritual World, we know man is Spirit. Then we know what physical death is. Man simply leaves his physical body entirely.

In physical birth, man passes from the Spiritual World into physical existence; and in physical death he passes from the physical world into Spiritual Existence. That is the CHANGE mentioned in the Bible.

We shall not sleep, but we shall be **changed** (1 Cor. 15:51, 52).

In this way we learn of the true nature of Man, which is Spiritual, and which goes through physical birth and physical death. Only then are we able to comprehend our whole being.

ASTRAL PROJECTION

The foregoing is the Spiritual Science that was taught by the Masters. It leads up to the secret of Astral Projection. Their writings on this subject were so completely destroyed by the early church fathers that only fragments have come down to us.

The secret of Astral Projection was used by the Masters in the Ancient Mysteries to demonstrate to the neophyte that he had Eternal Life. He was taught how to withdraw from his body and then look down at his body through his Astral Sight.

In the Egyptian "Book of the Dead" the Spirit of Osiris was pictured as a hawk or dove that was leaving the body and looking down at it. This was termed "the resurrection." In the Egyptian Drama Osiris said, "I am the resurrection and the life" (Jn. 11:25).

When the church fathers interpolated that phrase in the John gospel, they never anticipated that the original source of it would ever be found.

When some persons undergo an operation, while under the influence of the anaesthetic they experience a state of Astral Projection.

In 1936 Juliette Neel, of Texas, underwent an operation, and says that when she inhaled the ether to make her unconscious, a strange thing happened.

Of this experience she said:

"I heard the doctor talking in low tones as he ordered instruments, and suddenly I was no longer conscious of being in my body. I seemed to be above my body and looking down on the operation.

"I saw the doctor insert instruments into my body. Then I spoke and said, 'I know what you are doing to my body, but you will not believe me.'

"The doctor and nurses were startled, and for a moment did not move. I went on describing the operation and trying to prove that I was conscious of everything and was not in the body on which the doctor was working.

"When the operation was over, I returned to my body. There was an interval of unconsciousness, and when I awoke I found the doctor and nurses were amused by my description of the operation, given while under the effect of the ether.

"The operation was a minor one, the description was not complicated and they believed I had been only dreaming" (Condensed from Fate, October, 1953).

Margaret Linden, writing in Fate Magazine, says,

"I am certain that Life continues after (physical) death, because I was once permitted to cross the threshold between them."

She became ill and was rushed to a hospital for an operation. Not more than a couple hours after the operation, she says,

"I was back in bed and was reviving from the effect of the anaesthetic, and heard myself cry despairingly, over and over, 'Don't send me back!'

She continues:

"I can further remember trying frantically to move my inert body and being restrained by the doctor, who held both my hands.

"He was speaking quietly, insistently, striving to impress on my subconscious that it must hold fast to the remembrance of why I was begging not to be 'sent back.'

"The next day when I came back to full consciousness, the doctor was there, and asked me, 'Did I remember?' I did, and do now.

"At some time during the operation, I—my spirit—left my body. I remember that I was flying, and knew this was no dream. For I had died. I knew it, and welcomed it.

"It was far more wonderful than any dream. I was no longer imprisoned in my body. I was lighter than thought; had no weight, no substance at all. I knew I was no longer a (physical) person.

"I was just an essence, a vital spark, equipped with thoughts, feelings and senses. The feeling above all else was that of extraordinary happiness.

"I could hear magnificent music, and it seemed that I was the center of it.

"As I was savoring this ecstasy in its entirety, a voice in me commanded: 'You must go back; you must go back.'

"I felt as if I were being pushed downward. I cried, I implored, but again came that command: 'You must go back.'

"Down I came, faster and faster, until, with a crash,

I felt myself pushed into what seemed to be a coffin of lead, which my spirit knew was my body.

"After I told this to the doctor, he informed me that toward the end of the operation, I had no pulse, no heart beat, no breath. I was apparently dead. He had immediately inserted his fingers through the incision in my body, and from there was able to massage my heart, hoping to start its action. He succeeded—and I was alive again."
—Condensed from Fate Magazine.

Occultists have described various methods of Astral Projection. One of these advises the student to make the attempt for at least ten nights in succession, as follows:

"The student should select a quiet room where he can remain undisturbed. At exactly the same time each evening he should dim the lights, make himself comfortable in an easy chair, close his eyes, and mentally and physically become quiet, relaxed, and concentrate."

The student is advised to breathe deeply and quietly, relax, clear the mind of all thoughts, and when a state of relative mental emptiness is reached, he should try to visualize himself seated in the chair. This is difficult and apparently the most important single step in the process.

When the initial visualization is accomplished, the student should visualize himself rising slowly from the chair, in his normal physical fashion. If the image suddenly breaks off, he should compose himself and try again.

The experiment should be attempted each evening at the same time under the same conditions.

There is a strong effect on the Subconscious Department of Mind of identical efforts repeated at the same time, under the same conditions, every day—an adjustment, a conditioning process, occurs that makes each successive effort easier and more certain of ultimate success.

Finally the time will come, to many persons, when they will be able to turn their thoughts back upon themselves, and to see themselves clearly, mentally, as they appear seated in the chair.

Then it is a comparatively minor step to visualize oneself rising from the chair and walking slowly several paces.

The student must then learn to turn around carefully until he can look back, through his Astral Sight, at his body seated in the chair. From here on progress is rapid.

At first the student should practice walking around his closed room, then pass through doorways—not by walking through closed doors, but by reaching for the knob, turning it, and mentally pushing open the door as in the usual way.

This method is evidently recommended to avoid unbalancing the student's delicate sense of reality, which would trigger the conscious mind into pulling the Astral Body back into the physical.

The first Astral Journey should be short and in familiar surroundings. For example, a slow walk to a neighbor's house, going through the usual physical motions of opening and closing doors, walking up and down steps and quietly into the neighbor's presence—preferably at a time when he would be reading or writing.

Once in his friend's presence, the student should observe what he is reading or writing, so that he may later confirm his Astral Visit.

Only after repeated, careful and short Astral Journeys should the student try trips further afield, or pass directly through doors and walls.

He should also refrain from ever letting his Astral Visits become known to any one, and never to the unsuspecting subjects of his secret observations.

Of course, those seeking development and activation of their latent Psychic Powers should follow a course of natural living in clean country air, in order to purify blood, body, and mind.

They must practice rigid self-denial in all things, and develop divine love and gratitude for their present state of Spiritual Consciousness, and a realization of their attunement with Cosmic Spirit.

Gluttons, drinkers, smokers, and those living the regular conventional life, would only be wasting time to try this experiment. The same is true of those who fail to live a life of chastity. This last requirement is of the utmost importance.

Before any attempt is made at Astral Projection, the following steps should be taken:

1. After several months of chastity and a natural mode of living in clean, country air to purify blood, body and mind, look calmly and modestly at yourself in a mirror and mentally instruct your inner-self to return to the room and physical body at the desired time—never over an hour.

2. Visualize the astral-etheric bodies in union and mentally see them back in the room and your physical body at the desired time, alone and unencumbered by any outside entities.

3. Affirm solemnly and firmly that Cosmic Spirit and the Masters are guiding you. Repeat this affirmation until you have

an inner conviction that they are guiding you. Then relax, meditate, and request their protection.

The student should stop the experiment instantly, if he feels himself blacking out or losing consciousness. Promptly will yourself back into your physical body.

While entering the trance state, one should hold in mind the following suggestions:

I am (your name) ... I am strength and power. ... I will not be influenced against my will by force other than good. ... I can always return to myself when I so desire.

The Masters carefully warned their disciples against excessive introspection.

"Never go inside of your own head and examine its processes, or introspect for too long a time. Always keep an interest in external things and live, as it were, outside your head, in the external world all the time."

Never under any circumstances tell anyone your secret.

Lesson No. 57

Plate 1

Padmasana

AWAKENING OF KUNDALINI

At the lower end of the Sushumna Nadi is the "Lotus of the Kundalini." It is triangular in shape, and, in the symbolical terminology of the Masters, there coiled up is the dormant Kundalini (Serpentine) Fire.

When the Kundalini is aroused to activity by the force of man's spiritual will, whether by his conscious effort or unconsciously so far as his phrenic mind is concerned, it displaces the sluggish nerve force or neuricity and becomes the agent of the telestic or perfecting work.

As the fiery force flows upward from one ganglion to another, its voltage increases, the chakras acting like electric cells coupled for intensity. In each chakra it liberates more force which partakes of the quality peculiar to that chakra, and it is then said to conquer that chakra.

The Serpentine Fire, as specialized and intensified in the chakras, is called in the Apocalypse the Seven Pneumata (breaths), since they are differentiations of the Great Breath, the World-Mother, symbolized by the Moon.

Concurrent with these Seven Lunar Forces, symbolized as Stars in Revalation (1:16; 2:1; 3:1), are Five Solar Forces pertaining to the cerebro-spinal system, called the Five Pranas, Vital Airs, or Life Winds, which in the Apocalypse are termed "winds."

These twelve forces the Apocalypse represents as corresponding to the twelve signs of the Zodiac.

All occurrences in the spiritual and physical worlds are under the influence of Cosmic Impulses, the Prana. The activities of the human body, forming part of the whole, come under its control.

Cosmic Prana, as it operates in the body, is named according to the activity of the department it controls and the situation it occupies. Thus, the Yogi lists five kinds of vital impulses in the body, known as Pancha Pranas:—Udana, Prana (auxiliary), Samana, Apana, and Vyana.

Udana rules the region of the body above the larynx. This Prana keeps us on the alert as regards our special senses.

Prana (auxiliary) rules the region between the larynx and the base of the heart.

Samana rules the region of the body from the heart to the navel.

Apana has its abode below the navel and rules the automatic action of the kidneys, colon, rectum, bladder and genitals. It governs mostly the excretory mechanism of the body.

Vyana pervades the whole body and governs its movements due to the contraction, expansion and relaxation of muscles, both voluntary and involuntary, and the movements of the joints and adjacent structures.

Beyond the description given, little is known about these Pancha Pranas. Some occult students hold that they are the five important subsidiary nerve centers in the brain and spinal cord.

These centers are called Shaktis of the Chakras. Every involuntary act in the body is governed by them, and when their activities are balanced, there presence is not felt.

The Thalamus is the highest reflex center in the brain. As all impressions ascend to it, it is called the Udana-prana, and is said to rule the portion of the brain above this point.

The Yogi, by conscious control over the Udana-prana, suppresses all incoming and outgoing sensations in it. This suppression is necessary to prevent that distraction of the mind which he wants to control.

Prana (subsidiary) is situated in the medulla oblongata and governs the respiratory and circulatory functions.

These Pancha Pranas and the currents they generate are not normally under the control of the will. To establish such control is one of the most important achievements in the Science of Yoga.

As stated, these Pranas are the different controlling forces of the plexuses of the sympathetic nerve, but there is a Shakti that controls singly the activities of these plexuses; and that Shakti is the Vagus nerve, i.e., the Kundalini. By gaining control over this Kundalini with the will, one can subjugate not only the Pancha Pranas, but the whole of the autonomic nerve system, and thus suspend the katabolic activity of the body which disturbs the Mind.

This current of Kundalini is brought under control by practicing certain catches (Bandha) and by attitudes of the body (Mudra) during the process of Pranayama.

PRANAYAMA

Pranayama means the regulation of breathing. It is a series of breathing exercises by which the Yogi gains control of Prana.

Pranayama begins with regulation of the breath for controlling the Vital Force. It is control of the Vital Force through control of the Breath.

The chief aim of Pranayama is to unite the Prana with the Apana and take the united Prana-apana slowly upward to the brain. The effect is the awakening of dormant Kundalini.

H. Y. Pradipike, famous author on Kundalini, says:

"When the breath is irregular as it is in most cases,

300

the mind wanders, but when the breath is under control, the mind is also under control."

Also, as long as the Nadis(nerves) are not pure, the Prana cannot go through the Sushumna; and as long as Prana does not go through Sushumna, there is no success in raising Kundalini. As soon as the Nadis are purified, the Yogi succeeds in doing Pranayama, and then the Prana goes through the Sushumna.

There is no success without purification of the Nadis, and no purification of the Nadis without Pranayama.

When the Prana goes through the Sushumna, the mind becomes one-pointed. This is called Unmani Avastha (steadiness of mind).

Pradipike says: "When Pranayama, called Kevala Kumbhaka, has been mastered, there is nothing in the three worlds that cannot be attained."

During the Kumbhaka stage of Pranayama, when the inhaling of external energy with the oxygen is stopped, and exhaling of carbonic acid gas is prevented, the venosity of the blood increases, and this has a powerful effect in stimulating to action the origin of the Kundalini.

The longer the breath is held, the more powerful is the effect on the Kundalini.

By this process, the current that is generated flows through the whole length of Kundalini and distributes itself in Manipura-chakra, which is indirectly connected with the Swahishtana and Muladhara chakras.

Directing the vision at tip of nose in the process of Pranayama has the effect of stimulating the afferent sympathetic fibers of the Kundalini. In this exercise the Yogi wants the current of Kundalini to stop at a desired chakra to inhibit the function thereof. This is done by practicing certain Bandhas (catches) during the process of Pranayama and also by certain attitudes of the body called Mudra.

These attitudes of the body must not be confounded with postures of the body, called Asana.

While Mudra is a variety of Asana, it differs in having a certain contortion of the portion of the body above the neck. In Asana, that contortion is restricted to the portion below the waist.

There are three important Bandhas and many Mudras which a student of Yoga may practice to rouse the Kundalini.

The various Asanas, Bandhas or Mudras are said to deliver the body from the ravages of idleness and decrepitude, and thus defer death. They keep the body supple, and also prevent distraction of the mind, over which Yogi wants to gain control.

THE THREE BANDHAS

Plate II

Uddiyana-Bandha with condition of the
neck preliminary to Jalandhara-Bandha.

The three important Bandhas (catches) are Mula-bandha, Jalandhara-bandha, and Uddiyana-bandha. They are all to be practiced in one rhythm of Pranayama.

Mula-bandha is to be practiced at the beginning of the process of Pranayama.

In this Bandha, the center of the perineum (Yoni) is firmly pressed by the heel of the right foot. In Lesson Number 54 the student was advised to press the finger on the lower end of the spine. When this is properly done with the heel, the body appears to rest on that heel. The left leg then rests on the right thigh.

With the Puraka of Pranayama, i.e., with deep and prolonged inhalation, the anus becomes contracted and drawn upward, hands rest on knees, shoulders elevated, and head and neck depressed between them (see plate II).

While, in this attitude, Puraka is completed, Kumbhaka, i.e., retention of the breath is practiced with head bent forward, and chin is made to press firmly against root of neck. This causes submersion of Kantha-Mani in the depression caused by elevation of shoulders.

After this, the Rechaka process of Pranayama is gone into,

Plate III

Pose showing the three bandhas. Mula-Bandha, Uddiyana-Bandha and Jaland-hara-Bandha.

Plate IV

Siddhasana
or
Mula Bandha

and here the breath in exhaled, navel drawn upwards, with expansion of lower part of thorax until abdomen is flattened. This is called Uddiyana-bandha, and with these Bandhas a complete rhythm of Pranayama ensues.

The effect of these Bandhas on the nerve mechanism of the autonomic system is interesting to follow.

In Mula-bandha the pressure of the heel on the center of the perineum from below upwards, and the pressure of the body, which is made to rest on the heel, from above downward, stimulates the pelvic plexus (Muladhara chakra) to action. At the same time it blocks the downward and outgoing (efferent) impulses from it, but the upward afferent impulses, being unchecked, ascend through the connecting tissues to the Swadhisthana chakra, and thence, through it, to the Manipura chakra.

These plexuses being thus stimulated, there occurs an inhibition of function of the organs supplied by the sympathetic fibers from these plexuses.

The peristaltic action of the gastro-intestinal tract being inhibited by stimulation of the sympathetic fibers, gases accumulate and inflate it with consequent discomfiture. Also owing to the contraction of the blood vessels of the splanchnic area, there is dimunition of blood supply to the abdominal viscera, which checks the excretion of the gastro-intestinal tract.

This disturbance of the katabolic activity of the sympathetic system causes a general respiratory and circulatory disturbance: the heart beats faster, the blood vessels going to the muscles dilate, and the cutaneous blood vessels contract. Respiratory activity is increased, breathing becomes faster, and a feverish sensation occurs in the body.

All this activity of the sympathetic nerve system is described in weird and exaggerated terms in the old Yogic literature; but, in the main, it is true and correct.

This katabolic disturbance excites fear of illness in the initiate, and often makes him omit the practice of Pranayama with Bandha. If persisted in, this excessive stimulation of the sympathetic fibers automatically excites the parts of the Kundalini in the Manipura chakra, where she is said to lie dormant.

This is the unconscious activity of the Kundalini, not desired by a Yogi, who wants to become conscious of the work, and that is possible only if stimulation of the vagal center occurs through the posterior part of the spinal column (Sushumna Nadi), the **Nerve of Knowledge.**

By practice of Pranayama with these three Bandhas mentioned, a Yogi establishes conscious control over Kundalini, which is then easily acted upon by the will.

This conscious control may not last long. The Kundalini tries to resist it and begins to move in and out of the Medulla—begins to send and receive efferent and afferent impulses.

A Yogi's effort is not only to get conscious control of the Kundalini, but to keep her steady and inactive in her abode in mid-brain, so that she may remain impervious to efferent and afferent impulses, which have the power of influencing the Mind-stuff, which the Yogi call 'Chitta."

Kundalini is thus submerged in Chitta.

The submersion of Prana in the mind is Samadhi, i.e., super-consciousness, and does not prevent a Yogi from the worries of subsequent incarnations.

The submersion of Kundalini in Chitta, which is a further process of Samadhi, obtains for a Yogi the desire of his life, viz., liberation from rebirths, subsequent incarnations.

This is known as Nirvikalpa Samadhi, wherein a Yogi is one with that Cosmic Power which creates and sustained the Universe.

SHAKTICHALAN MUDRA

There are various Mudras for rousing Kundalini. The easiest of these is said to be the Shaktichalan Mudra.

The pose of Siddhasana having been assumed, both legs are taken hold of by the hands and made to press firmly on the perineum at the Muladhara Chakra. Then with strong in and out breaths the abdominal muscles are made to contract and expand, with corresponding contraction and expansion of anus.

Contraction of the abdominal muscles prevents the Apana impulse from ascending.

Inhalation generates the Prana impulse that meets the Apana impulse at the Manipura chakra.

This is the preliminary for consciously exciting Kundalini, which starts successive impulses of reflex action of the ascending and equipoising forces.

The next Mudra to be practiced is the Shanmukhi. In this Mudra, all external impressions, carried by the nine openings in the body to the brain, are stopped by the fingers and heels

These openings are eyes, ears, nose, mouth, anus and urethra. It is impossible to breathe when nose and mouth are closed, so the mouth opening should be only partially closed by protruding lips forward like the beak of a bird.

The pranayama process is then followed by concentrating and meditating on the six chakras from lowest upward.

The next Mudra is the Khechari. In this the tongue is rolled backward and upward, during the process of inspiration, behind the soft palate, so as to reach base of skull behind posterior nasal openings. Vision is fixed on root of nose.

The folding up of the tongue prevents stimulation of the vagal center through the afferent fibers from the buccal cavity and lungs, yet it stimulates it directly through its own afferent fibers. This closure of the larynx is again helpful in preventing the exit of the air from the Lungs. Also, this pose of the tongue lifts up the lower jaw and tends to keep mouth closed.

This use of the tongue during the process of inspiration practically blocks all expiratory channels, producing a vacuum in the buccal cavity (cheeks), and also keeps lungs inflated, which is necessary for the oxygenation of the venous blood, sent to the lungs from the heart.

Concentration is fixed upon the nerve to be worked upon to the exclusion of all others; then by continuous meditation on the object of one's desire, an afferent impulse is generated and carried up to the brain through the spinal cord, the Sushumna, the **Nadi of Knowledge.**

By this process, Kundalini can be made to flow through the six important chakras. This is known in Yogic literature as Shat-chakra-bheda.

It should be understood that the rising of the Kundalini Power does not mean that the dynamo leaves its location. The dynamo remains permanently in place, and the power which rises is that generated by the dynamo.

One author gives the following directions for awakening of Kundalini:

Take a deep breath, breathing first from bottom of lungs and then ascend to fill the top. Sit erect, pull chin down to chest, and with chest filled with air, compress chest from top down, forcing the air in lungs downward.

This forces Prana down, toward the pelvis. Then contract navel and draw in anus. The Prana is thus compressed in the pelvis. Press it in from all sides, with intense force. Hold it there. The Prana then releases its free electrons to the base of the spine. Electric energy is then generated there. With exhalation it ascends up the spine to the brain, and awakens the higher centers. This is called "Mudra," the secret practice of Yogis. It is the method to vitalize the brain with Prana.

Do this preferably just at sunrise, when the air has the most ultraviolet force or ozone. Sit with spine erect when doing it. Practice cautiously so as not to strain the heart. In this way Kundalini is awakened.

These practices are said to be dangerous if not properly performed, and it is better to have a personal teacher.

As the higher brain centers are electrified, a tiny radio apparatus in the brain is activated, and we discover that we are a Being apart from the body in which we dwell.

Still another author gives the following directions:

Seated comfortable in a chair with a straight back, or with spine erect, inhale deeply, hold a few seconds, then exhale very slowly. Do this four to seven times at first, holding breath longest on final inhalation.

The number of breaths as well as the length of time of inhaling, holding and exhaling may be increased from week to week, but slowly. Do not hold nose in this exercise, and allow arms to rest limp in the lap or on arms of chair.

At each inhalation keep thought fixed on realization that you are inhaling pure light. As you retain the breath, hold thought on the realization that the light is diffusing through entire body, filling it with light. As you exhale, fix mind on realization that you are exhaling all darkness and impurity from the body.

After a short rest, practice tensing and relaxing the muscles of the body, starting with toes and ending with muscles of neck, face and scalp.

Now take a deep breath and hold it while you tense and relax muscles of abdominal region, and think of the light as striking Kundalini, rousing her from her dormancy.

Do not contract the musculature too violently, but build up slowly, and do not hold breath too long.

The muscles should be alternately tensed and relaxed while the breath is held. Lift and lower the abdomen, contracting the muscles upward and downward and from side to side, giving play to all abdominal muscles.

Having held the breath while doing these exercises, exhale and rest, breathing in regular manner. Then take another deep breath and hold while working the abdominal muscles again. Do this not to exceed six to seven times at first.

Now relax entire body. The mantra "OM" helps the relaxing process, as does also "Om mani padme hum." "So ham" (He I am) is soothing and aids one in the relaxing process.

Now begin reciting the Kundalini rousing mantra, "Hum Sa." Repeat this over and over, consciously directing the sound to the central triangle in the Muladhara.

Relax body more and more after each exhalation until you are so thoroughly relaxed that it is an effort to repeat the mantra aloud.

Now continue the repetition of the mantra mentally, directing it as before, until it seems to be reciting itself.

While this is going on, relax to the point of sleep, keeping thought fixed on Kundalini. In this dim twilight zone between sleep and being awake the concentrated power of the will is very strong.

This exercise need not be performed perfectly at first, nor be persisted in too long.

If discomfort or uneasiness appears, discontinue until the next period. Once a day should be effective, but one should give oneself at least two or three practice periods per week. Adepts practice more often of course.

When the Kundalini awakens, it begins to flow upward through the Sushumna Nadi. As it rises, layer after layer of the Mind is opened and activated. Then come visions and paranatural powers to the neophyte, as described in the Apocalypse.

As the power rises to the Brain, the neophyte is detached from his physical body and free of all physical restrictions and limitations.

One may experience the elementary state of this condition but know it not. You may have been half-conscious of the body jerking and actually jumping when almost asleep. You have had the sensation of sinking, or rising or floating, whirling, vibrating.

These sensations appear as the result of the psychic body being freed from the physical, causing a disturbance of the nerve system.

Surrounding the physical body there is an exact counter part, composed of ethereal substance, of a higher rate of vibration. The substance of this body pervades all space and is termed the Astral Body. This is the vital part of man, the actual cloak of the Soul. The physical is merely activated by the Astral Force so that man is able to function on the physical plane.

When the psychic body is out of its physical counterpart, it is connected with the physical by what the Masters termed "The Silver Cord" (Eccl. 12:6), a current of force similar in intensity to an electric current.

The ancient alchemist said: "I give myself over to wisdom's smelting furnace (Serpentine Fire) as to a fire of purification, till all my vain desires and tares of earthly lust have burnt away, so that I appear in Spirit as Pure Gold.

The Philosopher's Stone symbolizes the Spiritualized Man who consciously and by choice is as little susceptible to carnal lust as is a stone in its still unawakened consciousness.

SPECIAL INSTRUCTION

It appears that leaders and teachers prepare their work in a way that leaves them an opening to come in. The fact that we are all of us at least ninety percent ignorant does make it necessary for the most of us to be instructed in very simple matters.

It is also true that the great majority of people, deceived and misled by those who use and exploit them, do need much instruction on how to live the better life that builds a sound mind in a sound body.

It is exceedingly difficult to find teachers who are competent and willing to do that. The great majority of those who claim to be such teachers, are exploiters and frauds and not to be trusted. And the doctors hate health and health teachers, for they live and thrive on man's miseries, not on his good health.

It does not appear reasonable that Cosmic Intelligence would make man and leave him so helpless that he needed special instruction to cause the organs and glands of his body to perform their legitimate and eternally ordained functions. His lungs, liver, heart, kidneys, stomach and all other organs and glands of his body do their allotted work properly and without any direction from him, or the guidance of a teacher or doctor.

Why do civilized man's spiritual organs fail? Why do any of his organs fail? Because of misuse and abuse of his body.

The positive and negative poles of the cells of his body become corroded so they cannot register the subtle vibrations of the astral plane; and, in most cases, they register more or less defectively the lower vibrations of the gross physical plane.

The spiritual organs fail first because they are the most delicate and sensitive. They go out early in this world of evil where few know how to live for health, and many resent all teaching on the subject because it interferes with their mode of living.

The student should study "Man's Miraculous Unused Powers," in Lesson Number 22 in which we mentioned the uncanny powers of certain wild Indians in South American, and those of birds and beasts. We are now explaining the basis of these powers.

It is the strange work of the Serpentine Fire. That power guides all vertebrate animals in their conduct called instinct. By instinct these animals know what to do and when to do it.

This fact shows that the power automatically rises from the dynamo in the sacral plexus and activates the chakras, when organs and glands are properly developed, and penetrates the glands in the brain of these animals without their having been instructed or directed, save by the Cosmic Intelligence instilled by the Creative Power of the Universe.

Certain authors admit that Kundalini has been awakened in those who know nothing about Nadis, Chakras, and the Serpentine Fire. One case is sufficient to show what is possible in a million other cases.

The well-known Vedantist writer Swami Vivekanada, in his book "Rajah Yoga," said:

"Whenever there is any manifestation of what is ordinarily called supernatural power or wisdom, there must have been a little current of Kundalini which found its way into the Sushumna."

This knowledge constrains some occultists to assert that what man actually needs is definite instruction on how to live the better life that builds a sound mind in a sound body.

Man needs no special instruction concerning the functions of his body, or how to win the rewards legitimately due him from his Maker. They come freely and quickly to him who is worthy and entitled to receive them.

It appears logical that for him who is worthy and able to open and to read the Mysterious Book of Life, the Seals thereof will open automatically.

PREPARATION

What we give here on the Awakening of Kundalini has been gleaned from the many works we have studied. We present them for the student's benefit, and warn him that we recommend none of the methods cited. We certainly would not advise doing anything that disturbs the body's regular functions to the point where "a feverish sensation occurs."

As stated in Lesson No. 54, danger appears when the Serpentine Fire is aroused by unnatural means before the body is prepared for it, and we advise no one to attempt it.

Put not the cart before the horse. Let the condition of the body become so good that the spiritual power will be naturally activated, as in the case of birds and beasts.

Man is naturally prepared for the higher functions of the Serpentine Fire by purity of Mind and Body.

When the body is naturally prepared and ready, no unnatural means are necessary to awaken the Spiritual Power. But the Power is dangerous when aroused by unnatural processes as taught in most works on the subject, none of which are written by the Masters, because they are restrained from so doing by their vow of secrecy.

Knowledge of the Serpentine Fire was wisely concealed from the masses for certain reasons, one of which was, that if the powerful sex force were aroused unnaturally in those who were not prepared and ready for it, who had not subdued their epithumetic nature, it would make them sex maniacs, of whom there are always too many.

The Serpentine Fire is a double-edged sword that cuts both ways. It exalts or degrades, improves or destroys, depending on the conditions. If aroused unnaturally from its slumber without the power to control, it would give its deadly sting to him in whom it were unwisely awakened.

When not controlled, it can "burn one to death," figuratively speaking. This power was symbolized by the bush that burned with fire, but was not consumed (Ex. 3:2; Acts 7:30).

Paul (Apollonius) referred to this "fire" when he said, "It is better to marry than to burn" (1 Cor. 7:9). The burning sensation is not present when the power is controlled and raised up to the brain, where it illuminates the Mind by activating dormant brain centers that are asleep in the average man.

In pursuing a regimen of purification for Mind and Body,

(1) the first step is rigid conservation of the creative essence of the generative system.

(2) The next is to replace the conventional diet with one of uncooked and unseasoned fruits, melons and tomatoes, and to drink only fruit juices and pure rain water that has not touched the ground.

3. The next and very important, is to seek that peaceful environment of Nature, where the turmoil of civilization is absent, and the air is pure and not polluted with hundreds of poisons.

(4) The final step is to lift one's thoughts up to a higher plane, and concentrate on the better things of life.

All great things are simple. All Nature is simple. The secret of regeneration is simplicity itself. It is far too simple to attract the attention of the average man, who thinks of regeneration as a strange process that depends on mysterious means.

Lesson No. 58

THAT GOSPEL CHRIST JESUS

Millions of people in the world worship a man whose whole history is contained in the New Testament; and yet there is

absolutely no authentic knowledge as to the life or history of
one single author of anything contained in the New Testament,
which says:

> "And immediately his fame spread abroad throughout
> all the region round about Galilee. . . . And he preached in
> their synagogues throughout all Galilee" (Mk. 1:28, 39).

That was not much of a region when it is known that Palestine is a small country, some 140 miles long and 30 to 80 miles wide—smaller than some counties in the state of Texas.

Considering the fame of Christ Jesus today, there is an amazing absence of information about him from his contemporaries.

During the period chronicled in the New Testament, the great philosopher Philo lived in Egypt, near Palestine. Much of his works have come down to us and may be found in the public libraries. He records many of the same things appearing in the New Testament. He must have met many men from Palestine and Galilee; but he never mentions a Jesus of Nazareth, or Jesus the Christ, nor any of the disciples of such a man.

Between Jerusalem and Galilee extended the main trade route of those days. It connected Egypt and Babylon, and a branch of it extended to a Palestine seaport, from which shipments were made to Rome.

In the days of Christ Jesus, men travelled over this road from every part of the Roman Empire. Writers went from Rome to Greece, to Palestine, and to Egypt. They recorded their impressions of many things they learned about the leading men they met.

In those days men could write and did write. Their histories, geographies, plays, poems, religious works, fables, jokes and numerous other writings have come down to us. They may be read in modern libraries. In all these works not one word about Christ Jesus appears. Of this most extraordinary man of their time, of the most extraordinary man of all time they wrote not one word.

In the year 38 A.D., there was born in Galilee a man named Josephus. He became deputy governor of Galilee under the Romans, and was delegated by the Emperor Titus to write the history of the Jewish Rebellion and the siege and fall of Jerusalem.

In seven volumes, Josephus detailed the life and acts of King Herod and his relatives, and described at great length the various political and religious issues that led up to the Rebellion. He gives an almost day-by-day eye-witness account of the seige of Jerusalem.

Yet Josephus, born four years after the latest date that can be set for the alleged crucifixion of Christ Jesus, also a ruler of Galilee, a writer of Galilee, never once, in these seven volumes, makes the slightest reference to Christ Jesus, nor to any of his so-called disciples.

After Josephus, more than two hundred years were to pass before Christ Jesus would be mentioned in the works of any writer outside of the New Testament.

Christ Jesus was the Great Teacher. He might be expected to have put his teachings in writing. But not even the church has claimed that a single line of the New Testament was ever written by him.

Even the New Testament fails us as we search for men who saw Christ Jesus. Not one of all the writers of the New Testament mentions seeing him, nor do they ever place themselves at the scene of the events they record.

The gospels were written long after the death of Christ Jesus. Nor are the gospels authorship claimed by the saints, but for them. It is not the Gospel of St. Mark, but the Gospel according to St. Mark.

We know that unless rehearsed beforehand, no two people will or can describe an event in the same words, the same lines, and in the same sequence.

In the case of the Synoptic Gospels, when we compare them we realize that two of the writers had a copy of the third one's work before them, or else all three of them copied from some manuscript.

Many dramas were written and presented in the centuries preceding the time of Christ Jesus, and also after that. Some of these were religious mystery plays, In them, the stage was set, the actors appeared, played their parts, and made their exits as they do in theaters now.

There is a striking suggestion of the mystery drama in the New Testament. None of the books thereof presents a biography of Christ Jesus, nor do all the books combined. In all of them we find the stage set, the Christ Jesus makes his appearance, speaks his lines, and makes his exit to reappear in a later scene.

AN ACTOR

Everything surrounding Christ Jesus strongly indicates that he was only an actor. His parts had been prepared for him. He merely acted them. Yet it hardly appears possible that an actor, or an imaginary man who never lived, could have affected the world so profoundly.

No man, whether mythical or actual, could affect the world so profoundly as has Christ Jesus.

Therefore, it is certain that he was not a man. It is just as certain that the world has been misled in regarding him as a man. It is far more reasonable to infer that he was used as a symbol to represent some Cosmic Principle of the Universe.

For instance, there are no dates of his birth and death, simply because they represent Universal Principles.

The birth and death of Christ Jesus came to be fixed at the time of the Winter Solstice and The Spring Equinox, thus symbolizing Cosmic Principles—the motion of the Earth and the course of the Sun.

The motion of the Earth produces the Four Seasons of the year. So the New Testament has Four Gospels.

On December 22nd the motion of the Earth halts and reverses, causing the Sun to appear to stop in its southward journey, and begin to move northward on December 25. Then the New Year is born.

In its apparently northward movement, the Sun crosses the Equator in March, that time being termed the Spring Equinox.

SYMBOLICAL GODS

It was a common custom of the ancients, and especially of the ancient Egyptians, to use imaginary gods to represent various principles and elements of Nature. In his masterful work titled "The Gods of the Egyptians," Budge presents, in two large volumes, a list of these symbolical gods and describes with great care what each represents.

The evidence is strong that the New Testament scribes pursued this ancient practice. They presented their Christ Jesus as a symbol of some Cosmic Principle. In doing that, they followed an ancient practice that has descended from the remotest times.

The suggestion is so engrossing that it is worthy of consideration. By such course we may be able to solve the mystery of the New Testament Christ Jesus.

It is well-known that the Sun God and the Serpentine Fire were the basis of the ancient religion that runs so far back in the night of time that no record of its origin now exists. These two factors represent Cosmic Principles, and not men nor gods.

314

History shows, beyond the shadow of a doubt, that at the Nicean Council in 325 A.D., these Cosmic Principles were personified in a mythical man that came to be known as Christ Jesus. Then more than seventy million people were slaughtered in the campaign, supported by the Roman Emperor Constantine, to force the world to accept this mythical man as the Lord and Savior of humanity.

After the Roman Church was firmly established, for more than a thousand years no one living in a Christian country dared question Christian doctrine except at the risk of his life. The first man in England who dared print the Bible in English, so that all might read and judge for themselves was burned at the stake and his work destroyed.

THE SUN GOD

When man first appeared on earth, millions of years ago, the Sun rose regularly, as it still does, like a god of the sky, bringing light and heat, and sank each day, like a retiring king, to return the next morning in the same array of majesty.

Men worship Immutability. It was the steady, immutable character of the Sun that men of antiquity worshipped. His light-giving and life-giving powers were secondary attributes. The grand inspiration that constrained worship was that characteristic of the Invisible God which men saw reflected in the Sun's light, and fancied they saw in its originality the never-changing Deity.

The Sun saw nations rise and fall, and earthquakes shake the earth and hurl down mountains. Beyond Olympus and the Pillars of Hercules He had gone daily to His abode, and returned in the morning to behold the temples men built to His worship.

Ancient man personified the Sun as Brahma, Krishna, Amun, Abram, Adonis, Apollo, Osiris, Bel, Malkarth, Mithras, Hesus, etc.

The nations that did so grew old and died. Moss grew on the capitals of the columns of the Sun's temples, and He shone on the moss. Grain by grain the material of His temples crumbled into dust and was borne off on the wind, and still He shone on the decaying structures. The roof fell crashing on the pavement, and He shone on the Holy of Holies with unchanging rays.

It is not strange that man, millions of years ago, worshipped the Sun as the visible representative of the Invisible God, and personified him in various ways.

The ancient Hindus called the Sun "Kris." In their religion,

Krishna was a personification of the Sun. As time passed this was forgotten, and Krishna evolved into an actual man, said to have been born of a virgin.

It came to pass that Krishna was imported to Europe, and the Greeks called him Christos. The Romans called him Christus, and the English called him "CHRIST."

The ancient Druids called the Sun "Hesus." At the Nicean Council the names were joined into Hesus Christus, and later changed by the English to Jesus Christ.

It requires only a knowledge of the name of the Sun-god in different languages to understand from whence came the name Jesus Christ.

SYMBOL AND ALLEGORY

Compilation of the New Testament involved much labor. The church fathers had access to all the ancient literature collected and filed in the great Alexandrian library, in which they did their work.

From that mass of literature they culled what they wanted and destroyed the rest. Then later the church had the library burned, the reason for the burning being that the church **"did not want the clergy to have their minds diverted from their holy work by studying heathen literature."** (Antiquity Unveiled, p. 59).

Was Christ-Jesus Man or Symbol? That we shall see as we proceed.

The Roman Emperor Constantine, presiding over the famous Council of Nicea in 325 A.D., "decreed as to how the New Testament Record should be worded," says Livingston (Book of David, p. 140).

Constantine's objective was to crush the Sacred Science of the Ancient Masters. The Masters were too clever to be outwitted by him. They met him at his own game, prepared the New Testament as he directed,—but they skilfully made the gospel Jesus play a double role.

So far as we know, this is the first attempt ever made, on a scale so elaborate, to show that the gospel Christ Jesus is a personification and symbolization of certain Cosmic Principles and of the Spiritual Powers and Processes of the Temple of God (1 Cor. 3:16), allegorized in the Bible and other occult works as the Serpentine Fire.

It is certain that those who compiled the New Testament were Initiates of the Ancient Arcane Science. They had to be to know what they knew of the secret traditional lore, handed down from times immemorial.

The record shows that the church fathers were Initiates of the Ancient Mysteries. They include Clement of Alexandria, Clement of Rome, Origen, Archelaus, Cyril, and Basil.

Like the Apocalypse and all other books of the Bible, they wrote the New Testament in symbol and allegory, so preparing it that it contains dual messages,—one for the exoteric and one for the esoteric.

Nothing new about that. It was a common custom of the Masters to have their sacred scriptures contain one message for the profane and another for the initiates and disciples.

Allegory is designed to inform the esoteric and mislead the exoteric. We get an example of that in the following:

God said unto Moses, "Make thee a Fiery Serpent, and set it upon a pole; and it shall come to pass, that every one that is bitten, when he looketh upon it, shall live" (Num. 21:8).

The Masters taught the neophyte that while the pleasure of copulation lasts but a short time, the damage it leaves behind is permanent. The Fiery Serpent on the pole was a symbol to keep that fact before him.

The phrase "every one that is bitten" was interpolated to mislead the exoteric by inference that it meant the serpent was actual instead of symbolical.

In the interpretation of the Apocalypse we saw that various empty words and phrases were interpolated here and there to make the context more puzzling to the exoteric, and to conceal better the real meaning of the message. The same practice was followed in preparing the New Testament.

For sixteen hundred years the church has given the world the message of the New Testament intended for the exoteric, to the effect that the hero is the Lord and Savior of Mankind,—and the esoteric have laughed in their sleeve.

For sixteen hundred years the many critics of the New Testament have exhausted every means of information and knowledge in their efforts to show that Christ Jesus is only a myth. M. J. Gauvin wrote:

"If Christ was an historical character, why was it necessary to forge documents to prove his existence? Did any one ever think of forging documents to prove the existence of any one who was really known to have lived? The early Christian forgeries are a tremendous testimony as to the weakness of the Christian cause" (Did Jesus Christ Really Live? P. 46).

None of these critics ever dreamed that there is an esoteric

317

message concealed in the Hidden Life of Jesus, and that it contains the secret of the Serpentine Fire.

We have prepared this work to give the student that esoteric message.

BIRTH OF JESUS

The Golden Oil, one of the basic constituents of the blood, in its purest state was termed "Chrism" by the Greeks.

This Golden Oil is the Light of the Logos, termed by the Masters the living, conscious, vital electricity of the body, the Serpentine Fire of the Bible, of which Christ Jesus was made a symbol.

This substance, with the fishy odor, flows down the spinal cord to the solar plexus (cave, manger—Lu. 2:4), where it is activated by the Sun (Helios, Holy) Breath (Ghost), and the Seed (Son) is born.

Every 29½ days in the life of man and woman after puberty, when the Moon is in the sign the Sun was in at the time of one's birth, there is a psycho-physical Seed born in the Solar Plexus, which in the ancient text is termed the "House of Bread," because it lies behind the stomach.

Jesus was born in Bethlehem (Mat. 2:1). Bethlehem is from Beth, house, and Lechem, bread; and Jesus thus becomes the "Bread of Life" which came down from heaven (head) (Jn. 6:35, 41).

Water symbolizes the body fluids that carry the Seed, with the fishy odor. So it was in order for the disciples to be fishermen, working round the water. The early Christians used a fish as their secret sign.

After birth, Jesus is taken down into Egypt. This is the descent of the Seed into the dark, lower part of the body, symbolized by the Masters as Egypt; and there it remains until the neophyte subdues his epithumetic nature, symbolized as the death of Herod. Then "Out of Egypt" have I called my Son" (Mat. 2:14, 15).

BATTLE OF ARMAGEDDON

The gospels are silent as to the activities of Jesus from birth until the age of 12, and then silent again until the age of 30.

Puberty usually comes at the twelfth year, and from there on to thirty occurs the process of developing the Serpentine Fire by living in harmony with the law and observing a continent life.

At the age of Puberty there comes the development in the

318

brain of the **Knowledge of Good and Evil** (Gen. 2:9, 17; 3:22).

And so at the age of 12 we find Jesus disputing with the doctors (Lu. 2:42, 46).

This symbolizes the fact that the Divine Consciousness, having ruled the young body thus far in peace, must now begin to dispute with the newly awakened fáculty of propagation in the brain, termed by the Masters as the Great Red Dragon (passion in the blood) that stands ready to devour man as soon as born (Rev. 12:1-4).

By means of masturbation that power of evil begins to devour many before they reach the age of 12.

Abuse of sex is the curse of all nations today. The people are debilitated and have fallen to a low level because of sexual excess. Nothing debilitates the body so much as the repetition of the nerve crisis in copulation; nothing else so exhausts the supply of nerve power.

This phychological secret is the basis of the Edenic Parable. This is the actual Battle of Armageddon (Rev. 16:16). This is the eternal struggle in the brain between the Cerebrum and the Cerebellum. This is the reason why the Masters called the Cerebrum the God-brain and the Cerebellum the man-brain.

Bellum means opposition, conflict; and there is constant conflict between the dual forces of the brain, the higher and the lower, the spiritual and the physical, with the physical usually victorious. Few are they in whom the spiritual force wins the fight.

JESUS IS BAPTIZED

In the Sacred Ancient Mysteries "baptism" meant much. In Christianity it is a conventional form of pure mockery that means little to the one baptized.

The canal in the center of the spinal cord is filled with a precious fluid. This stream was symbolized by the Masters as the "River of God." This is the Jordan in which Jesus was baptized (Mat. 3:13-15).

Jesus now becomes "my beloved Son" (Mat. 3:17), and his ministry begins.

"Repent: for the kingdom of heaven is at hand" (Mát. 4:17). **So the Talking Serpent of the Garden of Eden now goes into action.**

"For if ye believe not that I am he (Serpentine Fire), ye shall die in your sins," as stated in the Edenic Parable. "When ye have lifted up the Son of man (Serpentine Fire), then shall ye know that I am he" because of the illuminating effect on the Mind (Jn. 8:24, 28).

THE GOLDEN OIL

We have mentioned the Golden Oil that is deposited in the crystal lamp, and the shock of sudden light received by the neophyte when that Oil is raised up to the brain. "Then shall ye know that I am he."

In the case of man ruled by his epithumetic nature, under the controlled customs of the social pattern, living in the polluted air and degrading environment of civilization where health is impossible, the valves in the Spinal Cord suffer much damage along with all the rest of the body, and become subnormal and deficient in function. That condition obstructs the natural flow of the delicate Serpentine Fire between the sacral plexus and the brain, between the Muladhara and the Sahasrara chakras.

First, there is not in such persons much of the Serpentine Fire to flow. The little generated by the Kundalini dynamo is dissipated in sexual and other excesses, leaving a depleted, impoverished current to flow up to the brain.

When the Golden Oil is consumed in copulation, it does literally bring decay and death to the body.

The statement, "Our Lord (Golden Oil) was crucified in Egypt" (lower body) (Rev. 11:8), literally means the consumption of the Golden Oil in copulation.

When man subdues his epithumetic nature, is victorious in the Battle of Armageddon, and the Golden Oil, thus saved, is resurrected and raised up from the grave (solar plexus), it ascends to the Most High (Brain), and becomes the Savior and Redeemer of mankind.

"When ye have lifted up the Son of Man (Golden Oil),
then shall ye know that I AM HE." "If I be lifted up, I
will draw ALL MEN Unto Me" (Jn. 8:24, 28; 12:32).
Not just those who believe in me, but "all men."

The chemical formula of the Golden Oil with the fishy odor is J.O.H.N. To make the symbolism more complete, Jesus is baptized of John (Golden Oil with the fishy odor).

The Apocalypse covers, in symbol and allegory, the "Initiation of Ioannes." This word also means J.O.H.N. and Fish. So the church fathers made John the author of that work. He was the disciple whom Jesus loved (Jn. 20:2; 21:7, 30), and was said to be an ignorant and unlearned fisherman (Acts 4:13).

The physical proclivities of the Sun and its water-drawing power, were used by the Masters to symbolize the spiritual process, in which man's Divine Consciousness is raised, increased, illuminated, and drawn upward to the Spiritual Realm by the power of the Solar Force. So Jesus also symbolized that Force.

The Golden Oil is mentioned in the parable of the ten virgins who took lamps and went to meet the bridegroom (Mat. 25:1-9). It is also mentioned in Zechariah (4:11, 12) as the "golden oil" of the two olive branches (Ida and Pingala) on the right and left side of the candlestick (spinal cord).

When the Golden Oil is raised up and supplies the nerves which dip into the Optic Thalamus in the brain, it activates the Thalamus to stronger and more rapid vibration, producing that illumination in the brain which the Masters termed the Glorification of God.

When this occurs, it awakens millions of dormant brain cells and produces the phenomenon termed Spiritual Light. This shock of sudden light makes the neophyte feel a general upheaval in his body, mentioned in these words:

"And the temple of God (body) was opened in heaven (brain), and there was seen in His Temple the Ark of His Testament (womb, place of birth), and there were lightnings, and voices, and thunderings, and an earthquake, and great hail" (oil dripping into the thalamus) (Rev. 11:19).

RESURRECTION OF THE DEAD

Every practical "pyrotechnist" knows that the brain contains certain centers, including the Pineal and Pituitary Glands, the higher functions of which are almost entirely dormant in the average man, and such are termed in esoteric writings as "the dead." They are also the dead that are raised up and the dead that are resurrected in the regeneration (Mat. 11:5; 22:31).

So Christ Jesus, as the Serpentine Fire, refers to these "dead" and says, "I am the resurrection, and the life; he that believeth in me, though he were dead, yet shall he live" (Jn. 11:25).

Osiris, playing the part of the Serpentine Fire in the Egyptian Mysteries, made the same statement five thousand years before, according to Budge in his "Gods of the Egyptians," vol. 2, p. 141.

In the case of the Master, in whom the dormant brain cells are activated, the higher faculties become so acute that he is cognizant of the interior worlds, the planes of true being.

When the brain is aroused to fuller function by the action of the Golden Oil, it then becomes the Divine Androgyne, wherein occurs the immaculate conception and gestation of the self-born spiritual man, the "monogenes," who is in very truth "born from above" (Jn. 1:13; 1 Jn. 5:4, 18).

When the Golden Oil (Serpentine Fire) is conserved within the body through the process of transmutation, this Divine Esse permeates brain and body, producing a regenerative process, increases the vital force, sensitizing the nerves, and intensifies the consciousness, raising man to a higher plane.

THE SACRED LAMP

After the candidate was initiated and his mind flooded with spiritual light, the Masters regarded him as a Lamp: "Ye are the light of the world" (Mat. 5:14).

The light of the body is said to be the spiritual eye: If therefore thine eye by single (Optic Thalamus activated by the Serpentine Fire), thy whole body shall be full of light (Mat. 6:22).

As the Serpentine Fire, is was said of Christ Jesus that "He was a burning and shining light; and ye were willing for a season to rejoice in his light" (Jn. 5:35).

In Lesson Number 56 we stated that the Pineal Gland is phosphorescent, and when aroused from its dormancy by the Serpentine Fire, it glows with spiritual light that floods the Mind, illuminating the higher consciousness of him in whom this occurs.

So the talking Serpent of the Garden of Eden, in the person of Christ Jesus, speaks and says;

"I am the light of the world; he that followeth me shall
not walk in darkness, but shall have the Light of Life.
I am come a light into the world, that whoever believeth
on me will not abide in darkness" (Jn. 8:12; 12:46).

The radiance of the Golden Light (Gold of Ophir, 1 K. 9:28), is so powerful that it cannot be contained by the skull. It emanates from the head, especially from the back of the neck where the highest vertebra of the spine articulates with the condyles of the occipital bone.

This light, appearing in the aura around back part of head,

322

suggests the halos of saints and the nimbus so often used in religious art. This light, forming part of the human aura, indicates regenerative action.

The wise took oil in their vessels. And the foolish said unto the wise, Give us of your oil; for our lamps are gone out (Mat. 25:4, 8).

My head with oil thou didst not anoint; but this woman hath anointed my feet with ointment (Lu. 7:46).

The Golden Oil is the illuminating substance of the body. Without it there is no consciousness. When it is entirely exhausted, consciousness ends and decay of the body begins. Dr. George W. Carey says, "A total lack of oil in the body will, in itself, cause death" (p. 110).

This oil is not only easily affected, but the effects are carried by the blood into the tissues of the brain and all parts of the body, producing strange symptoms not understood by the doctors.

I (Chrism—Golden Oil) am come (back to the brain) that they (who conserve it) may have life, and that they might have it more abundantly (Jn. 10:10).

The Initiation of Ioannes, mentioned in Lesson Number 19, refers to the Golden Oil, flowing down (to the grave) through the spinal cord (Jordan) from the Source of the Life Essence in the Most High (Upper Brain), the heaved-up place, the heaven within the Temple of God.

The Kingdom of God is within you (Lu. 17:21). Knowing that in yourselves ye have in Heaven (Brain) a better and an enduring substance (Heb. 10:34).

Now to Abraham (Sun God) and his seed were these promises made, and to thy Seed which is Chrism (Gal. 3:16).

JESUS CRUCIFIED

And he bearing his cross went forth into a place called the place of a skull, which is called in the Hebrew Golgotha: where they crucified him, and two others with him, on either side one, and Jesus in the midst (Jn. 19:17, 18).

In occult anatomy, Golgotha is the base of the human skull, where the spinal cord enters the brain.

At this point occurs a double nerve crossing, made by Ida, Pingala and Pneumogastric nerves. In the allegory they are the St. George and St. Andrew Crosses, with the form of a man displayed thereon. Many Byzantine coins and frescoes show this esoteric symbol.

The Ida and Pingala Nadis extend down the right and left. side of the spinal cord to its base, and there converge into the

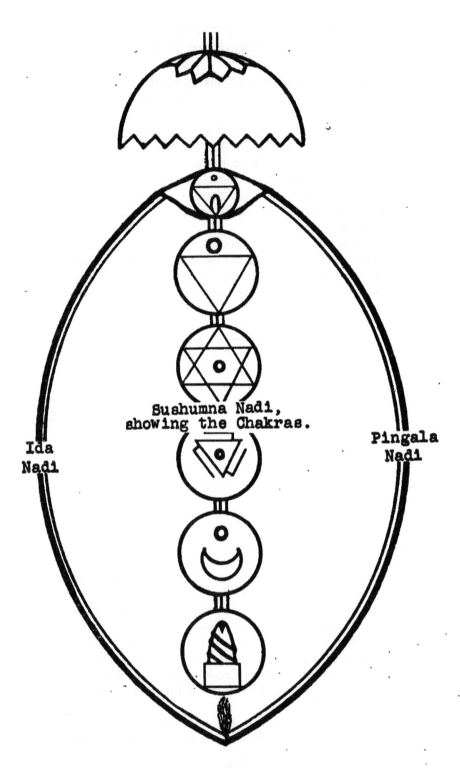

Ida
Nadi

Sushumna Nadi,
showing the Chakras.

Pingala
Nadi

324

body through the semiluna ganglion, allegorically termed the "Sea of Galilee." So there it was that Jesus did most of his work.

To crucify means to raise in power. When electric wires are crossed, their power is increased and they set on fire all inflammable substances near them.

When man refrains from copulation, the psycho-physical essence accumulates and flows upward to its throne in the brain. Ascending the central canal of the spine, it makes the crucial (crucifix) crossing at the base of the skull (Golgotha), and re-returns to the Optic Thalamus (Father). At this point it undergoes the final balancing and is transmuted into the substance that is deposited in the Crystal Lamp (Optic Thalamus).

As this fluid supplies the nerves that dip into this bowl from the Cerebrum, it produces that shock of sudden light which arouses millions of dormant brain cells and produces the phenomenon of Illumination.

In the allegory the scribe says that when the raised up seed crossed (crucifixion) the nerves in the skull (Golgotha) and its power was augmented by the ascension, the veil of the temple was rent, the earth (body) did quake, the graves were opened, and the dead (dormant brain cells) came forth (Mat. 27:51, 52).

In cosmic phenomena the ancient scribe recorded the shock the brain cells receive as they are activated by the raised up Serpentine Fire.

"Father, the hour has come; glorify thy Son (Seed),
that thy Son (Seed) may also glorify thee" (Jn. 17:1).

Glorify means to illuminate. The passing of the Serpentine Fire over the cross of nerves and into the Optic Thalamus does literally cause glorification,—that flash of spiritual light within which illuminates the Mind.

The nerve-crossing (crucifixion) of the raised up Seed gives power to vibrate the Pineal Gland at such a terrific rate that it causes the "Light of the Chamber" (skull) to fill the "whole body with light," and send its vibrations along the optic nerve to the physical eye.

In a previous lesson we stated that the vibratory rate of the force-emanation from the Pineal is beyond any rate of vibration capable of being registered by any instrument so far produced by science, and has been estimated to be in the billions of cycles per second.

THE TWO FORDS

Only two fords are mentioned in the Bible (Gen. 32:22; Jos. 2:7; Ju. 3:28; Isa. 16:2).

These crossings symbolize (1) the end of the Spinal Cord at the twelfth dorsal vertebra, where "Jesus was baptized," and (2) the base of the skull, where "Jesus" was "crucified."

When the Golden Oil is crucified (increased in power at the nerve crosses), it remains two and a half days (moon's period in a sign) in the tomb (cerebellum). On the Third Day it Ascends to the Pineal Gland, which connects the Cerebellum with the Optic Thalamus, the Central Eye in the Throne of God (Brain) (Mk. 16:19).

That is the Chamber overtopped by the hollow (hallowed) caused by the curve of the Cerebrum (Most High).

So it is written: "He that dwelleth in the secret place (Pineal) of the Most High (Brain) shall abide under the shadow of the Almighty (Cerebrum) (Ps. 91:1).

Hence, no man hath ascended up to heaven, but he that came down from heaven, even the Son (Seed) of Man which is in heaven (Jn. 3:13). What and if ye shall see the Son (Seed) of Man ascend up where he was before (Jn. 6:62).

THE TWO THIEVES

Why was Jesus crucified between two thieves?—Lu. 23:32; Jn. 19:18.

This is probably the strongest evidence presented to show that Jesus is only a Symbol of the Spiritual Processes of the Temple of God.

The three figures present a perfect picture of the Sushumna, the Ida and the Pingala Nadis.

The Ida and Pingala must be emptied of their Pranic Power, which thence passes into the Sushumna, the chief central channel, before the Serpentine Fire can be made to rise.

In this instance Jesus is a double symbol, representing both the Sushumna and also the Serpentine Fire which flows through it.

By the Yogins of yore, the Spinal Cord was called the Sushumna Nadi. It extends up from the Muladhara chakra to the Sahasrara, situated in the crown of the head, and was termed the "dwelling place of Shiva."

On its thousand petals are the letters of the Sanskrit alphabet twenty times. In side of it is the full Moon (Chandra-Mandala) containing the Trikona, mentioned in a previous lesson.

Even a mere novice in the Secret Science of the Masters would instantly recognize this picture for what it actually is—a definite Symbol of the Serpentine Fire.

It is amazing how perfect the Masters made the picture in words, and how baffling it has been to the exoteric.

But the gospel story of Jesus is not less puzzling and confusing than is the Apocalypse, which has baffled the best minds for a thousand years.

Then behold how simple it is to one who has the Key. So the gospel story of Jesus becomes just as simple to one who has the key.

Then the Savior of Mankind appears as a Symbol of the Serpentine Fire. And the Serpentine Fire is literally the Savior of Mankind. That makes the Symbolism perfect.

As the Serpentine Fire, Jesus is "crucified" and raised to the Crown of the Head, and "sat on the right hand of God" (Mk. 16:19).

RESURRECTION

After the "crucifixion," the "body" of Jesus is claimed by a mysterious Joseph, and by him taken into his own tomb, where no man had ever been laid (Mat. 27:57-60).

This man is symbolical of the Pineal Gland, the tomb where no man hath ever been laid.

For this is the First Seed of the neophyte that has been saved, lifted up, resurrected since he was born (Rev. 14:4; 20:5; 22:13).

In parabolic representation, the Son (Seed) is lifted up, resurrected, and returns to the Father (Pineal), the Most High, the Kingdom of God within (Lu. 17:21).

"And greater things than I do, ye shall do,"—is the message given to the body by the First Seed that is resurrected.

When the First Seed is saved, lifted up and illuminates the body, the entire body becomes improved, regenerated. It vibrates at a higher rate, and the fluids are of better quality and more highly refined.

In 29½ days another Seed is born. The material from which it is formed is of more refined substance, of greater power than the First Seed; and "greater things than I do ye shall do" (Jn. 14:12). Hence, when the next Seed is lifted up, crucified,- and resurrected, it is of greater power than the first.

When the Moon enters the sign at birth, the Seed is born every month in both man and woman. The Spiritual Force multiplies within the body as each new Seed is lifted up, crucified, and resurrected, and it is of greater power than the first, and so on with the next.

TOUCH ME NOT

After the resurrection of Jesus unto woman he said, "Touch me not; for I have not yet ascended to my Father" (Jn. 20:17).

O man! Consume not thy Vital Essence on the physical plane. Touch not woman in copulation, that she may not thus touch you; and then shall ye receive that illumination produced by the Golden Oil, termed the Glorification of God.

He that overcometh his epithumetic nature shall inherit all things that make life worth living; and I will be his God, and he shall be my son (Rev. 21:7).

The dead letter of the Bible and the distorted context lead one to believe that Paul (Apollonius) referred to the gospel Christ-Jesus when in fact he referred to the Serpentine Fire. He begins:

"It is reported commonly that there is fornication among you." "The body is not for fornication." "Flee fornication" (1 Cor. 5:1; 6:18).

These statements show that he was not referring to a man, not to Christ-Jesus, but directly and definitely to copulation and the raising of the Serpentine Fire. He continues:

"If the Serpentine Fire be not raised, your faith is vain; ye are yet in your sins" (1 Cor. 15:17).

He devoted much of the 15th chapter of 1st Cor. to this subject, but to deceive the masses the church fathers deleted Serpentine Fire and interpolated "Christ."

Paul (Apollonius) taught that marriage was not originally intended, but was instituted to prevent something worse. Writing of the unmarried and the widowed, he said:

"It is good for them if they abide even as I (single, unmarried). But if they cannot contain (control their lust), let them marry: for it is better to marry than to burn" (1 Cor. 7:8, 9).

He realized the greater damage connected with the sexual function was not in its use for propagative purposes, but in the gratification of carnal lust.

Christ Jesus lived 33 years, the number of bones in the spinal column, through which is raised up the Serpentine Fire, of which he is a symbol.

In those cases where Christ Jesus acted the part of an

328

actual man, the work was taken from the life of Apollonius (Paul), the great philosopher of the first century who wrote the so-called Pauline Epistles and the Apocalypse.

In his book on "Protestantism," the French pastor Bertrand wrote:

"The real newness of Christianity is that it does not offer its followers a law or a doctrine, but a person, a living, conscious ideal: Jesus Christ. Christianity is life with Christ."

He also missed the point as do all who write on that subject. They think the church fathers presented a man. They wanted the world to think that. What they did present was only a symbol of the ancient Serpentine Fire.

LAMB ON THE CROSS

If the man Jesus were crucified on the cross, why did the figure of a Lamb appear on the cross until the year 680 A.D.?

At the Sixth Ecumenical Council held at Constantinople in 680 A.D., it was ordained that in place of the Lamb, the figure of a man should be portrayed on the Cross. After that decree of the Council, the representation and worship of the Lamb on the Cross was prohibited, and the figure of a man was substituted in its place (Ant. Unveiled, p. 161).

The Popes through the ages have known that Christ Jesus is a fraud, and said so. Pope Leo X said:

"How well we know what a profitable superstition this Fable of Christ has been for us" (Doane, Bible Myths, p. 438).

Renan's "Life of Jesus" shows that the Christ Jesus as a man is a modern creation. The figure of a man did not appear on the modern cross until the year of 680 (Ant. Unveiled, p. 161).

Ralph Waldo Emerson, one of the most lovable of men, said: "We must get rid of that Christ."

Prof. Smith wrote, "The supernatural Christ of the New Testament is dead; but the priestcraft lives and conjures up the ghost of this dead god to frighten the masses of mankind."

ANCIENT PHILOSOPHY

In the middle of the fifth century A.D., Archbishop Chrysostom said:

"Every trace of the old philosophy and literature of the ancient world has vanished from the face of the earth" (Doane, Bible Myths, p. 436).

IMMORTALITY

It is easy to understand why the ancient philosophy was destroyed. It taught these two doctrines:

(1) The development of spiritual intelligence by raising the Serpentine Fire, and

(2). the passage on to Spiritual Life through the gateway of physical death.

Paul (Apollonius) stated that we do not sleep in death, but are changed to spiritual life in the process of physical death, in which we leave the gross physical body behind and rise to a higher plane of Consciousness (1 Cor. 15:51).

That ancient knowledge the church suppressed by destruction of the ancient literature because it makes priests and preachers useless by teaching man that he has and is Eternal Life without their aid or belief in their mythical Christ Jesus.

The literature we now have on the Serpentine Fire all comes from India. The rest was collected and destroyed as stated by Chrysostom, and it was done to keep people from understanding what the Bible actually teaches.

There would be none coming from India today had the church fathers been able to get hold of it during the Dark Ages when the church was all-powerful. But in that day travel was slow and India was far away. That saved the Serpentine Fire literature that we have now.

Only he who understands the secret of the Serpentine Fire of the Ancient Masters can understand the Bible. That parable begins in the first book of the Bible, runs all through the Bible, and ends with the last book of the Bible.

SEXUAL PROPAGATION

Some may ask, What would preserve the race from extinction if all people lived a continent life? C. J. VanVliet thought of that, and he wrote:

"A danger might be seen in the far-off possibility that those who entirely abstain from sex become so numerous as to form the great majority. But even then. . . .

330

"If perfect celibacy were chosen by man for the sake of spiritual evolution, this would indicate that the larger portion of the race had reached a stage above that of animal-man.

"Should Nature find that it was then becoming unpractical to continue the human species by the sexual method, she can be trusted to institute a new reproductive system in which sex plays no part. Thus the moment when all men will finally overcome carnal lust and become entirely chaste . . . will be the end of the historical process' . . . not necessarily the end of the human race.

"It may well be that attainment of the fully spiritualized state will raise mankind to the point where it can step out of the human into a higher evolutionary kingdom. That would mean the end of humanity as such. Not by suicide, but by what may be called its natural death— death in the same sense as a graduation from school may be called the death of the 'pupil' who thereafter, in a higher institution of learning, becomes a 'student.'

"Suicide of the race is the customary abuse of sex, because it threatens humanity with an untimely death from self-inflicted diseases.

"If mankind adheres to its present sexual behavior, 'it is likely . . . to perish by the various vicious abuses and excesses which it has used the powers of its superior reason to devise and indulge.' It threatens to degenerate and destroy itself by abuse of the very element by which it was intended to maintain and, by transmutation, to regenerate itself.

"There can be no question of racial suicide when humanity rises spiritually, and thereby rises above sex—and when, after attaining every purpose of human existence, it leaves the human for the supermannic life" (Coiled Serpent, p. 146).

Clements shows in his "Science of Regeneration" that complete mastery of man's epithumetic nature is the only Road to Redemption.

The body is altered and improved and its days are prolonged and pleasurified by saving the vital essence and raising the Serpentine Fire.

To him who resolutely pursues the path of purity and improvement, there will come the consciousness of Immortality and Spiritual Calmness.

There must also be concentration of Mind upon the Spiritual Man that is eternal, instead of upon the Physical Man that is temporal, being ruled by the alternating processes of Birth and Death.

This mental reversion is what Paul (Apollonius) referred to when he said, "Be ye transformed by the renewing of your mind" (Rom. 12:2).

From the first book to the last the Bible is devoted to this great secret of Life.

The writings of Ezekiel, Zechariah and the other Hebrew "prophets" are esoteric treatises on this psycho-physiological process of the body, thinly disguised as "predictions" to deceive the exoteric. In them, nations and personages play the parts that are acted by the heavenly bodies in the Apocalypse.

CPSIA information can be obtained
at www.ICGtesting.com
Printed in the USA
BVOW11s0549071016
464431BV00011B/258/P